WILDLIFE

WILDLIFE

PHOTOGRAPHY BY ROBERT B. SMITH

TEXT BY ROBERT M. STORM

International Standard Book Number 0-912856-27-0
Library of Congress Catalog Number 76-5667
Copyright© 1976 by Publisher • Charles H. Belding
Graphic Arts Center Publishing Co.
2000 N.W. Wilson • Portland, Oregon 97209 • 503/224-7777
Designer • Robert Reynolds
Text • Robert M. Storm
Printer • Graphic Arts Center
Bindery • Lincoln & Allen
Printed in the United States of America

All senses alert, a red fox stalks its prey in an Oregon forest. Among the smartest of our wild animals, they survive well in fairly populated areas.

Grizzly bear pauses to define the odors in the wind. Perhaps the most feared of North American predators, the grizzly is the largest meat-eating mammal on earth. Provocation usually causes bodily harm.

These grizzly bears appear to be deadly serious, but are probably only playing. The big brown bear of Alaska is now considered one and the selfsame species with the grizzly.

Young osprey receives daily ration of fish. Crane Prairie in central Oregon is natural habitat for osprey that nest in dead snags, killed by rising reservoir water from dam construction on the Deschutes River.

Deep in the forest, a pileated woodpecker feeds its young. Largest of our
living woodpeckers, it prefers old forests with snags for nesting and food.

Canada geese wing their way over a southeastern Oregon marsh. Their characteristic honking is music to ears of wildlife enthusiasts everywhere.

Canada goose herds her goslings into feeding waters. Adult geese feed mainly on land, but young family feeds largely on various water plants.

Male ruffed grouse produces his "drumming" sound warning other males off his territory. The sound is produced by rapidly moving the wings forward and upward. Described as thump-thump rup-rup r-r-r.

The picture of grace and beauty, a swallowtail butterfly alights on a flower. Several varieties occur in United States and southern Canada.

Yellow-headed blackbird proclaims ownership of this territory. The alarum of these birds has been compared to the creaking of a rusty gate.

Avocet prefers shallow ponds where it can wade, sweeping its up-turned bill from side to side through water, seeking aquatic animals.

Appearing somewhat dazed, a young cougar or mountain lion stares at the big world outside its den. Cougars are distributed more widely than any other American mammal, ranging from northern British Columbia to southern South America. It may reach eight feet in length.

Largest cat in most of North America, a mountain lion or cougar pauses in a forested clearing on slopes of the Cascade Range. Feeding mainly on available deer population, a cougar may range over 100 square miles.

Golden-mantled ground squirrel, on the alert for predators. Tourists
enjoy the friendly antics of these active visitors at picnics and camps.

Bison bull feeds on lush grass in Montana meadow. Once reduced almost to extinction, thousands now exist in parks, preserves and private herds. It can weigh a ton and is capable of running 30 miles per hour.

Dozing through the day, porcupine awaits the dark of night for its feeding activities. Well-protected against predators, porcupines are slow-moving and frequently quite conspicuous.

Preparing to pounce, a young bobcat practices the skills that will make it a successful hunter. Feeding mainly on smaller mammals, bobcats are able to kill full-grown deer. Adult males seldom reach 40 pounds.

Mother barn owl and her young peer from their nest in Willamette Valley barn. Feeding almost entirely on mice, owls are highly beneficial.

Barn owl searches for its food. A keen sense of hearing enables this bird to locate many mice, rats and other rodents in almost total darkness.

Eastern Oregon black-tailed jackrabbit ready to escape the grasp of an unfriendly coyote. A declining population of rabbits sometimes forces the coyote to seek other means of subsistence, provoking the stockmen.

Fierce gaze of this great horned owl seems to say "keep your distance." Some owls can see in light up to one one-hundredth of that needed by man.

Cluster of lump-nosed bats hang from the attic ceiling of an abandoned house in western Oregon. Bats are able to lower their body temperature while roosting and thus conserve energy. When flying most are harmless.

Western rattlesnake suns near its den in southeastern Oregon. Rattle-snakes need deep rocky crevices below the surface for their winter dens.

Mountain billy goat eyes the photographer from an alpine slope in Alberta. Older males are usually alone except for rutting season in late fall.

Mountain goat crosses a canyon wall in the Alberta Rockies. Although extremely sure-footed, on occasion miss their step and fall to their death.

Moose raises his head for a look around as he feeds on his favorite diet of underwater vegetation. A large bull moose may weigh up to 1,800 pounds, the largest antlered mammal known to have ever existed.

Relying on its camouflage coloring for protection, young spotted sandpiper peers from cover. These small shore birds may be observed along the edge of almost any stream or lake on the North American continent.

Becoming increasingly rare in the Northwest, a spotted owl rests on a limb in a western Oregon forest. They require large tracts of mature timber to successfully incubate and forage.

An inquisitive deer peers from a grove of birch trees in Alberta. One whiff of human scent and she will leap, as if by magic, into the sheltering brush. They are distinguished for grace of body and swiftness.

Swainson's hawk inspects her brood in eastern Washington. These hawks feed almost entirely on ground squirrels, mice and other rodents.

Showing his warning coat of black and white, spotted skunk searches for insects or mice. Locally known as "civet cat", usually are smaller and more active than the striped form.

Caught at the height of his display, a sage grouse goes through the ritual of attracting a female. Dozens of these birds may gather during the spring in a small area known as a lek.

Half-asleep, a great horned owl awaits darkness for his hunting. In areas where crows are abundant, owls remain concealed during the day, for they never fail to harass them.

Mallard drake displays his finery in central Oregon lake. These large
premier table birds have always been a favorite of wildfowl hunters.

Mallard hen ever-alert with her brood. She will never leave this family until they are able to fly, thus helping to guarantee their survival.

Red spotted garter snake searching for food. Confined to the Willamette Valley and adjacent coast of Oregon, this is one of the most beautiful of all snakes. More than 1500 species of snakes are known.

Faced with a decision, Swainson's thrush will provide choice morsels to the noisiest and most gaping mouth, thus feeding the hungriest nestling.

Eastern Oregon pronghorn antelope stares intently at some possible source of danger. Pronghorns warn others of their kind by erecting the white hairs of their rump into a conspicuous signal seen miles away.

Pronghorn antelope graze on bunchgrass in eastern Oregon. America's swiftest plains mammal, they have been clocked at 60 miles per hour.

Pacific shrew pauses briefly in its never-ending search for food. Members of this family are smallest living animals to suckle new born.

Adhesive toe disks permit tree frog to show off his climbing ability. Loud choruses of these small frogs can be heard throughout the far western United States from late fall to mid-summer, depending on the locality.

Velvet-antlered elk resting quietly in grassy meadow along the Northwest coast. Growing antlers are very soft and easily damaged, and seem to be carried with gallantry by the owners.

Bull elk battle for cows in a Wyoming meadow. Such contests are usually short and bloodless, but some have resulted in injury or death to one or both. Adult males weigh 550 to 750 pounds, females are less.

Young bighorn ram gazes across his Alberta mountain domain. Bighorns have superb eyesight and depend on their eyes to warn of danger.

Well-camouflaged in his summer plumage, this Alaskan willow ptarmigan will become all white in winter, except for black outer tail feathers. Ptarmigans reside in Arctic areas.

In full breeding plumage, a male American widgeon or baldpate rests on an Oregon lake. This species is an abundant nester in the Northwest.

Perhaps the most beautiful of our waterfowl, a male wood duck moves through the waters of a western Oregon river. Once reduced to low numbers, their population count now indicates a substantial increase.

Male bufflehead in the water of Tule Lake. Buffleheads are our smallest expert diving duck and they frequently pursue and feed upon small fish.

Short-tailed weasel or ermine forages on a Washington forest floor.
They turn white during winter except for those in the humid Northwest.

Safe on a limb in an Alberta forest, a red squirrel scolds an intruder. Also called chickarees or pine squirrels, they often fight viciously to protect their sphere of rule from one another.

Poised for flight, a young buck watches and listens in a northern California field. Mule deer are widespread over the West from southwestern Canada well into Mexico.

Rufous hummingbird broods her tiny nest, located in western Oregon rose bush. She will raise her two young alone without any help from the male.

Kestrel or sparrow hawk approaches its nest hole, probably an abandoned woodpecker nest. Kestrels subsist mainly on insects and mice.

Red-tailed hawk poses for a portrait. This much misunderstood hawk, comparatively harmless, feeds mainly on mice and other small mammals.

Belding ground squirrel, on the alert for predators. These squirrels may reside up to eight months in a semi-torpid state within their burrows.

Talons at ready, a golden eagle plunges toward its prey. Feeding mainly on rodents and rabbits, they are at home in the open areas of the West.

On the lookout for food, a gray jay looks over a small clearing in the forest. Usually called "camp robbers", these jays will frequently delight campers with their apparent boldness.

A pair of humpback whales cavort in icy water of Gastineau Channel near Juneau in apparent harmony with Alaska's snow-capped mountains.

Timber wolf moves alertly through a British Columbia forest. The wild areas of Alaska and Canada are perhaps the last stronghold of these magnificent animals. They stand over two feet high at the shoulder.

Chipmunk nibbles on some bits of food. Common throughout forested western Canada and the United States, chipmunks can be distinguished from ground squirrels by the stripes on their heads and lively antics.

An eye-to-eye confrontation with a yellow jacket. Known for constructing hanging papery nests, which they usually defend with painful stings.

Bald eagle with seven foot wing span is native only to North America.
His keen eyes have been known to spot prey three miles away. Liking
fish, they are known to rob osprey of their catch with razor sharp talons.

Fish securely grasped in its talons, a mature bald eagle rises from water near Juneau, Alaska. Alaska still has an abundant count of our national bird, which is becoming increasingly rare in the continental United States.

Male canvasback at edge of Siuslaw River near Oregon Coast. Nesting mainly in the prairie marshes of Canada, they are the rarest of North America's widespread game ducks.

Widespread through southern Canada and the United States, the mourning dove winters mostly in our southern states. In the western states this dove will frequently nest on the ground.

Perched over her nest, a red-winged blackbird is prepared to defend it. She and other blackbirds in the area will unite to drive away any predator.

Lustrous eggs of the cecropia moth on the underside of a leaf. They will hatch into a colorful caterpillar destined to reach four inches in length.

Raccoon appears "caught in the act" somewhere in western Oregon. These appealing animals are usually active at night, often visit suburban homes for handouts or available refuse. Raccoons do not hibernate.

With effortless ease, a new gull soars in a summer sky. Nesting in northern Asia, Alaska and western Canada, this small gull can be seen in winter along many areas of the Northwest coast with other shore birds.

Perched on a willow twig, a red-winged blackbird surveys his territory. Within this area he will claim two or three females to be his mates.

Occurring throughout the wilder forested areas of North America, the
black bear is wary and elusive outside the protection of National Parks.

Blue grouse hen searches for food in forest area of western Montana.
Called fool hens by westerners, they may seem absurdly tame at times.

Common flicker brings food to her nestlings. Flicker nest holes are often used by birds unable to build their own, like bluebirds and starlings.

In western America, a saw-whet owl scans the ground for mice. These owls are such sound sleepers during the day that occasionally they are captured without putting up resistance.

An arctic tern scans the waters near Juneau, Alaska, searching for small fish. This champion long-distance vagabond will winter near Antarctica.

Belted kingfisher with his latest catch. Kingfishers usually nest in perpendicular walls of stream banks, digging burrows as much as six feet deep.

Flock of migrating snow geese over Tule Lake in California. A few Canada geese appear at the top of this picture. Fall and spring migrations of snow geese number in the tens of thousands at Tule and Malheur Lakes.

Silver salmon encounter plunging water as they migrate up stream on the western slope of the Cascade Range. Having been at sea for three or four years, they are returning to the site of their birth for spawning.

A long-tailed weasel searches for prey. These miniature killers fear nothing, including man, and often have been known to attack a person who mars their movement, or aims.

Lone snow goose rises from Tule Lake in northeastern California. They will nest in the Arctic and are migrants to an expansive area of the United States.

Female bufflehead leads her brood across lake in central Oregon. They were probably hatched in a tree cavity, affording them ample protection.

Part of a nesting colony of Brandt's cormorants. Each bird will defend only the immediate perimeter around its nest from invasion by another.

Sea lions appear contented on coastal rocks north of Juneau, Alaska.
These are the smaller females; males may weigh up to 1800 pounds.

Canada goose escorts her young across pond in Malheur National Wildlife Refuge in southeastern Oregon. Canada geese will mate for life.

Common snipe perches near its nest in Oregon marsh. The long bill pierces and probes soft mud for earthworms and other invertebrates.

Sandhill cranes soar over the marshes of Malheur National Wildlife Refuge in southeastern Oregon. Once hunted almost to extinction, cranes are now making a comeback, but they still need close protection.

A half-submerged western grebe moves through the water of an Oregon lake. Like other grebes, they will nest on floating masses of vegetation.

Trumpeter swan appears to admire its reflection in a Yellowstone lake. Bordering on extinction, these birds have recovered to fair numbers in some of our national wildlife refuges.

Great blue heron retains eye on her nest while resting in pine tree,
above the Deschutes River in eastern Oregon. Several dozen pairs will
form a nesting colony, returning to the same site for many, many years
to raise their young. A fully-grown heron stands over four feet tall.

Among the largest of our North American moths is the cecropia, here possibly preparing to lay eggs. These are akin to silkworm moths of Asia.

Alaska fur seals cavort on a rocky shore of Pribilof Islands. Each year
a million plus will return here to breed, and give birth to their young.

Plump tufted puffins cling to a narrow ledge on sheer wall of the Pribilof Islands. At breeding time the male puffin dons a clownlike face to ready nesting burrow with its stubby beak.

Treasured sea otter appears relaxed along the shore of Resurrection Bay near Seward, Alaska. Hunted to near extinction at the turn of the century, small herds are now multiplying under government supervision.

Dall ram merits the title of elder statesman. Each dark ridge on the under-side of their horns defines a year's growth. Graceful and sure-footed, they can leap 12 to 15 foot chasms in their alpine territory.

Murres perch on a rocky cliff in the Aleutian Islands. Going fishing they will dive headfirst into water using their wings as oars below the surface.

Red-faced cormorant resting on flank of St. Paul Island in the Pribilofs. These birds seemingly reign unmolested in this area of the Bering Sea.

Caribou pauses for a moment on tundra slopes in Mt. McKinley National Park. These majestically antlered animals seldom hault in their meanderings except to sleep, chew their forage and drop their fawns.

Beaver pursuing natural instincts in pond within Mt. McKinley National Park. They prefer summer because their dark fur against the snow, is easy target for enemies. Heavy vegetation provides perfect camouflage.

Alaska brown bear, normally a vegetarian, turns fisherman in late summer on western Alaska river. The largest carnivores to walk the earth, adults may exceed a height of seven feet when standing erect.

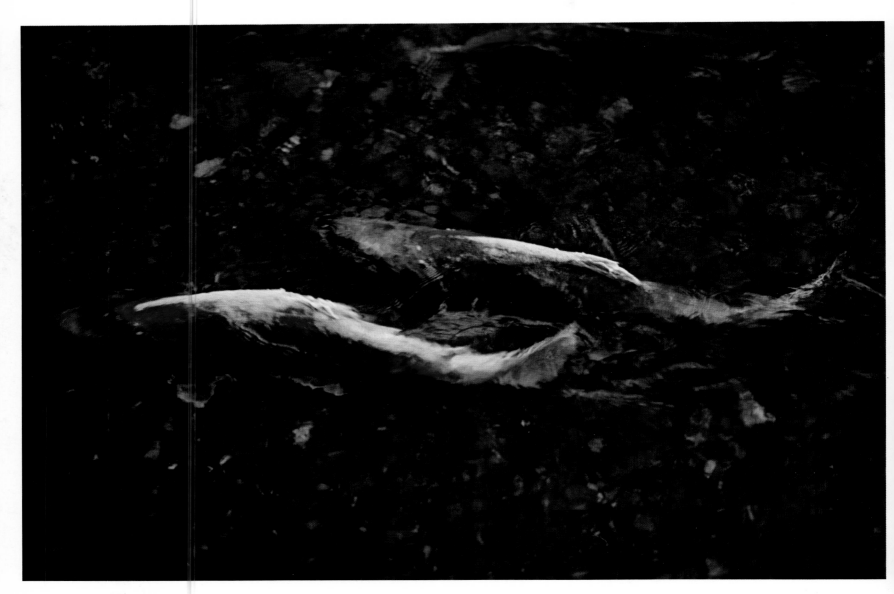

Salmon completing a gallant endeavor to reach the area of their birth. Schools may range the Pacific for 1,200 miles or more before homing in on their native waters. In rivers teeming with activity, they will make their upstream run, only to expire when spawning cycle comes to an end.

As I begin to write, I have the feeling that I have been witness to greater changes in the world of wildlife than a person of my age could possibly have seen. Then I realize that my grandfathers' stories to his teenage grandson have become part of my thinking, and in a way have stretched my life back into the 1800's. Grandfather Haley told stories of great flocks of passenger pigeons and of wild ducks and geese so plentiful that hunters would supply them to markets and restaurants. The passenger pigeons have been lost to us forever, but increasing concern for wildlife during the early 1900's has saved many other species from extinction. We can still enjoy the beauty of wild ducks and geese in flight or see them resting on the waters of our public parks and refuges.

There is no denying that many kinds of wildlife have suffered great losses of numbers and living places at the hands of man, and that this is continuing for many species. On the other hand, North America is still the home of an immense diversity of animals, and our people are gradually becoming more aware of these and taking better care of them.

Wildlife means many things to different people. To the apartment dweller among the man-made canyons of New York, it may be something unknown and vaguely terrifying, or it may be the ever-present pigeons. To the suburbanite, it is often the raccoons and opossums that make nightly visits to his garbage container. To the big game hunter it is a select group of horned or antlered animals and large predators such as bears and cougars. We could go on through a variety of meanings, but I prefer to think of wildlife as all the undomesticated and relatively free-roaming creatures around us. They may have backbones and we call them vertebrates, or we get more specific and call them fish or frogs or birds. We may know a few or many of them by name: bullfrogs, horned lizards, pheasants, moose, etc. They may lack backbones so we call them invertebrates, and we include such things as clams,

earthworms, butterflies and crabs. To me, all of these are wildlife, and although most of the pictures in this book are birds and furred animals (mammals), I may often bring other types of animals into my writings.

If you spend a day driving eastward from the Pacific shores, you will first enter the forested Coast Range. Today you see the steep hills of the Range covered by a variety of vegetation, from freshly-cutover areas supporting only grasses and weeds to areas of alder and various shrubs to stands of Douglas fir of various ages up to magnificent 200 to 300 year old giants. If any area in the Coast Range is cleared to bare ground it will begin to restore its vegetation by clothing itself with larger and larger types of plants until finally, if left alone for a century and a half, it will again be forested with giant trees. This process is called succession and the end vegetation that any area can support is called its climax vegetation.

As you move eastward from the Coast Range, you descend into the valley region, now a mosaic of towns, small to large ranches, and with winding ribbons of trees along the streams. Early explorers in the valley found its climax vegetation to be a head-high grass, with scattered oak trees. Ascending into the Cascade Mountains, you encounter a forest similar to that of the Coast Range, which changes at higher elevations to an evergreen forest of smaller tree species. Changes follow one another quickly now. Low on the eastern slopes of the Cascades, you suddenly enter a park-like forest of ponderosa pine which is followed by a belt of picturesque juniper trees, which give way to vast stretches of sagebrush.

This changing plant scene is largely due to varying amounts of rainfall, which in turn is a result of differences in elevation. The point of all this talking about plants is that they are the homes and food of animals, and different kinds of plants support different kinds of animals. A certain combination of plants and animals has developed together through millions of years of time and the interrelationships may be very close and very complicated. Thus it is that the little squirrels we call chickarees or pine squirrels feed only on the seeds within certain kinds of cones, and are limited to areas where trees bearing those cones occur.

Some animals have always been associated with climax vegetation and these are the kinds that are most likely to be reduced in numbers when forests are cut or prairies plowed up. Remember the passenger pigeon? The disappearance of that species was due in large part to the cutting down of the beech forests of the Northeast. On the other hand, a great many animals depend on successional plants, and since successional stages always follow disturbances of the vegetation, man-made or otherwise, these animals can maintain their numbers or even increase. Fortunately, many better-known forms are in this category. Marshes, burned or logged forests and many parts of agricultural lands are examples of successional situations. With a proper amount of human care and restraint, waterfowl, deer, elk and a great variety of songbirds thrive in these.

So, in a day's drive in the Northwest we have not just passed through a lot of different plant types; we have seen perhaps without knowing it, a great many different plant-animal associations. The relationship between animals and plants is so consistent that those who know wildlife know exactly where to go to see certain animals, and his or her clues are largely the vegetation. Almost everyone knows that robins require open moist lawn-like areas, but relatively few know where to look for Swainson's thrushes (damp brushlands) or hermit warblers (high in fir trees) or blackcapped chickadees (woods along streams). Every deer hunter worth his salt knows where to hunt his quarry, but few can go directly to the haunts of red tree mice or grey foxes.

Of course, there are a number of other things besides plants that have to do with an animal being where it is, but typical assemblages of plants and animals cover large areas of North America. These are often called things like life zones or biomes or biotic provinces. Much of the Northwest was once covered by a forest of Douglas fir, hemlock and red cedar. Logging has greatly reduced the extent of such forests, but where sizeable portions remain, a typical group of wildlife occurs. Here you may find such birds as Steller's jay, the western tanager, blue grouse and the spotted owl. Some resident mammals will be elk, blacktail deer, pine squirrels (chickarees), mountain beaver and spotted skunks. Similarly, other vegetation types have their characteristic animals.

Another thing that may have a direct influence on animal distributions is the nature of the soil. Soil can be heavy and compact like clay, it can be sandy, it can have a high humus content, etc. It can be wet or dry, or subject to periodic floods. Plants get the food they need for growth from soils and soils differ in the kinds of food they contain, having more or less decayed plant material in them, varying amounts of minerals, etc. For instance, deer grow the largest antlers in areas where soils are high in dissolved limestone content.

Many birds require soils of certain types. The robin in your yard strengthens its nest with mud that dries to a hard consistency, then lines it with soft grasses. Many other birds use mud in their nest-building; the cliff swallow constructs a gourd-shaped nest entirely of mud pellets brought one by one from nearby puddles or stream banks. Cliff swallows occur widely across the country but they can't all use the same kind of mud. In some areas, their mud is somewhat sandy and nests may fall during spells of wet weather.

A South American bird, called the rufous ovenbird, indirectly saved thousands of human lives. An incurable sickness called *Chaga's disease* is carried from person to person by an insect that lives in cracks in the walls of native huts. One doctor recalled that, as a boy he had thrown rocks at ovenbird mud nests, but they never cracked. Examination of the nests showed that the birds constructed them of a mixture of sand and cow manure. This mixture which fortunately proved to be odorless when dry was then used to plaster the interior of huts and, without cracks to live in, the disease-carrying insect disappeared.

Birds may actually build nests within the ground. Kingfishers and rough-winged swallows tunnel into vertical earthen banks, usually along streams, and these burrows in the case of the kingfisher may be up to six feet in length. Burrowing owls use the deserted burrow of some rodent or a badger and nest within these. Many mammals (mice, ground squirrels, badgers) find shelter for themselves and their families by digging burrows for living places. To the dismay of many a home owner, some mammals live entirely underground and can produce unsightly mounds of displaced dirt in an otherwise beautiful lawn. Moles are the main offenders; they raise little ridges as they move just below the surface in softer soils, searching for earthworms and other invertebrate animals. In firmer soils, their burrows are deeper, but the dirt taken from them is pushed to the surface like a miniature volcano.

Gophers likewise live almost entirely underground, and the mounds of dirt from their burrows heavily freckle many an otherwise green pasture in the Northwest. Gophers are plant eaters and have angered many a gardener, who discovers that his carrots are being pulled, not up, but down into a gopher burrow. Aside from his differences with man, gophers perform a valuable function by continually bringing deeper soil to the surface, where it can be mixed with richer soil and dead vegetation. As one might expect, gophers find living too difficult in lowlands that flood every winter and they are absent from such places.

Many desert animals live beneath the ground, and here the burrow serves not only as a place of concealment and a site for the young, but also as a means of getting along with the heat and dryness of the desert. Ground acts as an insulator so that temperatures within a burrow are more acceptable than those at the surface. On a fairly warm day, surface temperatures often exceed 120°F., but two feet down the temperature is nearer 90 degrees. The kangaroo rat is a common inhabitant of deserts and plains in the West, wherever the soil is loose enough for easy digging, but firm enough to hold up as a burrow. Kangaroo rats, as well as several other desert forms, roam the surface during the cool of the night then retreat to a burrow thus avoiding the heat of the day. To insure further the insulative properties of their burrow, kangaroo rats plug the entrance with loose soil.

Water is a problem in deserts because it is so hard to acquire and so easy to lose. Every living animal has to maintain a water balance in its body, by which we mean that the amount of water lost must be balanced by water consumed. The kangaroo rat is capable of getting all the water it needs from what seem to be dry seeds. These seeds contain a high proportion of carbohydrates, and when combined with oxygen in the animal's body, water is produced. A given amount of barley can produce about half its weight in water when oxidized in the body cells of this rat.

This seems like a rather risky way to depend on getting water, but they have quite a list of ways to keep their water. They have no sweat glands in the skin so they lose almost nothing there. When they are resting in their burrows, the air is fairly humid and little moisture is lost from the body. Much of their water is lost in the air they exhale, but they even have a clever device for reducing this amount. As air is exhaled, it cools the various membranes of the nose area; in the lungs, this air is warmed and filled with moisture. As exhaled, some of the moisture in the warm moist air condenses on the cooled nasal membranes and is absorbed into the bloodstream. Kangaroo rats also have remarkably capable kidneys, extracting water from urine so that it is five times more concentrated than that of man. Other desert animals may utilize other ways to maintain their water balance but in the arid areas of the Northwest, perhaps none is so capable as this individual.

Larger mammals such as pronghorn antelope and deer must utilize other means to maintain their water balance. For one thing, they frequently feed on vegetation containing some moisture. Depending on how dry their food is they must at certain intervals seek a source of drinking water. Waterholes in desert areas are privileged places for birds and mammals, especially in the evening or early morning. Hunter-wise buck deer often visit waterholes only at night.

Cold is a serious problem for wildlife in some areas where land animals must survive severe winters and aquatic animals must live in arctic waters. Birds and mammals are "warm-blooded", although scientists prefer the terms endothermic or homeothermic. Most of them are able to maintain their temperatures at a fairly constant rate at about the same point that man does, 98.6. Again we have a balance problem for heat gain must equal heat loss, and in cold areas the problem becomes one of increasing heat production and decreasing heat loss.

All of us have probably at some time or other experienced the feeling of increased warmth as we did some kind of exercise on a chilly morning. Exercise is one way of producing heat in the body, because it involves the oxidation or "burning" of substances in the body. When we get cold, we shiver, and this is an attempt by the body to produce more heat because it really means muscles are contracting and relaxing quickly—a form of exercise. Further heat can be produced by a complicated chemical process in deposits of special fat called brown fat. Brown fat occurs in several newborn mammals, including man, and is known to be present in some adult mammals.

One of the best ways for an endothermic animal to reduce heat loss is by some means of insulation because this keeps the heat in. In the case of birds, feathers are excellent insulation, and their effectiveness is increased by the bird's ability to fluff up its feathers. This produces dead air spaces between the feathers—a further insulation. Birds of cold areas often have more feathers than other birds, and penguins, inhabiting cold antarctic waters are the only birds that have feathers growing all over their body. Most birds actually have feathers growing in patches even though they grow in such a way as to appear to cover their body. Next time you prepare a chicken for dinner, scan the skin for the tiny pits where the feathers were; you will see that not all areas have these pits.

Fat is also an excellent insulator and many birds of arctic regions have heavy layers of fat. The feet and beaks of birds are not usually protected by insulating fat or feathers, and one wonders, for example, how ducks and geese can stand on ice for so long without freezing their feet. They do this by a device whereby blood flowing to the leg in an artery can pass directly into a vein for return to the heart without passing through the smaller vessels or capillaries of the feet or bill. Furthermore, roosting birds snuggle their feet up into their feathers and turn their head so the bill rests among the feathers of the back.

Arctic land mammals depend heavily on their fur for insulation. As trappers know, the best furs are available during the winter. In the arctic, a winter fur may be one and one-half times more effective as insulation than summer fur. Small mouse-sized mammals in the arctic utilize still another form of insulation—snow. They move around at the interface betwen snow and ground and the snow helps conserve their body heat. Small animals have a greater heat conserving problem than larger because they have more surface area in proportion to their volume. In fact, shrews are the smallest mammals possible because anything smaller would lose heat through its skin faster than it could produce it. The rate of energy change in a gram of house mouse tissue is 20 times that in a bison.

Arctic land animals use other devices to cut down on heat loss. Their ears, tails and limbs are shorter for one thing. For another, most of them possess what are known as counter-current heat exchangers at points where blood enters extremities such as paws. All these big words mean is that arteries and veins lie very close together so that heat coming from the inner body can pass across into the vein before it is carried into the cold paw and lost. Many of these animals are able to function properly with much lower temperatures in their paw pads, feet and even lower legs than within their body.

A mammal loses heat in the water at ten times the rate at which it would lose it in air. It is well known that humans cannot survive in near-freezing waters for more than a few minutes. Nevertheless, arctic waters are inhabited by such things as seals, sea lions, walruses and a number of kinds of whales (right whale, killer whale, narwhal, white whale, grampus, and others). Seals and sea lions may have both fur and thick fat as insulation, but the walrus and whales have only a thick layer of fat, or blubber, beneath the skin. In some seals and small whales, 25 to 45% of the total weight may be blubber. Blood supply to the blubber and skin can be controlled so that the temperature of the skin can be near freezing, but little or no blood is present to lose heat to the water. In addition, blood supplies to the blubber and skin are involved in multitudes of counter-current heat exchangers so warmth can pass from arteries to veins without going to the cold surface. In like fashion, blood to extremities (flippers, tail, etc.) is controllable in amount and passes through heat exchangers.

Another phenomenon that we tend to associate with animals and cold weather is hibernation. It is a subject that is worth looking at more closely. Not all warm-blooded or endothermic mammals maintain their temperatures at some given level. In fact, among bats, many varieties allow their temperature to drop to near that of their surroundings whenever they are inactive, usually during the day. Scientists call such animals heterotherms. The advantage of such a system to a small animal like a bat is that rather than use up the energy that it would take to maintain a high temperature, they can cool off periodically and use less energy. Remember here that small animals have a much greater problem in maintaining a temperature because of the greater amount of surface area they have compared with their body volume. The smallest birds are hummingbirds and they, too, let their temperature drop at night to conserve energy. Interestingly enough, the smallest mammals, the shrews, don't seem to have this ability, and must live where they have rich food supplies, which they must continuously "burn" or oxidize to produce heat. A shrew can eat its own weight in meat every two or three hours.

To get back to hibernation, the ability of an animal to change its temperature (heterothermy) seems to be necessary for hibernation to occur. Hibernation is a condition in which the temperature of the animal drops to within a degree or two of the surrounding temperature and the breathing rate goes down to perhaps one a minute, and there are lengthy periods of several minutes when the animal doesn't breathe at all. The animal feels cold to the touch and seems to be in a condition much deeper than sleep. The first time I saw a hibernating animal, a woodchuck, I thought it was dead.

Only certain North American mammals truly hibernate in terms of the conditions we stated above. These are some bats, marmots and woodchucks, most ground squirrels, and a group of mice called jumping mice. Within these groups, as cold weather approaches the animals begin to accumulate heavy layers of fat, which seems a necessity before the winter sleep. The picture is really much more complicated than this, however. A number of other mammals spend long periods in a kind of torpor or sleep during the winter, and it is probable that for some periods, at least, they come close to truly hibernating. The most famous of these are black bears. Bears den up during the winter, and remain in the den for several months. It has been found that their temperature doesn't drop very much, but their heartbeat goes down to about a quarter of its normal rate. Bears move around a great deal within their winter den. As further evidence that bears are not in a deep hibernating state, black bear cubs are born during their mother's winter sleep.

A further complication to the situation is that many mammals go into a state resembling hibernation during the summer. When this occurs it is called estivation, and here we run into a common problem, the exact meaning of words. As a matter of fact, there are animals that go into estivation in the summer but "sleep" right through into the winter and then they are hibernating. Belding's ground squirrel of the Great Basin may estivate in late July or August then never emerge until March or April. Somewhere along the way estivation or "summer sleep" becomes hibernation or "winter sleep". Before leaving the subject of hibernation, I should tell you that we know of only one North American bird that hibernates and this is a western species called the poorwill, which is related to the more familiar nighthawk.

Animals other than birds and mammals have little or no internal means of raising their body temperatures. Such things as snakes, lizards, frogs, newts and all the invertebrate animals are pretty much at the mercy of the temperature around them and we call them cold-blooded or ectotherms. In one way, the term "cold-blooded", is not truly appropriate, because a number of these forms, especially reptiles, have ways of getting their temperature up to a point very near that of man and we certainly can't say that their blood is cold. They do this mainly by means of their behavior. Imagine a lizard sitting on a rock. The sun is shining on the rock and the lizard can move to whatever surface of the rock gets more or less sun-heat. Once in position, it can turn its body at right angles to the sun's rays or parallel with them, thus controlling the amount of heat received by the body. Snakes can allow their entire body to be in the sun or only a portion of it.

In addition, many reptiles have the ability to change their general color from dark to light and back to dark by means of pigment cells in their skin. When they are cold, they tend to be dark, thus absorbing more heat. As they warm up, the skin becomes lighter and heat is reflected. By these simple means, a desert lizard may maintain its temperature within a degree or two of a given point, usually somewhere between 90 and 100 degrees Fahrenheit. Snakes can be fully active at lower temperatures and an average range for them would be approximately between 75 and 90 degrees Fahrenheit. Lesser animals are usually well-adapted to operate at the usual temperature of their surroundings.

In cooler or cold areas, hibernation is a necessity for ectotherms. As temperatures drop, they are unable to produce heat and without body heat they are increasingly unable to move. Through eons of time, such animals have become able instinctively to seek out hibernation sites that will protect them during the cold season. Earthworms retreat deep in the soil below the frost line. Salamanders move downward in rock crevices, old root channels or mammal burrows. Frogs may burrow into mud under the water of a lake or they may gather in groups and remain a sluggishly active gathering beneath the ice of a pond. Lizards usually retreat beneath rocks or get underground by burrowing, utilizing crevices or ready-made burrows.

Many snakes are more spectacular in their means of hibernation. Some species annually travel to rocky dens where they can retreat among cracks in the rocks to unfreezable levels below the surface. Rattlesnake dens are a common phenomenon throughout the

United States, and wherever they occur, local people are well aware of their presence. As the nights become cooler in the fall, rattlesnakes move toward these traditional dens from distances up to at least two or three miles away. At the den, they retreat downward at night, but emerge to sun during nice days, until oncoming winter forces them finally to gather in snakey masses in deep protected crevices or chambers. Rattlesnakes are frequently joined in their dens by other species, particularly gopher or bull snakes.

Now that we have talked about the distribution of wildlife and some of the ways in which they survive in different places, we can turn to an all important part of our wildlife story, the problems of getting a new generation started. Whatever level of wildlife we may be concerned with, insect or frog, earthworm or bird, lizard or mammal, the ultimate test of the success of that species in this world is whether or not it keeps its numbers up or increases them by reproduction. The majority of the animals we are concerned with come in two different sexes, male and female. Even though an individual earthworm is both male and female in a sense, the appropriate organs are arranged in such a way that two different earthworms must meet to carry on the species.

I suppose a logical question to be answered at this time is why have different sexes. Why isn't every individual animal able to produce its kind without the help of a different sex? The question isn't easy to answer, but I'll try. First of all, the typical characteristics of any kind of animal, the things that allow us to recognize it as a moose or a deer, are determined by submicroscopic particles called genes, thousands of which are carried on larger devices called chromosomes. Genes can change slightly from time to time, and when they do they often produce a slight to considerable effect in the characteristic they are responsible for. These slight changes have gone on for thousands and even millions of years to the extent that every individual animal carries a different set of genes from every other individual, even within the same species.

Consider what would happen if every individual could only produce other individuals like himself (no two sexes). From generation to generation, there would be very little change. Compare this with a two-sex system where genes from the father must combine with those from the mother to produce each new animal. Every time a new individual is produced, there is brought together a new combination of genes, which in turn will produce something a little different. This is most evident to us among domestic animals, because we are used to looking for certain characteristics. It also occurs in wild animals and even though a litter of baby mice or twin fawns or a nestful of young robins may look alike to our unpracticed eyes, they have slight differences. These may be in terms of size or other physical things or there may be differences in aggressiveness, craftiness, reproductive ability, etc. The main advantage then, of a two-sex or bisexual system is that it allows for more rapid change, which in turn tends to allow more rapid adjustment by the species to the conditions of its environment.

Most wildlife species have a yearly cycle of reproductive effort. In North America, the overall control for these cycles seems to be the changing lengths of the day throughout the year. This regular change in the amount of light or photoperiod apparently acts through the eyes to stimulate parts of the brain which control production of certain hormones, which then are responsible for the cycles. To appreciate these cycles, consider that young animals should be born at the best possible time to assure that they survive. This can mean that the weather must be favorable, food abundant, water available, and so on through other necessities. Further consider that young animals often take time to develop—within an egg, as a larva, or within the body of the mother. Whether it is a salamander whose eggs may take three months to develop or an elk that carries its young for 255 days, the time of the male and female coming together must be such that the young will emerge at the best time. Obviously, the timing of all this has become well-nigh perfect through a long period of adjustment to nature.

The nature of the reproductive cycle is such that when the eggs or ova have matured to a certain point within the female, she makes this fact known to males in the area, usually by means of special odors or behaviorisms. Some female moths at this time give off a substance into the air which can be detected by the antennae of the male in amounts as little as a ten-billionth of a gram. He then can follow this scent, through darkness, to the female. Female salamanders release certain odors into the water which are detected and followed up by the males. Odor is important in bringing together the two sexes of such varied animals as snakes and mammals. Behavior may be the important signal. A male lizard may recognize the differences between receptive and non-receptive females and males by the way they respond to his advances. The behavior of female birds at the time they are ready to mate serves as a signal to the male.

Looking over the various patterns of male-female behavior at this time one is struck by several that seem more impressive or different than most. Male sage grouse gather at traditional mating grounds called arenas or leks, which may be up to one-half mile long by 200 yards wide. In such an area, up to 400 males may gather, spacing themselves some 25 to 40 feet apart. Each male then displays repeatedly by momentarily inflating paired yellow balloon-like sacs on the neck, at the same time giving a low call. Females wander among these males and eventually select a male with whom mating is completed. In one study, 74% of 114 observed matings were done by only four males, referred to as "master cocks". Apparently, the females see something in these master cocks that is missing in the others.

This selecting of certain males from among many is a fairly wide-spread phenomenon among many animals and is often called sexual selection. In the long run, it means that the healthiest, strongest, or perhaps the most typical males carry on the species. In some mammals, males often fight for females. Bull elk battle one another for possession of several cows and although these battles occasionally end in severe injury or even death for one combatant, they are usually fairly brief and the weaker bull leaves. A powerful bull has been known to have as many as 60 cows in his "harem". Moose, on the other hand, do not collect harems, but stay with one cow for a few days at a time then move on to find another. At this time, bull moose are very pugnacious and quite ready to fight any rival bull. If the bulls are of about the same size, the battles can be quite bloody. Bulls of both elk and moose are quite dangerous to man during the breeding or rutting season.

For most back-boned animals (vertebrates), before actual mating occurs there is a preliminary period, known as courtship. The word is familiar to humans, and we are bound to notice similarities, but scientists try very hard not to put human feelings and thoughts into animal behavior. Among lower animals, courtship may involve many things. In addition to various poses and movements of the body, colors or patterns may be displayed, special odors produced or calls and songs employed. Various combinations of these produce the courtship behavior and it is important to note that each species has its own specific courtship pattern.

Whatever may be involved in courtship, the entire courtship procedure seems to do the following important things: it prepares and stimulates both sexes for the final act of transferring germ cells or sperms from the male to the female; and helps insure, through the fact that each species courtship pattern is different, that only males and females of the same species will mate. Among wildlife, there are very few mismatchings between species, and the intricacies of the courtship are one good reason for this.

The male salamander is drawn to the female by her specific odor or odors. Once they have met, the hours or even days will pass while he clings to her with his front or rear legs, all the time giving off odors and body movements characteristic of his species. The reluctant female gradually relaxes her attempts to escape and eventually becomes stimulated to follow the male when he releases her. He moves a short distance, stops and deposits from his vent or cloaca a tiny blob of jelly, topped by a bundle of sperm either underwater or on the ground in the case of many land salamanders. He then leads the female over this object and stops her at a time when the sperm bundle is picked up by her cloacal opening. The sperm are stored in a special pocket of her cloaca and can fertilize eggs up to months later.

The courtship of birds is probably the most conspicuous to us. I have already mentioned the display and sounds of the male sage grouse in his arena. Most birds, however, have a different system. The males usually arrive in the nesting area first, where each male establishes what is known as a territory. In many of the birds best-known to us, this is an area large enough to contain materials for building a nest and sufficient food to see nestling and adults through the nesting season. The male maintains the limits of his territory by chasing other males of the same species from it. Within his territory, he displays, sings or calls in notes characteristic of his species. The songs and displays advertise that the male has a territory; they warn other males away and serve to attract a female into the area. Once a female has moved in, the male frequently employs other displays and sounds for her as part of a pre-mating courtship. She, in turn, may signal her readiness by certain displays. Female house sparrows crouch down and flutter their wings just prior to mating.

Other bird species have different systems. The nesting territory of many gulls, terns and seabirds (auks, murres, puffins, etc.) may be only an area immediately around the nest, often the area within pecking range of the female as she sits on the nest. Consequently, such birds often nest in colonies of hundreds. Substitutes for song occur widely among birds. Snipe fly high over their territories, producing a winnowing sound as air vibrates their stiff outer tail feathers. Ruffed grouse advertise their territories by beating their wings rapidly to produce a drumming sound, whereas blue grouse give low muffled hooting notes, which are difficult to pinpoint as to location. Most species of woodpeckers beat out rolling tattoos on some reverberating dead limb. When a boy, I came upon a flicker that was utilizing the bottom of an old tin can, producing a most impressive sound. At my present home, sapsuckers find my T.V. antenna post to their liking.

So in a multitude of ways, wildlife will find a mate, male and female germ cells are united and a new generation begins. In the great majority of animals considering both vertebrates and invertebrates, eggs are produced. In most lower forms, these are cast into the waters, left in a cavity under a rock or buried in soil or rotting wood. Parental care shows up occasionally. Mother crayfish carry their eggs attached to the abdomen and young larvae remain attached for several days. Some centipedes guard their eggs until hatching. Many land salamanders remain with their small egg clutch, and their presence seems necessary to prevent the eggs from molding. As a rule, it is only when we get to the birds and mammals that parental care becomes the common thing.

Care for a time by the parents is probably a major reason for the success of birds and mammals over the world. The young can be raised to an age where they are more capable of caring for themselves, and during their period with the parents, they go through learning experiences, so necessary later on. This is not to say that a mother bird deliberately goes about teaching things to her young. More probably, the young may acquire part of their future pattern of living by imitating their parent or parents. We know that in many bird species, the ability to sing is inborn, but the details of song are learned from surrounding adults. Birds are creatures of marvelous instincts and most of what a bird does as an adult was entered into his genetic makeup when he was born.

In mammals, the dominant role of instinct is not so clear. Mammal parents, in many instances, clearly teach their young valuable skills—hunting for food, hiding, and even getting along with others of the species. The fact that we can teach our dogs or horses so many things is a clue to the fact that mammals learn. Witness how quickly seemingly wild animals become adjusted to the presence of man in a refuge or National Park. I'm sure many a camper in Yellowstone has cursed the learning abilities of black bears.

Another advantage of parental care is that it enables a species to keep its numbers up with the production of fewer young. Invertebrates or fish that pass their eggs into the waters of the ocean may produce eggs by the thousands or even millions in order to assure that some will survive. Freshwater habitats apparently are not as dangerous, for many salamanders leave only one to two hundred eggs each year. On the other hand, frogs apparently face greater dangers, for many frogs produce upwards of a thousand eggs. I hope that by now you are beginning to see that the number of young produced by a species has adjusted through time to the natural dangers faced by that group.

When we move from salamanders and frogs to reptiles, we encounter another drop in the number of young. In fact, most lizards lay less than ten eggs, leading one to believe that land situations are much safer places to leave eggs and young than the waters of ponds or marshes. Similarly, many snakes produce less than ten eggs. A phenomenon occurring in a number of reptiles that seems to have a bearing on numbers is that of retention of the eggs by the female, so that they develop within her body. Other things

being equal, such a reptile will usually produce fewer young than a similar egg-layer. This is probably a type of parental care in that the female can move around, sun herself and the eggs, and thus will protect them as best she can. Live-bearing lizards and snakes, probably because they can bring more total heat to their internal eggs, can inhabit cooler areas. The only reptiles on the Northwestern Coast are live-bearing garter snakes and alligator lizards.

The advantages of parental care are certainly apparent when one examines the number of young of birds and mammals. All birds lay eggs, but since birds are endotherms, the eggs must be kept warm or incubated through their development. After hatching, young birds take several days to weeks to develop full temperature control and during this time must be protected from heat or cold. Complicating this picture is the fact that young birds tend to fall into two groups. Either they are born quite helpless and unable to leave the nest for a period of weeks or months (perching birds like robins and crows, hawks, eagles, owls, etc.) or they hatch with the ability to move around and pick up their own food (pheasants, grouse, ducks and geese, shorebirds, etc.). Apparently, even though both are cared for by at least one parent, the latter group faces more dangers, because their egg clutches are larger on the average. Most perching birds, with helpless young, produce four to six eggs, whereas ducks and pheasant or grouse-like birds lay eight to twelve. On the other hand, seemingly to confuse my point, shorebirds usually have four eggs and perching birds like chickadees lay up to nine. We can only conclude that there are probably many things affecting clutch size in birds, so long as we remember that the number has probably adjusted through time to the dangers faced throughout the life of individuals of that species.

It is among mammals that parental care seems to have reached its highest point. Man has the most highly-developed brain of all the animals. In order to make use of this brain, a comparatively long period of learning is necessary, and this learning period is one reason for the lengthy parent-young relationship. Among non-human mammals, periods of parental care seem longest among those forms that we consider the most advanced in their mental abilities. Young chimpanzees are allowed to stay with the family clan for several years. Beaver young are allowed to remain within the family colony for up to two years. Young wolves remain with the family at least a year, until they are old enough to hunt on their own. On the other hand, young mice and rats leave their parents within days or weeks after birth, often in a sexually mature state.

Within a population of animals there are happenings which scientists call population dynamics. When we speak of a population of animals, we are usually referring to all the members of one kind of species of animal, living within whatever limits or area we define. Thus, we can talk about the roughskin newt population of a certain pond, the robin population of some town or the Dall sheep population of Mount McKinley National Park in Alaska.

A natural wild population of any animal has the ability to increase its numbers rapidly when it is living under fairly ideal conditions. The best way to show what populations are capable of is to give one or two examples. In the late 1930's, two male and six female pheasants were released on an island in Puget Sound. Within five years, the population of pheasants had increased to 1,325 birds. A meadow mouse or vole was observed to have 17 litters in one year, in captivity. Charles Darwin once estimated that starting with one pair of elephants, in about 750 years there could be as many as 19 million living elephants, all descendants of the first pair. The steady increase in the number of human beings over the world is another example of what we call reproductive potential.

Fortunately, most wildlife species seldom, if ever, build up their numbers so rapidly. As they increase, various factors act upon the swelling numbers to force a leveling off amidst their environment, such as shortages of food or space, or increase of animals that feed upon them. Forces within the population may also act to reduce the rate of increase. For one thing, increases in numbers may cause fewer young to be born at a time and fewer litters or clutches of eggs per year. A recent study of coyote population dynamics indicated that when the population was reduced by various controls to half its original size, average litter size doubled. The authors pointed out that killing about half the coyotes born every year does not permanently reduce their numbers, because the birth rate increases.

It has been known for many years that several animals in the northern parts of our continent go through regular increases and decreases of numbers. These have come to be known as population cycles and tend to fall into two main types. The first, known as the "mouse cycle", has an average length of four years. This means that every four years, northern mice, particularly lemmings and voles, increase their numbers to high densities. During the period of fastest increase, the mice have larger and more litters, and breed at an earlier age. Numbers are maximized during summer of the peak year. In the following winter, the mice begin to die in such numbers that the phenomenon is called a population crash, and there follow about two years in which the numbers remain very low, largely due to a very reduced reproductive output.

Animals that depend on mice or lemming for food also show an approximate four-year cycle. These include arctic foxes and birds such as rough-legged hawks and snowy owls. The same is true of the second, named the "rabbit cycle" because the main animal involved is the snowshoe hare. This cycle has a period of about ten years and was first noticed by a scientist who checked over the fur receipt records for the Hudson Bay company of Canada, going back some 200 years. He noticed that the take of lynx hides increased and decreased with about a ten year regularity, and this was eventually traced to the regular rise and fall of the lynx's main food item, the snowshoe hare. Red foxes, martens, fishers, and horned owls are involved in this cycle. The four-year cycle seems to occur among animals of the open tundra, whereas the ten-year cycle is limited to forest animals.

There is still no agreed upon cause for these cycles. It has been shown that most of the animals that die are not unusually diseased. Perhaps there are different causes for different animals and different areas. Long-term studies of lemming cycles in the Point Barrow region of Alaska showed that the cycle there had a three-year duration and that most of the die-off occurred during the third summer. Peak numbers of lemming during the preceding winter fed so heavily on vegetation beneath the snow that they had little or no cover when the snow melted. Bird and mammal predators moved into such areas in large numbers and contributed greatly to the rapid decline of lemming numbers. In other parts of their range, lemmings, at times of population highs become extremely aggressive toward one another and move away from their home area, usually always going downhill. In the process, they may encounter bodies of water, which they attempt to swim across and in which large numbers drown. There is no truth to the myth that they deliberately jump over cliffs or enter the sea in mass suicides nor are they trying to swim to some long-lost continent under the sea.

Other theories as to the cause of cycles that may have some basis in fact involve such things as a wearing out, at the time of the numbers decline, of hormone-producing glands, due to the increased stress brought on by the ever-increasing number of neighbors; or the idea that the genetics of the mice change because more aggressive mice survive, but the change to aggressiveness carries with it a lowered reproductive capacity. Eventually, we may know the answers to the mystery of population cycles, but these answers will probably raise more questions. Jackrabbits of the west

have an increase and decline in their numbers, but they do not fit a ten-year cycle. Mice occasionally build up to unbelievable numbers in certain areas, but not in a regular cyclic way. In 1907, it was estimated that there were 8,000 to 12,000 meadow mice per acre in Humboldt Valley, Nevada. Such outbreaks or eruptions are due to several years of very favorable climate and food supply.

With normal populations, the numbers of animals may change somewhat from year to year, but generally remain stable. The animals are still capable of reproducing at a high rate but as populations begin to build up, many things act to maintain a balance. One of the interactions between kinds of animals is that certain kinds feed upon other kinds. This is called predation, and is a very common phenomenon among wildlife. We humans do not hesitate to apply the name, "predator", to such things as cougars, coyotes and bobcats, perhaps because they often feed on animals of value to us, but lizards dining on grasshoppers or birds feeding on earthworms are certainly predators to the insects and worms.

Biologists, then, are used to predation as a means of an animal acquiring the food it needs to live. They see it all around them in the natural world as an expected part of the wildlife scene. The relationships between a predator and its prey may have gone on for millions of years. During this time, there would be a constant tendency for the predator to improve its methods of capture. At the same time, you could expect the prey populations continually to improve their methods of escape. The result that we see today is often a complex or efficient way of capturing food by the predator. Wolf packs have evolved effective ways of hunting as a group.

Successful predators have an impressive array of weapons that they have developed for capturing their prey. Spiders construct what seems to us to be fragile webs, but toss a grasshopper into the web of a large garden spider. The insect cannot escape the sticky tough strands and its struggles relay a message to the web owner. She emerges from her spun lair at the edge of the web, seizes the victim and begins to whirl it with her feet. As she does so, thick webbing pours from her abdomen, encircling and immobilizing the grasshopper. Then, or at a later time, she will sink hollowed fangs into the insect and extract its life-giving juices. The sticky, long tongue of frogs and toads, the fangs and venom of a rattlesnake, the talons of an eagle are a few of the impressive devices employed by predators.

As the hunting or capturing devices have improved, so have the defense mechanisms of the prey. Many animals have colors or patterns that blend into their surroundings. Female birds are usually dull-colored so that they are less visible on the nest. Many birds and mammals have sentry animals that remain alert while others feed. Alarm calls, recognizable not only by the species involved, but even by other species, are common among both birds and mammals. Prey animals have, in some cases, developed substances that are distasteful or even poisonous to a would-be predator. Such animals often also show bright colors or distinct patterns that appear to serve as warnings. There are many instances among animals of edible forms imitating the color or pattern of some inedible species, which tends to ward off predators.

Competition is another type of interaction between populations, occurring when each of two populations has an adverse effect on the other. This seems like a simple definition, but competition has had volumes written about it, and yet many of its aspects are still debated and not well understood. Competition can occur between members of the same species; for example, we have already noted that male birds select territories and chase away other males of their species. It can also exist between different species; a number of kinds of birds within a marsh may seem to all be feeding on the fish therein. By now, it should be more apparent that competition can be for food, space, water or any number of things an individual or species might need for its survival.

Many careful studies over the years have shown that where there appears to be competition, there are actually differences that reduce or minimize it. Studies of five kinds of small birds known as warblers, in eastern forests, revealed that although these species all fed on insects in the same trees, they concentrated their efforts in different parts of the tree. Grassland birds have different feeding patterns such that each may be picking up insects in different parts of grass clumps or in the spaces between. More obviously, swallows and bats both catch small insects on the wing. However, they divide this resource very nicely by one feeding only by day and the other only at night. Hawks and owls similarly separate their feeding times. Referring back to the marsh birds, it can well be that different sizes of birds are feeding on different sizes of fish. Furthermore, each species of bird probably has certain specific areas in which it catches fish.

The fact that all of these little differences in ways of feeding have developed is proof that competition exists in nature. It is the force behind constant adjustments by animals through time, to utilize the environment more fully without overly interfering with other animals. We say that each animal has its niche. Unfortunately, this word has been defined in many different ways, some of which are beyond the scope of this effort to explain. Perhaps we can be satisfied by saying that an animal's niche consists of all the conditions under which that animal can successfully replace itself. The food it requires, the space it needs, the materials for nests and homes, and the other things that enable it to live and reproduce its kind are all part of its niche. Niche overlap means that two animals are using the same resource to some extent, and this can be the basis for competition. In spite of the fact that predation and competition are an ever-present part of the wildlife scene, thousands of species continue to exist in satisfactory numbers. By now, perhaps one can visualize some of the age-old processes that have constantly adjusted the reproductive rate to the species needs, refined the quality of parental care, sharpened the hunting abilities of predators and the escape mechanisms of prey, and fitted species into niches, wherein their lives can continue in spite of the adversities of their living and non-living environment. There is no doubt that through millions of years thousands of species have dropped by the wayside, unable to adjust well enough, indicating this is a natural phenomenon. When man entered the picture, his abilities and ingenuities at capturing and growing food or utilizing resources like forests for homes and other things placed additional problems in the way of wildlife. Now that we have looked more closely at some of the intricate adjustments of wildlife to each other and to their environment in general, it is easier to understand why many species are so reduced in number when man so drastically alters their niche size and adds immeasurably and too suddenly to their competition pattern.

Energy, a subject presently of much concern to humans, is equally important to wildlife, although we can be sure that they are incapable of being concerned about it to the extent that man is. The source of energy for animals is the sun, but it reaches them indirectly. Only green plants can use the light from the sun to manufacture their tissues, through a complicated chemical processes involving the green chlorophyll of plants. In other words, plants can convert sunlight energy to plant tissue energy. This energy is secured by animals when they feed on the plants. High school physics students know that energy can neither be created nor destroyed, but it can be changed to a different form; for example, sunlight to plant tissues. However, whenever such an alteration occurs, it is to a less useful form, so that with each change, less energy is available to the next level.

In a community of plants and animals, plants are the primary producers of energy. Animals feed upon plants or upon animals whose food is plants. Animals for whom plants are the only source of energy are first-level consumers. Included are such animals as most insects, larval frogs or tadpoles, many lizards and turtles, several birds, most rodents and rabbits, and large grazing or browsing mammals such as cattle, pronghorn antelope, deer, elk and bighorn sheep. These animals are in turn fed upon by the second-level consumers, consisting of such things as some insects, spiders, frogs and toads, lizards and snakes, many birds and carnivorous mammals. A third-level consumer may feed upon second-level animals and this group includes mainly the larger bird and mammal predators. Such a system can be called a food chain, although in nature, feeding interrelationships are much more complicated and are called a food web. Because each change in the form of energy causes a loss in the energy available, each of the levels we have talked about contains fewer animals and the various levels (called food, trophic or nutritional levels) form a pyramid of numbers with a broad base of plants at the bottom and a few predators at the top. In terms of total weight, called biomass, the base is even wider and the top more narrow. In one study of the relationships between plant food, moose and wolves, it turned out that 762 pounds of plant food produced 59 pounds of moose a year, which in turn could produce one pound of wolf. In terms of energy, the losses of energy through the food chain are impressive. In another study, it was shown that only one percent of the total sun energy falling on an area was converted into usable plant tissue. Meadow mice consumed about two percent of the plants and weasels consumed 31 percent of the mice. It is estimated that only about ten to twenty percent of the energy in any given nutritional or trophic level is available to the next higher level. If 1000 units of energy (calories) are available to the primary producers (the plants), 100 to 200 of these are available to first-level consumers and only ten to twenty to second-level consumers. By the time we reach third-level consumers (the larger bird and mammal predators mentioned above), only as little as one or two units of energy may be available to them. The point of all this is that trophic levels cannot go on indefinitely, because eventually there isn't enough energy to support the top levels. In other words, the closer an animal can stay to the lowest trophic or nutritional level the more energy it will have available to subsist.

In these few pages, we have been able to present only a brief introduction to the study of wildlife, but hopefully enough so that you can go into the world of nature and look at wildlife with wiser eyes. If we have learned one thing, it is the interrelationships that exist between all living things, including man, and we are becoming increasingly aware of the effects of man's actions on his environment and that of wildlife. Over the years, there have always been strong advocates for wildlife refuges, parks and wilderness areas, and there are today a number of organizations whose members are dedicated to the preservation of wildlife and the places they live. Such groups as Audubon Society, Ducks Unlimited, Nature Conservancy, Izaak Walton League, National Wildlife Federation, Friends of the Earth, Wilderness Society and Sierra Club may seem like strange bedfellows to some, but all are dedicated to the preservation of wildlife and the environment. This legacy carries a heavy responsibility which requires a maximum degree of devotion and dedication. This we must pledge to exercise.

Grandfather Haley was a young boy when our first national park was established (Yellowstone, in 1872), and I am sure he would be astonished at the total acreage of parks, wildernesses, refuges and other public lands today. If we are to maintain wildlife as we see it in this book, much of these lands must be preserved in a condition wherein the animals can live out their normal and fascinating lives for generations to come.

INDEX

The Student Writer

Editor and Critic

Second Edition

Barbara Fine Clouse
Youngstown State University

With a Contribution by
Joy Johnson DeSalvo

McGraw-Hill Book Company
New York St. Louis San Francisco Auckland Bogotá Caracas
Colorado Springs Hamburg Lisbon London Madrid Mexico Milan
Montreal New Delhi Okalhoma City Panama Paris São Paulo
San Juan Singapore Sydney Tokyo Toronto

THE STUDENT WRITER: Editor and Critic

1 2 3 4 5 6 7 8 9 0   DOCDOC   8 9 3 2 1 0 9 8

ISBN   0-07-011412-9

See Acknowledgments on pages 419–420.
Copyrights included on this page by reference.

This book was set in Times Roman by Better Graphics, Inc.
The editors were Emily Barrosse and John M. Morriss;
the designer was Caliber Design Planning, Inc.;
the production supervisor was Leroy A. Young.
R. R. Donnelley & Sons Company was printer and binder.

LIBRARY OF CONGRESS
Library of Congress Cataloging-in-Publication Data

Clouse, Barbara Fine.
     The student writer : editor and critic / Barbara Fine Clouse.
         p.   cm.
     Includes index.
     ISBN 0-07-011412-9
     1. English language—Rhetoric.   2. Editing.   I. Title.
PE1408.C537 1988
808′.042—dc19   87-27981
                    CIP

*In loving memory of
Rose Lewin and
Chance Crago Tatman*

Contents

PART III   A Brief Guide to Frequently Occurring Errors

Preface

One assertion informing this text is that learning to write well means developing effective writing procedures. Thus, a primary focus of *The Student Writer: Editor and Critic* is helping students develop their own successful writing processes. To this end, the text helps students become aware of what they do when they write. It also helps them determine which aspects of their processes are effective and efficient and which are not. It describes a variety of ways to handle the different aspects of writing (idea generation, drafting, organizing, revising, editing, and proofreading), and it calls upon students to sample many of these procedures. After sampling alternative procedures, students assess their effectiveness to determine whether further sampling is in order. In other words, throughout the text students are considering what they do when they write, evaluating the effectiveness of their procedures, and trying alternative procedures in an ongoing effort to improve their processes.

Another assertion informing this text is that student writers need considerable work with revision. For this reason, revision is a second focus of *The Student Writer*. To help students become skilled at revision, the text targets two concerns: accurately judging the strengths and weaknesses of a draft and successfully effecting the necessary changes. Revision, then, is treated as a two-step process. To help students learn to judge writing reliably so they can make accurate revision decisions, the text includes a large number of student essays. These essays are of varying quality, but each has some strengths and some weaknesses. Students are asked to study these essays and assess their strengths and weaknesses. This experience develops students' critical abilities and helps them become reliable evaluators of their own drafts so they can make accurate revision decisions. To help students learn to revise effectively, many revision strategies are described throughout the text. Students are encouraged to try a number of these strategies in order to discover revision techniques that work well for them.

The two-stage focus on revision gives the text its subtitle: *editor* is used in its broadest sense to refer to one who makes change to improve writing; *critic* refers to one who evaluates writing to determine what changes need to be made.

In addition to focusing on process, *The Student Writer* also treats essay structure: Chapter 2 discusses essay structure in detail; each of the chapters in Part II includes material on essay structure; the questions that follow the professional writings speak, in part, to the structure of the essays. In fact, throughout the text, the dual concern for process and structure is evident.

Organization of the Text

The Student Writer: Editor and Critic is divided into three parts:

1. The Writer's Process and the Essay's Structure
2. Methods of Development
3. A Brief Guide to Frequently Occurring Errors

Part I concerns itself with both the student writer's process and the characteristics of an effective essay. It treats process by helping students identify their own processes and determine how they can improve them. It describes a wide range of techniques for shaping topics, generating ideas to develop those topics, determining purpose, establishing and assessing audience, and drafting. All of this is discussed in the context of writer-based activity. In the context of reader-based activity, Part I describes various ways to evaluate a draft, revise, edit, and proofread. This section also includes essays by professional writers Barbara Wright and Gail Godwin, essays that reiterate points made in Part I about the writing process.

Part I also concerns itself with product. It offers a detailed treatment of essay structure and the qualities of an effective essay, including logical organization, adequate, relevant detail, and effective sentences.

Part II discusses description, narration, illustration, comparison and contrast, process analysis, cause-and-effect analysis, definition, and persuasion. A full chapter is devoted to each. The chapters all have the same features, ones that attend to both process and product. Each chapter discusses content, structure, audience, and purpose. Each chapter also includes both professional and student samples to illustrate the principles discussed in the chapter. In addition, the student samples are the basis for activities that help students sharpen their critical abilities. These chapters also include writing topics as well as writing procedures students can sample as they work to improve their processes. Finally, each chapter closes with questions to help students evaluate the strengths and weaknesses of their current processes and to help them decide in what ways, if necessary, to alter their processes.

In additon, Part II includes a chapter on using researched material to develop essays. Rather than treat the traditional research paper, which has rightly been judged artificial, this chapter calls for students to use source material to develop their own essays. The focus here is on using source material as a portion of the writer's supporting detail. The chapter treats how to find material, document it responsibly, and incorporate it into an essay.

Part III of *The Student Writer* is a brief guide to frequently occurring errors. Rather than a handbook, this section is a concise explanation of fragments, run-ons, agreement, tense and person shifts, dangling and misplaced modifiers, parallelism, capitalization, and punctuation. It is intended as a quick editing reference for students who make occasional mistakes in these areas but not so many that comprehensive help is needed. The section also includes exercise material to allow students to apply the principles discussed.

An important feature of the text is Appendix I, which is a quick guide to solving writing problems. Most of the problem-solving strategies in this guide are explained in more detail in the body of the text, but the shorter appendix version makes a convenient troubleshooting reference.

Appendix II is another important feature. Here the student can study a student essay in progress to better understand the nature and importance of revision.

Changes in the Second Edition

In response to suggestions made by instructors who have used the first edition of *The Student Writer: Editor and Critic*, I made a number of additions to the second edition. Two chapters have been added, one on process analysis and one on cause-and-effect analysis. Also, I added discussions of frequently confused words, words and phrases to avoid, active and passive voice, use of the apostrophe, and use of parentheses. I expanded the discussion of comma usage and added a correction chart on the inside cover and an appendix that presents a student essay in progress. I eliminated the chapter on combining methods of development; reviewer consensus was that this chapter was rarely assigned.

Although users of the text unanimously applauded its relaxed style and supportive tone, they also called for tighter prose. Thus I have revised with an eye and ear toward a less discursive style. In so doing, I do not believe I sacrificed the style and tone that distinguishes the text. Similarly, users appreciated the evaluation questions in Part II but called for a shorter list so students could work through the questions more quickly. The evaluation questions have been shortened on average by a third.

Upon rereading the original preface, I realized I was addressing instructors more than students. In the second edition, ''To the Student'' explains why students should learn to write well, how they can accomplish this, and how they should use this book.

To freshen the text, I have changed approximately one-third of the examples and exercises. Most of the readings that were replaced were done so at the suggestion of users of the text. Some exercises and illustrative essays were added (for example, paragraphs to edit for fragments and run-ons were added to the existing exercises, as was an essay to illustrate organization).

Finally, to update the terminology, *coordinate clauses* are now called *main clauses*, and ''The Standard Pattern of Organization'' is replaced with the more accurate ''A Useful Pattern of Organization.''

Like most writing, *The Student Writer* is a work in progress. The second edition is better than the first because it incorporates the changes instructors and their students have called for. I hope to continue responding to the needs of those who work with the text, so please write to me or McGraw-Hill with your responses and suggestions.

Acknowledgments

Composition texts are not written in isolation, and this one is far from an exception. Many studied the manuscript in its various stages and offered valuable advice and direction. I am particularly indebted to the following reviewers, who showed patience and wisdom: Thomas Amorose, State University of New York, Potsdam; Jay Balderson, Western Illinois University; Nancy Culberson, Georgia College; Linda Donahue, Mattatuck Community College; Todd Duncan, Wayne State University; Harvey Kail, University of Maine; Wayne Losano, University of Florida; Lawrence J. McDoniel, St. Louis Community College at Meramec; Janet McReynolds, Southern Illinois University at Edwardsville; Robert Perrin, Indiana State University; Mark E. Rollins, Ohio University; Herbert J. Roth, Southwestern Adventist College; June W. Siegel, New York City Technical College; Richard Stoner, Broome Community College; Ellen L. Tripp, Forsyth Technical College; Ralph Voss, University of Alabama; Marjorie Wells, San Antonio College; and David Willard, Bakersfield College. In addition, a special thanks must go to Michael S. Kearns, Ohio Wesleyan University, whose criticisms were particularly astute.

I am also grateful to Mary Louise Quisenberry, who types with efficiency, speed, and good humor. Her graciousness made this project more pleasant. To my parents, Lucille and Irvin Fine, as always, I owe more than I can repay, for it is they who are responsible for my love of language and education. To my husband Dennis and my sons Gregory and Jeffrey, I offer grateful thanks for their understanding and unfailing patience.

For her contribution to the first edition I must thank Joy DeSalvo of Youngstown State University. She is a respected colleague, a superior teacher, and a cherished friend.

To the Student

What I am about to tell you I believe completely: Learning how to write well is vitally important. I am not talking about writing well so you can survive college, although I admit that's part of it. I am referring to another truth: Knowing how to write well will make a difference in your life outside the classroom. On the job, people write often. Those in business routinely write letters, reports, memos, and grant proposals. Those in science write research grants, lab reports, research papers, and reviews of scientific literature. Those in education write reviews of methodology, research reports, book reviews, committee reports, lesson plans, and reports to parents and colleagues. Those in the arts write grant requests and reviews. So necessary is writing to any profession requiring a college degree that one cannot name a degree-related job that does not require some writing.

When you write on the job, you make a statement about your competency. No matter how good your ideas are, if you do not present them well, your reader will question your ability. That is a hard fact of life. Imagine yourself for a moment on the job after graduation. And imagine that your boss has asked you to write a report outlining ways to improve efficiency in your department. You may know just the things to do, but if your report is poorly written your boss will doubt your competence.

In your personal life, too, writing will be important. You may write business letters of varying kinds—letters of inquiry, letters seeking redress, and letters of praise or complaint. The organizations you belong to may involve you in writing committee reports, addresses to the membership, newsletters, or proposals. You may read something in a magazine or newspaper that prompts you to write a letter to an editor. Or you may want to share an observation or an experience with someone or try to influence how someone thinks or acts.

Let me share here two recent experiences I had. Not too long ago I bought a faulty product which the store would not take back. I wrote a letter to the manufacturer and received a refund as a result of that letter. However, if my letter had been poorly written, I might have been viewed as just another crank and might not have gotten my refund. Less recently, the teachers in my community went on strike, and a group of citizens got together to work to resolve the problem. One of the things we did was send letters to the teachers' union and members of the board of education describing what we felt should be done. Our comments were taken seriously, largely because our letters presented us in a reasonable light and because our ideas were effectively written.

There you have it: Writing is important outside the classroom. In other words, people write because they expect their writing to accomplish something, but poor writing probably will not have the desired effect.

Now let's deal with writing for academic survival. Yes, you must learn how to write well to pass your writing course, to handle essay examinations, and to write research papers and reports. But once you become a confident writer, you will discover an interesting thing happening. You will welcome opportunities to write as more than chances to show your teachers what you have learned. You will notice that as you write, you are doing *more* than recording what you know—you will find that the act of writing helps you discover ideas, sharpen reactions, and refine your thinking, because the act of writing is a discovery process. Writing is a series of stages that gets your mental wheels spinning so you can explore ideas, test relationships, and develop your thinking. More than anything, this is why writing is such an important part of the college curriculum. In short, writing is thinking. To be an educated person, you must write to record your ideas *and* to discover what they are in the first place.

To learn to write well, you must draw on a number of resources close at hand. First, you have this book. If I have done my job well, it will help you improve your skills. More important, you have your teacher. She or he will offer guidance, make suggestions, and comment on your work. Take everything your teacher says to heart. Study the comments on your papers. Be sure you understand them all, know how to repeat the strengths noted and overcome the weaknesses pointed out. If you have questions, *ask*. Your teacher will be glad to clarify. Try to apply what you learn to the next essay you write. Talk to your classmates. Form a network. Discuss techniques you have tried and share successful procedures. Read and comment on each others work. Ask people—classmates, your teachers, your boss—what they do when they write, and try some of their procedures. Gradually, you will improve, and the key word here is *gradually*. Nothing as valuable as learning how to write will happen quickly. Your goal should be slow, steady progress.

Now a word about how this book operates. The goal of *The Student Writer* is to help you become a better writer by helping you discover writing procedures that work well. Throughout the book a variety of procedures will be described. It is your responsibility to try a range of these procedures and evaluate their effectiveness. You should incorporate into your writing process the procedures that work well. Try alternative procedures to replace the ones that do not work well. In other words, you will read about many writing techniques. You should experiment with many of these techniques until you are satisfied that you have found procedures that yield effective writing. If you are ever unsure about the success of your procedures or how to alter them, talk to your instructor.

Another goal of *The Student Writer* is to help you become an accurate judge of the strengths and weaknesses in a piece of writing. Once you can reliably judge an essay's strengths and weaknesses, you will be able to make wise decisions about how to change your own drafts. One way this book helps you become a reliable judge is by providing a number of student writings for you to evaluate. Some of these writings are better than others, but all have strengths and weaknesses. As you study these writings, you will become more skilled at judging the qualities of effective writing so you can determine what changes to make in your own drafts.

As you work this term, remember the significance of your endeavor. Learning to write is important, and writing well is satisfying. If at times the going gets rough and you feel frustrated (that can happen when you are learning a skill), talk things over with your instructor. By the end of the term, you will feel proud of your progress.

Barbara Fine Clouse

I

The Writer's Process and the Essay's Structure

1

Shaping Topics and Discovering Ideas

Writers need ideas. They need ideas so they can decide what to write about, and they need ideas so they can develop whatever it is they *do* decide to write about. That's pretty obvious, but it raises a question: just where do these ideas come from?

Many people believe writers get their ideas in a flash of inspiration. They believe there is a magic moment when all the right ideas explode in the brain, and the writer is swept forward by the force. And that happens at times. But more often, writers cannot depend on inspiration because inspiration does not make scheduled appearances—often it does not arrive at all.

So if people are not inspired, does that mean they cannot write? Fortunately, it doesn't, for when ideas do not come to the writer, there are ways the writer can go after the ideas. And that is what this chapter is all about—ways you can discover ideas when inspiration does not arrive just when you need it.

The Writing Subject and the Writing Topic

Sometimes you do not have to choose your writing topic because it is chosen for you by an instructor, boss, or situation (as when you want to respond to a particular editorial with a letter to the editor). However, when this is not the case, the first stage of the writing process will be topic selection.

If it falls to you to shape your own writing topic and you are not inspired, you can take steps. Before discussing those steps, let's consider for a moment the difference between a writing subject and a writing topic.

A *subject* is a broad area you decide you want to write about. A *topic* is the narrow territory within that subject area that you stake out as the specific focus for your writing. For example, say you want to write about presidential elections. That's a subject area because *presidential elections* takes in quite a bit. If you settle on the wisdom of electing the president by popular rather than electoral vote, then you have a topic—a narrow focus for your essay. In the most general sense, topic selection involves choosing a subject area and paring it down until you have a narrow topic.

Anything Can Be a Subject

Anything, and I mean *anything,* can be a writing subject. As proof of this, consider the variety of subjects that appear in syndicated columns in newspapers. For example, Andy Rooney writes a syndicated column that appears in over 150 newspapers, and he also appears regularly on *60 Minutes.* Among his honors are Emmys, Writers Guild Awards, and the Peabody Award. Here are some of the subjects Mr. Rooney has written on: chairs, soap, warranties, directions, sizes, catalogs, mail, fences, street names, bank names, signs, hair, eyeglasses, gender, telephones, dirty words, calendars, and ugliness.

You may think that these are unlikely subjects to write about, but remember—there is nothing that cannot be shaped and narrowed into a fine topic.

Finding a Subject

As Andy Rooney illustrates, anything can serve as the subject for an essay. However, when you are casting about for your own subjects, there may not be much comfort in knowing that you can write about *anything.* You need to discover which of the many "anythings" you want to write about. Fortunately, writers can do several things to find subjects for their writing. These techniques are described for you below.

1. Try Some Unfocused Freewriting

Freewriting is a technique that helps writers shake loose ideas by freeing themselves of the constraints of proper form, clarity, organization, and even logic. To freewrite you take 10 minutes and write nonstop. You record everything that comes to mind, even if it seems absurd or irrelevant. If you cannot think of anything to write, then write anything: the names of people you know,

"I don't know what to say," the alphabet—anything. Soon ideas will occur to you and you can write them. Keep writing them until there are no more ideas, and then return to writing names, numbers, nonsense, whatever. Freewriting is not for sharing, so you do not stop to correct anything, nor do you polish as you go. Just get your ideas down any way you can or want to. After 10 minutes of this, read your pages over and you are likely to find at least one idea for an essay subject. Sure this idea will be rough—as everything in your freewriting will be—but you can take that rough idea and shape it. Freewriting works because it stimulates thought. It allows the writer to unload many ideas in a burst—ideas that can be sorted through, evaluated, and polished later. If you like, you can begin your unfocused freewriting this way: "I have to find a writing subject. Let's see, there's . . ." For an example of freewriting, see p. 12.

2. Browse through a Dictionary

You may not want to write about aardvarks or Zyrian, but there are many entries in between that you may wish to discuss. Or perhaps an entry will trigger your thinking because it is associated with something you would like to write about. Who knows? The *balloon* entry might remind you of that summer day at the fair when you were 6, and your first helium balloon escaped your grasp.

3. Read Your Local and Campus Newspapers

The events, issues, controversies, and concerns reported in newspapers can be subjects for essays. Tax hikes, building projects, curriculum changes, pending legislation, demonstrations, actions of officials or citizens or students—all of these and more are reported in the papers, and they can prompt interesting, worthwhile subjects.

4. Keep an Essay-Subject Notebook

Get a small spiral notebook to keep in your pocket or purse. During the day you will have thoughts and experiences that at some time could serve as essay subjects. If you write these down, you can refer to them later when you are searching for things to write about.

5. Fill in the Blanks

It is possible to discover a subject by filling in the blanks in key sentences like these:

I'll never forget the time I _____.

_____ is the most _____ I know.

After _____ I was never the same again.

College can best be described as _____.

Is there anything more frustrating (interesting/exciting) than _____?

This world can certainly do without _____.

What this world needs is _____.

_____ made a lasting impression on me.

After _____ I changed my mind about _____.

My biggest success (failure) was _____.

Life with _____ is _____.

Life would be easier if only _____.

I get so angry (annoyed/frightened) when _____.

_____ is better (or worse) than _____.

The main cause of _____ is _____.

The main effect of _____ is _____.

Most people do not understand the real meaning of _____.

The best way to do _____ is _____.

6. Give Yourself Enough Time

Sometimes people think they cannot arrive at a subject simply because they do not have any luck in their first 10 minutes. Deciding on a writing subject can take time, so be fair to yourself. Allow yourself a day or two for ideas to surface. If you go about your business for a while with a portion of your brain considering what you experience and observe during that time, you may be inspired. For example, a routine walk across campus may not ordinarily prompt an essay subject. But if one day you take that walk aware that you need a subject, you might see the library you pass every day in a new light: you might see it as the subject for an essay, perhaps one about the different ways people study in the library.

Shaping the Topic

When you are shaping a topic, keep the following points in mind.

1. Shape a Topic That Will Have an Impact on Your Reader

A topic should interest you as the writer, but it should also have some significance for the reader. After all, you are writing something that will be read by someone else, and you don't want your reader to be bored.

To shape a topic that will have some impact on your reader, you must get outside yourself a bit. That is, you cannot expect a reader to be enthusiastic about your topic just because *you* are. To determine whether your topic can have an impact on a reader, ask yourself the following questions:

1. In what ways can the topic inform a reader?
2. In what ways can the topic entertain a reader?
3. In what ways can the topic influence a reader to think or act differently?
4. In what ways can the topic arouse a reader's emotions?
5. Why would the topic interest a reader?
6. How can I make my topic interesting to a reader?

If a topic that interests you is not likely to affect a reader in at least one of the ways suggested by the above questions, then it probably is not a suitable topic, and you should reshape it or find another one.

2. Shape a Topic You Know Enough About

There is no quicker way to build frustration and failure into your writing than to try to squeeze 500 words out of a subject when you only have 200 words of knowledge about it. Try to shape a topic you have some first-hand experience with or one you know through observation, reading, classwork, or watching television. It makes little sense, for example, to write about saving the whales if you did not know they were in trouble until you saw a bumper sticker yesterday.

If you are not sure whether you know enough about a topic to develop an essay, answer the questions below. They can serve both as a way to generate ideas to include in your writing and as a way to discover whether your knowledge is sufficient.

1. What have you experienced that relates to your topic?
2. What have you observed that relates to your topic?
3. What have you read that relates to your topic?
4. What have you heard that relates to your topic?
5. What have you learned in school that relates to your topic?
6. What have you seen on television that relates to your topic?

If you come up with little after answering the above questions, then you probably do not know enough about your topic to develop an essay, and you should reshape your topic or find another.

3. Shape a Topic That Can Be Handled in an Appropriate Length

As you shape a topic from your subject area, remember this guideline: it is better to treat a narrow topic in depth than a broad topic superficially. A superficial treatment will never satisfy a reader because the essay will be vague and general. The reader will be left feeling that the writer did not come to grips with the topic.

If your topic takes in too much territory, then to develop it appropriately you would be forced to write a very long piece. For example, how would you like to be stuck writing an essay about why *Star Wars, The Return of the Jedi,* and *Close Encounters of the Third Kind* are better movies than *Star Trek: The Movie, Star Trek: The Voyage Home,* and *The Empire Strikes Back?* If you did that in 500 words, you wouldn't treat any of these movies adequately. If you gave each movie adequate development, you would probably write an essay so long that three of your friends would have to help you deliver it to your instructor. However, if you narrowed your topic to showing that the character development in *Return of the Jedi* is superior to that in *Star Wars,* you could treat this aspect of two movies well—and in a comfortable length.

How to Narrow Your Topic

Often, restricting a topic will require a series of narrowings. Let's say, for example, you have decided to write about unemployment. There is quite a bit to be said on that subject, and it is unlikely you can—or would want to—treat it all in one essay. But unemployment does give you a subject area. Now you must narrow this subject to something that can be managed in a reasonable length. You could narrow first by deciding to write about the effects of unemployment. That's narrower, but still a bit broad for a single essay. So narrow some more. You could write about the causes and effects of the high unemployment rate in our country. Yet it is unlikely one essay could say everything about the causes and effects of unemployment in this country, so yet another restriction is necessary. You may settle on a discussion of the causes *or* of the effects. These are narrower, but they still take in quite a bit, so another narrowing is in order. Perhaps you could narrow to discuss the effects of your father's unemployment on your family. Or if you feel there is too much to say about that topic, you could narrow once more to discuss the effects of your father's unemployment on you. Such a topic would be narrow enough for treatment in a single essay.

If you need help narrowing a topic, try one of the following procedures.

1. Freewrite

Perhaps you did some freewriting to arrive at your subject, perhaps not. In either case, 10 or 15 minutes of freewriting that focuses on your subject can help you discover ways to narrow for a topic. (See pp. 4 and 11.)

2. Make a List

Write your subject at the top of a page and below it list every aspect of the subject you can think of. Do this quickly (but without rushing) and jot down everything you think of, without pausing to evaluate the worth of the items. A list for the subject *football* might look like this in part:

players   **Football**
fans

professional
college
high school
television
training
scholarships
NFL
Canadian

Sometimes this list is enough to prompt a topic. You might look at it and decide to use as your topic "Too much football is televised on weekends." Other times you might need a second list. Perhaps you look at the first list and narrow to televised football. That's a step in the right direction, but "televised football" is still rather broad and without a specific focus. You could try a second list, which might, in part, look like this:

college
professional
all day Saturday, Sunday
Monday night
commercial time is expensive
families aren't together on weekends
interferes with holidays
children encouraged to see players as heroes
viewers witness violence

Televised Football

You could study a second list like this and settle on one of several topics, perhaps "Televised football as a disruptive influence on family life."

3. Ask Questions
Another way to go from subject to topic is to ask some key questions about your subject. Among the most useful questions are:

What is it like?
Why is it important?
What is it different from?
What does it mean?
What should change?
How does (did) it happen?
What are its good and bad points?
What are its causes?
What are its effects?

The answers to questions like these reveal various aspects of your subject to help you discover ways to narrow. For a more extensive list of questions, see p. 17.

Points to Remember about Shaping Topics
1. Sometimes writers first identify a broad subject they are interested in and then carve a narrow topic from that broad area.
2. Techniques to help the writer find subjects and topics include:
   a. Freewriting
   b. Browsing through a dictionary
   c. Reading newspapers
   d. Filling in the blanks in sentences
   e. Keeping an essay-subject notebook
   f. Thinking and observing
   g. Making lists
   h. Asking questions
3. Suitable essay topics should
   a. Have an impact on the reader
   b. Be narrow enough to be treated with penetration in a reasonable length
   c. Be something the writer knows enough about

Exercise: Shaping Topics

1. Identify five subjects you might like to write an essay about. If you cannot arrive at five after some thought, try one or more of the techniques for finding subjects listed in the box above. If you use any of these techniques, indicate which ones yielded which subjects.
2. For each topic below, write a *B* if the topic is too broad to be handled with penetration in a 500- to 700-word essay. Write an *N* if the topic is narrow enough to be handled in a 500- to 700-word essay.
   N a. The day I learned a lie can be less harmful than the truth
   B b. My favorite people
   B c. Being the oldest of six children has dozens of disadvantages
   N d. Being the oldest of six children has two chief disadvantages
   N/B e. It's a mistake to teach children to read in kindergarten
   B f. Cigarette smokers have their rights too
   B g. Our public schools are deteriorating in every way
   B h. How to teach a 6-year-old to ride a bike
   N i. There are more similarities than differences among modern religions
   B j. Computer science should be taught in elementary school
   N k. Television soap operas present an unrealistic and potentially dangerous view of the ways people relate to each other
   B l. For pure fun, nothing is better than watching a Japanese monster movie
3. Using three of the five subjects you gave as your response to number 1 above, shape three suitable essay topics. Refer to the box above for a reminder of the qualities of a good topic. If necessary, use one or more of the techniques listed in the box to help you arrive at a topic. If you use any of these techniques, note which ones produced which topics.

4. Below are five broad writing subjects. Select two of them and write one narrow topic for each.
   a. Studying for exams
   b. Team sports
   c. The changing role of women (or men)
   d. Difficult decisions
   e. Interesting (or unusual) people

Discovering What You Have to Say

After shaping a topic, you are ready to begin writing your essay. So you pour yourself a cold drink, empty the last of the potato chips into a bowl, and push the clutter on your desk to one side. You get comfortable, reach for some fresh paper, and begin—and idea after idea tumbles forth as you write through your first draft, right? Well, yes, if you are lucky enough to be inspired. No, if inspiration is too busy helping the redhead in the third row to bother with you. So once again, if ideas do not come to you, you must go after the ideas.

All writers (not just students) experience writer's block. Sometimes we draw a blank—not a single idea comes to mind. Sometimes we have a hazy idea but it's too vague to get us anywhere. Often we find ourselves saying something like, "I know what I want to say, but I can't explain it."

Fortunately, writer's block can be dealt with, because there are techniques to stimulate thought and start the flow of ideas. These techniques for idea generation come under the broad heading of *prewriting*. Although the term "prewriting" seems to indicate that the techniques occur *before* writing, in truth the techniques are themselves a form of writing. These are writing procedures that stimulate ideas that can be refined and included in an essay. Actually, you already know something about prewriting because the techniques you learned for discovering and shaping topics are forms of prewriting. The next pages, however, will offer ways to use prewriting to overcome writer's block.

Freewriting

As you now know, freewriting is a prewriting technique that can help the writer searching for subjects and topics. However, it can also be useful to the first-draft writer who needs ideas to develop a topic. To freewrite for ideas to develop a topic, write down anything and everything that occurs to you about your topic without evaluating the worth of the ideas. You can shift direction abruptly to pursue a new idea that suddenly strikes you, or you can pursue a single idea as far as you can take it. You can make random, wild associations. You can be flip, serious, or angry. You can experiment and play with words. Just be relaxed, and go with your flow of thoughts. If you run out of ideas, write the alphabet or write about how you feel until new ideas strike you. Remember, the emphasis in freewriting is on *free,* so do not be concerned with grammar, spelling, logic, and such.

After 10 or so minutes, read what you have (most likely you will have filled about two pages). What you have down will be rough, but you will notice at least one or two ideas that can be polished and developed in an essay. Sometimes this is enough to start you off on an outline or draft. Other times you might need a boost from a second freewriting. If this is the case, write for 10 more minutes, this time focusing on the ideas you underlined in the first freewriting. When you are done, read your material and again underline the good ideas. Between the two freewritings, you may generate what you need to get started.

A Sample Freewriting

One freshman did a freewriting in response to the question, "What am I getting out of this?" The result appears below and on the next page.

"What am I getting out of this?" That's the question. Sure we all ask it. Seems so selfish. Like we're all out for ourselves. Cliche. I hate cliches. Are they true, it doesn't matter. Do students have to get something out of everything they do? Yes yes yes. So what? They shouldn't have to but I don't know why. Seems like the right (write — hah) thing to say. Like what your minister or mother would say. I don't know if I care about this I'm stuck stuck stuck A B C D here we are at Romper Room. I need a cig. How does she expect me to think of something important when I can't smoke in here, where was I? Do I need to get something out of everything? Yes. I changed my mind that's not bad. Why? why not. I know, because no I don't know. The thing is teachers expect you to think something's important because they do. Pretty pompous. Pompous profs. Pomp-ass — that's appropriate. Back to it now. What does anyone get from anything? What they put into it. Another cliche. Not true. I put a lot into calc and only got a C. God but Harris was a lazy prof, just stood up there and read the book — I *think we should have gotten more from him. I changed my mind—what am I getting from this is a fair question cause if I don't get enuf I should demand more and everything would improve like Harris, Ferris, Paris, 1 2 3 4 5 6 7 8 Gordon was lousy too in History. Showed slides all the time & gave unfair tests. Then there was Dibitz—she was dumb dumb dumb. Maybe students need a union so they get ther money's worth. My fingers hurts I'm getting a callous. Is it time yet? If students demand to get something they won't be cheated. I need a cig. enuf.*

Evaluating Freewriting

A close look at the previous freewriting shows that some interesting and useful things occurred while it was written. First, the student clarified his thinking. In the beginning he felt it was somehow bad to always ask, "What am I getting out of this?" but he was not sure why. He just sensed it was the proper point of view (the way a minister or the writer's mother might regard the issue). As he wrote, however, the student discovered what he *really* believed—that this was a valid question.

Second, the freewriting led the writer to discover *why* he held his particular view. He felt that if people didn't ask what they were getting—indeed, if they didn't demand to get something—then they were likely to end up with little or nothing. This seemed to be what happened to the writer in his calculus class.

Another useful result of the freewriting is that it helped the student sharpen and narrow his focus. He began discussing the question as it applied to people in general. Rather quickly, he refined his focus to students, and finally he centered on students' rights and the wisdom of a union for students.

So what did the freewriting do for the student? It helped him clarify his thinking, discover a narrow topic, and generate some ideas to support that topic. As a result, he wrote an essay advocating that students unionize to demand and ensure quality instruction. To support his view that some instruction is quite poor, the student cited as examples his past instructors who performed badly, the same instructors that showed up in the freewriting.

List Writing

You have read about list writing as a technique for shaping topics from subjects. This prewriting activity is also helpful for generating ideas to develop these topics. For this purpose, list writing works like this: in a column list every idea that occurs to you about your topic. As with freewriting, do not stop to decide whether you like these ideas or whether they will "work" in your essay.

When you run out of ideas, review your list. Now you can evaluate whether or not each idea is suitable for your essay. Perhaps you will find ideas that do not seem relevant to your topic or do not seem worthy of inclusion for some other reason. If so, simply cross these ideas out.

Next, study the first idea remaining on your list. Think about it a few moments. As you do, you may discover one or two related ideas that can be added to your list. Proceed this way down your list, studying each idea and adding thoughts. When you are done, you will have a list of ideas you have judged suitable for inclusion in your essay.

Many writers find that this list writing meets their needs. Others, however, like to go one step further by turning their list into a *scratch outline*. To turn a prewriting list into a scratch outline, group together the ideas that are related to each other. For example, say you have a list of ideas for an essay about the day you baby-sat for 2-year-old twin boys. You want the essay to explain that the experience was one of the most nerve-wracking of your life. When you look over your list, you discover that three of your ideas pertain to feeding the children lunch, four of them pertain to trying to bed them down for a nap, and five of them pertain to keeping them out of mischief. If this is the case, you make three lists—one of ideas about lunch, one of ideas about the nap, and one of ideas about mischief.

When you group ideas in this way, you are forming a scratch outline because you are determining which points will be discussed together in your essay. That is, you are doing just a bit more than listing your ideas; you are also organizing them.

A Sample List

Below is a list one student developed before writing an essay about the trauma he experienced when his family moved to a new town, and he had to change schools.

loved old school
comfortable with friends — knew them 12 years
at new school I was outsider
everyone belonged to a clique
sleepless nights for weeks before the move
asked if I could live with my aunt so I wouldn't
  have to move

my parents tried to reassure me (crossed out)
I knew I would never see my old friends again
scared to leave familiar for unknown
new school was ugly
I resented my parents for transplanting me (crossed out)
I became argumentative with my parents (crossed out)
I was behind in my school work at new school
I didn't get on basketball team at new school

Some of the ideas in the list are crossed out because after reviewing the list the writer decided he did not wish to treat these ideas after all, probably because they focused on his relationship with adults, and he wanted to center on his adjustment to the school and his relationship with his classmates.

After the writer eliminated ideas he judged unsuited to his purpose, he reviewed his list and added ideas he thought of. After this step, the list looked like this:

loved old school
comfortable with friends — knew them 12 years
at new school I was an outsider
everyone belonged to a clique
sleepless nights for weeks before the move
asked if I could live with my aunt so I wouldn't have to move
my parents tried to reassure me (crossed out)
I knew I would never see my old friends again
scared to leave familiar for unknown
new school was ugly
I resented my parents for transplanting me (crossed out)
I became argumentative with my parents (crossed out)
I was behind in my school work at new school
I didn't get on basketball team at new school
new math teacher tried to help me adjust (crossed out)
at new school I was stared at like a freak
I would skip lunch because I didn't know anyone to sit with

I was popular & respected at old school—at new
  I was a nobody
new school was old, needed repair—describe ugly
  classrooms
math & science classes were way ahead of my
  old ones & my grades suffered
I was center on basketball team before—at new
  school I didn't make team
I couldn't go to games & cheer for a team I wasn't
  playing on & felt no loyalty toward

After adding his new ideas to the list, the writer decided to form a scratch outline by grouping together the ideas that seemed to relate to each other. The result appears below and on the next page.

Before Move

loved old school
comfortable with friends—
  knew them 12 years
sleepless nights for
  weeks before the move
I knew I would never
  see my old friends
  again
asked if I could live
  with my aunt
scared to leave familiar
  for unknown

After Move

Classmates
I was outsider
everyone belonged to clique
stared at like a freak
skipped lunch cause
  had no one to sit with
I was a nobody instead of
  popular & respected

Basketball
didn't make team—was
  center before
couldn't go to games &
  cheer for a team I wasn't
  playing on & felt no
  loyalty toward

Surroundings
new school was ugly
new school was old &
  needed repairs
describe classrooms

School work
I was behind
math & science classes
way ahead of me
& my grades suffered

The ideas in your list will not necessarily cover every point, example, and piece of detail that you will include in your essay. Instead, the ideas in your list can serve as your starting point.

Asking Questions

Asking questions about your subject, you have learned, is one way to move from subject to topic. Similarly, asking questions about your topic is one way to generate ideas for developing that topic. Some of the most useful questions are the standard journalistic questions: Who? What? When? Where? Why? How? These questions can be shaped in a variety of ways, according to the nature of your topic. Here is just a sampling.

Who is involved?
Who is affected?
Who is for (or against) it?
Who is interested in it?
What happened?
What does it mean?
What causes it?
What are its effects?
What is it like (or different from)?
What are its strengths (weaknesses)?
When does it happen?
When will it end (or begin)?

When is it important?
Why does it happen?
Why is it important?
Why is it interesting?
Where does it happen?
How does it happen?
How does it make people feel?
How does it change things?
How often does it happen?
How is it made?
How should people react to it?

The list of questions here is by no means complete, and you will discover quite a few others to ask yourself.

Sample Questions and Answers

Below are the questions a student asked herself for an essay about why she started, and later stopped, using marijuana. Notice that not all the questions ask who, what, when, where, why, or how; the student shaped questions appropriate to her topic.

1. What happened?
   I started smoking grass.
2. Why did it happen?
   Pressure from friends & my bosses.
3. What was the effect?
   At first, I became paranoid about getting caught & then I got leery of people who didn't smoke.
4. What was the effect of the paranoia?
   I started hanging out only with people who smoked. I worried a lot about getting caught & about my parents finding my stash.
5. Did you like to smoke?
   Not at first. Then I relaxed and enjoyed the highs.
6. How did you feel when you smoked?
   Light, airy, giddy, relaxed, happy.
7. How often did you smoke?
   Eventually — every day.
8. Where did you smoke?
   At home — alone or with friends.
9. What was the effect of smoking every day?
   My life revolved around pot, who had it, how to get it, where to hide it, where to get the money to buy it.
10. Why did you quit?
    When I was broke & couldn't afford to buy any grass, my friends stopped coming around. I realized they weren't very good friends if all we had in common was smoking. Also, I realized I couldn't concentrate at work & my grades fell to near flunk-out point. Got scared.

11. How did you quit?
I gradually lengthened the time between joints until I was going months at a time without any.

12. Was it hard to quit?
Not really. At first I wasn't sure what to do with myself & I seemed to have a lot of time on my hands.

13. Do you smoke now?
Rarely. At a party I might take one hit.

14. How do you view your experience?
When I think of all the time I wasted smoking dope, I feel like a fool.

15. Do you miss it?
No.

16. What is the effect of quitting?
I feel proud when someone offers me a joint & I say no without any regret.

17. Do you think marijuana should be legalized?
I don't begrudge anyone their right to smoke. There probably should be a minimum age though.

18. Are you still pressured to smoke?
Yes, but I can handle it. Especially since a lot of my old friends have been busted for possession or dealing.

19. What is the significance of all this to you?
I'm not paranoid anymore. I'm my own person who doesn't have to smoke to fit in. My friends & I have important things in common. My grades are better. I use time more wisely. I'm proud that a drug doesn't control my life & actions.

20. What is the significance to others?
If you smoke, be careful. It can take over your life & make you think everything's fine when it's not.

When the student wrote her essay, she did not use all the points that resulted from her questioning. Also, her essay included ideas she developed along the way, after her questioning. However, the questioning and answering that she did provided many ideas to refine and develop in her essay.

Asking questions can be especially helpful when done with a partner. Have another person ask you questions on your topic.

Letter Writing

Sometimes writers have trouble generating ideas because they do not relax enough to allow a free flow of thought. If this is ever the case for you, try letter writing, which is a prewriting technique that often relaxes the writer. This method of idea generation is really quite simple. You write a "letter" to someone you are close to, someone you feel comfortable with and can open up to easily. The subject of your letter, of course, is your essay topic. Use this letter as an opportunity to express and explore ideas about your topic. Since you are writing to someone you are close to and comfortable with, you will not feel the need to hold anything back. Of course, this is all just a way to stimulate your thought, so there is no need to actually mail your letter.

It is interesting that some people like to write letters to themselves rather than to others. If this appeals to you, give it a try. After all, when it comes to prewriting, anything that works is a good technique.

To discover ideas for developing her topic—the changing roles of women—a student wrote the letter that appears below. The letter explores some difficulties the writer faces meeting the demands of her various roles.

Dear Liz,

I guess I'm what you'd call a modern woman, but I'm not sure I like it very much. I know this is what I asked for, but it's a lot rougher than I expected and frankly less exciting.

The kids are 10 and 13 now, so they are fairly independent, but they still make a lot of demands on my time. Katie's adolescence has her turned inside out, and half the time she's crying and the other half she's mad at me for something. She's really on my mind a lot. Jenny is pretty together, but her gymnastics, Camp Fire activities, and swim meets really keep me on the fly. She makes a big demand on my time.

Then there's the job. I know it's only part-time, but those 20 hours really eat up my week. I can't keep up with the cleaning or the kids. And poor Jim really gets shortchanged. Actually, I feel pretty guilty that he works all day and then has to come home and help with laundry, dinner, and things. He doesn't mind, but I do. I feel like he's always picking up my slack and I'm not pulling my weight.

To top it off, now I'm in school. I must be crazy to make my work load even heavier than it already is. Still, I want my degree badly. I don't know, maybe I'm just in a slump, but I feel like I'm not doing anything well. Being liberated is not all I thought it would be. It's really very hard. I think I'm paying a big price for being a modern woman.

Love,
Marge

Thinking without Writing

Freewriting, listing, questioning, letter writing—these prewriting techniques are structured activities aimed at stimulating thought. But often our thinking does not need such prodding. Often, if we just allow enough time, ideas surface on their own.

If your prewriting is to be thinking without writing, there are some hints to keep in mind:

1. Allow yourself plenty of time to think. As soon as you discover you have a writing task, begin thinking about it. Don't wait until the last minute.
2. Think about your writing project while you are involved in your normal routine. As you are cooking, shopping, walking to class, showering, and so forth, turn a corner of your brain to the writing task.
3. Think about your writing before falling asleep at night. While you are sleeping, your mind will work on the task, and you may wake up with an idea or two.
4. Although this is thinking without writing, it's a good idea to jot down ideas that occur to you. This is insurance, in case you forget on Wednesday what you thought of on Tuesday.

5. Do not expect your ideas to come to you in perfect form. Just as the written idea-generation techniques will yield rough ideas to be polished later, so will your thinking often produce just the seeds of good ideas.

Additional Points to Remember about Prewriting

Regardless of the prewriting techniques you favor, some generalizations can be made.

1. The writing process seldom progresses in a straight line from step 1 to step 2 to step 3, and so on. Most often, writers find themselves going forward and then stepping back to reshape something that already occurred. This reshaping affects what happens when the writer goes forward again. Because writers can step back several times, the final paper is often very different from what the writer first had in mind. This fact has important implications when we settle on subjects, shape topics, and generate ideas for development. It means that subjects, topics, and ideas can be abandoned, refined, or altered at any point. Wise writers are sensitive to what each new step brings to their writing, and they are prepared to step back and make changes when necessary.

2. Idea generation takes time.

3. Although each prewriting technique is described separately in this chapter, many writers rely on a combination of these techniques. You too may find that a combination of prewriting activities yields more ideas than one technique by itself.

4. It is wise to experiment with all of the prewriting techniques. When you do, you may settle on two or three that work the best for you.

5. Even if you decide you prefer certain prewriting techniques over others, these favored techniques may not work for you every time. If a technique that has been successful for you in the past does not work in a particular instance, switch to another technique. You can try the favored approach again next time.

Exercise: Generating Ideas

1. When you write, how do you usually get your ideas? Have your past procedures been successful? Explain.

2. When you responded to number 3 and number 4 of the exercise on p. 10, you shaped a total of five essay topics (if you did not complete this exercise, do so now). For each of these topics, generate at least four ideas worthy of inclusion in an essay. To generate these ideas, try each of the idea-generation techniques described in this chapter (freewriting, listing, questioning, letter writing, and thinking without writing) at least once.

3. For each idea you generated for number 2 above, note the technique that yielded the idea. Which technique(s) do you think worked the best for you? Which are you likely to use in the future?

Purpose

Several factors govern which details writers use in their essays and which they leave out. Two of these factors are the writer's purpose and the writer's audience.

Early on you should ask yourself just why you are writing a particular piece. The answer to this question will form your *purpose*. Perhaps you want to express yourself, to share your feelings or observations. This self-expression and sharing can be a purpose. Or perhaps you wish to make your reader aware of something. In that case your purpose would be to inform your reader. Maybe you desire to convince your reader to think or act a certain way. This means your purpose would be to persuade your reader. In the most general sense, writers can establish one or a combination of four broad purposes for their writing:

1. To share feelings, ideas, and/or experiences with the reader.
2. To inform the reader of something.
3. To persuade the reader to think or act a certain way.
4. To entertain the reader.

It is important for writers to have a clear purpose in mind because the reason for writing will influence what is said. Let's say, for example, your writing topic is the difficulties you encountered during your first term at college. If your purpose is to share your experiences with a reader, you might include accounts of what went wrong for you, along with descriptions of your emotional reactions to these happenings. If your purpose is to inform your reader, perhaps to make him or her aware that college life is not as easy as it seems, you might provide explanations of the problems you encountered, without a discussion of your reactions. If your purpose is to persuade your reader that a better orientation program is needed, you might offer only those unpleasant experiences that could have been avoided if a better orientation program existed. And if your purpose is to entertain your reader, you would tell only amusing stories based on the difficulties you encountered.

Even this does not fully indicate how clearly purpose should be established, for it is usually necessary to be even more precise by asking yourself *why* you want to share or inform or persuade or entertain. Let's return to the purposes mentioned for writing about the difficulties encountered during the first term of college to see how asking "why" can sharpen your purpose. If you ask why you want to share your experiences of the first term, you might answer, "To vent frustration and/or earn some sympathy." If you ask why you want to inform your reader that college is not as easy as it seems, you might answer, "So my reader understands better what college life entails," or "So my reader knows what to expect when he or she begins college." If you ask yourself why you want to persuade your reader that a better orientation program is needed, you might respond, "So pressure is applied on the administration to institute the program." If you ask yourself why you want to entertain your reader, you might answer, "To help my reader appreciate the humor or absurdity of a situation."

If you have trouble establishing your purpose, try answering the following questions:

1. Can I share my ideas, feelings, and/or experiences with my reader? If so, what do I want to share, and why?
2. Can I inform my reader? If so, what do I want to inform my reader of and why do I want to do so?
3. Can I persuade my reader to act or think a certain way? If so, what can I persuade my reader of and why do I want to do so?
4. Can I entertain my reader? If so, in what way, and why do I want to do so?

Audience

Like your purpose, your audience will affect your writing. An essay about freshman life may need a great deal of explanatory background information if it is written for someone who knows little about college. However, such background would not be necessary if the reader is someone who recently attended the same school you do and understands how things work on your campus. Similarly, if you wish to convince the administration to improve the orientation program and they claim there is no money to do so, then you would have to show that the program's cost is affordable. Such cost information might not be necessary if you were writing to persuade the student council to run the program and the council had the money. To convince the council, though, you might discuss how such a program could increase student support for council-sponsored activities. This latter fact, however, would not appear in writing aimed at the administration.

You might be thinking that because you are in a writing class, your audience is your instructor. And, of course, you are right. Yet composition teachers are able to assume the identities of different readers, so you are free to write for different audiences. It is also possible to identify your audience as "the average, general reader"—someone who knows something about your subject, but less than you do. You might think of the average, general reader as the typical reader of a large daily newspaper.

If you have trouble deciding on a suitable audience for your writing, answer the following questions:

1. Who could learn something from my writing?
2. Who would enjoy reading about my topic?
3. Who could be influenced to think or act a certain way as a result of reading my writing?

4. Who shares an interest in my topic or would be sympathetic to my point of view?
5. Who would find my topic important?
6. Who needs to hear what I have to say?

Once you have identified your audience, you will need to assess the nature of that audience so you can provide the kind of detail that will fill your reader's needs and help you achieve your purpose. To determine the nature of your audience, answer the following questions:

1. What does my reader already know about my topic?
2. What will my reader need to learn to appreciate my point of view?
3. Does my reader have any strong feelings about my topic?
4. Is my reader interested in my topic or will I have to arouse interest?
5. How receptive will my reader be to my point of view? Why?
6. Will my reader's age, sex, level of education, income, job, politics, or religion affect reaction to my topic?

Exercise: Determining Purpose, Establishing Audience, and Generating Ideas

1. Shape an essay topic about campus life, using one or more of the techniques described in this chapter. Then establish a purpose for an essay on this topic by answering the questions on p. 24.
2. Establish the audience for this essay by answering the questions on pp. 24–25.
3. Determine the nature of the audience by answering the questions above.
4. Select any two of the idea-generation techniques described in this chapter and use them to generate at least five ideas that could be included in an essay with the topic you selected for number 1 above. After generating the ideas, determine whether they are compatible with the audience and purpose you have established.
5. If some of your ideas will not work with your audience and/or purpose, what options do you have?

An Essay to Write

When you completed the above exercise, you shaped an essay topic about campus life. In addition, you determined a purpose for this essay, established and assessed audience, and generated at least five ideas. Now it is time to develop this material into an essay. As you do so, keep the following points in mind.

1. Nothing is sacred about the material you have already developed. Any or all of it can be changed. You can even start over with a new topic if you like.
2. You may have to generate additional ideas to include in your essay.

3. To plan your essay, consider listing your ideas in the order you think they should appear.
4. Write a rough draft from this list of ideas. Do not be concerned about the quality of this draft; just get your ideas down the best way you can without worrying about anything, particularly grammar, spelling, and such.
5. Leave your rough draft after you write it. Stay away for at least a day. Then go over your work and make necessary changes. To decide what changes should be made, you can ask yourself the following questions:
   a. Is each idea clearly explained?
   b. Is each idea well developed (backed up with examples and/or explanation)?
   c. Are all ideas related to the topic?
   d. Do ideas appear in a logical order?
6. After making changes in your draft, recopy it and ask two classmates to read it and make suggestions.
7. Check your work for correct grammar, spelling, and punctuation.
8. Type or copy your essay carefully and proofread it for errors.

2

Structuring the Essay

When you are prewriting for subjects, topics, and ideas for support, your focus is on *you,* and that is the way it should be. In the early discovery stages of prewriting, your primary concern is with what *you* want to write about, with what points *you* want to make, with what purpose *you* want to achieve, and with what audience *you* want to address. Yet even though your primary focus is on yourself at this point, you still give some thought to the reader: you identify your audience; you shape a topic that will have an effect on the reader; you generate and/or evaluate your ideas with an eye toward their appropriateness for your reader. In fact, throughout the writing process you will find yourself making many decisions on the basis of this dual concern for writer and reader.

Writers must concern themselves with their readers—that is, they must be aware of their readers' needs and meet those needs—or they will not communicate their thoughts successfully. In short, it is not enough for us to have fine subjects and worthwhile ideas. We must also present these ideas in a way the reader understands and appreciates.

One way writers meet the needs of their readers is to organize their ideas in a logical way, in a way that allows the reader to understand easily how all the writer's ideas relate to each other.

From Prewriting to Organizing

During prewriting, thinking itself is often disorganized. We make random associations, travel roundabout, double back over the same path, and test offbeat relationships. This, illogical though it may seem on the surface, can be very productive—when we are *thinking*. When we are writing, however, the reader can have a pretty rough go of it if we expect him or her to follow such twists, turns, repetitions, and leaps. Thus, once you have your ideas formed and have settled on which of them to include in your writing, you are obligated to discover and reproduce on the page some logical organization for them.

Before actively working to order your material, evaluate your ideas and make preliminary decisions about which to use and which to reject. You make these decisions on the basis of which ideas best develop your topic, suit your purpose, and accommodate your audience. After your evaluation, you may discover you have rejected quite a few ideas. Or you may decide to alter your topic, purpose, or audience. If this happens, more ideas may be needed and you can find yourself prewriting and evaluating again. Actually, this prewriting and evaluating process can occur any number of times until you are satisfied that your topic, purpose, audience, and ideas are established well enough to form a comfortable departure point. Then it is possible to think about ways to organize your ideas.

The chart below shows what can occur before writers give serious thought to organizing their ideas.

Prewriting Chart

Idea Generation
1. Writer discovers subject.
2. Writer shapes topic.
3. Writer discovers supporting ideas.

Establishing Audience and Purpose
1. Writer may establish audience and/or purpose before, or at any point during, idea generation.
2. Writer may establish audience and/or purpose after idea generation.

Evaluation
1. Writer considers subject, topic, supporting ideas, audience, and purpose to be sure all are compatible with each other.
2. If necessary, writer adjusts subject, topic, supporting ideas, audience, or purpose (any or all) to make them compatible.
3. If changes are necessary, the writer may prewrite again to discover ideas for effecting these changes or adjusting material to accommodate them.

Notes:
a. The process continues until the writer feels he or she has enough to proceed. How much of this framework must be in place before the writer advances will vary from writer to writer.

b. The nature of the writing process is such that writers often find themselves stepping back before moving forward. This means that generating support can lead to a new topic, establishing purpose can alter detail, altering detail can shift audience, and so on.

When to Move On

At some point during prewriting, you will feel "done." You will sense that you have enough groundwork laid. Usually this means you are satisfied that you have a workable topic, a viable purpose, a clear and appropriate audience, and enough satisfactory ideas to form a departure point.

Being "done" with prewriting will mean different things to different writers. Some writers are not comfortable advancing until they are certain of every idea they want to include in their writing and how they are going to develop each of those ideas. For those who feel this way, prewriting may take longer because it must yield more. Others require less of prewriting. These are the writers who do better with only an awareness of some of the major points they will cover. Such writers feel constrained if they predetermine too much; they prefer to discover only some of their main points during prewriting (or maybe only one main point) and let the rest emerge in the flow of their later writing.

How much you require of prewriting to ensure a successful piece only you can decide. You may already have a sense of how much groundwork you must lay before moving on. If not, try prewriting both ways—extensively and less extensively—for separate writing tasks and evaluate which way works better for you. Keep one thing in mind, however: if after prewriting you have trouble going forward, it is possible you have not yet laid enough groundwork. Try additional prewriting in that case, and you may find yourself advancing more readily.

What to Move On To

After prewriting, some writers like to plunge into a first draft. They may have some notion of how to organize their ideas, or they may not. Those who do not, prefer to get a draft down so they can see where their ideas are going. They may like to get everything down in some form—no matter how rough—and then go back and change things when necessary to achieve logical organization. Some writers have the capacity to organize mentally by reviewing their ideas from prewriting and arranging them logically in their heads. But this usually works when there are not many ideas to deal with. Some writers organize as they write their first draft. They decide which idea to treat first, write through it, and then decide what comes next when they get there. Other writers are more successful if they plot their organization in a separate outlining step between prewriting and the first draft. Regardless of whether you go from prewriting to draft or from prewriting to outlining, at some point you will have to concern yourself with the logical organization of your ideas.

There is no single way to organize an essay, for many different organizational strategies are at the writer's disposal. It is even possible to take the same ideas and organize them effectively in more than one way. Sometimes our ideas clearly suggest the best organization (as when we are telling a story and move from what happened first to what happened second, and so on), but often we must give the issue careful thought.

Although there is so much variety to essay organization, it is possible to make many generalizations by discussing one useful pattern of organization. This pattern can be varied in many ways and even abandoned altogether, but a discussion of it serves two purposes. First, it provides us with a useful model. The pattern can serve in so many situations that understanding it allows the writer to organize almost any writing effectively. Second, the pattern provides a handy departure point. Understanding how it works can make you more aware of ways to vary your organization and still be logical and effective.

A Useful Pattern of Organization

Here's something you already know: every essay has a beginning, a middle, and an end. In the pattern of organization presented here, the beginning is the introduction; the middle is the body; and the end is the conclusion. Let's take an overview of each of these three parts and then deal with each in more detail.

The first paragraph (or paragraphs) of the essay forms the *introduction,* which serves two purposes: it lets your reader know what your essay is about, and it arouses your reader's interest in your topic. That's your beginning.

Next comes the middle. This is two or more *body paragraphs.* The purpose of your body paragraphs is to present detail to develop your topic. It is the body paragraphs that form the real meat of the essay.

The end of your essay is the *conclusion.* This final paragraph serves to bring your essay to a satisfying finish.

Before looking in more detail at the function and structure of the three parts of the essay, read the essay in the next section. It illustrates the pattern of organization that is discussed in the rest of this chapter.

The essay here was written by a student. The notes in the margins call your attention to the structural features of the essay, features which will be referred to throughout the rest of this chapter.

All Creatures Great and Small

Gladys Kline stared at her TV in abject horror. Before her eyes lay a gross caricature of a man. His face and hair were discolored, his body disfigured by grain alcohol. He seemed to be having a tantrum—jaw working wildly, arms flailing at his sides. That man was Gladys Kline's son. All at once, memories flooded through her mind—the banners in his bedroom, Saturday night football games, the subscription to *Sports Illustrated*. Like countless others, Gladys Kline never thought it would turn out this way. Nonetheless, it had happened: Her son had deteriorated into the vilest of all beings—a bleacher creature.

One of the first symptoms of the deterioration is his disgusting appearance. Let us consider Bobby Ray Kline as an example. Bobby Ray's sweatshirt always exposes about a 2-inch span of rather flaccid flesh protruding over his waistband. The front of his shirt is commonly adorned with today's stadium mustard and yesterday's spaghetti sauce. Bobby Ray's innovation in hair styling is to knot dog bones in his hair. He would advise you that the greasier your hair, the more manageable the style. In tribute to the Cleveland Browns, Bobby Ray had his hair dyed orange and white. Bobby Ray is very proud of his neon locks, for they help him get noticed by the television cameras—much to the chagrin of his mother. To top off his appearance, Bobby Ray applies makeup to his face. From the top of his forehead to the tip of his chin, urban graffiti is sprawled in vibrant colors. The obscene words Bobby Ray expertly sketches upon his skin would stop a nun dead in her tracks.

Under bleacher creature code, obscenity on the face must translate into profanity in speech. A bleacher creature must be well versed in the seven deadly words. Not only must he be familiar with the terms, he must be able to utilize them in a variety of ways. For instance, he must be able to apply the words to the mother, brother, or any living relative of the person he intends to insult. This task apparently becomes easier as the level of beer consumption rises. After downing the first twelve-pack, most creatures are considered to be at their verbal peak. During this stage, verbal barrages lasting 10 to 15 minutes are not uncommon. Usually, they are directed at some poor, unsuspecting line judge. There are exceptions to this rule, as when intercreature conflicts arise.

These conflicts bring into focus the major credo of the bleacher creatures: Thou shalt show a consistent lack of consideration toward others. Under this rule, a blatant disregard for the neighbor is a must. A bleacher creature has to possess the ability needed to spill beer on many of his less fortunate counterparts at the same time he is whistling shrilly through his teeth. When throwing empty beer cans into the crowd, a very talented creature can make the containers ricochet off two or more spectators. Staggering back to the concession stand for refills, he then must proceed to knock down, knock into, or knock out any or all bystanders in his way. All these actions should be performed with gleeful smiles, to leave no doubt the creatures are sincere in what they do. There is a more tender side to these animals. When confronted by a member of

The first paragraph is the introduction. The last sentence is the thesis, which tells what the essay is about (bleacher creatures are vile). The rest of the introduction stimulates reader interest with description.

Paragraph 2 is a body paragraph. The first sentence is the topic sentence, which tells what the paragraph is about (the appearance of the bleacher creature). The rest of the paragraph is the supporting detail, which develops the topic sentence idea. In all, the paragraph helps support the thesis idea.

Paragraph 3 is a body paragraph. The topic sentence (the first) tells that the paragraph will focus on obscene speech. The rest of the paragraph (the supporting details) develops the topic sentence idea. The paragraph helps develop the thesis idea.

Paragraph 4 is the last body paragraph. Its topic sentence (the first) notes that the paragraph will discuss the creature's lack of consideration. The rest of the paragraph is supporting detail, which develops the topic sentence idea. The paragraph helps prove the thesis.

the opposite sex, the creatures will begin burping loudly to gain the attention of the female. Virility is proven not only by the vulgarity of the burps, but by the rapid succession in which they are delivered. As for Bobby Ray, he has yet to muster the gastric power needed to be a contender in this field.

At 33 years of age, Bobby Ray was sure his mother would miss him terribly if he ever married and left home. Little did he know that back at the Kline homestead, Gladys was busily throwing all his possessions on the front lawn. Her lease had a no-pets clause, and Gladys always followed the rules.

Paragraph 5, the conclusion, brings the essay to a satisfying finish.

The Introduction

We don't always like to admit it, but first impressions are important. Often our initial reactions to something dictate our responses—even though we might react differently if we waited and formed our impressions more slowly, after gathering more information. Think about it a moment. Have you ever dropped a course after attending only one class session? Have you ever made an excuse to walk away from a person you have just met? Have you ever selected a restaurant solely on the basis of its name? We all do such things, and we do them in response to first impressions. Because first impressions are so important, the introduction of your essay must be carefully handled to ensure that your reader's initial reaction is favorable. (Reread the introduction of "All Creatures Great and Small." Notice how well it stimulates reader interest.)

In addition to creating a first impression that can please or displease your reader, there is another purpose the introduction can serve. It can let your reader know what your topic is—that is, it can tell your reader what your essay is about by including a statement that reveals the topic. This statement is called a *thesis*. Below are three introductions written by students. In each introduction the thesis statement that presents the essay topic is underlined.

Introduction 1
The compact disc player, introduced only a few years ago, has become extremely popular. The compact disc system utilizes the most advanced technology available to reproduce recorded music. <u>As a result of this technology, the compact disc system offers excellent sound quality, amazing longevity, and convenient features.</u>

Thesis indicates the writer will discuss the excellent sound quality, amazing longevity, and convenient features of the compact disc system.

Introduction 2
There was a blistering wind howling outside my van window as I was driving to my early-evening English class. The snow began to fall rapidly, blowing and swirling in the air before it reached the road in front of me. <u>Once I</u>

had reached my destination, YSU's campus, I had to struggle to search out and snare a parking space.

Thesis indicates that the essay will explain what the writer went through trying to find a parking space on campus before English class.

Introduction 3

What is a woman? Well, if all that propaganda out there is correct, a woman is someone who delights in serving. Her husband, her children, her house—taking care of these is woman's ultimate purpose in life. And if she doesn't relish it, then surely something is wrong—with her. Most women were brought up firmly grounded in the belief that their major role in life is to marry, have children, and keep a clean house and beautiful home. From the time little girls are big enough to mimic Mother, they are taught in subtle ways that the never-ending battle with dirt, dust, and grime should be their major concern in life. Well, personally, I find housework frustrating.

Thesis indicates the writer will discuss the fact that she finds housework frustrating.

If you look again at the thesis statements in the above three introductions, you will notice that they present the writers' topics in a particular way: each thesis indicates what the writer's broad subject is and what narrow territory within that broad subject the writer has staked out for treatment. This is charted for you below.

Thesis 1
broad subject: the compact disc system
narrowing: It has excellent sound quality, amazing longevity, and convenience.

Thesis 2
broad subject: campus parking
narrowing: It's a struggle.

Thesis 3
broad subject: housework
narrowing: It's frustrating.

You have probably noticed that in each of the sample paragraphs, the thesis is the last sentence of the introduction. While it is not necessary to place the thesis there (it can work well at the beginning or in the middle of the introduction), many writers find it convenient to place the thesis at the end of the introduction.

Below are examples of introductions with thesis statements at the beginning and in the middle. The thesis statements are underlined for you.

Introduction 4

If Marcus Norris wins the mayoral election, our city will not recover from its current economic slump. Norris is on record as advocating layoffs of city workers, which will swell our unemployment ranks. He also favors increased deficit spending, which will strain our city budget to its limit. And most troubling of all, he plans to scrap the economic recovery program begun by our current mayor.

Introduction 5

Psychologists have devised many sophisticated tests for determining the kinds of personalities people have. They need not have bothered, for there is an easier way. It is possible to determine people's personalities from the cars they drive. Whether a person is aggressive, retiring, success-oriented, failure-prone, sexy, or drab—these traits and others are reflected in the individual's choice of automobile.

It is not uncommon for the introduction of an essay to be written without a thesis. In fact, this is frequently the case in narrative essays (essays that tell a story). When an essay lacks a stated thesis, the writer's subject and narrowing must be strongly implied elsewhere in the essay. For an example of an essay with an implied thesis, read "Look Out, Here She Comes" on p. 56.

Shaping the Thesis

The thesis of an essay is important to both the writer and the reader. It is important to the writer because it provides the focus for the essay and hence guides the writer, serving as a kind of touchstone. A writer selecting details and deciding how to express those details will weigh them against the thesis to be sure everything functions to develop the thesis and fulfill its promise. Similarly, the thesis is important to the reader, who views it as a statement of what is to come in the essay. A reader develops expectations for an essay according to what the thesis promises. An essay that fails to deliver what the thesis promises will disappoint a reader. Thus, because the thesis is important to both writer and reader, it must be shaped carefully. This means that when you shape your thesis, you should keep the following points in mind.

1. The Thesis Should Be Narrow Enough to Allow an In-Depth Discussion in a Manageable Length

In Chapter 1 you learned of the need to find a narrow topic, and this applies directly to the thesis (see p. 8). A thesis that is too broad will force the writer into a vague, superficial discussion. And such a discussion will never satisfy a reader because it will never get beyond statements of the obvious. The following thesis statement is too broad.

The role of women has changed drastically in the last fifty years.

Because this thesis is so broad, it would present a problem for the writer. Fifty years is a long time; to discuss in depth all the changes in that time span would require far more pages than the typical college essay runs. If the essay were to run a more manageable length, the writer could do little more than skim the surface and state the obvious. Below is a more suitable thesis, one that is sufficiently narrow.

> The role of women in politics has changed drastically in the last ten years.

This thesis is better because it is narrowed to include only one role of women and because the time span is more reasonable.

2. The Thesis Should Usually Include Only One Subject and Only One Narrowing
More than one subject or more than one narrowing will cause the thesis to be too broad. The following thesis, for example, has more than one subject.

> The Nontraditional Student Center and the International Student Union are two university organizations that serve students well.

This thesis forces the writer to treat two subjects, the Nontraditional Student Center and the International Student Union. Unless the same points can be made about both, the writer will have too much territory to cover. Either of the following would make a more manageable thesis.

> The Nontraditional Student Center serves students well.

> The International Student Union serves students well.

Now consider the following thesis with two narrowings.

> Divorce would be less traumatic if custody laws were revised and if attorneys counseled their clients more carefully.

This thesis suggests two narrowings, which would be a problem for a writer with a great deal to say about both of these focuses. The following thesis statements have only one narrowing each, and thus they are more manageable.

> Divorce would be less traumatic if custody laws were revised.

> Divorce would be less traumatic if attorneys counseled their clients more carefully.

3. The Narrowing Should Be Expressed in Specific Words
Because the reader relies on the thesis for a clear indication of what the essay is about, the narrowing should be expressed in specific words. The following thesis, for example, has a vague narrowing.

> It is interesting to consider the various meanings of *love*.

The word *interesting* is vague, and as a result the reader cannot be sure how the writer is narrowing the subject. In the following revision, however, the narrowing is stated in specific terms, so the reader has a clear sense of the focus of the essay.

A consideration of the various meanings of *love* reveals that we apply this word to a broad spectrum of emotions.

There is one other point to make about your thesis. When you shape it for inclusion in your final paper, avoid forming it into a formal announcement, such as "This paper will show why I've always hated team sports" or "The next paragraphs will present the reasons I enjoy collecting rocks." A thesis that is a formal announcement can appear in your drafts if you like, but it is considered poor style in your final essay.

Exercise: The Thesis

1. In the following thesis statements, identify the broad subject and the narrowing.
   a. Just ask any mother and she will tell you that there can be no more exasperating experience than taking preschool children to the grocery store on a Saturday to do a week's worth of shopping.
   b. My brother, Jerry, taught me the meaning of courage.
   c. Television news does not adequately inform the U.S. public.
   d. It has been said that Benjamin Franklin was a great diplomat; however, no one is more skilled at diplomacy than people who make their living selling clothes.
   e. Many people believe a little white lie can be better than the truth, but I have learned that even these seemingly harmless untruths can cause trouble.
2. Below are pairs of subjects and narrowings. Shape each pair into an interesting thesis. The first one is done for you as an example, and from it you can tell that you may use your own words and add ideas.
   a. subject: blind dates
      narrowing: they don't work out
      After four blind dates this year, I've concluded that such dates are usually disastrous.
   b. subject: final exams
      narrowing: create too much anxiety
   c. subject: the military
      narrowing: a good choice for those undecided about their careers
   d. subject: television game shows
      narrowing: contestants make fools of themselves
   e. subject: living alone
      narrowing: it has its advantages
3. Below are four broad subjects. Select two of them and write a thesis for an essay about each. Narrow so that you are treating a topic manageable in 500 to 700 words.
   example: Saturday morning cartoons—If parents took the time to watch Saturday morning cartoons with their children, they would be surprised by just how violent these programs really are.
   a. Little League
   b. large parties
   c. a childhood memory
   d. surprise quizzes

Creating Interest in Your Topic

An introduction, you now realize, can present your topic in a thesis and arouse your reader's interest in what you have to say. Below are five approaches you can take to your introduction in order to stimulate your reader's interest. Each approach is illustrated with an introduction taken from a student essay.

Approach 1: Provide Background Information

I have been a serious bodybuilder for 7 years now, and during that time I have worked out in quite a few gyms, from posh to no-frills, from homemade basement gyms to top-of-the-line health spas. However, I will never forget one gym, because it was so dreary and rundown.

Approach 2: Tell a Pertinent Story

Hurray, it's Saturday! But my hopes of spending a perfect day off relaxing and enjoying the outdoors are instantly dampened when I look out the window and see a rainy, cold, and altogether dreary day. Clomping downstairs in my bathrobe and fuzzy slippers, and finding my husband's and son's eyes glued to Thundarr the Barbarian does not help cheer me up. My husband, noticing my depression during a cereal commercial, suggests I go shopping. Perfect! Flying upstairs, getting dressed, and putting my makeup on in record time, I'm off to the mall for a glorious day of shopping. Certainly, shopping must be the best way to spend a day.

Approach 3: Explain Why Your Topic Is Important

The recent tuition hike proposed by the Board of Trustees has serious implications for everyone on this campus, students, faculty, and staff alike. If tuition goes up 45 percent as expected, fewer students will be able to attend school, which will mean fewer faculty and staff will be employed. Once the cost of school becomes prohibitive for all but the wealthy, then this university will begin a downward spiral that will eventually mean its demise. There is only one way to solve our economic woes. We must embark on an austerity program that makes the tuition hike unnecessary.

Approach 4: Present Some Interesting Images or Use Description

It was a cool, crisp October morning. Sunrise was complete, the countryside awake and responding to another day. As I turned and slowly made my way into the woods, I had no idea what lay ahead on the path I was to follow that day. (Note: "All Creatures Great and Small" uses this approach.)

Approach 5: Present an Intriguing Problem or Raise a Provocative Question

Are you a Dr. Jekyll who transforms into Mr. Hyde the minute you get behind the wheel of a car? Are you a kind little old lady who becomes Mario

Andretti's pace car driver the instant you hit the freeway? Are you an Eagle Scout by day and a marauding motorist by night? The chances are you are because people's personalities change the moment they strap on that seat belt and head out on the highway.

The approach you take to your introduction is partly influenced by your audience and purpose. Let's say, for example, you are writing to persuade your reader that capital punishment is not immoral. An introduction that includes a funny anecdote would not be appropriate to your serious purpose. Similarly, let's say you are writing to inform your reader that some types of day care centers are harmful to children. If your reader is a mother with children in a day care center, you would not need to provide background information on the purpose of a day care center. Thus, when considering ways to handle your introduction, keep your audience and purpose in mind.

Points to Remember about Writing Introductions

1. Your introduction is important because it forms the first impression your reader gets.
2. An introduction can
   a. Present your topic.
   b. Arouse interest in your topic.
3. The introduction can present your topic in a thesis.
   a. The thesis need not be the last sentence of the introduction, but it is often convenient to place it there.
   b. The thesis presents your topic by stating your subject and your narrowing in specific terms.
   c. Both the subject and the narrowing must be restricted.
   d. For your final draft do not shape a thesis that reads like an announcement.
4. You can create interest in your topic several ways. Five of these are
   a. Providing background information.
   b. Telling a story.
   c. Explaining why your topic is important.
   d. Presenting images or using description.
   e. Presenting a problem or raising a question.
5. Your approach to your introduction will, in part, be determined by your audience and purpose.

The Writing Process and Introductions

Sometimes writers write their introductions first—and sometimes they don't. Let's look for a moment at where writing introductions can fit into your writing process.

Often during prewriting your concern is to develop ideas to support your thesis; you may not give much thought to how you will create interest in that thesis in an introduction. In this case, when you write a first draft you may be stumped about how to begin. So what do you do?

Actually, you have two choices. First, you can skip your introduction and begin drafting with your second paragraph. By the time you finish your draft, a suitable approach to your introduction may suggest itself. If you skip your introduction, you should draft a tentative thesis to provide a focus, something you can check your detail against to keep yourself from drifting off into unrelated areas.

Your second choice is to prewrite for your introduction in a separate stage. (Of course, you can do this too if you skip your introduction and find when you return that you are still stuck.) To prewrite, you might try the following:

1. Shape a thesis by writing a sentence that includes your subject and your narrowing.
2. Ask yourself whether your audience needs background information to appreciate your topic or point of view. If so, list the background points that are needed.
3. Decide whether you could tell a brief story that would interest your particular audience and pave the way for your thesis.
4. List the reasons your topic is important to you, and list the reasons it should be important to your reader.
5. Decide whether you can describe anything related to your topic that would engage the interest of your reader.
6. Ask questions or raise problems that would interest or arouse the curiosity of your reader.
7. Review your responses to numbers 2–6 and decide (considering your audience and purpose) which material will make the best introduction. That material, along with a form of the thesis you wrote for number 1, may be enough to serve as a departure point for your introduction.

Exercise: Three Introductions to Rewrite

Below are three introductions written by students. Although each one has the potential to be effective, each one has problems. Revise each introduction so that it stimulates interest and has a suitable thesis.

1. It was snowing when I boarded the plane. But I was terrified. I have always been afraid of air travel, and hopefully I will someday overcome this fear.

   Suggestions for revision: Create some images. You might describe the weather in a bit more detail. Specify the kind of airplane and explain more carefully the feeling of terror. Also, does the thesis present one or two narrowings? It should only present one.

2. I set the alarm two hours earlier than usual and spent the morning cleaning like

crazy. At 11:00 I went to the grocery store and bought all the necessary food. All afternoon I cooked; by 5:00 I was dressed and ready; but still the first meal I cooked for my in-laws was terrible.

> Suggestions for revision: You might try to be more specific. What time did the alarm go off? Give an example or two of the cleaning you did. What food did you buy? Was it expensive? What did you cook? How bad was it? Can you find a word or words more specific than *terrible?*

3. Does crime pay? Does justice win out? Do the police always get their man? The day I shoplifted a box of candy I learned the answers to these questions.

> Suggestions for revision: Try substituting more interesting questions for these trite, rather boring ones—perhaps some questions that focus on the writer's feelings, such as: "Have you ever wondered what a criminal feels when he or she gets caught?" Create some interest by naming the brand or type of candy and giving its price and by giving the name of the store.

Exercise: Three Introductions to Write

1. Using one of the thesis statements you shaped when you responded to number 3 on p. 36, establish an audience and purpose and write an introduction for an essay that might use that thesis. If you wish, feel free to alter the original thesis somewhat. Also, you might want to check "Points to Remember about Writing Introductions" on p. 38.
2. Below is a list of four subjects. Select one of them and shape a narrow topic from it. (If necessary, do some prewriting to find a suitable topic.) Then establish an audience and purpose. Next, write an introduction for an essay that discusses that topic. You might want to check "Points to Remember about Writing Introductions" on p. 38.
   a. A first experience
   b. A disagreement with a friend
   c. A pleasant (or unpleasant) surprise
   d. The best (or worst) feature of your university
3. Write a second introduction using the thesis, audience, and purpose you shaped for number 2 above, only this time use a different approach to the part that stimulates reader interest. That is, if you told a story the first time, try something else—say, creating images—this time. If you wish, you may state your thesis differently in this second introduction. (As an alternative to this exercise, you may select a subject different from what you used for number 2. Just be sure to narrow, establish audience and purpose, and use a different approach than you did for the first introduction.)

The Body Paragraphs

The paragraphs after your introduction form the body of your essay. The purpose of the body paragraphs is to present the detail that supports, explains, defends, describes, illustrates, or otherwise develops the idea given in your thesis. Obviously it is the body that is the real core of a piece of writing, for it is here that you present the material to convince your reader of the validity of your thesis.

In the organizational pattern we are discussing in this chapter, each body paragraph has two parts: the topic sentence and the supporting detail.

The *topic sentence* presents the point the body paragraph will deal with. This point will be one aspect of the thesis. While the topic sentence can appear anywhere in the body paragraph, many student writers find it easiest to place the topic sentence first. After the topic sentence comes the *supporting detail*. This is all the information that explains, illustrates, defends, describes, supports, or otherwise develops the idea presented in the topic sentence. Look again at the body paragraphs of "All Creatures Great and Small" and notice the topic sentence and supporting details.

Adequate Detail

For your essay to be successful, your supporting detail must be *adequate*. For your essay to have adequate detail, you must have enough body paragraphs to develop your thesis adequately and enough detail in each body paragraph to develop each topic sentence adequately.

Put yourself in your reader's place. You cannot expect a reader to understand and appreciate the point of view stated in your thesis if you do not provide enough convincing support for that view. Let's say someone walked up to you and said, "This town stinks." You respond by asking why. The first person replies, "It's really awful here; I hate it. I'm going to leave, and you should too." Well, would you leave? Would you agree that the place is awful? I doubt it, because you were not given convincing evidence to support the claim that the place stinks. And that is the way it is with supporting detail: without enough of it, no reader will accept as truth the idea in the thesis.

One way to ensure that you supply adequate detail is to remember that as a writer you can't just *tell;* you must also *show*. Thus, the person who *told* by saying that the town stinks should also *show* by providing specific evidence, such as there is no symphony or museum, there is only one theater, the local government is corrupt, the public schools are inadequately funded, the roads are in disrepair, and the people are snobs.

When writers show rather than tell, they are *supporting generalizations*. A generalization is a statement offered as truth. The support for the generalization is what is offered as proof of the generalization. Say, for example, that you believe registration at your school is too much of a hassle. That would be your generalization—your statement of truth. Now if you wanted to convince me that registration is indeed a hassle at your school, you would have to do more than just make the statement. After all, why should I accept your statement as fact just because you make it? If I am to believe registration is a hassle, you will have to prove it to me. Here is a list of some evidence you could provide to support your generalization about registration:

long lines
crowded facilities
too few classes offered
confusing procedures
inaccessible advisers

If you were writing an essay about the hassles of registration, you could write one body paragraph on each of the points in the above list. However, you would have to support every generalization in every body paragraph by showing in addition to telling. Thus, the paragraph about crowded facilities must describe the nature and extent of the crowding in enough detail that the reader comes away from the paragraph believing that crowding really exists. This need to support generalizations would hold for every generalization you make everywhere in the body of your essay.

Look again at "All Creatures Great and Small" on p. 31. Notice that the author supports the thesis generalization by providing this evidence in the topic sentences of the body paragraphs:

The bleacher creature's appearance is disgusting.
The bleacher creature's speech is profane.
The bleacher creature lacks consideration for others.

Now look at the body paragraphs and notice how carefully the author develops each topic sentence generalization by giving examples. For instance, to show that the bleacher creature's appearance is disgusting, the author makes these points:

Fat belly hangs exposed over the belt line.
Sweatshirt is food-stained, and not all the stains are fresh.
Dog bones are in hair.
Hair is greasy (unwashed).
Hair is dyed orange and white.
Obscene words are written on face.

Ways to Develop and Arrange Supporting Detail

Now you know that writers must prove the truth of their thesis statements by providing adequate detail. In Part II you will learn that writers can take a variety of approaches to developing detail, including describing, telling a story, giving examples, explaining similarities and differences, telling what something means, showing how something is done, and explaining causes and effects.

Writers must also decide on an effective order for their details. There are several arrangements possible, and these will be discussed in detail in Part II. Three of the more useful arrangements are: (1) chronological, (2) spatial, and (3) progressive. A *chronological* ordering of ideas means that the writer begins with what happened first, moves to the second event, on to the third, and so on. This can be a useful order for the storyteller. A *spatial* arrangement means the writer moves through space in some logical way, say top to bottom, outside to inside, left to right. When writers describe, they frequently use a spatial arrangement. A *progressive* arrangement means that the writer moves from the most important (surprising, convincing, or representative) idea to the least important. Or the arrangement can be from least to most significant point. Persuasive writers often find themselves following a progressive order.

All this is discussed in more detail in Part II. For now, however, you should be aware that detail in body paragraphs is arranged and developed in some logical, effective way.

Relevant Detail

In addition to being adequate, your supporting detail must also be *relevant*. This means that every bit of information you place in a body paragraph must be strictly and clearly related to the topic sentence of that paragraph. Thus in "All Creatures Great and Small," the first body paragraph (about disgusting appearance) could not describe clean, neat designer jeans and polished Italian shoes. Since these are not disgusting, they are not relevant. Sometimes writers fall into the trap of including detail that is not relevant because they become so concerned about supplying *enough* detail, they overlook the need to include the *right* detail. You know the feeling, that sense that if you only write enough, in there somewhere you will say something that's terrific. Well, as common as that impulse is, it is a dangerous one that can lead you to write ideas that do not belong in a paragraph because they are not related to the topic sentence.

There is another aspect to the relevance issue. In addition to being sure that the detail in a paragraph is relevant to its topic sentence, a writer must also be sure that each topic sentence is relevant to the thesis. If you have a topic sentence—and hence a paragraph—that does not pertain to the thesis, then you will end up with a whole portion of your essay that has strayed from the stated topic. For this reason, "All Creatures Great and Small" cannot include a topic sentence that says bleacher creatures are nice to children—such a statement would not be relevant to the thesis, which presents the creatures as vile.

The best way to ensure relevance in your writing is to think of your thesis as a contract between you and your reader. It guarantees that your essay will be about what the thesis says it will be about. Run a careful check on both your topic sentences and your supporting detail to be certain you have not violated the terms of the contract.

Take some time now and reread "All Creatures Great and Small." Notice that every topic sentence is clearly relevant to the thesis. Also notice that all the supporting details in each body paragraph are directly related to the paragraph's topic sentence.

When to Paragraph

Most often, writers begin a new paragraph each time they begin discussion of a new point to develop the thesis. However, there are some exceptions to this, and these are noted below.

1. Writers sometimes begin a new paragraph to give the reader's eyes a rest. If the detailed discussion of a point requires a very long paragraph, the writer can break up the discussion into two or more paragraphs as a courtesy to the reader, who may find one long paragraph taxing. Because a paragraph indentation serves as a momentary break, it keeps the reader from feeling bogged down in a paragraph that runs on for the better part of a page or more.

2. Sometimes a writer will begin a paragraph to emphasize a point. If a point can appear in a paragraph along with other ideas, but the writer wants that point to receive special emphasis, it can be placed in a paragraph of its own.

3. Writers sometimes place an extended example in its own paragraph. A writer may use one body paragraph to make a point and then illustrate that point with a long example or a series of short examples. If including the example or examples in the paragraph that makes the point would create an overly long paragraph, then the example(s) can appear in a separate paragraph.

Points to Remember about Body Paragraphs

1. The purpose of body paragraphs is to present detail that demonstrates the validity of the point made in the thesis.
2. In the pattern of organization discussed here, body paragraphs have two parts: the topic sentence and the supporting detail.
3. The topic sentence tells what the body paragraph is about; it presents the aspect of the thesis under discussion in the body paragraph.
   a. A topic sentence can appear anywhere in the body paragraph, but it is often convenient to place it first.
   b. The idea presented in the topic sentence must be relevant to the thesis.
4. The supporting detail for a topic sentence develops the point presented in the topic sentence.
   a. The writer must support all generalizations by showing and not just telling.
   b. The supporting detail in a body paragraph must be relevant to its topic sentence.

Evaluating Your Supporting Detail

How can writers be sure their detail is adequate and relevant? A number of ways to evaluate your detail are noted in Part II. For now, you might find the following evaluation techniques helpful.

To Evaluate the Adequacy of Your Detail

1. Go through your draft and underline every generalization. Then bracket off the specific details that support each generalization. Next, go back and read

your first underlined generalization. Look at the bracketed material that supports it and ask yourself if you are *showing* the truth of the generalization in enough detail. Continue this way throughout your draft.

2. Ask someone who can be objective about your work to read your draft. Have that person note in the margin any additional information he or she needs to appreciate your point of view.

3. Count the number of sentences in each of your body paragraphs. If you have a paragraph with fewer than five sentences, ask yourself if you have developed your topic sentence adequately.

4. For each body paragraph in your draft, answer the following questions:
   a. Why would my reader find the information in this paragraph helpful?
   b. How does the information in this paragraph advance my purpose?
   If you cannot justify the inclusion of certain details, then these details are probably not appropriate.

To Evaluate the Relevance of Your Detail

1. Examine each of your topic sentences against your thesis and ask yourself if each is clearly related to the thesis.

2. Examine each sentence of every body paragraph and ask yourself if each is clearly related to its topic sentence.

3. Ask someone who will be objective about your work to read your draft and underline any detail that does not seem relevant.

Exercise: Body Paragraphs to Evaluate

Below is an essay written by a college freshman. The essay has definite strengths, but it also has a problem or two. Read the essay and then answer the questions that follow. These questions are meant to help you understand the points made in this chapter about body paragraphs.

Exhaustion

All of my friends told me it would be hard for me to attend college at my age because I was eighteen years removed from any study habits that I may have once had. However, I'm finding that the hardest part of attending college is not lack of study habits but coping with the exhaustion from trying to keep up with attending classes, working 40 hours a week, raising a family of three exuberant boys, and taking care of household chores.

A typical day starts for me at 6:00 in the morning when I crawl out of my toast-warm bed and stumble over the dog. Flicking on the lights in each of the boys' rooms, I grope my way carefully down the stairs, with eyes half open. My first encounter is with three hungry, mewling cats and a dog who lets me know he has to be let out. Next I grab a cup of coffee and gulp half of it down so I can pry my eyes open enough to take care of all the urgent matters of the morning. Gulping coffee and grabbing quick puffs of my cigarette, I stumble around packing school lunches. Now it's time for the real work, pushing the boys to get ready for school. "Greg, don't forget to brush your teeth."

"Bob, take that shirt off. I don't care if it is your favorite; you wore it yesterday." "Mike, you can't comb your hair like that; it makes you look like Alfalfa." By the time I get them out the door, I'm ready to go back to bed, but work is waiting and I have no time to lose. Eight-thirty finds me on the job, brushed, curled, and ready to begin.

The hands on the clock finally reach twelve and it's time for my lunch hour. Lunch? What is that? I have one hour to do my grocery shopping for the day and pay any bills that need paying. I rush home, put my milk and bread away, take care of the pets again, and hurry back to work by one o'clock.

Work is filing, typing, taking payments, balancing my money drawer, and putting my data on the computer as fast and efficiently as possible so I can exit quickly at 4:30 p.m.

My first class in the evenings at college starts at 5:40, and I live 40 miles from campus, so my trip usually takes 45 to 50 minutes. By the time I find a parking place, I barely make it to class on time. Algebra class is over at 9:30. I then have a 45-minute drive home.

Packing lunches for the next day, bathing and washing my hair, finding something to eat, and relaxing enough to go to sleep usually puts me in bed as late as 1:00 a.m. Most of the time I fall asleep immediately because I am so worn out.

I knew attending college and working would be hard, but I did not realize it would be this exhausting. However, I feel that when I graduate it will have been worth the exhaustion to achieve at last a degree which I have always wanted.

1. What is the thesis of "Exhaustion"?
2. When you finished the essay, did you feel there was enough detail to demonstrate the validity of the idea presented in the thesis? That is, is the thesis adequately developed in the body paragraphs? Explain.
3. What is the topic sentence for each body paragraph? Are all these topic sentences relevant to the thesis?
4. Which topic sentence receives the most development?
5. Which topic sentence receives the least development? What effect does the paragraph with that topic sentence have on you?
6. Do any topic sentences need additional supporting detail? Is the author telling without showing in any of the paragraphs?
7. Are any details in any body paragraphs not relevant to the appropriate topic sentence?

Exercise: Two Body Paragraphs to Write

1. Assume you are writing an essay with one of the following thesis statements:

The best thing about _____ is _____ (you fill in the blanks).

The worst thing about _Nursing school_ is _the paper work_ (you fill in the blanks).

First, decide which thesis you will use, and then prewrite until you have discovered two main ideas for developing that thesis. For example, if your thesis is, "The best thing about college life is meeting interesting people," you might describe the people you meet in class and the people you meet in your dorm. Or develop one paragraph about Chris, the guy you met from Zimbabwe, and another about Dr. Sorenson, the prof who got you interested in cellular biology.

    After you have settled on your two main points, develop each one in a body paragraph. As you do this exercise, remember the following:

  a. Write your thesis across the top of your page to serve as a guide for the rest of your writing.

  b. Consult "Points to Remember about Body Paragraphs" on p. 44.

  c. You may want to prewrite a second time to discover supporting detail for your topic sentences.

  d. You will probably revise your paragraphs (maybe more than once) before you are satisfied with them.

2. Bring your completed body paragraphs and thesis to class and exchange them with a classmate. After reading each other's work, write a note to the person whose paragraphs you read, and in the note, answer the following questions:

  a. Are the topic sentences relevant? If not, what specifically is the problem?

  b. Are all the supporting details relevant? If not, what detail is not relevant? Why?

  c. Is the supporting detail adequate in each paragraph? If not, where is detail needed? What kind of detail should it be?

  d. Are there any unsupported generalizations? If so, which ones?

  e. Is the method of development effective? If not, what is wrong?

  f. Is the order of details logical? If not, what is wrong?

3. When you get back your paragraphs, study your classmate's responses. Decide whether you agree with the evaluation. If not, discuss your disagreement with your teacher to determine whether you or your classmate is correct.

The Conclusion

The conclusion of an essay is important because it influences your reader's final impression. We have all had the experience of watching a movie that starts out strong and then fizzles at the end. Typically we do not react well to this, and when we remember the film, we tend to recall the weakness at the end more than the strength at the beginning. Writing works much the same way. Even if it has a strong introduction and body, an essay with a weak conclusion will leave your reader feeling let down, perhaps even frustrated or annoyed. For this reason, the same care that goes into your introduction and body should also go into your conclusion.

    Consider, for a moment, the conclusion a student wrote for an essay with the thesis, "The way Mr. Wang communicated with students, challenged them, and spent his own time with them made him the teacher I respected most." The essay with this thesis had three body paragraphs, one on communicating with students, one on challenging students, and one on spending his own time with students. The conclusion ran like this:

> Therefore, Mr. Wang is the teacher I most respected because of the way he communicated with students, the way he challenged them, and the way he spent his own free time helping them.

This conclusion is certainly logical enough in its approach, but how do you react to it? Do you find it boring? Are you annoyed by the blatant repetition of the thesis? Boredom and annoyance would be valid reactions to this conclusion. Actually, the student's essay was well organized with interesting detail, but the writer did not craft his conclusion carefully, and as a result the reader comes away from an otherwise well-written essay feeling disappointed.

Now react to a conclusion handled with more care. This conclusion was for an essay describing a night spent at the beach. Interestingly, throughout the essay the writer likened the beach to a lover. Here is the conclusion:

> As the sun rose to signal the start of a new day, I walked away, not feeling at all tired but instead fulfilled. The beach had offered me all of her beauty, and the night we spent together would remain a pleasant memory always.

Clearly the approach to this second conclusion is more interesting than the unnecessary repetition of the first. For this reason, a reader will come away from the second essay feeling more satisfied than he or she would after reading the first. The point to be drawn from all this is that like first impressions, final reactions are significant.

Now look again at "All Creatures Great and Small" on p. 31. Is the conclusion effective? Why?

Ways to Handle the Conclusion

The conclusion of an essay can be handled a variety of ways. Some of these are described below.

1. Leave the Reader with an Overall Reaction

With this approach, the writer extracts from the major points of the essay some overriding impression, observation, or reaction. This kind of conclusion often leaves the reader with a final sense of how the writer feels about things. The conclusion of "Shame" on p. 173 is an example of this approach.

2. Summarize the Main Points of the Essay

For this approach, the writer recaps the major ideas in the essay. A word of caution is needed here, however. Save a summary conclusion for those times when a brief review would be helpful to the reader. If you have written a relatively short essay with easily understood and easily remembered ideas, your reader does not need a summary and may grow annoyed at unnecessary repetition. On the other hand, if your essay is long and has many ideas, some of which are complex, your reader will appreciate a summary of main points at the end. For an example of a summary conclusion, see "Togetherness: Before Children and After" on p. 250.

3. Introduce a Related Idea

Often an effective conclusion can be built around an idea or ideas not appearing elsewhere in the essay. For this approach to work, the idea or ideas introduced must be clearly and closely related to the ideas that appear in the body. It would be disconcerting for a reader to encounter ideas in the conclusion that seem to spring out of nowhere. The conclusion of "Seniors in the Night" on p. 180 is an example of introducing a related idea.

4. Draw a Conclusion

Frequently the ideas in the body of an essay lead to some significant conclusion. When this is the case, the final paragraph(s) can be used to state and explain what that conclusion is. An example of this approach appears in "Friends at Work" on p. 277.

5. Restate the Thesis or Another Portion of the Introduction

It is possible to conclude an essay by repeating the thesis or another part of the introduction. However, a word of caution is in order because when this approach is used at the wrong times, the effect is most unsatisfactory. The conclusion you read on p. 47 (about Mr. Wang) seems lazy; it is certainly not very interesting. Yet this approach *can* succeed if you keep two things in mind. First, if you decide to repeat the thesis or another part of the introduction, it is often best to restate the idea using different language. That is, restate the ideas in a new way. Second, the restatement is best used to achieve the kind of dramatic effect that comes from repetition. For an example of restatement in a new way, read "Locating a Buck: The Key to Success," on p. 224.

6. Use a Combination of Approaches

Often a conclusion combines two or more strategies. Sometimes the restatement of the thesis is followed by a summary. A conclusion can be drawn and be included with an overall reaction. A related idea can appear with a restatement. Any combination of approaches is possible. The conclusion of "Look Out! Here Comes a New York Driver!" on p. 254 includes new and related ideas and a summary.

Not only can the approach to a conclusion vary from essay to essay, but so too can the length. At times you may find that a single sentence serves very well. Other times you may shape a paragraph of several sentences. Sometimes a conclusion of more than one paragraph is in order. Regardless, the function of a conclusion is to bring your writing to a satisfying finish. Effective writing does not screech to a halt but closes off neatly.

There is another note on the conclusion: it is best not to begin this final paragraph with "In conclusion." This phrase has become a cliché of sorts and stands a good chance of annoying a reader.

The Writing Process and Conclusions

Sometimes when writers begin their first draft they already have a sense of how they want to handle their conclusion—maybe they have even outlined this portion of the essay. Probably more often, writers determine their approach to the conclusion after their body paragraphs are complete, and this makes sense for two reasons. First, sometimes writers find that just the right approach suggests itself once the body is drafted. Second, a conclusion can be shaped by the character of the essay's body. This means it may not be possible to know what is best for the final paragraph until after the body is written.

To make decisions about how to handle a conclusion, you might try the following procedure:

1. Ask yourself these questions:
    a. Would my reader appreciate a summary or find it unnecessary?
    b. Would a restatement of the thesis provide emphasis or dramatic effect? Or would it seem lazy and boring?
    c. Would my reader better appreciate my point of view if I closed with an overall reaction?
    d. Are there any ideas related to my thesis that do not appear in my introduction or body? Would closing with any of these ideas help my reader appreciate the significance of my topic or advance my purpose?
    e. Can I draw any conclusions from the points in my body paragraphs that would help fulfill my purpose or help my reader appreciate my point of view?
2. The answers to the questions above can help you discover suitable approaches to your conclusion. If more than one approach appears possible, consider combining approaches or choose the one you like best or the one that seems the easiest to handle.
3. Try writing more than one conclusion, each with a different approach. Then you can judge more easily which approach is the most effective.

Points to Remember about the Conclusion
1. Because final impressions significantly influence how readers view your work, your conclusions must be carefully crafted.
2. The function of a conclusion is to bring your essay to a satisfying finish.
3. Among the possible approaches to the conclusion are
    a. Leaving the reader with an overall reaction
    b. Summarizing your main points if your essay is long and/or has complex ideas
    c. Introducing a related idea
    d. Drawing a conclusion from the ideas in your essay
    e. Restating the thesis or another part of the introduction, possibly in a new way, for emphasis or dramatic effect
    f. Combining approaches
4. The length of the conclusion can vary.
5. Avoid beginning your conclusion with "In conclusion."

Exercise: Three Conclusions to Evaluate

Read "The Old Ball Game" on p. 322, "What It Means to Be a Friend" on p. 297, and "Going Back" on p. 205. Answer the following questions about the conclusion of each of these essays.

1. Does the conclusion bring the essay to a satisfying close? Explain.
2. What approach is used for the conclusion? Is this approach effective? If not, explain why.
3. Is the length of the conclusion appropriate? If not, explain why.
4. Does the conclusion leave you with a positive final impression? If not, explain why.

Exercise: A Conclusion to Write

Below is a clever, entertaining essay written by a freshman. The conclusion has been omitted, so write your own. In class take turns reading your conclusions and note the variety of approaches. You will find it interesting to see how many different ways the conclusion can be handled. You might also note the various strengths and weaknesses of the different conclusions you hear.

Beware the Body Brigade

I honestly believe that if all the health fanatics were piled in one big heap, the mound would make Mount Everest look like an anthill. These joggers and protein-poppers seem to be banding together armed with sweatsuits and wheat germ to descend upon the junk food junkies and those chumps whose only exercise is climbing in and out of bed morning and night. The poor slovenly souls in the latter group struggle to defend themselves against the psychological tactics of what I call the "Body Brigade." Disguised as run-of-the-mill let's-get-a-pizza people, they are actually brainwashers. Take your Big Mac and run the other way if you come face-to-face with a Body Brigader. The breed works in potent ways.

Take for instance the health food nut. The health food nut will weaken your resistance and convert you to a Body Brigade Believer by threatening you with immediate, self-inflicted death if you continue eating "whatever that awful stuff is you're feeding yourself." As you open your lunchbox, empty stomach growling, and begin to gobble your bologna sandwich, he or she will grab your arm, yank the sandwich from between your teeth, and proclaim, "You're *killing* yourself eating that junk. Don't you know they put *rat meat* in bologna?" Because you now believe that you will not rise from the lunch table upon consuming your rat bologna, the carrot sticks and plain, natural yogurt your patron Brigader offers you begin to look appetizing. Watch out, Burger Barn addict—you are beginning to weaken.

If you ever hear a pair of sneaker-clad feet running up behind you—don't turn around. You are being chased by the jogger. The jogger will snare you by pounding into your head the "I used to look *like you* before . . ." line. A common conversation goes something like this: "You take the bus to work? And it's only 5 miles to your office? You have to be kidding." Mr. Addidas here believes that you should run the "short 5-mile jaunt" each morning, despite the fact that walking just the two blocks from your doorstep to the bus stop leaves you gasping for air. The next line is "I used to look *like you*" (and the Brigader puckers up his face on the "like you") "before I started running each morning. I used to have a pot belly just like you do, and look at me now." You do look at the jogger—no gut. You look at yourself—big gut. Never worried before about your pot belly, now you feel as if you have an overblown beachball beneath your shirt. The self-disgust maneuver is working on you, and you begin to feel inferior to the Brigader.

A Useful Pattern of Organization: An Illustration

Below is an essay written by a freshman to express some of the frustration of eating at Courtney's on his campus. The essay is well written and follows the pattern of organization discussed in this chapter.

So you can study how the pattern works, there are numbers throughout the essay to refer you to notes at the end of the essay. These notes call your attention to key features of the organization to illustrate how this organizational pattern operates.

Lunch at Courtney's

Every Tuesday and Thursday I have a 2-hour break in the afternoon at which time I am plagued by shooting stabs of hunger pains. To help ease this misery, I stroll over to Courtney's to get a little sustenance.[1] Even though the food is always great, more often than not eating at Courtney's is a big hassle.[2]

One of the biggest hassles at Courtney's is trying to order the food.[3] The long, twisting lines of hunger-stricken college students create ridiculous delays and a jam of people pressed together shoulder to shoulder. Half the time the people have not decided what they want to order by the time they make it up to the counter. This lengthens the wait while students ponder the wisdom of choosing a roast beef with cheese rather than a turkey club. By this time my stomach is so hollow, I would be grateful for a measly french fry. After deciding at last what they want, some students create problems because they order so much they do not have enough money to pay for it all. Then the rest of us wait while the ones short of funds beg an extra dollar off of their friends in varying spots throughout the lines. Of course if they fail to come up with the extra money, the rest of us cool our heels waiting while the poor ones decide which of the ordered food they won't take after all. This confusion is all made worse by the coming and going of people who cut through the lines on their way somewhere else or by folks who have no interest in food but want to hang out in line and chat with those who do.[4]

An even bigger hassle is finding a place to sit and eat.[5] At most times of the day, this can be about as hard as school is. Sometimes I stand around for as much as a half an hour waiting for a table. By this time my food is cold, my shake has melted, and eating does not seem as appealing as it once did. But then I feel another stab in my stomach, so I decide to see this through. Occasionally I will spot an empty seat across the room, race over balancing my loaded tray, books, and notebook, only to arrive a few seconds behind the first-place finisher. I have even stooped so low as to hover around someone who seems ready to finish up, so I can hurry the person along and grab the vacated seat. I always try to look my pathetic best, but invariably the person takes a last bite and then announces, "I'll be here awhile; I'm waiting for someone." Starved and frustrated, I heave a sigh and head for the outdoors. Lunch on the grass isn't bad, unless the grass is buried 3 inches under the snow.[6]

The biggest pain of all is not getting the right order.[7] This can happen because of all the confusion behind the counter. With so many people to serve, it is not unusual for the receipts with the orders on them to get mixed up. Actually, I never understood why people took so long to decide what they want to eat, since the chances are good they will get something else anyway. Of course no one ever seems to discover the mistake until after they have gone through the hassle of finding a seat. Then there are only two choices. Eat what you've got, or get back in the crazy line and wait. Personally, I recommend eating what you've got, since there is no guarantee that once you have waited in line a second time you will get the correct order.[8]

Well, the food is good, even if it is not what you ordered, and you find yourself consuming it in the midst of the construction for the new football stadium. I suppose that's why I have not yet taken to bringing my own peanut butter and jelly sandwich in a little brown bag.[9]

1. The first two sentences of the introduction create reader interest with background information.
2. The thesis is the last sentence of the introduction. It presents what the essay is about by giving the subject (Courtney's) and the narrowing (eating there is a hassle).
3. The first body paragraph begins with a topic sentence that reveals the first aspect of the thesis to be developed (the hassle of ordering food). The topic sentence is relevant to the thesis.
4. The supporting detail for this body paragraph comes after the topic sentence. This detail is adequate because it shows that ordering food is a hassle. That is, the generalization in the topic sentence is supported. All the support is relevant to the topic sentence; there is no straying. The method of development in this paragraph is description and illustration (examples); the hassle of ordering is described and illustrated to establish the validity of the topic sentence. The ordering of details is, in part, chronological.
5. The topic sentence for the second body paragraph is placed first. This topic sentence is relevant to the thesis, and it presents the second aspect of the thesis to be discussed (the hassle of finding a place to sit and eat). The topic sentence suggests that the chronological ordering of details continues (one eats *after* the food is ordered); however, the words "an even bigger hassle"

reveal that the order of details is also progressive—from big to bigger hassles.

6. After the topic sentence for the second body paragraph comes the supporting detail, all of which is relevant to its topic sentence. The detail is adequate; the writer *shows* it is hard to find a place to eat by using examples and some description as the methods of development. In part, the order of details is chronological (first he waits and the food gets cold; then he feels a stab of hunger and decides to persist; then he races for a seat and loses; then he goes outside). The details also have a progressive arrangement from racing for a seat to acting pathetic to get a seat to giving up and going outdoors—this shows progressively the lengths the writer must go to.

7. The topic sentence for the third body paragraph appears first. It is relevant to the thesis and reveals the third aspect of the thesis to be discussed. The topic sentence furthers the progressive arrangement with the words, ''the biggest pain of all.'' However, the chronological arrangement is also present, since a person does not discover the incorrect order until after the seat is found.

8. After the topic sentence for the third body paragraph comes the supporting detail, all of which is relevant to the focus of the topic sentence (not getting the right order). This supporting detail is developed in part with a cause-and-effect pattern (cause: confusion, effect: incorrect order; cause: discovering incorrect order, effect: eat order or return to line). This paragraph also follows a progressive order with the climactic idea that despite all the hassle, people do not get what they ordered.

9. This last paragraph is the conclusion, which brings the essay to a satisfying close by restating part of the thesis (the food is good), summarizing part of the essay's ideas (incorrect orders and inadequate seating), and introducing a new but related idea (the reason the writer continues to eat at Courtney's). The conclusion also leaves the reader with a positive final impression.

Varying the Pattern of Organization

The standard pattern of organization can work well in a variety of situations. For this reason, it makes sense for you to understand it so you can use it if you want—and you will probably find yourself using this format on many occasions.

However, there is another reason to understand the workings of the standard pattern: once you appreciate how this basic organization functions, it is not hard to vary it in ways that suit any piece you are working on. Let's look, then, at some of the more common ways writers can vary the standard pattern. Below is a chart of common departures.

Variations of the Pattern

I. Introduction

   A. Sometimes there is no separate introduction; instead the essay begins with the writer's first main point.

      1. When there is no separate introduction, the thesis can be strongly implied in the rest of the essay or stated in the conclusion.

      2. Narrative essays (ones that tell stories) often begin with the first chronological event rather than a formal introduction.

   B. The thesis statement can be taken from more than one sentence in the introduction.

   C. The thesis can be at the beginning or middle of the introduction rather than at the end.

   D. Sometimes the first paragraph begins with the thesis but there is no formal part aimed at arousing reader interest. Instead, after the thesis the writer begins development of the first main point. This development forms the remainder of paragraph 1.

II. The Body

   A. Sometimes a body paragraph does not have a stated topic sentence. Instead, the aspect of the thesis under discussion is strongly implied.

   B. A stated topic sentence can appear in the middle or at the end of a body paragraph.

   C. A single aspect of the thesis can be discussed in two or more body paragraphs.

   D. Two closely related aspects of the thesis can be treated in the same body paragraph.

III. The Conclusion

   A. Sometimes there is no separate concluding paragraph.

      1. This can be the case when the discussion in the last body paragraph provides sufficient closure.

      2. This can also happen when a concluding sentence forms the last sentence of the last body paragraph.

   B. When there is no stated thesis in paragraph 1, the thesis can appear in the conclusion.

   C. The concluding paragraph can include the last (and frequently the most significant) point to develop the thesis.

Note: An essay can incorporate any one or combination of the above variations. The student and professional essays in the rest of the text illustrate many of these variations.

Variations of the Pattern: Illustrations

To appreciate some of the ways writers can vary the useful pattern of organization, read the following three essays written by students. There are notes in the margins to call your attention to the variations.

Look Out, Here She Comes

Every morning at 8:30 a.m., there enters a short, overweight, middle-aged woman through the front doors of the Valu King where I am employed, even though we do not officially open for business until 9:00. This lady is always dressed in the same out-of-style, dirty-looking outfit. Her hideous legs are so fat they are fortunate to be supported by a pair of old, black, high-heeled pump shoes. Her gray hair is unsuccessfully dyed with red. From her appearance you would assume that she can't afford new clothes or health and beauty care. The lady is Nora Tompkins.

Introduction has no specifically stated thesis that reveals topic. Instead, it is implied that essay is about Nora Tompkins in Valu King.

Nora starts every day off by browsing through the produce section, searching for discolored, old, or bruised fruits and vegetables. Once she has discovered some items, she asks us if she can have them reduced. Sometimes she practically begs us to mark the price down for her. If we do not mark the produce down enough to suit her, Nora throws the items back in the display and wheels her cart away in a huff.

As Nora exits the produce section and enters my dairy department, she slowly grabs a few of my sale items, looking at them to see if they are her idea of real bargains. If she notices some milk products are reduced, she will usually buy all of them, even though the expiration date is near.

The day-old bakery items are her favorites. Upon arriving at the day-old rack, she starts glancing over it for bargains. Most of the time, she fills her cart with these reduced items. But first she demands they be reduced even more. I have seen her stand there and argue about the price with the bakery women. She has even taken a swing at one of them for not reducing the day-old pastries more.

There are only two things she looks at in the grocery department: generic products and sale items. These are the only items she will buy, and she usually does not want just one or two of each of these products. She usually asks us if she can buy a full case, regardless of what our ad says is the limited purchase on these items.

Inexpensive fresh cuts of meat are all she buys out of the meat cases. She picks up a piece of meat that she might want and inspects it better than a health inspector. The meat cutters have found meat packages with holes in them because of Nora's finger inspection. She even has enough nerve to ask the meat cutters to trim off minute pieces of fat for her. Other times she has asked them to cut one thick piece of beef into two thin pieces of meat for her.

Topic sentence of body paragraph is implied: Nora behaves just as badly in the meat department.

Over time, everyone in the store, including the cashiers, has come to hate Nora. Now most of the employees avoid her by staying in the back room or slipping into an aisle she has already passed. She wants to be friends with everyone so that she can save a penny, but no one even says hello to her anymore. More than once Nora has asked cashiers not to charge her for some of the food, but they do anyway. It's not a matter of honesty. They really hate the woman.

We are all relieved when Nora leaves. When she finally does go, she takes all of this discount food to her $150,000 home in a suburban development. Then, after she cleans, cooks, or repacks most of the food, she drives out to a roadside stand, sells these lower-priced items to people at a higher price, and pockets the profit.

Rather than a standard conclusion, final paragraph presents the last (and perhaps main) point of the essay.

The Ball Game

It was midsummer and the Little League baseball playoffs had begun. Many teams from the area participated in them, including the one I coached. My team was made up of 9- and 10-year-olds, all relatively the same size and build, with one exception. Jimmy was much smaller and had much less athletic ability than the others. Still, he was very excited about the playoffs. Jimmy's father was also worked up over the playoffs, maybe too worked up.

When my team went on the field for the pregame warmups, it was easy to pick Jimmy out of the crowd. His uniform was much too big. He was always tripping over his long pants or pulling his sleeves up to throw the ball. His cap was continuously falling over his eyes, blocking his vision. Still, Jimmy was as proud and happy to be a part of that team as the next boy. He never complained about anything; he just went along with what was asked of him.

It was in the third inning of our first game that I sent Jimmy in to bat. He was so excited when I told him that he ran out on the field without the bat. But when he came back to get it, I reminded him to calm down and take his time. His first swing at the ball brought a solid single; it was his first hit all year. The big, gleaming smile on Jimmy's face showed how proud he was. But his father, who was watching the game from the side of the dugout, stood still. He neither clapped nor smiled. The look on his face seemed to say, "Is that all?"

Jimmy's second at-bat was not at all good. He struck out in three straight pitches. As he slowly turned around to make that lonely walk back to the dugout, I could see the disappointment all over his face. I went out to meet Jimmy and started to console him, when suddenly I was pushed from behind and knocked several feet away from him. It was Jimmy's dad who pushed me. It was also Jimmy's dad who was yelling and screaming at Jimmy in front of everyone in the ball park. Everyone tried to ignore the scene Jimmy's dad was making. The players in the dugout began to talk to each other, coaches looked at the roster sheets, fans stared up at the sky, and Jimmy just looked down at the ground, crying ever so slightly so no one would notice.

Essay has a two-paragraph introduction that provides background information. There is no stated thesis.

After several minutes, which seemed more like hours, Jimmy's dad finally walked off the field and left the park. Jimmy walked slowly back to the dugout and sat on the end of the bench for the rest of the game. He stared blankly into the ground, not once looking up, as big round tears rolled slowly down his embarrassed cheeks.

We lost the playoff game that day, but no one seemed to mind that much. We all realized that Jimmy had lost something more important, something it would not be easy to get back. In just a few minutes of cruel and thoughtless yelling, the little bit of pride and confidence that Jimmy had gained was lost.

Body paragraph has no stated topic sentence.

Conclusion presents thesis idea: that a few minutes of yelling caused Jimmy to lose pride and confidence. A larger thesis is implied by the essay: Little League parents can do more harm than good.

The Stranger from My Past

Would time never pass? The taunting chimes of the grandfather clock filled the room, and my eyes were drawn by its magnetic powers. I had been unable to keep from watching the hands slowly move around its face. Time had not moved so slowly in the past. I could no longer stand the loud ticking of the clock, so I stepped out through the door to await the arrival of my guest.

The sun felt warm and soothing. My eyes squinted against the brightness of the afternoon, and as they slowly focused, I scoured the long gravel drive. Vague, shadowy images flickered in and out of my mind. What would he be like today? Was it age that put pressure on us to reunite, to bring our lives together once again? Why had we waited so long?

My mind traveled back over the years. I was walking to school. My head was bent to hide the tears hanging on my lashes. I felt frightened and alone. Then a hand lightly touched my shoulder, but I was afraid to look. I did not want a classmate to see the tears. I turned slowly and looked up into caring brown eyes of an unexpected friend. I tried to speak. He stopped me with a gentle smile of understanding. We continued to walk together, his gentle strength filling me with love and security.

The love we shared grew over the years. I marveled at the accomplishments he made in life. He became a man who would walk in places other men only dream of. Yet he remained the compassionate young man that had taken time to calm a little girl's fears. Nature etched and polished his qualities into a fine edge. Through the years his achievements led him down a different path, and my friend moved so far away. Suddenly a flash of light, reflecting off a car, snapped me back from the past.

The quiet hum of a car motor and crunching of tires on gravel filled my ears. My legs trembled as I approached the car. I saw his silhouette through the bright windshield. At last the motor was quiet, and the sound of the car door opening filled the air. As the car door swung slowly out, the man stood to reveal himself. Was this stranger my friend of long ago?

My eyes took in every detail of the distinguished gray-haired man. He looked so different. I tried to conjure up those shadowy images to compare to this stranger. As I hesitated, he reached out and embraced me with loving arms. I still had doubts and did not respond. He stepped back holding my

There is no separate introduction; the essay begins with the first event in the narration.

The body paragraphs do not have topic sentences; the time sequence of the narration provides structure and focus for the details.

There is no separate conclusion; the last event of the story provides adequate closure.

shoulders at arm's length. He looked at me with misty eyes and said, "Sis, do you not know your own brother?" Tears rushed forth as shadowy images of the past merged with the man before me.

An Essay to Write

You have read about how writers can generate and organize their ideas. Now it is time to try your hand at writing an essay. The broad subject for this essay is how you feel about writing and/or taking a writing course and why you feel as you do.

Your audience for this essay is your composition instructor, a person who is interested in your thoughts and feelings about this subject. The purpose of your writing is to communicate honestly and accurately the attitude you are bringing to your writing course in order to help your instructor better understand your current feelings about your work this term.

Before you begin work on your essay, review the following suggestions. You may want to try some of them, although you are not obligated to do so.

1. To generate ideas, consider your past experiences with writing and writing classes, whether you have enjoyed writing in the past, how successful your past writing has been, the kinds of writing you do and do not enjoy, what you hope to learn this term, what you see as your strengths and weaknesses, whether you are glad to be in a writing course, what you perceive as the purpose of your writing class, how good your previous writing instruction has been, what you think your chances of doing well are, and so on.

2. If you have trouble generating ideas for support, use some of the prewriting techniques described in Chapter 1.

3. After generating ideas, review what you have and decide which ideas you want to include and which you will reject. If necessary after this, generate some additional ideas.

4. Once you feel you have enough ideas to bring to a draft (and different writers will vary in their needs here), number your ideas in the order you wish to handle them. Most likely, you will find that a progressive order (see p. 43) will work the best, but other arrangements are possible.

5. If you feel the need, make decisions about how you will handle your introduction and conclusion (see the discussions beginning on p. 32 and p. 47 to make these decisions). Otherwise, you can make these decisions when you draft.

6. Write your first draft, but let it be a rough one. Just get your ideas down the best way you can without worrying over anything. Try to go from start to finish in one sitting. If you have trouble getting started, skip your introduction and return to it after everything else is drafted.

7. After writing your draft, compare it against the charts on p. 38, p. 44, p. 50, and p. 55. Make any changes in your draft that you deem necessary after looking at these charts.
8. Type your reworked draft and ask two of your classmates to read it. Have your readers respond in writing to the following questions:
    a. Does the introduction hold your interest? If not, why?
    b. Is there a stated or strongly implied thesis? What is it?
    c. Are all generalizations adequately supported? If not, where is more detail needed?
    d. Are there any relevance problems? If so, what are they?
    e. Is there any detail not appropriate to the audience or purpose?
    f. Are there enough body paragraphs to develop the thesis adequately?
    g. Is there anything you do not understand? If so, what?
    h. Is the conclusion appropriate, and does it leave you with a positive final impression? If not, what problems exist?
    i. What are the chief strengths of the draft? The chief weaknesses?
9. Rework your draft, taking into consideration the reactions of your readers. If you question the validity of a reader response, ask for your instructor's opinion.
10. Check your essay slowly and carefully for spelling, punctuation, and grammar errors.
11. Type or copy your essay into its final form and then check it carefully for typing or transcription errors.

3

From Ideas to Essay

In Chapter 1 you learned ways to shape writing topics and discover ideas to develop those topics. In Chapter 2 you read of the need to organize and present your ideas logically so your reader can understand what you are saying. But at what point do writers organize their ideas? For that matter, at what points do they check relevance, or polish their sentences, or write a first draft, or check spellings, or make sure they are being clear, or make sure that they are providing adequate detail? At what points do writers do all of the many things they do? And more importantly, *how* do writers do these things?

When we ask what writers do and when they do it, we are really asking about the *writing process*. We are asking how writers move from idea generation to finished pieces. We are asking what goes on when people take their own thoughts and prepare them for public viewing. In short, we are asking what happens when people write.

It is the writing process that is the focus of this chapter. Its purpose is to lay groundwork to help you discover the writing procedures that work well for you so you can approach your writing in ways that are both effective and efficient.

What You Should Know about the Writing Process

Put twenty successful writers in a room, ask them what they do when they write, and you could well get twenty different answers. This is because different people approach their writing in different ways. Put one successful writer in a room, ask that person what happened when he or she wrote twenty different pieces, and once again you could get twenty different answers. This is because the same person does not always do the same things when writing. Thus, we can make two important points about the writing process. First, there is no *one* process, and each varying approach can work well. Second, the same person does not always use the same procedures—an individual may change the process for a number of valid reasons.

Now what if I told you it is possible to identify steps in the writing process? "Ah," you might say, "this is not as tricky as I was starting to think. I just learn the steps and perform them in order, right?" Actually not. You see, the nature of the writing process is such that writers often find themselves stepping back before going forward. Let's say, for example, you have shaped a topic and generated ideas that please you, so you begin to consider ways to arrange your ideas. But while you are arranging, you discover a relationship between your ideas that had not occurred to you before. And this discovery prompts you to go back and shape your topic a bit differently. This would amount to stepping back before going forward, and it illustrates that the writing process is not linear (advancing in a straight line through the steps) but *recursive* (advancing with some doubling back and more advancing—perhaps in a new direction).

What, then, can we say for sure about the writing process? Three things, actually, and they appear in the following chart.

Points to Remember about the Writing Process
1. The procedures writers follow can vary from person to person.
2. The same person might use different procedures for different writing tasks.
3. The writing process is recursive rather than linear.

Discovering Your Own Writing Process

Obviously, the goal of a writing course (and a writing text) is to help you improve your writing. At the same time, however, a writing course and text should help you discover writing procedures that work for you. If you can learn what to do, how to do it, and when to do it, then your writing is bound to improve. However, writing well is just part of what we are after here. We also want to help you write efficiently, in ways that bring good results with a minimum of wheel spinning. To learn to write effectively *and* efficiently, you will be working toward discovering your own productive writing process.

You may be wondering how you can find out which procedures work best for you, when the writing process varies from writer to writer. The answer lies in experimentation.

Throughout this text, you will be exposed to a variety of ways to handle the various aspects of writing. To discover the best writing process for yourself, you should sample several of the different techniques described. Afterwards, evaluate the success of what you sampled and make a decision about whether to retain a procedure because it worked well or try something else. If you experiment and evaluate in this fashion throughout the term, you will go a long way toward improving your writing process—and hence your writing.

Before discussing the writing process any further, let's identify what it is you currently do when you write. The following questionnaire will help you do this.

A Writing Process Questionnaire

Answer the following questions as completely as possible.

1. How do you get ideas to include in your writing?
2. How do you establish your audience and purpose?
3. How do you decide what order your ideas should appear in? When do you decide this?
4. Do you typically write more than one draft? If so, how many?
5. How do you decide what changes to make in your drafts? At what point do you decide this? Do you outline?
6. Do you ask other people to read your work before you submit it? If so, who?
7. What do you do when you get stuck?
8. Under what circumstances do you produce your best work (in a quiet room, at night, a week before deadline, with a special pen, etc.)?
9. Do you write a piece all in one sitting or do you leave your work and come back to it? If you do the latter, when do you leave and when do you return?

Your answers to the questions above will give you a sense of what you currently do when you write. However, it is also important for you to identify how successful your current process is. For this reason, answer the following questions:

1. Which features of your process produce satisfactory results in a reasonable amount of time?
2. Which features of your process take too long and/or fail to produce satisfactory results?

Your response to question 2 will indicate aspects of your process that you need to improve. Keep a list of these aspects, and the next time you write, try techniques described throughout this text to handle these aspects (you can consult the index to find the discussions of techniques you are after under the following headings: Topic selection, Idea generation, Audience, Purpose, Outlining, First draft, Revising, Editing, Proofreading). After trying a new technique, evaluate its effectiveness and determine whether you need to experiment further. Also, in Part II there are postwriting evaluations to help you further identify aspects of your process that need to be improved.

Six Areas of the Writing Process

Even though writers do different things when they write, it is possible to identify six areas that most successful writers turn their attention to sometime between the point they set out and the point they finish. These six areas are as follows:

1. Generating ideas, establishing purpose, and identifying audience
2. Ordering ideas
3. Writing the first draft
4. Revising
5. Editing
6. Proofreading

Since it is known that successful writers deal with these six areas, you may be wondering why there is so much variance among the writing processes of different writers? Can't we just say that writers perform the six tasks identified in the list? No, we cannot, because while successful writers attend to these six areas, they vary in the way they handle each individual area. Furthermore, they attend to these areas in different orders, and sometimes they attend to two areas at once. And this is what explains the variety of approaches to writing.

What all this means, then, is that your efforts to discover the process that works best for you will involve you in understanding each of the six areas, becoming aware of the various approaches to handling each of the areas, and experimenting to learn which of the approaches in what sequence works for you. Then you will have discovered your *own* effective, efficient process.

Now look again at the list of six areas, but this time let's group the areas to shed more light on the writing process.

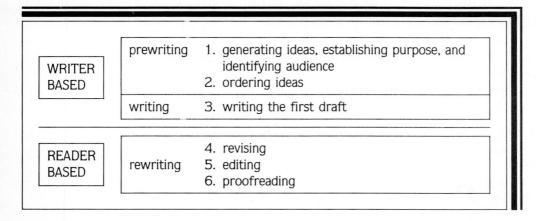

WRITER BASED	prewriting	1. generating ideas, establishing purpose, and identifying audience 2. ordering ideas
	writing	3. writing the first draft
READER BASED	rewriting	4. revising 5. editing 6. proofreading

The above chart illustrates that the six areas in the process can be divided into two groups: *writer-based activities* and *reader-based activities*. In other words, as writers move from idea to finished piece, they first concentrate on what *they* want for their writing and then move to what their *readers* need in their writing. Of course, during writer-based activities the reader is still considered, and so too is the writer's orientation a concern during reader-based activities. The division really represents the *primary* focus of each of the six areas of the process.

The chart also shows that the six areas can be grouped into three categories: *prewriting* (activities performed prior to writing the first draft), *writing* (writing the first draft), and *rewriting* (making changes in the first draft to get the piece ready for a reader). Prewriting and writing are primarily writer-based activities, while rewriting is primarily reader-based.

As you study the chart, remember the recursive nature of the writing process: you will not find yourself moving sequentially through the areas; instead you will frequently be stepping back as work in one area prompts you to make changes in an area handled earlier. And these changes will affect what you do when you go forward again.

This pretty much ends the safe generalizations about the writing process. Any further discussion gets us into the various ways writers can deal with the six areas, and this is precisely what we will turn to next. As you read about these six areas, their purposes, and the ways they can be handled, do so with an eye toward techniques you want to try as you experiment to develop your own effective, efficient writing process.

Generating Ideas, Establishing Audience, and Determining Purpose (Writer-based/Prewriting)

Chapter 1 had a great deal to say about generating ideas, establishing purpose, and identifying audience, and now would be a good time to review that material. As you recall from Chapter 1, the earliest stage of the writing process involves the writer in shaping a topic and generating support for that topic. To help you do these, several idea-generation techniques were described. As you work to develop your writing process, try several of these techniques to discover which are the most productive for you.

When writers generate ideas in this early stage, it is a time of discovery, a time to learn what is at the front of the brain and what is lurking further back in the recesses. It is a time for shaking loose ideas to discover what you can and want to say. Obviously, then, idea generation is a highly writer-based activity because the focus is on discovering what the *writer* wants to say.

Yet this time before writing the first draft is not solely writer-oriented, for the writer must also consider who the reader will be. Once the reader is identified, the writer must assess that reader to determine his or her needs. The nature of the writer's audience will significantly influence idea generation. For a review of how to establish and assess audience and a review of how audience affects detail, see the discussion beginning on p. 24. In addition, Part II of this text describes specific techniques for establishing and assessing audience.

In addition to being affected by audience, idea generation can be influenced by the writer's purpose. As you know from Chapter 1, early in the writing process a person must decide the reason for his or her writing. Let's say you are discussing the writing program at your school. Well, what is your purpose? Do you want to describe the program? Explain your experience in the program? Convince the reader that changes should occur in the program? Compare the program to another one? Do you want to share with the reader, inform the reader, or persuade the reader? Answering questions like these will help you discover your purpose, and your purpose, in turn, can affect the ideas you generate. Since you as the writer settle on the purpose you want, this is another writer-oriented activity. However, you may decide on your purpose with the reader in mind, which makes this a partially reader-based activity—as when you decide not to describe the program because your reader knows what it is like and choose instead to explain your experience so your reader can understand how the program affects students. For a review of purpose, see the discussion beginning on p. 23. In addition, Part II of this text describes specific techniques for establishing purpose.

Considering the Process

The points in this section identify some of the ways writers vary in their approaches to generating ideas, identifying audience, and establishing purpose. As you read these points, consider your own techniques to determine what, if anything, you might handle in a better way.

1. Writers vary in the number of ideas they must generate before they are comfortable moving on. Some writers determine main points without generating ideas for developing those main points. Other writers feel the need to generate as many ideas as possible to develop their main points. There are even some writers who do not generate more than one or two main points. Then they go on to their first draft to see where these ideas take them. These writers prefer to plunge into a draft as quickly as possible, feeling they cannot know what they want to say until they have said it.

2. Some writers prewrite only to shape a topic and perhaps settle on audience and purpose. From this point they go directly to a first draft, which can resemble an extended freewriting because it includes most of the ideas that occur to the writer. For these writers, writing the first draft is itself a form of idea generation.

3. As a general rule, the more planning (prewriting) done prior to the first draft, the less reworking the draft will require. This is not to suggest there is anything wrong with even the roughest of first drafts. Rather, it is to indicate that some writers do better by putting more effort into prewriting, which usually means less revision to do, while others do better putting less effort into prewriting and more into revising.

4. Some writers identify their audience and/or purpose when they shape their topic, while others do this in a separate step before or after idea generation.

Some writers do not discover their audience and/or purpose until they write their first draft.

5. Because the writing process is recursive, idea generation can prompt a change in topic, audience identification can necessitate additional idea generation, establishing a purpose can lead to selecting a different audience, and so on. In short, any one discovery or decision can mean a change in one or more aspects of topic, detail, audience, and purpose.

6. If you are not sure yet how you want to approach the first area of the writing process, try this sequence:
   a. Shape topic.
   b. Establish purpose and identify audience (reshape topic if necessary after this).
   c. Generate enough ideas for your main points (alter topic, purpose, and/or audience if necessary after this).

An Essay in Progress: Generating Ideas, Establishing Audience, and Determining Purpose

Directions: After completing this exercise, save your responses. They will be used later in this chapter as you work toward a completed essay.

1. Assume you have won a writer's contest. As first-prize winner, you may write a five-page, typed article that will be published in the magazine of your choice. You may write on any topic. What topic will you write about? (Remember to use the idea-generation techniques described in Chapter 1 if you have trouble shaping a topic.)
2. For what purpose will you write this article? (If necessary, determine your purpose by answering the questions on p. 24.)
3. What magazine will you publish your article in?
4. What are the typical readers of this magazine like? (If necessary, answer the audience-assessment questions on p. 25.)
5. Generate as many ideas as you can to include in this article. Try using at least two of the idea-generation techniques described in Chapter 1.
6. Study the ideas you have generated. Do they suggest you should alter your audience (magazine choice) or purpose in any way? If so, do that now.

Ordering Ideas (Writer-based/Prewriting)

When writers turn their attention to ways to order their ideas, they are still involved in writer-based activities because they are deciding in what order *they* want to present their ideas. At the same time, however, deciding on order is partly reader-based because it is necessary to find an arrangement that will help the reader appreciate what the writer is communicating and how ideas relate to each other.

The methods of development you settle on can at times determine how you order your ideas. (See p. 42 for a discussion of ways to order ideas.) If, for example, you decide to use narration, then chronological order is suggested. If you decide to describe, spatial order may be indicated. At other times, though, you will have to consider carefully to determine the most effective arrangement of details. If you cannot decide what arrangement to use, try drafting or outlining for two or more different arrangements to see which works the best. Arranging details is discussed in more detail in Part II of this text.

Outlining

An outline is a useful tool for the writer making decisions about the order of ideas. Yet many students resist outlining because they see it as time-consuming, difficult, and somehow unnecessary. But the truth is that outlining does not deserve this reputation because it can be a critical factor in ensuring the effectiveness of writing. Furthermore, outlining can be much less time-consuming and difficult than many realize. And finally, writers who outline regularly report that any time and effort put into an outline is worthwhile because outlining makes the first draft go more quickly. So before you decide whether or not to build outlining into your writing process, consider carefully this discussion of the purposes for and methods of outlining.

The purpose of an outline is to ensure a well-organized essay by allowing the writer to plot ahead the order and grouping of ideas. Because no essay can be effective if its details are not presented logically, a writer must determine at some point what order to present ideas in and how to group ideas. The arrangement of details is simply too crucial to be left to chance. This, then, is the issue a writer works through when he or she outlines.

Writers may outline more than once. Sometimes it just takes several attempts before a writer develops an organizational strategy that ''works''— that is, one that is both logical *and* effective. Yet the fact that a writer may have to take more than one run at outlining before developing an effective, logical organization should not discourage you from outlining, for two reasons. First, arranging details effectively can be a complex task, so it is unreasonable to assume that you can always manage it in a quick 5 minutes or in one attempt. Second, your details must take on a logical organization at some point if your writing is to succeed. Typically this means that if you don't organize by outlining, then you must do so at some other point in the writing process. Usually this ''other point'' is when the first draft is written. Sometimes it can be when the first draft is revised. Yet many writers discover that organizing at either of these times can complicate these two processes. Further, organizing at these times can take a writer's attention away from the typical concerns of first-draft writing and revision. So, organization is really a matter of ''sooner or later.'' And many writers discover it is more efficient ''sooner'' with an outline than ''later'' with a draft or revision.

The detail you include in your outline, whether it is everything that will appear in your first draft or just the main points, for the most part will come from the ideas you generated while prewriting. However, you will also discover that the outlining process stimulates thought. As a result, new ideas may occur to you. If so, include these ideas in your outline. Similarly, outlining may lead you to reject ideas that you earlier expected to include, and that's fine too. In other words, outlining does not mark the end of idea generation.

Which of the several outlining techniques you settle on will depend on which works the best for you. Further, you may use one technique in some situations and another in other situations. Try all the techniques described below to find the one or two that yield the best results.

The Formal Outline

Outlines can be formal or informal, highly detailed or sketchy. Usually, the more formal the outline, the more detail there is. You are probably familiar with formal, detailed outlines, the ones with all the roman numerals, letters, and numbers. One way to approach the formal outline is to follow the organization described in Chapter 2 and place your details where they logically fit. Below is an example of a formal outline, written for "All Creatures Great and Small" on p. 31. To the right of this outline is an outline of the organization described in Chapter 2. By comparing the two outlines, you can see how the details and arrangement of the student's work parallel the organization described in Chapter 2.

Student's Outline	Useful Pattern of Organization

I. Introduction
  A. Mother seeing her son on TV
  B. The son as a vile bleacher creature
	I. Introduction
	  A. Material to generate reader interest
	  B. Thesis

II. Body paragraph
  A. Bleacher creature's appearance is disgusting
  B. Beer belly
  C. Stained shirt
  D. Hair
    1. Dog bones
    2. Greasy
    3. Dyed
  E. Face painted with obscenities
	II. Body paragraph
	  A. Topic sentence
	
	  B. Supporting detail
	  C. Supporting detail
	  D. Supporting detail
	
	  E. Supporting detail

III. Body paragraph
  A. Speech full of profanity
  B. Swears to insult people
  C. Swears more when drunk
	III. Body paragraph
	  A. Topic sentence
	  B. Supporting detail
	  C. Supporting detail

IV. Body paragraph
   A. Bleacher creature lacks consideration toward others
   B. Spills beer on people
   C. Throws can at people
   D. Knocks into people
   E. Burps

V. Conclusion
   A. Mother throws bleacher creature out
   B. Pets aren't allowed

IV. Body paragraph
   A. Topic sentence

   B. Supporting detail
   C. Supporting detail
   D. Supporting detail
   E. Supporting detail

V. Conclusion

Although the outline above follows the organizational scheme described in Chapter 2, a formal outline can be used for any pattern of organization. Also, the outline does not include every idea that forms the supporting detail, but instead arranges only the main points. Whether you include just the main points or all your ideas is one decision about your writing process you can make by experimenting to determine what works best for you.

Outline Cards—Method I

Outline cards have many of the advantages of the formal outline, but they often simplify matters because the writer does not have to be concerned about roman numerals, letters, and numbers. As with the formal outline, the amount of detail can vary according to the writer's needs. The person who prefers to have every detail determined and placed prior to the first draft can plot everything; the person who needs only an awareness of major points and their placement can plot just these.

To outline using cards, you need several large index cards (or you can use sheets of paper). Use one card to plan your introduction, one separate card for each body paragraph, and one card for your conclusion. Each card will plot a separate section of your essay. On your introduction card, list the details you will include to arouse your reader's interest along with a preliminary version of your thesis. On each body-paragraph card, write a preliminary topic sentence along with a list of the points that will develop the topic sentence. On your conclusion card, list the details you will use to bring your essay to a satisfying close. On each of your cards you can list your details in the order they will appear in your first draft or not, as you prefer.

One advantage of outlining cards is flexibility. A writer can easily shuffle body-paragraph cards into different sequences to examine alternative arrangements. Also, it is easier to rework parts of the outline when cards are used. A writer can throw out one or two cards and redo just those without having to rewrite the entire outline.

Outline Cards—Method II

An interesting form of outlining was shown to me by one of my students. She would take every idea she generated, whether a main point or a subpoint, and place it by itself on an index card. If she had twelve ideas, then she had twelve cards. Next she would examine each card and place it in a pile. A card with an idea related to something on another card would go in the same pile as that card. If she encountered a card that could go in more than one pile, she made the appropriate number of duplicate cards and placed them in the appropriate piles. After all her cards were sorted, she decided which pile to handle first, second, and so on. Then she studied the cards in the first pile to be handled and arranged them in the order she wanted the ideas to appear. This she did for each pile of cards. When an idea appeared in more than one pile, she decided whether the repetition was called for. If not, she decided which duplicate card to eliminate from which pile. Finally, she stacked her cards and wrote her draft from them. The student also explained that if she discovered her organization was not working, she would rearrange the order of her cards and try again.

Outline Worksheet

The outline worksheet, like outline cards, allows writers to plot organization in as great or as little detail as they require. Also like outline cards, the worksheet does not make use of roman numerals, letters, and numbers. While it is not as easy to rework parts of the outline when the worksheet is used (this is the advantage of cards), it is easy to get a clear overview of your organization (this is one advantage of the formal outline).

Below is a sample outline worksheet. To use it, fill in the blanks with complete detail or main points, whichever works better for you.

Sample Outline Worksheet

Introduction

Detail to generate reader interest _____

_____

_____

Preliminary thesis _____

_____

Body Paragraph I

Preliminary topic sentence _____

_____

Support _____

_____

_____

_____

_____

Body Paragraph II

Preliminary topic sentence _____

_____

Support _____

_____

_____

_____

(*Note:* The number of body paragraph sections will correspond to the number of body paragraphs planned for the first draft.)

Conclusion

Detail to provide closure _____

_____

_____

The Informal Outline

The informal outline, sometimes called a ''scratch outline,'' is far less structured and usually less detailed than a formal outline, outline cards, or outline worksheet. Writers who prefer to come to the first draft with only an idea of the main points that will be made and the order they will be made in often favor the informal outline. The informal outline does not usually include much of the detail that will develop main points, so writers who use it must have in mind how their ideas will be supported, or they must determine this later. Or they must be writers capable of developing their subpoints as they write their first draft. Below is an informal outline that could have been put together by the student who wrote the formal outline on p. 69.

Informal Outline
Bleacher creature is vile.
Appearance is disgusting (describe hair, clothes, and makeup).
Bleacher creature swears a lot.
Bleacher creature is inconsiderate (give examples).
Bleacher creature gets thrown out of house (conclusion).

There are two things to notice about this informal outline. First, there is very little detail. Instead the outline suggests a thesis, major points to develop the thesis, and an approach to the conclusion. There is nothing to indicate how the reader's interest will be aroused, what development will be given the major points, where paragraphs begin and end, and specifically what will appear in the conclusion. For some writers such an outline would not be very helpful because too little is brought to the first draft. For others this is the preferred approach. These latter writers are the ones who find a more detailed, structured outline to be constraining. These writers do better when less is determined prior to the first draft, and they can "create" as they move through the draft. Another thing to notice about this outline is the material in parentheses, which serves as a reminder to the writer of the approach to the development of an item.

Considering the Process

As you experiment and make decisions about your own writing process, consider the following points about ordering of ideas.

1. Writers vary in the amount of organizing they like to do before the first draft. Hence some writers require detailed outlines that amount to a blueprint of the essay, while others do better with only a rough sketch. Other writers prefer not to outline at all, feeling it stifles their creativity. These writers order their ideas the best way they can when they draft and then adjust their organization afterward as necessary.
2. Some writers like to outline after they have written their first draft. They do this when they did not write an outline earlier, when they find they have deviated from their original outline, or when their original outline was sketchy or informal. To outline after the first draft is written, a writer goes through the draft and places each detail in a formal outline with roman numerals, letters, and numbers. In this way, the writer can study the outline to be sure each detail has a logical placement.
3. In general, the more detailed the outline, the more quickly the first draft goes and the less revision the draft requires.
4. During outlining writers often think of new ideas or make discoveries that cause them to step back and alter their topic, audience, purpose, ideas for support, or plan for organization.
5. If you're unsure about the best way to proceed, experiment first with a scratch outline that includes your main points and an idea or two for developing each.

An Essay in Progress: Ordering Ideas

Directions: When you complete this exercise, save your responses. They will be used later in this chapter as you work toward a completed essay.

1. Select the outlining technique that most appeals to you and outline the ideas you generated when you completed the exercise on p. 67.
2. Now select a different outlining technique and outline your ideas a second time.
3. Do you like one of the outlining techniques you tried better than the other? If so, which one and why? Do you think a third technique might work even better?
4. Do you think the outlining you did will help ensure a well-organized essay, or would you prefer to skip outlining and go on to drafting? Explain.
5. As a result of outlining, do you feel the need to return to an earlier stage of the process to alter topic, audience, or purpose or to generate ideas? If so, do that now.

Writing the First Draft (Writer-based/Writing)

Regardless of your approach to prewriting, when your planning is complete, you are ready to write a first draft. Although drafting moves you out of prewriting and into writing, this activity is still writer-based because your focus is less on getting your writing ready for a reader than it is on expressing your ideas the best way you can at the time.

A first draft is commonly known as a *rough* draft. It is an early effort to transform the ideas and organization of the outline into a form that resembles an essay, without worrying about grammar, usage, spelling, and such. This early effort is tentative, subject to changes of every kind. It can be loaded with errors and rough spots, but still it forms a base—material to shape and alter until the desired product is reached. And by the time the final product *is* reached, so many changes may have occurred along the way that it bears little resemblance to the original draft.

Writers who work from highly detailed, structured outlines may have to do little, if any, idea generation and organizing while writing the first draft. However, the less detailed and structured the outline, the more support writers will have to develop while drafting and the more organizing they will become involved in. With no outline at all, the writer may be doing a great deal of organizing and idea generation.

Of course, while drafting you may have new ideas occur to you, or you may see new relationships among your ideas. This is because idea generation can continue through the drafting stage. If new ideas occur, include them in your draft the best way you can.

If you get stuck—that is, you cannot get your ideas down in any way at all—then simply skip the troublesome section and go on, leaving space for the omitted part to be added later. Many writers use this strategy for their introductions. If you just cannot get started, no law says that you cannot begin with body paragraphs and return to the introduction later.

Sometimes the expression and development of a particular idea in a body paragraph proves troublesome. If this happens, leave space and push on. If you have an idea about how you want to approach this difficult part but you cannot get the words down, make a note in the margin to remind you later of what you had in mind. Also, if you cannot find the right word, leave a blank or use an alternative and underline it for later revision.

Skipping troublesome sections of a first draft is a useful strategy because it prevents you from becoming bogged down at one point. If the first-draft process is halted while you agonize over one section, then you are slowing your progress considerably. Also, you are building in frustration by focusing on what you cannot do instead of what you can. Also, if you skip a troublesome part, you may find when you return to it that it is no longer hard to manage. Somehow the words you needed surfaced while you were working on other parts of the essay.

Considering the Process

In addition to what you have already read about the first draft, the following points should be considered as you make decisions about your own writing process.

1. Some writers do not handle a first draft as a rough draft; they prefer to revise as they go. Such writers really combine the first-draft and revision steps. They are uncomfortable with rough copy, so they write a paragraph or perhaps just a sentence or two and then go back over what they have to shape and refine it. These writers push on in better fashion when they know that what they have left behind is in pretty good shape.
2. Some writers have very strong feelings about their introductions. When they are writing a first draft, they have to get this opening paragraph close to perfect before they can go on comfortably. These writers will revise or start over repeatedly until they are satisfied with their introduction, and then they go on to produce the rest of the first draft in far rougher form.
3. Some writers like to come to their first draft with little more than a topic. As already noted, this approach combines the first draft and prewriting. How much planning you do before your first draft is a decision you will need to make about your writing process. You can base that decision on how much you need to have predetermined before you are comfortable writing. Some people feel constrained if they plan too much, and some people feel overwhelmed if they plan too little.
4. Idea generation occurs during first-draft writing, so be receptive to new ideas and discoveries, and be prepared to go back and alter decisions made before the first draft if necessary. Also, if you discover while drafting that you need more ideas, return to the idea-generation phase.
5. In general, the more planning done prior to the draft, the less revision the draft will need. This is not to say that it is better to plan extensively. What is best is what works for the writer.

An Essay in Progress: Writing the First Draft

Directions: After completing this exercise, save your draft. You will use it later in this chapter as you work toward your completed essay.

1. Using one of the outlines you wrote when you completed the exercise on p. 74, write a first (rough) draft in one sitting. Do not worry about getting anything down in perfect form; just write your ideas the best you can without laboring over anything. Skip any sections that prove troublesome.
2. Study your draft. Does it suggest you should return to an earlier stage in the process? If so, which one(s) and why? Return to those stages now and do what is necessary.
3. Were you comfortable with writing your first draft? If not, what will you do differently the next time you draft? Why?

Revising (Reader-based/Rewriting)

Once the first draft is written, the writer has completed the work that is primarily writer-based, and it is time to begin getting the piece ready for a reader: the job of rewriting (revision) begins.

No matter how rough the first draft is, once it is done the writer has a substantial amount of material to work with. There it is on the page—the first expression of the writer's ideas, ready to be shaped and refined into polished form. There are rough spots, gaps, errors, and lots of things that are not working, but it is raw material that can be transformed into something that satisfies the writer and engages the reader. This process of reworking is known as *revision*.

Of all the steps in a writing process—*any* writing process—revision is the most important. In fact, revision is the very essence of the writing process. There is simply no way to overemphasize the crucial role revision plays in a successful piece of writing. Yet despite the importance of revision, not every writer understands its nature and function.

Many students, for example, say how frustrated they feel after completing a first draft. When they read their work over and discover it is nowhere near ready for a reader, they question their ability to write well and seem surprised that they have written so many pages but none of them is "right" yet. This, they sometimes conclude, means they cannot write.

Are these students correct? Is it true that their inability to produce polished first drafts means they cannot write? Absolutely not. Instead, what this means is that these students are expecting too much of themselves by looking for a finished product too soon. It is the rare writer who can get it right the first time. Most of us produce first drafts that need a major overhaul.

Some writers recognize the need to revise but fail to appreciate how much time and effort must go into the process. They think that revising means simply going through the draft to fix spellings, insert some punctuation, and change a few words. Sure, there are a blessed few who write quickly and produce near-perfect first drafts, but most people must make significant changes in content and wording before turning a piece over to the reader.

Typically, then, first drafts require much revision, and this revision takes time and effort. Let's examine the revision process to see what it entails.

How to Revise

The word *revision* (re-vision) means "seeing again." The revision process calls upon writers to look again at their work. And because revision marks the point when writers cross the line from writer-based to reader-based activity, revision involves us in seeing our work from the reader's point of view. This is the time when writers work to get their writing ready for a reader, the time when writers take their first draft and shape and refine it.

How, you may be wondering, can writers view their work as their readers will? And how do writers know what to change in their drafts? These are questions that go to the heart of the revision process, and the following suggestions will help you answer them.

1. After completing a first draft, writers should leave their work for a good chunk of time—several hours at least, a day or more if possible. In fact, the longer the writer can stay away, the better. This distancing is important because while generating ideas, outlining, and drafting, we become very close to our work. We have so firmly in our minds what we wanted to say that we can see this on the page—whether it is there or not. We know what we mean so well that we may not recognize when we have failed to clarify an idea for a reader who does not have the same awareness. Distancing is also important because the time you spend away provides a necessary transition that will help you make the very important shift from writer to reader.

2. As you are revising and viewing your work from your reader's point of view, your chief concerns should be *content*, *organization*, and *effective expression*. You should take a hard look at your first draft to determine whether you have met your reader's needs by expressing your ideas clearly, by providing enough detail, and by avoiding irrelevant detail. You should examine your work to be sure your organization is logical and effective and to be sure each idea flows logically from the one before it. Finally, you should evaluate the effectiveness of your sentences to be sure you create the effect you are after. (Chapter 4 discusses how to craft effective sentences.)

   On p. 80 there is a revising checklist that notes what should be looked at during revision. As you use the list, you will notice that matters of grammar, usage, and punctuation are not included. These details are attended to later, during editing.

3. A good way to see your work in a new light is to type the first draft after it is written. This distances you and helps you view your work from the reader's position because it removes you from the personal associations of your own handwriting. Typing your work is helpful also because your writing comes

to resemble printed matter, which makes it easier to view your writing as "someone else's work," an orientation which lends objectivity. Finally, when you view your work in type, it is easier to spot problems with detail, organization, and expression. Sometimes such problems leap out at you, as when you see that a paragraph is running only two typed lines, an indication that your detail may not be adequate.

4. Still another way to come to your writing with a fresh perspective is to read your work out loud. When you do this, you are approaching your work from the sense of sound rather than sight. It is not unusual for writers to hear problems while reading aloud that they overlooked before.

5. Show yourself no mercy when you evaluate your draft. If you encounter something of doubtful quality, you may be tempted to overlook the problem. You may discover detail not relevant to your thesis but want to keep it anyway because you like the way the idea is expressed—well, show no mercy and strike the irrelevancy. You may notice that your organization could be improved but you spent ages on your outline and you hate to redo it—well, redo it anyway. The harder you are on yourself, the better your essay will be.

6. To see your work as objectively as possible, assume the identity of one of the following as you study your draft and make revision decisions:
   a. A magazine editor who will decide whether or not to publish your essay
   b. An enemy who would delight in finding weaknesses in your essay
   c. A potential employer who will hire you at $80,000 a year if you can write well

   If you view your work from the point of view of one of these people, you can see with the fiercely critical eye the revising writer needs.

7. Often writers can get valuable advice about what needs to be changed in their drafts by asking others to read their work. You can give your draft to someone and ask that person to tell you what he or she thinks about it. Even better, ask your reader to write comments in the margin.

   Many writers feel they get their most helpful responses if they supply their reader with a list of questions to answer about the draft. You can form your questions around the specific concerns you have about the draft, or you can use this list:
   a. What is the thesis of the essay?
   b. Is there anything that does not pertain to the thesis?
   c. Are any ideas unclear?
   d. Do any ideas need more explanation?
   e. Do any ideas get too much explanation?
   f. Is there any place where the order of ideas seems illogical? Is there any place where you do not see the relationship between ideas?
   g. Is there any place where the writing does not hold your interest?
   h. Are there any sentences that you do not like?

   When you allow another to react to your writing, you have the benefit of an actual reader's point of view. There are, however, some cautions that go along with this technique. First, try to pick readers who will view your work objectively and offer constructive criticism. If your mother likes everything you do no matter what, she may not be a valuable reader. Second, evaluate your reader's responses carefully. Do not automatically accept everything your reader says. Weigh out the reactions and accept or reject them in a discriminating way. Finally, get several readers to react to your work. That way you can better evaluate responses by looking for consensus. Perhaps you could form a group of several of your classmates with whom you can regularly exchange and evaluate drafts.

Considering the Process

As you experiment and make decisions about your writing process, consider the following points about revision in addition to what you have already learned.

1. Some writers are able to move through their first draft evaluating and revising everything at once. For many others revision goes more smoothly and yields better results if the draft is examined for only one or two things at a time. If you prefer to revise this way in stages, try the following sequence:
   a. Read through your draft and make any changes that can easily be handled. Also, if you left blanks in your draft, made marginal notes, or used question marks, attend to these as best you can without agonizing over anything.
   b. Go back through your draft to check that everything is relevant to the thesis and appropriate topic sentence. If something is not relevant, strike it no matter how much it hurts.
   c. Check next to be sure all your points are clear and adequately developed. Make sure all generalizations are supported.
   d. Check your organization next to be sure your points follow logically from one to the next.
   e. Look at your introduction and conclusion. Does the former create reader interest, and does the latter bring the essay to a satisfying close?
   f. Go back and attend to anything you were unable to handle earlier.
   g. Finally, review your sentences for effectiveness. Chapter 4 explains the principles of sentence effectiveness.
       As an alternative to the above sequence, start at the top of the revising checklist on p. 80, and rework your draft until you can answer yes to every question on the list.
2. Writers who revise in stages often distance themselves after each stage to restore objectivity. When they return to their work, they often evaluate their rewriting and make further changes before going on.
3. Some writers like to revise one paragraph at a time, evaluating and rewriting until one paragraph is polished before going on to the next.
4. Some writers rely heavily on marginal notes when they revise. They study

their drafts, noting in the margin what revision is needed. The marginal notes can be anything that reminds the writer of what needs to be done. Phrases such as "explain this," "add examples," "tighten prose," "check facts," "establish relevance," and "move this to paragraph 3" can be used. Sometimes writers make all their marginal notes before they begin rewriting, and sometimes they reserve marginal notes for only the more difficult or extensive revisions, the ones they want to tackle later.

5. Some writers make their changes directly on the first draft by crossing out, writing above lines and in margins, drawing arrows, and so on. These writers often write on every other line when they draft to allow room for their changes. Other writers like to revise by writing a second draft on fresh paper. These people often feel it is too awkward or sloppy to revise directly on the first draft.

6. Writers often rewrite until they have completed several drafts. It is impossible to know how many drafts a person will write for a particular piece.

7. Some writers cut and tape when they revise. If they decide to alter the sequence of sentences or paragraphs, they can easily move them to a new location.

8. When writers revise, they must look very hard at their work to see what changes they must make before going forward.

9. If you are unsure of the best revision process for you, experiment first by going through the revising checklist below. Follow this with asking three readers to react to your second draft by answering the questions on p. 78.

Revising Checklist

This checklist can guide you as you revise your essays. Before you consider the revision process complete, you should be able to answer yes to every question on the list.

1. Did you distance yourself from your work before you began to revise and after each complete revision?

2. Did you view your work from your reader's point of view?

3. Is your introduction geared to engage your reader's interest?

4. Does your essay have a clear, narrow thesis (stated or implied) that accurately conveys what your essay is about?

5. Do you have at least two body paragraphs?

6. Does each body paragraph have a topic sentence (stated or implied) that clearly and accurately conveys what the paragraph is about? Is each topic sentence relevant to the thesis?

7. Are all your points suited to your audience and purpose?

8. Is your supporting detail in each body paragraph adequate? Have you supported every generalization?

9. Is your supporting detail in each body paragraph relevant to its topic sentence?
10. Do you have enough support in enough body paragraphs to adequately develop your thesis?
11. Are all your ideas clearly expressed?
12. Are your body paragraphs presented in a logical order?
13. Are the details in each body paragraph in a logical order?
14. Did you use transitions to link ideas? (See Chapter 4.)
15. Did you write a conclusion geared toward leaving your reader with a positive final impression?
16. Are your sentences as effective as you can make them? (See Chapter 4.)

An Essay in Progress: Revising the Draft

Directions: After completing this exercise, save your revision. You will use it later in this chapter as you work toward your completed essay.

1. Review pp. 77–80 and make a list of the revising techniques you would like to try—the ones that seem like they might work for you.
2. Use the techniques in your list to revise the draft you wrote in response to the exercise on p. 76.
3. Did your revision activities prompt you to return to any earlier stages of the process? If so, which ones?
4. Were you comfortable with the revision procedures you followed? If not, what will you do differently the next time you revise? Why?

Editing (Reader-based/Rewriting)

When you edit, you are looking for mistakes—mistakes in grammar, usage, capitalization, punctuation, and spelling. Editing is a reader-based activity because readers expect writing to be error-free. It is important for writers to find their mistakes because even the most tolerant readers can grow dismayed by misspellings, lack of punctuation, faulty subject-verb agreement, and such. This means that no matter how good your ideas, development, and organization are, if your work contains frequent and/or serious lapses in grammar and usage, your reader will grow annoyed and frustrated. It is also possible that your reader will lose confidence in what you have to say because if the reader questions your ability with grammar and usage, he or she is only a short hop from questioning the validity of your ideas. Thus, errors in grammar and usage can alienate a reader.

Furthermore, it is important that writers follow the grammar and usage rules because readers expect them to. The rules are there, and it is conventional behavior to follow them. Break the rules and you are behaving in an unacceptable way. Behave unacceptably and there is a price to pay. There is really nothing new here; you conform to convention all the time. For a job interview, you dress well because it is expected. Show up in jeans and a dirty T-shirt and you can expect to pay the price of making a bad impression. In other words, grammar and usage rules exist and serve a purpose. If we disregard them, the price we pay is negative reader reaction.

How to Edit

Many of the techniques suggested for revising can also be used for editing. For example, it is important that before you begin to edit you distance yourself to clear your head and restore objectivity. By the time you reach the editing stage, you will be so aware of what you wanted to say that you may see it on the page whether it is there or not.

When you return to your work after distancing, you will be looking for errors in grammar and usage. These errors can be of two kinds: those you have a tendency to make and those that are just slips. It is helpful to go over your work twice to find and edit mistakes. The first time through, look for the kinds of mistakes you typically make (fragments, lack of parallelism, or whatever), and the second time through you can identify and edit errors that may have occurred due to carelessness. Because people, even the best of us, make mistakes all the time, editing for error is very important. After all, a mistake is not really a problem if you catch it before your reader does. Part III of this book is an explanation of some of the more frequent errors in grammar and usage. You should consult this section on points you are unsure of.

Some writers can find their errors by reading through their work slowly, studying each word and punctuation mark. Other writers are more successful if they read their work out loud or speak it into a tape recorder to listen for mistakes. If you try these latter techniques, be very careful to speak *exactly* what appears on the page. It is easy to speak a plural form, for example, when a singular form was actually written; it is very easy to speak the word *feel* when *fell* is on the page. The best way to avoid this kind of substitution is to speak *very* slowly, focusing for a second on each word. If you choose to speak your words to check for error, you should also remember that certain kinds of mistakes cannot be heard. You cannot hear misspellings, nor can you hear certain punctuation. This means that at least once you should go over your work to check for mistakes visually.

When revising was discussed, you learned that writers can gain a fresh perspective on their work by typing one of their drafts. This advice also holds true for the writer at the editing stage. Errors are much easier to identify in typed copy, probably because handwriting, even our own, can be deceptive. It is easier to misread handwriting than typed copy. Also, typing can depersonalize your work, which makes it easier to spot mistakes.

Another revising technique that is helpful when editing is using a reliable reader. Professional writers have copy editors who check for errors in grammar and usage that the author may have overlooked. You can follow the professionals' lead by asking someone to review your work for mistakes. However, be sure your reader is someone knowledgeable enough to spot mistakes. Also, you cannot relinquish your own responsibility to learn and apply grammar and usage rules by assuming someone else can always correct your errors for you. Ultimately, the responsibility to find your mistakes rests with you. A reliable reader functions only to catch the errors that get by you.

After you have checked for grammar and usage mistakes and edited accordingly (this can usually be done directly on the revised draft), type or copy your work into its final form, the form for submission. If you are writing for an instructor, he or she may have some requirements for the final manuscript. Be sure you understand and fulfill these requirements, which may speak to such things as margins, placement of name and title, the amount of crossing out permitted, the kind of ink and paper to be used (or whether the essay must be typed), and so on. It is important that you conform to these requirements so that you fulfill your reader's expectations.

Considering the Process

As you experiment to improve your writing process, give some thought to the following points about editing in addition to what you have already learned.

1. Some writers combine revising and editing. As they rework their first draft, they consider grammar and usage at the same time they deal with content, organization, and effective expression. To do this, a writer must have strong grammar and usage skills. A writer weak in grammar and usage would run a risk by combining revising and editing because there would be too much to examine at once and a danger of missing something.
2. Writers who rarely have trouble with grammar and usage may skip a separate editing stage. Instead, when they proofread their final copy, they look for the occasional mistake. However, those who make grammar or usage mistakes with some regularity should never bypass separate editing because there is too much of a chance that mistakes will go unnoticed.

Proofreading (Writer-based/Rewriting)

Once you have edited your writing and copied or typed it into its final manuscript form, you are ready to run one last check for errors by proofreading. Proofreading is a necessary final step because it is quite possible to make mistakes when copying or typing the edited work into its final form. It is easy to leave a word out, lapse into a misspelling, inadvertently add an inappropriate plural form, and so on.

Proofreading can be handled much the same way as editing. The first step is to leave the final version for a while, for the same reason that writers distance at earlier stages of the writing process—to clear the head and regain objectivity. Remember, at no other point are writers as close to their work as here at the end, so the tendency to see what was *intended*, rather than what *is*, is now the most pronounced.

Because of this tendency, when you return to proof your final copy, you must go quite slowly, one word or punctuation mark at a time. A quick reading through of your work is not proofreading. Use your pen to point to each word and punctuation mark as you read to keep yourself from building up speed that can cause you to overlook an error. If you read your work aloud, run a second check for the kinds of mistakes that can only be seen. As was the case when you edited, look both for the kinds of errors you typically make and for the occasional slip-up.

If you discover an error while proofreading, most instructors will allow you to ink in the correction neatly. However, use your judgment. If you have quite a few corrections on a page, copy or type it over. The overall appearance of your work can affect a reader's reaction. If you do recopy or retype a page, remember to proof the new page for mistakes.

An Essay in Progress: Editing, Proofreading, and Evaluating Your Process

1. Consider for a moment how frequently you make errors in grammar, usage, spelling, capitalization, and punctuation. Do you make them often enough to warrant editing in a separate step?
2. If you do not need to edit in a separate step, which do you believe will be more efficient for you: combining editing with revising or combining editing with proofreading? Explain your answer.
3. Using procedures you already know work for you or ones described in this chapter, edit the draft you revised for the exercise on p. 81.
4. Distance yourself from your edited draft for at least half a day and then recopy or type your essay. Proofread the final version using procedures proven successful for you or ones described in this chapter.
5. If you completed all the "Essay in Progress" exercises in this chapter, you sampled procedures for each stage of the writing process. Which of these procedures (if any) worked well enough for you to use in the future? Which of these procedures (if any) will you not use again? Which procedures might you try in place of the ones that did not work well for you?

Writing Realities

As you experiment to discover your own effective, efficient writing process, keep in mind some points I call "writing realities," listed below.

1. Writing Is Usually Hard Work

Sometimes students think that while they are straining over the page, the rest of the world is out there merrily writing away with no trouble. On the contrary, writing is seldom easy for anyone. Sure, there are a few who write easily and well, but they are the exception. For everyone else, writing is hard work.

2. Writing Takes Time

Nothing difficult can be done quickly, and writing is no exception. Think for a minute about the writing process. If you are to attend to all the stages and distance yourself at strategic times, you simply must have time on your side. Furthermore, you must allow yourself enough time to step back before going forward when this becomes necessary. If you wait until the last minute to tackle your writing, you will build in frustration and failure.

In addition, writing often goes better if you allow yourself enough time to break it down into manageable steps. This way, you can establish intermediate goals and experience success each time one of these goals is achieved. And each success can propel you forward with a boost of confidence that makes for better writing.

3. Everyone Gets Stuck Sometimes

When this happens to you, leave your writing for a time and refresh yourself by doing other things. When you return to your work, you may have the solution to your problem. If not, try to discover why the problem exists by asking the following questions:

Is my topic too broad?
Am I trying to write about something I do not know enough about?
Am I worried about getting everything "right" too soon?
Do I need a different organization?

If these questions do not lead you to discover a way to solve the problem, ask a reliable reader to review your work and try to identify a way around the problem. The appendix beginning on p. 403 suggests other strategies you can try if you get stuck.

4. More Than Anything Else, Writing Means Revision

Writers are unfair to themselves if they expect their first efforts to be top quality. Unfortunately, first efforts are seldom completely satisfying. Professional writers are always tinkering with their work or making wholesale changes as they strive for the results they are after, and if pros must revise, amateurs certainly cannot expect to get it right the first time. So if you look at an early effort and discover everything is not what it should be, do not despair or conclude that you cannot write. Instead, get in there and revise.

5. Writing Can Start Out as One Thing and End up as Another

When we revise, we make changes. Sometimes these changes are minor, yet a series of minor changes can add up to a major alteration in the character of the essay. Sometimes the changes are more sweeping, and these too will change the overall character of the essay. Thus, when the revision process is complete, you may discover that you have ended up with something very different from what you initially had in mind.

6. Sometimes a Writer Must Start Over

Even though you may have planned carefully and executed your plan to the best of your ability, you may discover that what you have is not working. This unpleasant discovery can be made at any point in the writing process. When you realize you have major problems and no attempts at revision seem to help enough, then you may have to begin again. It is also possible that as you revise you discover you should have been doing something else all along, and the only way to get on track is to start fresh. This can be frustrating, but if you determine that it is necessary to start again, take a deep breath and do it. When you have a final essay that is much better than the first one ever could have been, you will be glad you did.

7. It Is Helpful to Keep Your Writing in Mind While You Are Doing Other Things

It is not true that people write only when they are at a desk. You can be thinking about your work while you are cleaning the bedroom, walking the dog, or stuck in a traffic jam. Anytime your mind is not fully occupied, you can think of ideas, toy with approaches to your introduction, consider different organizations, and so on. If you do this, you are mentally planning ahead, so when you do sit down to your paper, it is likely the writing will move along more smoothly. Thinking about your writing in this way can be especially helpful when you have hit a snag. As you pursue other activities, let a portion of your brain consider solutions to your problem.

8. Writers Have Instincts That Must Be Sharpened and Relied Upon

Over the years we have heard, read, spoken, and written our language so much that a great deal of what we know about it has been internalized. As a result, we sometimes function with language more by instinct than by a conscious awareness of all the principles. When it comes to writing and reading our own writing, we often have an intuitive sense of what is and is not working. Sometimes we may sense a trouble spot even if we cannot identify why the problem exists. Thus, you should trust your instincts and assume there is a problem when you sense one. Of course, you should also trust your instincts when you sense that something is effective. If you suspect that your intuitive sense could stand some sharpening, get in the habit of reading a little bit every day. Subscribe to a weekly newsmagazine or read books about subjects of interest to you. Regular exposure to effective writing will help you internalize the kinds of awarenesses about our language that will make your instincts ones that can be relied on.

How to Improve Your Writing Process

In Part II of this book, you will be called upon to write a number of essays. Since one of your goals is to make your writing process more effective and efficient, each time you write you should strive to improve your process. Already you have identified strengths and weaknesses in your process by answering the questionnaire on p. 63 and by answering question 5 on p. 84. When you completed these activities, you also identified specific strategies you will try the next time you write. In order to gradually and steadily improve your writing process, try the following:

1. The next time you write, implement at least one of the changes in your process that you have identified as desirable.
2. Complete the postwriting questionnaires at the end of the chapters in Part II, after writing each of the essays called for in these chapters.
3. When you write again, implement the changes you decided upon when you completed the postwriting questionnaires.
4. Be aware of what you do when you write and how successful your techniques are. Continue to experiment with the techniques described throughout this text until you are satisfied with the effectiveness and efficiency of each stage of your process.
5. To find techniques to try, consult the following headings in the index of this text: Topic selection, Idea generation, Audience, Purpose, Outlining, First draft, Revising, Editing, Proofreading.
6. Talk to successful writers in and out of your class; ask them what they do when they write and try some of their strategies.
7. Confer with your instructor for ideas about handling the stages of writing that prove troublesome for you.

   Note: It is possible that you will have to try several approaches to a given stage in your process before you discover the technique best for you.

Writers on Writing

In the following selections, two professional writers comment on various aspects of writing and their writing processes. These selections make a number of important points you should keep in mind as you consider your own process and ways to improve it.

"The Watcher at the Gates"

In "The Watcher at the Gates" Gail Godwin writes of the "inner critic," the restraining voice in writers that can interfere with inspiration and creativity if not held in check in the early stages of writing. Yet Godwin makes it clear that the inner critic should be set free to exercise vigilance during revision and editing. Finally, Godwin confesses to the reason she, like many student writers, errs by turning the inner critic loose too soon.

The Watcher at the Gates
Gail Godwin

I first realized I was not the only writer who had a restraining critic who lived inside me and sapped the juice from green inspirations when I was leafing through Freud's "Interpretation of Dreams" a few years ago. Ironically, it was my "inner critic" who had sent me to Freud. I was writing a novel, and my heroine was in the middle of a dream, and then I lost faith in my own invention and rushed to "an authority" to check whether she could have such a dream. In the chapter on dream interpretation, I came upon the following passage that has helped me free myself, in some measure, from my critic and has led to many pleasant and interesting exchanges with other writers.

Freud quotes Schiller, who is writing a letter to a friend. The friend complains of his lack of creative power. Schiller replies with an allegory. He says it is not good if the intellect examines too closely the ideas pouring in at the gates. "In isolation, an idea may be quite insignificant, and venturesome in the extreme, but it may acquire importance from an idea which follows it. . . . In the case of a creative mind, it seems to me, the intellect has withdrawn its watchers from the gates, and the ideas rush in pell-mell, and only then does it review and inspect the multitude. You are ashamed or afraid of the momentary and passing madness which is found in all real creators, the longer or shorter duration of which distinguishes the thinking artist from the dreamer . . . you reject too soon and discriminate too severely."

So that's what I had: a Watcher at the Gates. I decided to get to know him better. I discussed him with other writers, who told me some of the quirks and habits of their Watchers, each of whom was as individual as his host, and all of whom seemed passionately dedicated to one goal: rejecting too soon and discriminating too severely.

It is amazing the lengths a Watcher will go to to keep you from pursuing the flow of your imagination. Watchers are notorious pencil sharpeners, ribbon changers, plant waterers, home repairers and abhorrers of messy rooms or messy pages. They are compulsive looker-uppers. They are superstitious scaredy-cats. They cultivate self-important eccentricities they think are suitable for "writers." And they'd rather die (and kill your inspiration with them) than risk making a fool of themselves.

My Watcher has a wasteful penchant for 20-pound bond paper above and below the carbon of the first draft. "What's the good of writing out a whole page," he whispers begrudgingly, "if you just have to write it over again later? Get it perfect the first time!" My Watcher adores stopping in the middle of a morning's work to drive down to the library to check on the name of a flower or a World War II battle or a line of metaphysical poetry. "You can't possibly go on till you've got this right!" he admonishes. I go and get the car keys.

Other Watchers have informed their writers that:

"Whenever you get a really good sentence you should stop in the middle of it and go on tomorrow. Otherwise you might run dry."

"Don't try and continue with your book till your dental appointment is over. When you're worried about your teeth, you can't think about art."

Another Watcher makes his owner pin his finished pages to a clothesline and read them through binoculars "to see how they look from a distance." Countless other Watchers demand "bribes" for taking the day off: lethal doses of caffeine, alcoholic doses of Scotch or vodka or wine.

There are various ways to outsmart, pacify or coexist with your Watcher. Here are some I have tried, or my writer-friends have tried, with success:

Look for situations when he's likely to be off-guard. Write too fast for him in an unexpected place, at an unexpected time. (Virginia Woolf captured the "diamonds in the dustheap" by writing at a "rapid haphazard gallop" in her diary.) Write when very tired. Write in purple ink on the back of a Master Charge statement. Write whatever comes into your mind while the kettle is boiling and make the steam whistle your deadline. (Deadlines are a great way to outdistance the Watcher.)

Disguise what you are writing. If your Watcher refuses to let you get on with your story or novel, write a "letter" instead, telling your "correspondent" what you are going to write in your story or next chapter. Dash off a "review" of your own unfinished opus. It will stand up like a bully to your Watcher the next time he throws obstacles in your path. If you write yourself a good one.

Get to know your Watcher. He's yours. Do a drawing of him (or her). Pin it to the wall of your study and turn it gently to the wall when necessary. Let your Watcher feel needed. Watchers are excellent critics after inspiration has been captured; they are dependable, sharp-eyed readers of things already set down. Keep your Watcher in shape and he'll have less time to keep you from shaping. If he's really ruining your whole working day sit down, as Jung did with his personal demons, and write him a letter. On a very bad day I once wrote my Watcher a letter. "Dear Watcher," I wrote, "What is it you're so afraid I'll do?" Then I held his pen for him, and he replied instantly with a candor that has kept me from truly despising him.

"Fail," he wrote back.

"How I Wrote 'Fat Chance'"

In the following selection, Barbara Wright makes many important points about the writing process. She notes the occasional necessity to begin again, the reality of writer's block, the fact that writing is hard, the usefulness of writing ends before middles, the purpose and nature of revision, the fact that writing takes time, the need to distance, the unreliability of inspiration, the fact that writing is a form of discovery, the fact that final versions can vary greatly from first drafts, and the role of instinct and how to sharpen it.

How I Wrote "Fat Chance"
Barbara Wright

Writing a short story, I find myself changing things from the moment the first word is committed to paper until the last word of the final draft is typed. Even as I proofread, I see changes I want to make. The only thing that saves me is that I am too lazy to retype the story. Someone once said that a work of art is never finished, only abandoned. I agree.

Although the process of some writers seems to fit in neat categories with the first, second, and third drafts on pink, blue, and yellow paper, the process I go through is haphazard, totally chaotic. I usually start with an image of the main character and an ill-defined intent. I never know what is going to happen in my stories until I have finished one draft, which takes an average of a month, writing three hours every day except Sunday.

In "Fat Chance" I started out to write a story with an unreliable narrator named Jenny, a nineteen-year-old, 250-pound woman who goes to a weight reduction clinic and meets one of the waiters in the dining hall, who she deludes herself into thinking is attracted to her. I wanted to make the reader know more than the first-person narrator, to play with the tension between Jenny's fantasy and the reality.

Before beginning I read several books on obesity to find out how fat men and women perceive the world, the prejudices they encounter, how they view their fatness, and the problems they have in trying to reduce. Then I sat down and in two three-hour sessions wrote fifteen pages on Jenny's childhood, how she was taken advantage of by people in her high school, how they would use her to tell all their problems to, but wouldn't invite her to go on beach weekends because, as they told her, they didn't think she could swim. I wrote of the time she passed an anti-abortion activist on the street who didn't hand her a pamphlet, assuming that no one would sleep with her, so she wouldn't need any information.

Rereading what I had written, I realized that all of this was background information. There was no story. Nothing had happened. Those pages were necessary for me to write in order to get to know the character better, but they had nothing to do with the story I was about to tell, although I didn't know what that story was. However, I did discard the idea of the unreliable narrator. The Jenny who emerged on the page was different from the character I originally intended to create. This character was vulnerable, and tried to cover her vulnerability with tough language and humor, but she was basically honest and would never delude herself into thinking someone liked her if he didn't.

What had happened thus far was this: I had started with an intent, but in writing, was forced to discard the intent, although I hadn't replaced it with another. So there I was with fifteen pages that had to be thrown out.

I was able to salvage about three pages from different parts of the original and started from there. Now came the difficult part. For the next month, I worked on the first draft.

To explain why it takes me so long to write, I must divulge one of my dirty little secrets: I have writer's block, a mild form that makes it difficult for me to sit down and commit myself to paper.

In *Writing with Power* (New York: Oxford University Press, 1981) Peter Elbow identifies two kinds of difficulties in writing. The first he compares to carrying an unwieldy load across a stream on slippery rocks. This is the most noble, productive difficulty because it involves working through language, figuring out thoughts, developing ideas. One is struggling with the writing itself, and the task of mastering words and ideas can be overwhelming, thus causing the block (p. 199). This kind of writer's block derives from the fear of the unknown. When I know that a good idea is being formed, however inchoate and messy, as new ideas always are, there is a sense of real engagement, but also a pulling back, a terror of the unknown that causes me to panic, afraid I am going to blow the idea.

The second kind of difficulty is more neurotic, and, sadly, I suffer from it more than anything else. Peter Elbow describes it this way: "You are trying to fight your way out from under a huge deflated silk balloon—layers and layers of light gauzy material which you can bat away, but they always just flop back again and no movement or exertion gets you any closer to the open air" (p. 199). In this type of block, the writer has no sense of direction and keeps going around in circles. Elbow attributes this behavior to fear of the generalized audience some writers carry in their heads.

The dangerous audience in my head is composed of two factions. To stage left are all my critics, past, present, and future: the junior-high-school English teacher who read one of my essays in a voice like Bullwinkle's; all the people who have looked at my work and said something noncommittal, unable to disguise the screaming subtext; my eighty-year-old Quaker grandmother, whose heart may not be able to withstand the shock of sex scenes and vile language; people who may think they recognize themselves among my characters.

To stage right are my supporters, equally dangerous. These are people who think I have talent, who think I am going to make it. I am afraid I am going to disappoint them, make them reassess their view of me, expose the *real me*. Both these groups form a Gestapo, and I can't shake what one writer called "the feeling that the Gestapo is going to come to my door and arrest me for impersonating an intellectual."

So this is the audience for the drama that happens every morning as I sit down to write. The principal actors are the angel, the demon, and me. The props: a desk and a typewriter.

Angel: It's nine o'clock. Time to sit down and write.

  Me: But I can't think of anything to say. I have no idea what my character is going to do. I've got to get Jenny out of the fat farm and downtown so she can meet Marvin.

Demon: The plants need watering.

Angel: Don't do it. You know you'll waste ten minutes.

Demon: Well the least you can do is clean up this mess. I mean, it's disgusting—coffee stains, flakes from the white-out, eraser dust, paper on the floor. We can't write in this filth.

Angel: Don't listen to him. Why don't you just get started?

  Me: I don't know. I sit down to write and nothing quite . . . you know . . . jells. Maybe if I clean up . . .

Angel: Try freewriting. You can throw it away. No one is going to see it but me and . . . (whispers) . . . him.

  Me: It only depresses me. I sit down and write ten minutes worth of crap, and nothing can be salvaged. It only makes me feel worse.

Demon: You'd better check the mail. There's probably another rejection slip.

Angel: (Ignoring him) Okay, then just write one sentence and see if that leads you to another.

  Me: I can't seem to do it. When I write letters, they are full of life, everyone loves to get them—and I'm not counting my mother. But when I write a story, it never quite . . .

Angel: So write some background information on Marvin. You don't know what kind of a guy he is yet.

  Me: Okay. (Sigh. Write a sentence, rip it out of the typewriter carriage, crumple it up, aim at the wastebasket and miss.)

Demon: (Taunting) You're going to have to say something difficult, aren't you? You don't know if you have the talent to do it, do you? I saw that pitiful, decaffeinated sentence you just wrote. And you call yourself a WRITER? I've got news for you, Toots. That's never going to pass muster.

Angel: (To demon) Will you cut the clichés? (To me) If you absolutely have nothing to say, then just sit down and stare at the blank paper. It's not going to hurt. What is it that you're afraid you're going to do?

Demon: Fail.

Considering this daily drama, the brouhaha of the audience in my head, and my own expectations, which are always higher than I can ever meet, the wonder is not that I write so little, but that I write at all.

For a long time I thought my difficulty with writing was nature's way of handing me a rejection slip, but I have since learned that others share this. When asked if he enjoyed writing, William Styron said, "I certainly don't. I get a fine warm feeling when I'm doing well, but that pleasure is pretty much negated by the pain of getting started each day. Let's face it, writing is hell."[1]

Yet the fine warm feeling is worth the pain, especially when one has the heady experience of the writing taking over and writing itself. These rare moments, gifts from the unconscious, are to be cherished. In "Fat Chance" this happened to me on the last three pages. I had been working on the first part of the story, describing what goes on at Dr. Bonner's rice clinic where Jenny goes to reduce. I had also been tinkering with a later section in which Jenny meets a black waiter named Marvin in a railroad-car diner when she goes in to order black tea. Marvin was still vaguely defined and I didn't know exactly what was going to happen between him and Jenny, but I knew it would be something horrible to make her abandon her diet and go on a super-binge. For some reason, I felt I had to write the last scene before I could go on with the middle part. Every morning for two weeks I wrote and rewrote the ending. The results were abysmal, depressing. The garbage can was overflowing with discarded pages. I couldn't get it right. Not even one sentence was redeemable. For me it was not a problem of what to say, but how to say it; the two are indistinguishable in fiction. Some days I would sit for three hours and produce nothing. At this point in my life, nothing was going right. The freshman English classes I was teaching were uninspired, I was not doing good work in my graduate-school classes, and my personal life was dormant. All these problems were aggravated by my inability to produce even one good sentence after two weeks of solid work. I knew that I had to get the ending right before I could go on.

Then, one night after teaching, I came back from school and decided that instead of studying or reading I would take a walk to relax. I could feel the pressure building up from all points in my life. When I came back, I felt an urgency to sit down at the typewriter, even though I had already done my three-hour stint and rarely write twice a day. Typing as quickly as I could, I wrote the entire last scene in ten or fifteen minutes. It appears in

---

[1]*Writers at Work: The Paris Review Interviews* (First Series), ed. Malcolm Cowley (New York: Penguin Books, 1977), p. 271.

the final draft almost exactly as I wrote it. I was typing full speed when suddenly, out of nowhere, the image of a phoenix tattooed on Jenny's stomach appeared. As she gorges herself on junk food, she imagines the red and green wings blurring as her stomach expands until the tattoo is no longer recognizable as a bird. Clacking along, I typed: "But no one would see it but me. No one would ever see it but me." I came to an abrupt stop. I knew that I had the last line. And I knew I had the ending to the story. There was an immediate feeling of ecstasy. One of those rare moments in writing that make up in intensity what they lack in frequency.

Popular misconception has it that writers' inspiration falls from the sky and thwacks them over the head. Actually, the moments of clarity are born of hard work, false starts, discarded efforts. It is only through the struggle that what was brewing in the unconscious is able to shoulder its way through to consciousness.

Often the conscious mind needs a rest, needs to regroup. When the final breakthrough occurs, it seems so simple, and we wonder how we could have been so stupid as to miss it. The reason is that we were not psychologically ready to see it.

This is why I write every day. Inspiration is infrequent, and the periods of drought are frustrating and debilitating, but necessary to make creative breakthroughs possible.

After the ending to "Fat Chance" was written, I had to create a catalyst for Jenny's binging. This time, the unconscious deserted me. The first draft ended up like this: Jenny and Marvin go to the movies. She invites him back to her room. On the way there, two thugs from the Ku Klux Klan stop them, insult Marvin, tell him he's hard-up to be going out with a fat woman, then beat him up. Jenny runs to call the police. By the time the police get there, Marvin has disappeared. He quits his job and won't talk to her. Jenny goes to his house but his sister slams the door in her face. Then she goes on the binge.

By this time I had been working on the story so long I had lost all critical faculties, so I asked the help of a friend, an excellent critic whom I trust. She made the following observations: the voice was inconsistent, the first three pages, which were from the initial fifteen I had written, were irrelevant, and the whole bit about the thugs was fake and depended too much on plot. Also the symbolism of the tattoo didn't work.

Armed with this information, I went back to work. Usually, after the painful first draft, I work more quickly. I started the story in the middle of page four. I rewrote sections to make the voice consistent and tried to make the tattoo work. In the first draft, I had written one paragraph about the one time Jenny had been rebellious and got a phoenix tattoo on her stomach. This didn't do the trick, my friend told me, because her motivation for doing so wasn't clear. Now I added a scene in which Jenny's mother takes her to the department store on her sixteenth birthday to buy her a dress. Jenny tries on the largest size, but it is too small. Her mother humiliates her in front of the clerk, saying that they would take the dress anyway, since it would give Jenny incentive to reduce. Jenny changes in the cubicle, leaves the dress in a heap on the floor, then leaves without her mother, taking the subway home. On the way, she passes a tattoo shop and decides to get a phoenix tattooed on her stomach.

In this version, her motivation was still not clear. So finally I added a section in which she looks in the window of the shop and sees a life-sized photo of an obese oriental man stripped to the waist with a two-headed dragon tattoo winding up his stomach. Jenny remembers her mother's looking at the photo several weeks before and saying, "Can you imagine anyone showing off their blubber like that?" Now, juxtaposed against the department-store scene and the fact that her mother is always taking potshots at fatsos, the motivation is—I hope—clear. It is an act of self-hatred to get back at her mother.

To find the details of the tattooing, I called a friend who had had a tattoo put on her chest. She told me about the reclining dentist-type chair and how the needles sounded and felt.

Next I completely rewrote the catalyst for Jenny's binge. Now she goes to the restaurant where Marvin works. They overhear his friends in a booth, saying he must be hard-up to be going out with an obese woman— and white at that. Marvin jerks his hand away from hers and goes to the front of the store. Jenny leaves and calls him from Pizza Hut, but he doesn't say anything and she can't think of anything to say either, so she hangs up. Trapped in Pizza Hut, thick with the smell of oregano, tomatoes, and dough, she thinks a fast food fix will make it easier for her to think clearly. This is the start of the binge.

Most of what appears in the final draft was not in the first draft. Yet I was able to write it in two weeks. The first draft was so difficult because I didn't know what was going to happen, who the characters were, or even what my intent was. I started out with an intent, a preconception of what the work would be. But through writing I was constantly reassessing the intent, adapting and changing it to fit what the writing produced. At other times the preconception forced a revision of the writing. Each time I reworked a scene, a paragraph, or even a sentence, it caused a restructuring of the whole. Everything was in flux. Fiction writers, more than any other kind of writers, are familiar with Keats' negative capability and are used to swimming in uncertainty and doubt, without the ability to grasp onto something firm.

After the first draft, when one aspect of the writing had stabilized—in this case, the intent—it was much easier for me to work. Thus, I was able to complete the second draft in half the time.

In revision, the only help I have to make changes is an internal Geiger counter that registers when something is not quite right. This Geiger counter is partly intuitive, partly educable. When it starts registering dissonance, I have to stop, diagnose the problem, and decide what to do about it: whether to modify the intent or the writing.

For example, toward the end of the first draft, I was having trouble revising the scenes at Dr. Bonner's clinic. I tried to put them in past tense, but they seemed awkward and unnatural. So I asked myself to whom and how soon after the incident was Jenny relating the story. I realized that she had to be relating it soon after the binge because the sense of self-hatred that comes out in the scene would have to be relatively fresh. I decided that she was telling the story while she was still at the clinic, having had to stay longer after the setback of her super-binge. She would be telling the story to someone who hadn't been to the clinic, but who knew she was still there. Thus the reader would have to put himself in the position of being a confidant. Walter Ong talks of writers who "fictionalize their audiences, casting them in a made-up role and calling on them to play the role assigned."[2] In my case, this tactic is often intuitive. Only when problems arise do I consciously analyze these relationships.

The more I read literature and the more I work on my own fiction, the more sensitive my Geiger counter becomes, and the more often it registers dissatisfaction. I feel worse about my writing after two years of graduate school than I did when I first started, because the development of my Geiger counter has outdistanced the development of my writing. I can see the possibilities of what can be done with the short story form, and have become increasingly frustrated with my inability to reach the goal.

In her study of children's rewriting strategies, Lucy Calkins found that one group of third graders, whom she called transitional children, would start and abandon piece after piece of writing. Nothing seemed to satisfy them. Calkins writes: "As children develop high standards for themselves and become more self-critical, they become more and more frustrated with what they have done, and more and more unwilling to reread, recopy and refine what they view as 'lousy' to begin with."[3]

I find that when my freshman writing students do their best work at the end of the semester, they are invariably the most uncertain, the most self-critical. This is because over the course of the semester, they have learned what good writing is and how to identify the problems, but are not yet confident of their ability to solve the problems. Their Geiger counters have developed more rapidly than the skills to quiet them.

Even though it seems the longer I write the more dissatisfied I become, I know that my only chance is to write regularly to develop the craft.

[2]"The Writer's Audience Is Always a Fiction," *PMLA*, 90 (1975), p. 17.
[3]Lucy McCormick Calkins, "Children's Rewriting Strategies," unpublished manuscript, University of New Hampshire, p. 18.

4

Revising for Sentence Effectiveness

During revision, writers rework their pieces to get them ready for their readers by evaluating the various parts of their work and reshaping them as necessary. A quick glance at the revising checklist on p. 80 shows you the individual elements that must be viewed and shaped by the revising writer.

However, it must be remembered that while writers work with the individual parts of their piece, it is what these parts contribute to the whole that really matters. So when writers study their organization, it is to determine how that organization can best serve as a framework for the whole essay; when writers evaluate the adequacy of their detail, it is to be sure there is enough support so that the essay demonstrates its point; and when writers look at how effectively they have expressed their thoughts, it is to be sure their writing says what they want it to without boring or alienating the reader.

When writers look at their individual sentences to revise them for effectiveness, the same principle still holds—they evaluate and shape these sentences so that they contribute as much as possible to the essay. It is possible to identify three ways sentences can contribute to an essay: they can contribute to the adequacy of detail; they can clarify organization; and they can make for an appealing style. In the next sections of this chapter, we will examine each of these three areas so that when you revise for sentence effectiveness, you can do so with an awareness of what and how individual sentences contribute to your writing.

Sentence Effectiveness and Adequate Detail

When you read about adequate detail (see p. 41), you learned that writers must do more than *tell* that something is so—they must *show* that it is so. This means that writers must support every generalization with specific details in order to demonstrate the validity of the generalization. One way writers can support generalizations is to provide specific explanation and examples to back up the generalizations. However, there is something else writers can do to be specific: they can craft sentences that have specific words in them.

Using Specific Diction

Diction means "word choice." Some words are general and some are specific. *General words* present a broad (and often vague) sense of our ideas, while *specific words* present a more precise sense of our ideas. Very often, writers use general words, particularly when they are presenting a generalization. However, more often writers should strive for specific words, because they give the reader a more precise, accurate understanding of the writer's ideas— and in this way specific diction contributes to adequate detail. Consider, for a moment, the following sentence:

I walked across campus, feeling good about the test I just took.

The word *walked* is general and vague. Consider some of the more specific alternatives to *walked*, the ones that would be accurate when combined with *feeling good*. Some possibilities include:

strolled	strutted	bounced
sauntered	trotted	lilted

If we pick a more specific word for *walked*, one sentence we could get is

I strutted across campus, feeling good about the test I just took.

Now we have a more accurate sense of how the writer moved across campus, because of more specific word choice. But there is still room for improvement. The word *good* is vague and general. If we find something more specific, the sentence can convey an even more accurate sense of the writer's idea. Here are some of the many possibilities:

positive	elated	at ease	delighted	jubilant
pleased	satisfied	exhilarated	cheerful	optimistic

Now let's select a word that works with *strutted*. We need something that conveys lots of good feeling because we strut when we are really feeling up. For example, if we select *exhilarated*, we get:

I strutted across campus, exhilarated by the test I just took.

Now that is a more effective sentence than what we started out with because it is a more precise representation of the writer's idea.

Exercise: Specific Diction

1. Assume that you have just written this sentence:
   I walked across campus, feeling bad about the test I just took.
   a. List some more specific alternatives to the word *walked*. Then list some more specific alternatives to the word *bad*.
   b. Next, select one word from your first list and one from your second list and write a more effective sentence. Be sure that the two words you select work well together.
2. Below are some sentences with vague, general words. Revise these sentences to create more effective ones by substituting specific words for the general ones. In some cases, you may want to substitute several words for one general word and add additional detail.
   example: The boy ran down the street.
   revision: The paper boy sprinted down Ford Avenue, pleased that he had finished his route an hour early.
   a. The room was a mess.
   b. By afternoon the child was feeling terrible.
   c. The food tasted awful.
   d. The way that person was driving his car, he almost caused an accident.
   e. The sound of that baby's cry really got to me.

Using Concrete Sensory Detail

Concrete means "specific," and *sensory* means "pertaining to the senses" (sight, sound, taste, smell, touch). Using *concrete sensory detail*, then, means shaping sentences with specific details that appeal to the reader's senses. Concrete sensory detail can contribute to adequate detail because it helps the reader get a specific sense of the writer's idea. Consider, for example, the following sentence:

I heard someone coming down the stairs.

There is really nothing "wrong" with that sentence. But you must admit, it is not terribly specific either. One of my students did some revising, and she came up with this:

I heard the staccato clicking of high heels descending the stairs.

This revision is a far more interesting sentence, largely because of the effective use of concrete sensory detail. The words *staccato* and *clicking* convey specific sounds. (Also, there is the more economical *descending* substituted for *coming down*.)

Now consider another example.

> The bird stopped for a moment in midair and then flew away.

Again, there is technically nothing wrong with this sentence. But compare it with the following student revision.

> The sparrow hovered momentarily and then vanished into the rafters.

The revised sentence makes better use of concrete sensory detail. The specific *sparrow*, *hovered*, *vanished*, and *into the rafters* all appeal to the sense of sight. (The sentence is also made more effective by substituting the more economical *momentarily* for *for a moment*.)

One reason concrete sensory detail makes a sentence more effective and contributes to adequate detail is that it gives the reader a sharper mental picture. In both of the above cases, the revised sentences provide the reader with a clearer mental picture of what happened than the original sentences do. These mental pictures are known as *mental images*. Thus, when the writer uses concrete sensory detail, he or she is helping the reader form clear mental images.

Writers who strive for concrete sensory detail to create mental images focus primarily on their nouns, verbs, and modifiers. Instead of general nouns, such as *magazine*, *shoes*, and *dog*, they will write the concrete *Newsweek*, *loafers*, and *terrier*. Similarly, writers who appreciate the vividness that concrete sensory detail can give will avoid general, vague verbs, such as *said*, *moved*, and *drank*. Instead they will choose the more concrete *blurted out*, *bolted*, and *sipped* to create clearer mental images.

Sometimes it is desirable to clarify an image by describing a noun or verb. Such descriptive words, or *modifiers*, must be chosen carefully. Let's say, for example, you have written the following sentence:

> Cans and candy wrappers are on the floor.

You study it and recognize a need for concrete sensory detail, so you make the nouns and verbs more specific to get:

> Coke cans and Milky Way wrappers are scattered across the floor.

The more specific words do convey a clearer mental image, but let's say you want to sharpen the image even more. To do so, you might add some modifiers, some words to describe the nouns and verb. The result could be something like this:

> Smashed Coke cans and crumpled Milky Way wrappers are scattered across the floor.

The addition of the modifiers *smashed* and *crumpled* creates more concrete sensory detail and hence a more specific sentence with a clearer mental image.

When using modifiers, writers must be careful not to load their sentences with too many of them. Too many modifiers can lead to a bulky sentence with an overwhelming effect. Consider the following:

> Dozens of smashed, twisted, red-and-white Coke cans, lying bent on their distorted sides and at least forty crumpled, brown, wadded-up, misshapen Milky Way wrappers

representing two weeks of my traditional midnight sugar intake are scattered messily in heaps everywhere across the green, plush-carpeted floor of my small, third-floor bedroom with its green walls and white ceiling.

When it comes to concrete sensory detail—particularly modifiers—a writer must know when to stop.

Does all this mean that every sentence we write should have concrete sensory detail? Not quite. While it is true that we should strive for the most specific words possible, we will not always be writing sentences that call for sensory words. However, when it is appropriate and desirable to create mental images for the reader, concrete sensory detail will do the job.

Exercise: Concrete Sensory Detail

Below are some ideas for you to write in sentences. Strive to create clear mental images by using concrete sensory detail. (You may need to revise a number of times before you are satisfied.)

example: the pleasant ringing of church bells
sentence: The melodious ring of St. John's bells announced the start of morning worship.

1. a squirrel running back and forth across a branch
2. the smell of brownies baking in the oven
3. the sound of rain on a roof
4. a woman wearing too much flora scented perfume
5. walking barefoot and stepping on a sharp stone

Sentence Effectiveness and Organization

As you know, writers must present their ideas in a logical order so that the reader can follow the progression of thought. Writers must also make clear how one idea leads to the next if their essays are to be effective. One way writers can demonstrate the relationships among their ideas—and hence help the reader appreciate their organization—is to write sentences using coordination, subordination, and transitions.

Coordination and Subordination

A group of words with both a subject and a verb is a *clause*. If the clause is complete enough to stand as a sentence, it is a *main clause*, but if the clause cannot stand as a sentence, it is a *subordinate clause*.

main clause: this year's citrus crop was seriously damaged by the late frost
explanation: The above word group has the subject *citrus crop* and the verb *was damaged*. It expresses completeness and thus can be a sentence when a capital letter and period are added.

subordinate clause: because this year's citrus crop was seriously damaged by the late frost

explanation: This word group has a subject and verb, but it does not express completeness and hence cannot be a sentence.

Two main clauses can appear in the same sentence if they are connected by one of the following *coordinate conjunctions:*

and	nor
but	for
or	so
yet	

When writers connect two main clauses in the same sentence, the technique is called *coordination*. Coordination allows a writer to demonstrate a specific relationship between ideas in the clauses. This relationship is identified by the coordinate conjunction used to connect the clauses, as described below.

1. If the main clauses are connected by *and*, the idea in the second clause functions in addition to the idea in the first.

   example: The mayor urged a 14 percent budget cut, and he suggested a freeze on municipal hiring.

2. If the main clauses are connected by *but* or *yet*, the idea in the second clause shows contrast to the idea in the first.

   example: The temperatures have been unusually warm for December, but (yet) it is still possible we will have snow for Christmas.

3. If the main clauses are connected by *or*, the idea in the second main clause is an alternative to the idea in the first.

   example: Your research papers must be handed in on time, or you will be penalized.

4. If the main clauses are connected by *nor*, the idea in the second clause is a negative idea functioning in addition to the negative idea in the first clause.

   example: Unless the levy is passed, the school board cannot be expected to raise teacher salaries, nor can it renovate the high school buildings.

5. If the main clauses are connected by *for*, the idea in the second clause tells why the idea in the first clause happened or should happen.

   example: Television talk shows are on the decline, for viewers have grown weary of watching celebrities talk about themselves.

6. If the main clauses are connected by *so*, the idea in the second clause functions as a result of the idea in the first clause.

   example: Dr. Wesson was ill last week, so our midterm exam is postponed until Thursday.

Punctuation note: When two main clauses are joined by a coordinate conjunction, a comma appears before the conjunction.

When writers connect a subordinate clause and a main clause in the same sentence, the technique is called *subordination*. Subordination allows a writer to demonstrate the specific relationship between the ideas in the two clauses. This relationship is identified by the subordinate conjunction used to introduce the subordinate clause. Below are some common subordinate conjunctions, the relationships they signal, and some representative examples. Notice that subordinate clauses can come before or after main clauses.

because in order that since	to show why the idea in the main clause occurs or occurred

example: Because the traffic signal on Dearborn is out, cars are backed up for two blocks.

after whenever as while before when	to show when the idea in the main clause occurs or occurred

example: Before undergraduates can enroll in upper-division courses, they must get permission from their academic dean.

where wherever	to show where the idea in the main clause occurs or occurred

example: Janine always attracts attention wherever she goes.

as if as though	to show how the idea in the main clause occurs or occurred

example: Jim was out partying last night as if he didn't care that he was flunking out of school.

if provided once unless	to show under what condition the idea in the main clause occurs or occurred

example: Once the additional computer terminals are in place, we can complete the mailing lists in half the time.

although even though though	to admit a point

example: Although it is true that enrollment in literature courses has been down in the last five years, lately the trend is beginning to reverse.

Punctuation note: When a sentence begins with a subordinate clause, a comma appears after the clause. When the subordinate clause comes at the end of the sentence, a comma is used before the clause if it shows separation from the rest of the sentence.

Exercise: Coordination and Subordination

For each of the subjects below, write one sentence with coordination and one with subordination to demonstrate the specific relationships indicated. Try to place some of your subordinate clauses before the main clauses and some of them after. Also, remember the punctuation notes on pages 102 and 103. The first one is done for you as an example.

1. *exams:* (a) coordinate to show contrast; (b) subordinate to admit a point
   a. I studied for my European history final for a solid week, but the questions were so tricky I doubt that I did very well.
   b. Although Dr. Manolio is known for giving difficult tests, her exams are always fair.
2. *spring:* (a) coordinate to show addition; (b) subordinate to show when
3. *your best friend:* (a) coordinate to show contrast; (b) subordinate to admit a point
4. *your favorite restaurant:* (a) coordinate to show an alternative; (b) subordinate to show why
5. *your first day of college:* (a) coordinate to show a result; (b) subordinate to show when
6. *a miserable cold:* (a) coordinate to continue a negative idea; (b) subordinate to show under what condition
7. *the first day of summer vacation:* (a) coordinate to show why; (b) subordinate to show when
8. *a party:* (a) coordinate to show addition; (b) subordinate to show where
9. *your favorite teacher:* (a) coordinate to show why; (b) subordinate to show how
10. *a movie you have seen:* (a) coordinate to show result; (b) subordinate to admit a point

Transitions

Like coordination and subordination, *transitions* demonstrate the relationships among ideas, and thus they are an aid to effective organization. Transitions are connective words and phrases that can show the relationship between ideas in the same sentence, between ideas in different sentences, and between ideas in different paragraphs.

Transitions are important in writing because without them there can be abrupt, annoying shifts. Consider, for example, the following sentences taken from an essay a student wrote about what she experienced when her boyfriend, Dave, broke their engagement.

For weeks I wondered what I had done wrong until friends helped me realize that I was not necessarily responsible. Dave's explanation that "people change" became more acceptable to me.

The movement from the first to the second sentence is abrupt and annoying, and as a result a large measure of effectiveness is lost. Now look at what happens when a transitional phrase is used to bridge the gap between the two sentences by clarifying the relationship between the ideas in the first sentence and those in the second.

> For weeks I wondered what I had done wrong, until friends helped me realize that I was not necessarily responsible. As a result, Dave's explanation that "people change" became more acceptable to me.

In the above example, the transitional phrase *as a result* is added at the beginning of the second sentence. This word group signals that the ideas in the first sentence function as a cause, and the ideas in the second sentence function as the effect of that cause. By demonstrating this cause-and-effect relationship, the transition smooths the flow of ideas and helps the reader understand how the writer is connecting thoughts.

In addition to connecting ideas in different sentences, transitions can clarify the relationship between ideas in the same sentence. The following sentence is an example of this.

> In her campaign speech, the senator claimed she favored economic aid to the unemployed and the elderly; however, her voting record demonstrates otherwise.

In this example the word *however* functions as a transition that indicates contrast. That is, the transition signals to the reader that what comes after it is in contrast to what comes before it.

Transitional words and phrases can be used to signal a variety of relationships. The chart that follows presents these relationships and some of the more common transitions used to signal them.

Transition Chart

Relationship Signaled	Transitions That Signal the Relationship	Example
addition	also, and, and then, too, in addition, furthermore, moreover, equally important, another, first, second, third . . .	The mayor fully expects the city council to approve his salary recommendations for city employees. *In addition*, he is certain he will gain support for his road-repair program.
time sequence	now, then, before, after, afterwards, earlier, later, immediately, soon, next, meanwhile, gradually, suddenly, finally, previously, before, next, often, eventually	*Before* an agreement can be reached between the striking hospital workers and management, both sides must soften their stands on the economic issues.

Relationship Signaled	Transitions That Signal the Relationship	Example
spatial arrangement	near, near to, nearly, far, far from, beside, in front of, next to, beyond, above, below, to the right, to the left, around, surrounding, on one side, inside, outside, across, opposite to, far off, behind, alongside, there	As you leave the fair grounds, turn right on Route 76. *Just beyond* the junction sign is the turnoff you need.
comparison	in the same way, similarly, just like, just as, in like manner, likewise	The current administration must not abandon its commitment to the poor. *Similarly*, it must not forget its promise to the elderly.
contrast	but, still, however, on the other hand, yet, on the contrary, nevertheless, despite, in spite of	*In spite of* the currently depressed housing market, there is still money to be made in real estate.
cause and effect	because, since, so, consequently, hence, as a result, therefore, thus, because of this	*Because of* this year's frost, almost 30 percent of the state's fruit crop was lost.
purpose	for this purpose, so that this may occur, in order to	*In order to* pass the school levy, the school board must make clear just how desperately additional money is needed.
emphasis	indeed, in fact, surely, undoubtedly, without a doubt, certainly, truly, to be sure, I am certain	Adolescence is not the carefree time some adults view it to be. *In fact*, it can be the most unsettled period in a person's life.
illustration	for example, for instance, as an illustration, specifically, to be specific, in particular	Most of the parents complained that the schools were not tough enough. They said, *for example*, that their children were rarely assigned homework.
summary or clarification	in summary, in conclusion, as I have shown, in brief, in short, in other words, all in all, that is	The used car Joshua bought required brake pads, shocks, and a fuel pump. *In other words*, it was in terrible shape.
admitting a point	although, while this may be true, granted, even though, while it is true that	*While it is true that* too many Americans cannot read and write, this country's literacy rate is among the best in the world.

Repetition to Achieve Transition

The transitional words and phrases in the chart above are frequently used to increase sentence effectiveness by connecting ideas. There is, however, another way to achieve this goal—by repeating key words. At some point, you have probably heard the caution against repetition. Repeating yourself, you may have been told, is annoying to the reader and a waste of words, and quite often this is true. However, there are times when deliberate repetition is appreciated by the reader because it clarifies the relationship between ideas, bridges gaps, and hence aids comprehension. Consider the following pair of sentences:

> Exam anxiety is more prevalent among students than many instructors realize. Many students who understand the material may be prevented from demonstrating their knowledge.

These sentences have a relationship to each other (cause and effect), but that relationship is not revealed as clearly as it could be. Also, there is an awkward gap between the sentences. To alleviate both of these problems, some strategic repetition can serve as a transition.

> Exam anxiety is more prevalent among students than many instructors realize. Such anxiety may prevent many students who understand the material from demonstrating their knowledge.

In the above pair of sentences, the relationship between ideas is clarified by the repetition of the word *anxiety* at the beginning of the second sentence. This repetition also smooths the flow from the first sentence to the second.

It is also possible to create transitions by repeating a key idea rather than a key word. To understand this, first look at the following sentences:

> Mr. Ferguson, driving at close to 60 miles per hour, took his eyes off the road for only a second to light a cigarette. A three-car pileup put two people in the hospital.

The relationship between these two sentences is not as clear as it could and should be. Further, there is a gap that creates an abrupt shift, and both of these facts undermine the effectiveness of the sentences. The repetition of a key idea can serve as a transition and solve these problems.

> Mr. Ferguson, driving at close to 60 miles per hour, took his eyes off the road for only a second to light a cigarette. This momentary lapse caused a three-car pileup that put two people in the hospital.

At the beginning of the second sentence are the words *this momentary lapse*. This phrase refers to eyes taken off the road for only a second, and hence it repeats that idea to achieve transition.

One other way to achieve transition is to use synonyms to repeat an idea. Consider these sentences:

> Jenny has been in bed with strep throat for a week. Her illness may force her to drop her courses this term.

Notice that the second sentence begins with *her illness*. The word *illness* is a synonym for *strep throat*, which appears in the first sentence. This synonym repeats a key idea to achieve transition.

Transitions to Connect Paragraphs

Transitions can link ideas between the end of one paragraph and the beginning of the next. When transitions are used in this way, they tighten organization by demonstrating how the ideas of one paragraph relate to those of another, and they improve the flow of paragraphs by eliminating any abrupt shifts that occur between them.

The transitional devices you have learned so far—using transitional words and phrases, repetition of key words, repetition of key ideas, and using synonyms—can all be used to bridge paragraphs. Below are examples of how transitions can be used to show the relationship between ideas in different paragraphs.

1. *End of one paragraph:* Transitions function to show how ideas relate to each other.
   Beginning of next paragraph: There is, additionally, another use for transitions.
   Transitional device: The transitional word *additionally* signals that the idea in the second paragraph functions in addition to the idea in the first paragraph.
2. *End of one paragraph:* It is easy to understand why teacher burnout is such a serious problem.
   Beginning of next paragraph: Unfortunately, teacher burnout is not the only serious problem facing our schools.
   Transitional device: Repetition of the key words *teacher burnout* and *serious problem* signals the connection between the two paragraphs.
3. *End of one paragraph:* For the first time in years, the American divorce rate is beginning to drop.
   Beginning of next paragraph: The reasons for this new trend deserve our attention.
   Transitional device: In the second paragraph, *this new trend* is a repetition of the key idea in paragraph 1, *the American divorce rate is beginning to drop*.
4. *End of one paragraph:* All signs indicate that the safety forces strike will continue for at least another week.
   Beginning of next paragraph: If the work stoppage does last seven more days, the effects will be devastating.
   Transitional device: In the second paragraph, *work stoppage* is a synonym for *strike*, which appears in the first paragraph. Also, in the second paragraph, *seven more days* is a synonym for *another week*, which appears in the first paragraph.

Exercise: Transitions

A. Write sentences and supply transitions according to the directions given. The first one is done for you as an example.

1. Write two sentences about the way women are portrayed in television commercials. Link the sentences with a transitional word or phrase signaling contrast. Underline the transition.

   Television ads do not depict women realistically. <u>However,</u> today's commercials are an improvement over those of five years ago.
2. Write one sentence about final exams that has a transitional word or phrase of addition to link two ideas. Underline the transition.
3. Write two sentences about your favorite television show. Link the sentences with a transitional word or phrase signaling emphasis. Underline the transition.
4. Write one sentence about Thanksgiving that has a transitional word or phrase of contrast. Underline the transition.
5. Write two sentences that describe the location of things in your bedroom. Link the sentences with a transitional word or phrase to signal spatial arrangement. Underline the transition.
6. Write one sentence about a campus issue with a transitional word or phrase for admitting a point. Underline the transition.
7. Write two sentences about someone you enjoy being with. Link the sentences with a transitional word or phrase of illustration. Underline the transition.
8. Write two sentences, each about a different relative. Link the sentences with a transitional word or phrase of either comparison or contrast. Underline the transition.
9. Write two sentences about what you do upon waking in the morning. Link the sentences with a transitional word or phrase to show time sequence. Underline the transition.
10. Write two sentences about the toughest instructor you have had. Link the sentences with a transitional word or phrase of clarification. Underline the transition.

B. In the following sentences, fill in the blanks with one or more words according to the directions given. The first one is done for you as an example.

1. *repeat key word:* I never was comfortable with the principle behind life insurance. Basically <u>such insurance</u> means I am betting some giant corporation that I will die before my time.
2. *repeat key word:* Over the years the registration process has become increasingly complex, causing students to become confused and frustrated. This _____ is now being studied by campus administrators in an effort to streamline procedures.
3. *use a synonym:* Because so many students found it impossible to complete their term papers by Friday, Dr. Rodriguez was willing to give an additional week to work on them. _____ helped everyone feel more comfortable with the assignment.
4. *repeat key idea:* The Altmans returned from their weekend trip to discover their house had been broken into and ransacked. _____ was so extensive, it took them two full days to get everything back in order.
5. *repeat key idea:* According to the current charter, the club's president can serve for

only one term. _____ was meant to ensure that there would be frequent change in leadership.

Sentence Effectiveness and Style

It is not enough to develop ideas adequately and organize them logically. Writers must also express themselves in an appealing way if they are to hold their readers' interest. The ways writers craft their sentences to achieve appealing and effective expression constitute their *style.*

Actually, you have already learned about several stylistic considerations. When you use specific words and concrete sensory detail, you improve your style by creating more vivid, interesting sentences. When you use transitions to connect ideas, you improve the flow of your sentences, which improves your style.

When you are revising for sentence effectiveness, there are other things you should concern yourself with. These concerns are discussed on the next pages.

Simple Diction

Sometimes writers believe that to have effective, sophisticated sentences they have to choose big, twenty-dollar words. These are the people who use *pusillanimous* when *cowardly* would do just as well—even better, actually. And if these writers do not have words like *egregious* or *inveigle* in their vocabularies, they pull them out of a dictionary or thesaurus and plunk them into their writing.

Writers who believe "the bigger the words, the better the sentence" have not stopped to think that a sentence cannot be effective if the reader cannot understand it. Also, they do not appreciate that they can be specific and accurate by using the wealth of simple, clear words they have at their disposal. Consider for a moment the following sentences taken from student essays.

The impetuous drive of youth mellows into the steady pull of maturity.
The car vibrated to a halt.
Unnoticed, light filters in beneath the blinds.

These sentences are interesting and clear. They are effective, and their effectiveness is largely because of the specific word choice. Yet although specific, the words chosen are simple ones that are part of our natural, everyday vocabularies. It is words like *filters, mellows, impetuous, drive, pull, vibrated,* and *halt*—words as simple as these—that can make for highly effective sentences. So do not for a minute believe that you need to hunt for highflown, twenty-dollar words, because specific yet simple words create an appealing style. On the other hand, when writers use unnecessarily big words, the reader is put off by a style that seems pretentious and unnatural.

Wordiness

As you revise for sentence effectiveness, you can improve your style by avoiding wordiness. In general, unnecessary words that either repeat meaning or fail to supply additional meaning undermine the effectiveness of a sentence.

Consider the following two sentences from student essays.

When I worked at a local grocery store, my boss made me or required me to work overtime three nights a week.

Most people notice right off that Melanie is a sarcastic type of person.

In the first sample sentence, the difference between *made me* and *required me* is so slight that including both makes for annoying repetition. The solution, of course, is to eliminate one of the repetitious phrases to get:

When I worked at a local grocery store, my boss made me work overtime three nights a week.

[OR]

When I worked at a local grocery store, my boss required me to work overtime three nights a week.

In the second student sample, *type of* contributes no meaning to the sentence; remove these words and the meaning stands just as it did with the words in:

Most people notice right off that Melanie is a sarcastic person.

Writers should work to eliminate wordiness, but it is possible to carry this principle too far. If we pare our sentences down too much, the result is a style that is stark and dull or stiff and overly formal. Also, extra words can be used to achieve a particular flow or balance. Sometimes words that could be cut out are left in because the sentence works better that way with the sentences before and after it. The trick is to eliminate *annoying* wordiness while using words to achieve a relaxed, readable style that comes from each sentence flowing well from the previous one. Thus whether a writer uses ''Most people notice right off that Melanie is a sarcastic person'' or ''Most notice immediately that Melanie is sarcastic'' will depend in part on which reads better with the sentences before and after.

Exercise: Eliminating Wordiness

The following are students' sentences that would be more effective if wordiness were eliminated. Revise these sentences to eliminate annoying wordiness.

sample original: The most frightening experience that I think I ever had occurred when I was 15.

sample revision: The most frightening experience I had occurred when I was 15.

[OR]

My most frightening experience occurred when I was 15.

1. The only audible sound to be heard was the blower of the heater motor as it worked to produce a soft, low hum.
2. The reason I feel our nation is so great is that both men and women of the species have opportunities to excel.
3. Until that day I did not realize or consider that people such as Karen are the most dangerous of all because they are so extremely selfish.
4. In my opinion it seems that a physical education requirement for college students is a complete waste of time.
5. This particular kind of sport is ideal for the person who desires exercise but is not in the best physical condition in the world.

Clichés

A *cliché* is a tired, overworked expression that people are weary of hearing and reading. At one time, a cliché was a fresh, interesting way to say something, but as a result of overuse, it has become worn and dull. Below is a list of some clichés you have probably heard.

scarce as hen's teeth	black as night
sadder but wiser	over the hill
cold as ice	the quick and the dead
crawl out from under	free as a bird
dry as a bone	tried but true
free and easy	bright-eyed and bushy-tailed
cried like a baby	drank like a sailor
vim and vigor	soft as silk
clear as a bell	hard as nails

For the most part, you should avoid clichés and find a more interesting way to express your ideas. Take a look at the following student sentence.

When my father accepted a job in Ohio, my heart sank.

As readers we have no trouble determining what the writer of this sentence means: he felt bad about his father taking a job in Ohio. Still, the cliché *my heart sank* creates two problems. First, it is vague. Just how bad did the writer feel? And was the writer depressed, scared, or what? Second, the sentence lacks interest because the cliché is dull.

Now react to the following revision:

When my father accepted a job in Ohio, I lost sleep worrying about whether I would be able to make new friends.

With this revision, the reader understands both the nature and the extent of the writer's negative feeling. Thus, the revision is the more effective sentence.

Note: Sometimes student writers have trouble appreciating that clichés are dull, and as a result they have trouble understanding why they should be avoided. This is because they lack experience with clichés. A person who has not encountered many clichés is not likely to view them as overworked expressions. If you are someone who does not see clichés as a problem, keep in mind that a seasoned reader will. This, by itself, is a good enough reason for you to avoid them.

Exercise: Revising Clichés

The sentences below contain clichés, which are italicized for you. Revise the sentences to eliminate the clichés and create sentences that are more effective and interesting. Keep in mind the principles for writing effective sentences that you have learned so far, and remember that you may revise several times before your sentence reads the way you want it to. Also, feel free to add any detail you wish.

example: My sixth-grade teacher was *mad as a hatter*.
revision: My sixth-grade teacher was so eccentric that she wore the same faded green dress from September until Christmas break; then from January until June she wore the same black skirt and white, ruffled blouse.

1. Cassandra is never bored because she is always *busy as a beaver*.
2. *It's a crying shame* that rainy weather spoiled your vacation.
3. Anyone who can sit through Professor James' lectures deserves a medal, because the man has a *voice that would shatter glass*.
4. John is *happy as a clam* because he got an *A* in calculus.
5. Poor Godfrey is so clumsy he is *like a bull in a china shop*.

Passive Voice

When a verb is in the *active voice*, the subject of the sentence *performs* the action indicated by the verb. When a verb is in the *passive voice*, the subject of the sentence *receives* the action indicated by the verb.

active: The optometrist examined the child's eyes. (The subject, *optometrist*, performs the action.)
passive: The child's eyes were examined by the optometrist. (The subject, *child's eyes*, receives the action.)

Most of the time, a writer should use active voice rather than passive voice, because active voice is more vigorous and less wordy than passive voice, as the following examples reveal.

passive: The ball was thrown into the end zone by the quarterback.
active: The quarterback threw the ball into the end zone.

Another reason writers favor active over passive voice is that the latter may not indicate who or what performed the action:

passive: The workers were criticized for their high absentee rate. (Who did the criticizing?)
active: The new corporate vice president criticized the workers for their high absentee rate. (Now we know who did the criticizing.)

Although you should usually choose active over passive voice, sometimes the passive voice is more appropriate. This is particularly true when the performer of the action is either unknown or unimportant:

appropriate passive voice: After germination, the plants are thinned so they are spaced 6 inches apart. (Who thins the plants is not important.)

appropriate passive voice: The chicken was baked until it was tough and tasteless. (The person who baked the chicken is unknown.)

Sometimes a writer or speaker uses the passive voice to hide information. Be wary of this technique.

passive voice used to conceal: I have been told that someone is stealing from the cash register. (The writer or speaker does not want to reveal who did the telling.)

Exercise: Revising Inappropriate Passive Voice

Five of the following sentences use verbs in the active voice, five in the passive voice. First indicate whether each verb is in the active or passive voice. Then rewrite the passive voice verbs in the active voice.

1. The elaborate sand castle was built by Tina, Jerry, and their father.
2. By noon, high tide had washed away most of their creation.
3. While I was shopping in the mall, my purse was snatched by a teenager dressed in torn blue jeans and a green sweatshirt.
4. The police reported that someone matching that description had stolen three other purses the same day.
5. The antique necklace I wear so often was given to me by my favorite aunt.
6. Aunt Sadie collected antique jewelry and gave me a piece every year for my birthday.
7. A surprise birthday party was thrown for Rhoda by three of her closest friends.
8. Unfortunately, Rhoda did not arrive when she was expected, so she ruined the surprise.
9. I asked my academic advisor how to improve my calculus grade.
10. I was told by my advisor to spend two hours a week in the math lab.

Troublesome Words and Phrases

Below is a list of words and phrases likely to annoy an experienced reader. Study them and vow to eliminate them from the final version of your essays.

1. Eliminate phrases like "*as this paragraph will explain*," "*my paper will prove*," "*as I have shown*," and "*the following paragraphs will tell*." These phrases read like formal announcements of intent. They are common conventions in certain business, scientific, and technical writing, but in informal essay writing they are considered poor style because they are intrusive.
2. Eliminate the phrase, "In conclusion." Over the years, this expression has

been so overworked that the thoughtful reader is likely to find it trite and annoying.

3. Do not refer to people with the relative pronoun, *which*. Instead, use *who*, *whom*, or *that*.

   avoid: Donna is the woman which won the essay contest.
   use: Donna is the woman who won the essay contest.
   use: Donna is the woman that won the essay contest.

4. Do not use *plus* as a synonym for *and*.

   avoid: My car needs new tie rods plus shock absorbers.
   use: My car needs new tie rods and shock absorbers.

5. Avoid using *etc., and more, and so forth*, and *and such*. Usually these expressions will annoy a reader because they suggest you could say more but do not want to. While there are times when one of these expressions is appropriate, usually you should eliminate the expression or go on to say whatever it is you *could* say.

   avoid: For his camping trip, Kevin bought a tent, a sleeping bag, a lantern, etc.
   use: For his camping trip, Kevin bought a tent, a sleeping bag, a lantern, a stove, and a first aid kit.

6. Do not use *etc.* with *such as*. *Such as* suggests you are listing only representative items in a group, so there is no need to use *etc.* to indicate other things are included.

   avoid: For his camping trip, Kevin bought several items, such as a tent, a sleeping bag, a lantern, etc.
   use: For his camping trip, Kevin bought several items, such as a tent, a sleeping bag, and a lantern.

7. Do not use *and etc. Etc.* means *and so forth*, so *and etc.* means *and and so forth*.

8. Avoid phrases such as *I believe, in my opinion, it seems to me*, and *I think*. Because you are writing the essay, the ideas expressed are clearly your beliefs, opinions, and thoughts. Reserve these expressions for distinguishing your ideas from another person's.

   avoid: In my opinion, the mayor's refusal to endorse the safety forces' pay raise is short-sighted.
   use: The mayor's refusal to endorse the safety forces' pay raise is short-sighted.
   use: The city council president believes that the mayor is right to criticize the pay raise for the safety forces, but I believe the mayor's refusal to endorse the raise is short-sighted.

9. Do not use *irregardless*. This form is nonstandard usage; use *regardless* or *irrespective of*.

10. Avoid *a lot* and *a lot of*. Replace these forms with *many*, *much*, or *a great deal of*.

    avoid: Henry earned a lot of respect when he told Peter he would not cheat for him.

use: Henry earned a great deal of respect when he told Peter he would not cheat for him.

If you do find it appropriate to use *a lot*, remember that it is two words.

11. Eliminate *at this point in time* and *in today's world*. These phrases are annoying to the experienced reader, so use *now* or *currently* instead.

    avoid: At this point in time our public schools need more financial support.

    avoid: In today's world, our public schools need more financial support.

    use: Our public schools currently need more financial support.

12. Eliminate *the reason is because*. Use *the reason is that* or *because* instead.

    avoid: The reason fewer people are becoming teachers is because teacher salaries are not competitive.

    use: The reason fewer people are becoming teachers is that teacher salaries are not competitive.

    use: Fewer people are becoming teachers because . . .

13. Do not use *very* to intensify things that cannot be intensified. The temperature can be *hot* or it can be *very hot*, but some words are as strong as they can get. Words like *dead, gorgeous, incredible, outstanding, unique*, and *perfect* cannot be made stronger by adding *very*.

14. Avoid using *so* as an intensifier unless it will be followed by a clause beginning with *that*.

    avoid: After studying for midterm exams, I was so tired.

    use: After studying for midterm exams, I was very tired.

    use: After studying for midterm exams, I was so tired that I slept for 12 hours.

15. Eliminate *vice versa*. If you want to indicate that the opposite is also true, write out exactly what that opposite is.

    avoid: My mother is always criticizing me and vice versa.

    use: My mother is always criticizing me, and I am always criticizing her.

16. Avoid *being as* or *being that* as synonyms for *since* or *because*.

    avoid: *Being that* final exams begin next week, I must take a leave of absence from my job to study.

    use: *Because* final exams begin next week, I must take a leave of absence from my job to study.

    use: *Since* final exams begin next week, I must take a leave of absence from my job to study.

17. Avoid the use of *can't hardly*. This form is ungrammatical because it is a double negative.

    avoid: I *can't hardly* wait for Leonard to arrive from Tulsa.

    use: I *can* hardly wait for Leonard to arrive from Tulsa.

    use: I *can't* wait for Leonard to arrive from Tulsa.

18. Avoid using *expect* as a synonym for *suppose*.

    avoid: I *expect* dinner will be ready in an hour.

    use: I *suppose* dinner will be ready in an hour.

19. Avoid *more importantly*; use *more important* instead.

    avoid: *More importantly*, Andrews favors tax incentives for new businesses.

use: *More important*, Andrews favors tax incentives for new businesses.

20. Do not use *of* to mean *have*.
    avoid: He could of (should of, would of) gone if he had the time.
    use: He could have (should have, would have) gone if he had the time.
21. Avoid using *real* to mean *very*.
    avoid: The weather was *real* hot in Arizona.
    use: The weather was *very* hot in Arizona.
22. Use *try to* rather than *try and*.
    avoid: Try and understand my position.
    use: Try to understand my position.
23. Avoid modifying nouns and adjectives with the suffix *-type*. Find the accurate word for what you mean.
    avoid: She likes a desert-type climate.
    use: She likes a desert climate.
24. Avoid unnecessary qualifications with such words as *really*, *different*, and *particular*. They add no meaning to your sentences, but make them wordy.
    avoid: In this particular case, I agree.
    use: In this case, I agree.
    avoid: She served three different kinds of sandwiches.
    use: She served three kinds of sandwiches.

Frequently Confused Words

Certain words are often misused by writers. Although mistakes with these words are common, they are still errors likely to disturb a knowledgeable reader. Therefore, you should study this list and refer to it as you need to.

accept, except
> *Accept* is a verb that means "to receive" or "to agree to."
> > Mary was pleased to *accept* the scholarship.
> > I *accept* the conditions of employment you explained.
> *Except* is a preposition that means "excluding."
> > *Except* for the color, Joe liked the car.

advice, advise
> *Advice* is a noun that means "a recommendation."
> > Harriet always values Jan's *advice*.
> *Advise* is a verb that means "to recommend."
> > I *advise* you to quit while you are ahead.

affect, effect
> *Affect* is a verb meaning "to influence."
> > The trade deficit *affects* the strength of our economy.
> *Effect* is a noun meaning "result."
> > The *effects* of the drug are not fully known.
> *Effect* is a verb meaning "to bring about."
> > The new company president plans to *effect* several changes in corporate policy.

all right, alright
> A knowledgeable reader is likely to prefer *all right*.

allusion, illusion
> *Allusion* is a noun meaning "indirect reference."
>> I resent your *allusion* to my past.
> *Illusion* is a noun meaning "something false or misleading."
>> Having money can create the *illusion* of happiness.

already, all ready
> *Already* means "by this time."
>> I would stay for dinner, but I have *already* eaten.
> *All ready* means "prepared."
>> Now that I have packed, I am *all ready* to leave.

altogether, all together
> *Altogether* means "thoroughly."
>> The teacher was *altogether* convinced that Sam could read better if he had glasses.
> *All together* means "everyone or everything in one place."
>> Clear the table and put the dishes *all together* on the counter.

among, between
> *Between* is usually used to show the relationship of two things.
>> The animosity *between* Charles and Lorna has existed for years.
> *Between* can be used for more than two things when it means "within."
>> The floor *between* the stove, refrigerator, and table is hopelessly stained from years of wear and tear.
> *Among* is used to show the relationship of more than two things.
>> The friendship among Kelly, Joe, and Jean began in third grade and has continued for 15 years.

amount, number
> *Amount* is used for a unit without parts that can be counted individually.
>> The *amount* of suffering in the war-torn Middle East cannot be measured.
> *Number* is used for items that can be counted.
>> The *number* of entries in the contest will determine the odds of winning the grand prize.

anxious, eager
> *Anxious* means "fearful."
>> Jeffrey becomes *anxious* whenever he goes to the dentist.
> *Eager* shows strong interest.
>> We are all *eager* for the first signs of spring.

are, our, hour
> *Are* is a plural form of the verb *to be*.
>> The teachers *are* certain to get a raise in September.
> *Our* is a plural possessive pronoun.
>> *Our* efforts will not go unrewarded.
> *Hour* refers to 60 minutes.
>> In one *hour* the plane will land in Denver.

beside, besides
> *Beside* means "next to."
>> Dad put his book down *beside* his glasses.
> *Besides* means "in addition to" or "except for."
>> *Besides* a crib, the expectant parents bought a changing table and a dresser.
>> I have nothing to tell you *besides* watch your step.

breath, breathe
> *Breath* is a noun.
>> The skaters held their *breath* as the judges announced the scores.
> *Breathe* is a verb.
>> At high altitudes it is more difficult to *breathe*.

choose, chose
> *Choose* means "to pick."
>> *Choose* the one you want so we can leave.
> *Chose* is the past tense of *choose*.
>> I *chose* the one I wanted, and then we left.

clothes, cloths
> *Clothes* means "garments."
>> The vagrant's *clothes* were torn and filthy.
> *Cloths* are pieces of fabric.
>> Clean diapers make the best cleaning *cloths*.

coarse, course
> *Coarse* means "rough."
>> Because wool is *coarse*, I do not like to wear it.
> *Course* means "path," "route," or "procedure."
>> To speed your progress toward your degree, summer school is your best course.

complement, compliment
> *Complement* means something that completes.
>> Red shoes will *complement* the outfit nicely.
> *Compliment* is "praise" or "flattery."
>> Your *compliment* comes at the right time because I was beginning to doubt myself.

conscience, conscious
> *Conscience* is an awareness of right and wrong.
>> When in doubt, follow your *conscience*.
> *Conscious* means "aware."
>> Darryl is always *conscious* of the feelings of others.

dessert, desert
> *Dessert* is the sweet at the end of a meal.
>> Ice cream is everyone's favorite *dessert*.
> *Desert* means "abandon."
>> Kim is a good friend because he never *deserts* me in my time of need.
> *Desert* is dry, sandy land.

When driving across the *desert*, one should have a survival kit in the car.

different than, different from

Experienced readers are likely to prefer *different from*.

disinterested, uninterested

Disinterested means "impartial."

In labor disputes, a federal mediator acts as a *disinterested* third party.

Uninterested means "lacking interest" or "bored."

Joyce is *uninterested* in my problem because she has troubles of her own.

farther, further

Farther refers to distance.

It is not much *farther* to the restaurant I told you about.

Further means "in addition" or "additional."

The senator believed *further* that the tax bill was favoring the rich.

Any *further* discussion *is a waste of time*.

fewer, less

Fewer is used for things that can be counted individually.

There were *fewer* As on the test than I expected.

Less is used for one unit without individual members that can be counted.

The *less* you know about what happened, the happier you will be.

hear, here

Hear refers to sensing sound with the ear.

I *hear* the distant ringing of church bells.

Here means "in this place."

Here is the picnic spot we have always enjoyed.

hole, whole

Hole is an opening.

The street department dug a *hole* in my yard to repair the gas line.

Whole means "entire."

The *whole* class agreed that the test was fair.

human, humane

Human refers to men and women and the qualities men and women possess.

If we did not make mistakes, we would not be *human*.

Humane means "compassionate."

Our society is not known for *humane* treatment of the elderly.

imply, infer

Imply means to suggest something without stating it.

Your attitude *implies* that you do not care.

Infer means to draw a conclusion from evidence.

I can *infer* from your sarcasm that you do not agree with me.

it's, its

It's is the contraction form of *it is* or *it has*.

It's unfair to accuse Lee of lying without proof.

It's been 3 years since I saw George.

Its is a possessive pronoun.

The dog buried *its* bone at the base of the oak tree.

know, no

Know means to understand or be aware of.

I *know* it is only October, but I am starting my Christmas shopping.

No is a negative.

There is *no* way I can finish the report by Friday.

loose, lose

Loose means ''unfastened'' or ''not tight.''

Joey's *loose* tooth made it impossible for him to eat corn on the cob.

Lose means ''misplace.''

Every time I buy an expensive pen, I *lose* it.

maybe, may be

Maybe means ''perhaps.''

Maybe I can help you if you explain the problem more clearly.

May be means ''might be.''

If her plane lands on time, Julia *may be* here for dinner.

passed, past

Passed means ''went by.''

Summer *passed* far too quickly.

Past refers to a previous time.

The *past* week was hectic because I had to work overtime at the store and study for final exams.

precede, proceed

Precede means ''to come before.''

A preface *precedes* the main part of a book.

Proceed means ''continue.''

I am sorry I interrupted you; *proceed* with what you were saying.

principal, principle

Principal is a school administrator (as a noun); as an adjective *principal* means ''first in importance.''

The *principal* suspended the students for fighting on the playground.

The *principal* issue here is whether we can afford to spend the extra money.

Principle is a truth or a moral conviction.

There is a basic human rights *principle* to consider here.

quiet, quite

Quiet means ''with little noise'' or ''calm.''

Jake needs a *quiet* place to study.

The sea is *quiet* despite the earlier storm.

Quite means ''very.''

I am *quite* happy with my new job.

set, sit

Set is a verb that takes a direct object.

For daylight saving time, set your clock ahead one hour.

Sit is a verb that does not take a direct object.

Sit near the door, and I will find you when I arrive.

stationary, stationery

Stationary means "unmoving" or "unchanging."

This fan is stationary; it does not rotate.

Stationery is writing paper.

More men are using pink stationery for personal correspondence.

than, then

Than is used for comparisons.

The car I bought is more fuel efficient than the one I traded in.

Then is a time reference; it also means "next."

I went to college in the 1970s; students were politically active then.

Spade the ground thoroughly; then you can plant the seeds.

there, their, they're

There indicates place. It is also a sentence opener when their or they're does not apply.

I thought my car was parked there.

There are 12 people going on the ski trip.

Their is a possessive pronoun.

Children rarely appreciate what their parents do for them.

They're is the contraction form of they are.

Kelly and Jim said they're coming, but I will believe it when I see them.

threw, through, thorough

Threw is the past tense of throw.

The pitcher threw the ball to third base.

Through means "finished" or "into and out of."

We should be through by noon.

When I drove through the Lincoln Tunnel, I forgot to put my headlights on.

Thorough means "complete."

In the spring, many people give their houses a thorough cleaning.

to, too, two

To means "toward." It is also used with a verb to form the infinitive.

After 5 years, Kathleen finally saved enough money to go to Florida.

Too means "also" or "excessively."

The child whined because she did not get to go ice skating too.

When the curtain went up, Jake was too frightened to say his lines.

Two is the number.

Lenny gets along well with his two roommates.

weather, whether

Weather refers to climate conditions.

The weather this March has been unseasonably warm and dry.

Whether means "if."

Whether I go depends on my health.

were, where

Were is a past tense form of *to be*.

Our trips to London and Rome *were* exciting.

Where means "in which place."

Where are my car keys?

whose, who's

Whose is the possessive form of *who*.

Whose books are on the kitchen table?

Who's is the contraction form of *who is* and *who has*.

Who's going with you?

Who's been in the cookie jar?

your, you're

Your is the possessive form of *you*.

Your car is parked in a tow-away zone.

You're is the contraction form of *you are*.

Let me know if *you're* coming with us.

Sentence Variety

To have an appealing style, writers must pay attention to the way their sentences flow from one to the next. That is, they must revise to achieve a rhythm that is neither choppy nor singsong. To achieve a pleasing rhythm, writers strive for *sentence variety* by varying the sentence structures they use to avoid the monotonous rhythm that comes from too many sentences with the same pattern. The following paragraph lacks the necessary sentence variety. As you read it, notice how you react.

My son is in third grade. He told me yesterday that he was one of twelve students selected to take French. Greg is delighted about it. I am annoyed. I feel this way for several reasons. The French classes will be held three days a week. The students will have French instead of their usual reading class. I believe at the third-grade level reading is more important than French. I do not want my son to miss his reading class. The teacher says Greg reads well enough for his age. I maintain that there is still room for improvement. Some people might say that learning French at an early age is a wonderful opportunity. They say students will be exposed to another language and culture. This will broaden their awareness. This may be so. I do not think students should be forced into French for this. They should have a choice of languages to study, the way they do in high school. Greg might be more interested in German. He cannot pick German now. He will learn French now. This means in high school he will probably pick French again. He will think it will be easier because he already knows some. He will never be exposed to German or whatever other language he might like. This is not broadening awareness. This is narrowing the field. I am concerned about a third-grader learning a new grammar. He does not have English grammar down pat yet. It would be better to get one thing right before moving on to another. I suspect Greg will get the two grammars confused. Teaching French to third-graders in place of reading does not make sense to me.

Most readers come away from the above paragraph frustrated and perhaps annoyed because the flow is choppy at some points and singsong everywhere else. The paragraph has such an unsatisfactory rhythm because all the sentences begin the same way, with the subject. That is, the paragraph lacks the sophistication that would come from the rhythm and balance of varied sentence structures, and as a result it loses a great deal of effectiveness. The lesson to be learned from this paragraph is that no matter how good your ideas and organization, you must achieve sentence variety or you will seriously undermine the effectiveness of your writing.

To achieve sentence variety, include a mixture of sentence structures by following several of the suggestions below.

1. *Use coordination in some of your sentences.*
   examples: a. Gregory is delighted to be learning French, but I am annoyed about it.
   b. Third-graders are not ready for a foreign language, and I doubt they will profit much from it.

2. *Begin some sentences with subordinate clauses.*
   examples: a. While I believe the study of French can be beneficial, I do not feel it should be taught to third-graders at the expense of reading instruction.
   b. If my son is to learn another language, I prefer that he choose the one he wishes to study.

Note: For a more detailed discussion of coordination and subordination, see p. 101.

3. *Begin some sentences with one or two "-ly" words (adverbs).*
   examples: a. Excitedly, Greg told me of his opportunity to take French. Patiently but [yet] firmly, I told Greg I did not want him to take French.
   b. Loudly and angrily, I told Greg's teacher I did not want Greg to take French.
   c. Slowly, thoroughly, Greg's teacher explained why Greg should take French.

When you use two -*ly* words to begin a sentence, these words may be separated in one of four ways: with a comma, with *and*, with *but*, or with *yet*.

punctuation note: Two -*ly* words are separated by commas when *and*, *but*, or *yet* is not used. If one of these words appears, no comma is placed. In addition, an introductory -*ly* word or a pair of *two* introductory -*ly* words is followed by a comma if the writer wishes to signal a distinct pause between the word or words and the rest of the sentence.

examples: a. Wearily, I explained to Greg for the fifth time why he would not be taking French.
   b. Loudly and irritably I argued with the principal about the wisdom of teaching French to third-graders.

explanation: The comma in the first sentence signals a pause, while the lack of a comma in the second sentence indicates no pause.

4. *Begin some sentences with the -ing form of a verb.* The *-ing* form of a verb is the *present participle*, and it can appear alone, in a pair, or with a phrase.
example: Sobbing, Greg explained that all his friends were taking French, and he wanted to also.
example: Whining and crying, Greg left the room convinced that I was a cruel mother.
example: Understanding his disappointment, I finally agreed to the French instruction.
caution: When you begin a sentence with a present participle—whether it appears alone, in a pair, or with a phrase—be sure the participle and any accompanying words are immediately followed by a word or word group the participle can logically refer to. Otherwise you will create an illogical, or even silly, sentence.
example: Still having trouble with English grammar, it is not the time for Greg to learn French.
correction: Still having trouble with English grammar, Greg is not ready to learn French.
explanation: In the first sentence, the participle and phrase refer to *it*, which causes the sentence to express the idea that *it* was having trouble with English grammar. However, Greg was the one having trouble, so the word *Greg* must appear just after the participle phrase.

5. *Begin some sentences with "-ed," "-en," "-n," or "-t" verb forms.* These verb forms are the *past-participle* forms of verbs, and they can function alone, in a pair, or with a phrase.
example: Exasperated, Greg stormed from the room.
example: Spent from the long discussion with Greg, I took a nap for an hour.
example: Stricken with grief, Greg cried for an hour because he could not take French.
example: Frustrated and defeated, I finally allowed Greg to take the French class.
caution: When you begin a sentence with a past participle, whether it is one, part of a pair, or in a phrase, be sure the word or word group immediately following the structure is something the participle can logically refer to. Otherwise the result will be a silly, illogical sentence.
example: Delighted by the idea of learning a new language, French class was something Greg looked forward to.
correction: Delighted by the idea of learning a new language, Greg looked forward to French class.
explanation: In the first sentence, *French class* appears just after the past participle with its phrase. As a result, it seems that the

French class was delighted. In the revision, a word that the participle can sensibly refer to appears after the phrase.

punctuation note: An introductory past participle—whether alone, in a pair, or with a phrase—is followed by a comma.

6. *Begin some sentences with "to" and a present-tense verb.* When *to* is used with the present-tense verb form, the structure is called an *infinitive.* Infinitives can appear alone, in pairs, or with phrases or modifiers, but often they appear with phrases or modifiers.

example: To understand my reaction, you must realize that I value reading above all other school subjects.

example: To be effective, a foreign language curriculum should offer students a choice of languages to study.

example: To appreciate and to accept my view, you must agree with me that reading is more important than French.

punctuation note: An introductory infinitive—whether alone, in a pair, with a phrase, or with a modifier—is followed by a comma only if the infinitive and any accompanying words are followed by a main clause.

example: To study French in third grade, Greg would have to miss his reading class.

example: To study French in third grade seems foolish to me.

explanation: In the first sentence the infinitive phrase (*to study French in third grade*) is followed by a main clause, so a comma is used after the infinitive phrase. In the second sentence the infinitive phrase (*to study French in third grade*) is not followed by a main clause, so no comma is used after the phrase.

7. *Begin some sentences with a prepositional phrase.* A *preposition* is a word that signals direction, placement, or connection. Some of the common prepositions include:

about	among	between	from	of	over	under
above	around	by	in	off	through	with
across	before	during	inside	on	to	within
along	behind	for	into	out	toward	without

A *prepositional phrase* is a preposition plus the words that are functioning with it. The following structures are examples of prepositional phrases:

across the bay	of the United States
before the rush hour	to me
at the new shopping mall	without the slightest doubt

To achieve sentence variety, you can begin some of your sentences with one or more prepositional phrases:

examples: a. For a number of reasons, I oppose French instruction at the third-grade level.

b. By my standards, reading is more important than French for third-graders.

8. *Vary the placement of transitional words and phrases.* Many transitions can function either at the beginning, in the middle, or at the end of a sentence. To achieve sentence variety, vary the placement of these structures.
   examples:

       a. *Indeed*, Greg was disappointed that I would not allow him to take French.

       b. He was so disappointed, *in fact*, that I felt compelled to give in.

       c. This does not mean my belief has changed, *however*.

9. *Begin some sentences with the subject.* Do not assume that it is ineffective to have subject first sentences, because this is not the case at all. Sentence variety refers to mixing sentence structures to avoid the monotony of repetition. So by all means, begin some of your sentences with the subject.

10. *Strike a balance between long and short sentences.* Sometimes it is effective to follow a long sentence with a much shorter one, or a rather short sentence with a longer one. While it is never necessary to follow this pattern throughout an essay, on occasion it can enhance rhythm and flow.
    examples: a. While I explained to Greg repeatedly why I believed he was better off taking reading rather than French, he never came to understand my point of view. Instead, he was heartbroken.

              b. I did my best. I reasoned with him, bribed him, and became angry with him, but still I could not convince Greg that he would be better off to wait a few years before studying a foreign language.

Exercise: Revising for Sentence Variety

Rewrite the paragraph on p. 123 to give it the sentence variety it needs. While you should keep in mind the ways to vary sentence structure described on pp. 124–127, it is not necessary to include every one, or even most, of these techniques in your version. Instead, strive for an adequate mix of structures, using as many patterns as you find necessary. Also, you may alter the existing wording somewhat, and you may add words (transitions, for example). Of course, there is no one way to revise the paragraph. There may be as many different effective revisions written as there are people in your class.

Considering the Process: Effective Sentences and Revision

Crafting effective sentences is largely a matter of revision. Some writers revise their sentences for effectiveness at the same time they consider organization and detail. Some have a separate revision stage devoted solely to effective expression, and some consider the effectiveness of their sentences in stages—

say, word choice first, transitions next, and sentence variety last. It is even possible and sometimes desirable to break down these considerations even further into more stages—wordiness, precise word choice, economy, and so forth. How should you proceed? That is something only you can determine as you experiment to discover your own effective writing process. But as you work to discover this, remember: the crafting of effective sentences will involve revision. Furthermore, one revision may not be enough. A sentence may undergo a succession of refinements before it satisfies the writer.

Sentence Effectiveness: An Illustration

The following essay was written by a student and illustrates the principles discussed in this chapter. The questions at the end of the essay are meant to point out the principles of sentence effectiveness that the student writer followed.

They're Off and Running

Waterford Park is a rather remote horse-racing track wedged between the mountains of West Virginia. I go there often, not so much to test my luck as to observe the fascinating people.

Upon entering Waterford Park, a person first encounters a sign that reads, "Lucky Louie's Daily Selections." Beneath the sign sits the founder, selling his "winners" for 1 dollar. A portly man, Louie is usually dressed in an outlandish plaid sports jacket accessorized with a shirt and tie bearing the remains of his meals for the past week. A smoking cigar clenched between decayed teeth juts from his mouth, emitting a stench that keeps his clientele on the move. Every so often in his sandpaper voice Louie emits a garbled announcement: "Get your winners here!"

Another character frequently seen at Waterford Park is the inebriated bum. He looks like he stumbled down from his moonshine still in the mountains to gamble his last 2 bucks. Clothed in a pair of grimy overhauls and a stained jacket of indeterminate color, the sot can usually be found sleeping it off in a sheltered area of the grandstand, his nip bottle in one hand and his tattered ticket in the other. More often than not the bum loses, and when he does, he begins staggering around cursing the ponies for his rotten luck.

Of course there are those who have worries other than money: the flamboyant and well-heeled. They have their own club on the premises, known as the Cap and Whip. As the grandstand crowd eat their sausage sandwiches and guzzle their beer, this elite group dines on filet mignon and Asti Spumante served at their reserved tables. Protected from the elements, they sit back for a night of racing. There is no need for them to challenge the betting lines, since they have their own courtesy betting service. They lavishly toss two or three hundred dollars into the hands of the club steward who places the bets for them. Beautifully tailored three-piece suits and designer evening gowns are the standard attire of these affluent people. The air around them is heavy with the scent of Giorgio perfume and the aroma of Cuban cigars.

The hustlers, the sots, and the privileged can be viewed on any given evening at Waterford Park. By 7 p.m., they are all in their places as the familiar cry echoes over the track: "They're off and running!"

1. Which senses does the writer appeal to with his concrete sensory detail?
2. Cite one example each of a specific noun, verb, and modifier in paragraph 2.
3. Cite one example each of a specific noun, verb, and modifier in paragraph 3.
4. Cite one example each of a specific noun, verb, and modifier in paragraph 4.
5. Which mental image do you think is the sharpest: Lucky Louie, the sot, or the flamboyant and well-heeled? Explain.
6. What transitional device is used in paragraph 3, sentence 1? In paragraph 4, sentence 1?
7. How is sentence variety achieved in paragraph 3?

II
Methods of Development

5 Description

Description evokes images and impressions. It can allow a reader to experience something new; it can renew a reader's appreciation of the familiar; or it can lead a reader to perceive the familiar from a fresh perspective.

For the writer, description also has its rewards. There is the satisfaction that comes from sharing perceptions with the reader. There is the sharpening of impression: as we work to discover the words that accurately convey our perceptions, we find ourselves looking closer at what we are describing. The more we revise and refine our descriptions, the closer we must look. The inevitable result of these closer inspections is a greater awareness of and appreciation for our surroundings.

Description can form part of an essay that is predominantly developed using some other method, say narration or illustration. In this case, the description creates vividness, adds specific detail, provides vitality, and creates context. Other times, the description is the chief method of development. While the principles of descriptive writing discussed in this chapter hold true in either case, it is description as the primary method of development that will be discussed here.

Purpose

Writers who set out to describe want to share their perceptions with their reader, and they can do this for a variety of reasons. Sometimes descriptive writers want the reader to understand *why* their perception is what it is, and sometimes they want the reader to understand the effects the perception has on them. In either of these cases, the writer's goal is to open up to the reader by sharing reactions. Sometimes descriptive writers want their audience to experience something new or come to a fresh appreciation of the familiar. If either of these is the goal, the writer's purpose is an informative one—to help the reader achieve a new awareness. And sometimes descriptive writers strive to convince their reader to view something the same way they do. When this is the case, the writer's purpose is a persuasive one.

The purpose for your description will influence your detail selection. Let's say, for example, you wish to describe your car, and let's also say that you want your reader to understand that the car is a reflection of your outgoing personality. In this case, you might choose to describe the flashy colors, custom dash, unusual hood ornament, elaborate sound system, and so forth. Now let's say you want your reader to come to a fresh appreciation of the familiar. In this case you might describe the features of your car that show it to be a marvel of engineering. If, however, you want to convince your reader to view your car as you do (as, say, something that does more harm than good), you might describe the features that contribute to air and noise pollution, the features that make us lazy, the features that can kill, and so on. And so it is that the reason writers describe will affect the features they choose to include in their description.

To determine the purpose or combination of purposes for your descriptive essay, you can ask yourself the following questions:

1. Can I help my reader understand why I perceive my subject a particular way?
2. Can I help my reader understand the effect my perception has on me?
3. Can I help my reader appreciate something he or she has not experienced before?
4. Can I help my reader achieve a fresh appreciation for something familiar?
5. Can I convince my reader to view something the same way I do?

Audience

Your audience, like your purpose, will affect your detail selection, so it is important that you clearly identify your intended reader. How much your reader knows about your subject, how your reader feels about your subject, how interested your reader is in your subject—these factors can influence your choice of details. For example, say you plan to describe the beauty of your campus commons in winter. If your reader is from a warm climate and has never seen snow, you will have to provide more details to create mental images than you would if your reader were familiar with snow. If your reader hates winter, you will have to work harder to help him or her appreciate the beauty than you would if your reader enjoyed winter.

In order to establish a suitable audience for your description, you can ask yourself the following questions:

1. Who would enjoy reading my description?
2. Who would learn something from my description?
3. Who shares an interest in my subject?
4. Who could be persuaded to view my subject as I do?
5. Who would I like to share my perceptions with?
6. Who would find my subject important?
7. Who could come to appreciate my subject as a result of reading my essay?

Once you have answered the questions above, you can establish your audience by selecting any response, as long as it is compatible with your purpose. You would not, for example, choose a reader who already views your subject as you do if your purpose is to convince your reader to share your perception.

After establishing your audience, you will need to identify the nature of your reader so you can gear your detail to his or her needs. Answering the following questions can help you.

1. How much experience has my reader had with my subject?
2. How does my reader currently view my subject?
3. What does my reader need to know about my subject?
4. What strong feelings does my reader have about my subject?
5. How much interest does my reader have in my subject?
6. How receptive will my reader be to my point of view?

Selecting Detail

Let's say that the attic of your grandmother's house has intrigued you since the time you were a small child, and as a result you decide to write a descriptive essay about it. Or let's assume that your grandmother herself has always interested you, and you decide to describe *her* in an essay. In either event, one thing is clear: whichever subject you choose for your description, you cannot describe *everything* about it. If you tried to include every detail about your grandmother or her attic, the result would be an unwieldy essay. But how do writers decide what to include and what to omit? You already know part of the answer to this question: writers base their detail selection on their audience and purpose.

There is, however, something else you can do to keep from describing everything about your subject: you can settle on one impression of your subject and describe only those features that contribute to that impression. For example, if your grandmother's attic has always intrigued you because it is eerie, full of reminders of the past, and unusual, pick only one of these three impressions to form the focus of your description. Then describe only those features of the attic that convey the impression you have settled on. Similarly, if your grandmother is interesting because she is enthusiastic, eccentric, and young-at-heart, decide which of these three qualities will be your focus and then describe only features that convey that impression.

To see how description can focus on one impression, read the following paragraph written by a freshman.

The Fruit Cellar

It was late last night as I reluctantly took the steps down to the gloomy fruit cellar. Its dark, dusty shelves are located behind the crumbling basement walls. I fumbled in the dark for the lifeless screw-in light bulb and managed to twist it to a faint glow. With that the musty room was dimly lit, and long dark shadows lurked on the ceiling, picturing enlarged, misshapen jars of fruit. Water condensed and dripped from the ceiling, shattering the eerie silence. Cobwebs suspended in every corner hid their makers in a gray crisscross of lines. Hesitantly I took a step, my sneakers soaking up the black water lying 2 inches deep on the floor. A rat darted through a hole in the wall, and jars of fruit peered at me with their glassy eyes. The rotting shelves looked as if at any moment they would fall to the floor. The cold, gray walls reminded me of an Egyptian tomb forgotten long ago. Yet mummies don't decay, and I distinctly smelled the odor of something rotting.

"The Fruit Cellar" illustrates how descriptive detail can be chosen to convey a single impression. In this case, the student writer's impression of the fruit cellar is that it is gloomy, so the writer described only those aspects of the cellar that convey that sense of gloom.

When you decide on the impression to convey, this determines in large measure what details will be selected—the ones that best convey the impression. Any details that do not convey this impression can be safely excluded.

If you have trouble determining an impression to convey, try filling in the blanks in the following sentences:

1. My subject makes me feel _____ .

2. My subject is important to me because _____ .

3. My first impression of my subject is _____ .

4. The word that best describes my subject is _____ .

5. When I am near my subject, my mood is _____ .

Concrete Sensory Detail

The descriptive writer shares perceptions by creating vivid mental images (pictures in the mind) for the reader. These mental images are created by following many of the principles for crafting effective sentences discussed in

Chapter 4. Of these principles, the most crucial to the creation of vivid mental images is using concrete sensory detail (see p. 99).

Concrete sensory detail refers to specific words that appeal to the senses (sight, sound, taste, smell, touch). If you look back at "The Fruit Cellar" you will notice many strong mental images created with concrete sensory detail. Take, for example, the sentence, "Cobwebs suspended in every corner hid their makers in a gray crisscross of lines." The detail here is *sensory* because it appeals to the sense of sight. It is also *concrete* (specific) because of such specific words as *suspended* and *crisscross of lines*. The result of this specific detail that appeals to the sense of sight is a clear picture in the mind of the reader, a picture much more vivid than one that would be formed from something like "cobwebs were in every corner hiding their spiders."

Notice too in "The Fruit Cellar" that the writer employs more than just the sense of sight. He also includes sound (water "shattering the eerie silence"), smell ("the odor of something rotting"), and touch ("feeling the dampness at my back"). While it is true that description typically relies more on one sense than the others, impressions are most clearly conveyed when the writer brings in as many senses as are pertinent to what is being described. A word of caution is in order here. It is true that the success of a descriptive essay depends largely on concrete sensory detail to create vivid mental images. However, too much of anything is no good.

With too much concrete sensory detail you bombard your reader with mental images; too much of it and your reader is likely to think, "Enough already; give it a rest." To realize that this is true, read and react to the following sentence:

> The small, fluffy, gray terrier danced and jumped with excitement and pleasure as her master took the hard, crunchy, brown dog biscuit from the large red-and-white sack.

The sentence is a bit overdone; it illustrates that descriptive writers must exercise some restraint. Of course you want to describe vividly, but recognize when enough is enough.

This same principle of restraint holds true in paragraphs as well. Often when you have a complex, highly descriptive sentence in a paragraph, it is wise to have a more simple, less descriptive one next to it. This pattern gives the reader a momentary rest and allows the individual mental images to influence the larger impressions without constant bombardment. Take, for example, the following two sentences which appear together in a descriptive essay called "The Sounds of the City" on p. 140.

> Trash cans rattle outside restaurants. Metallic jaws on sanitation trucks gulp and masticate the residue of daily living, then digest it with a satisfied groan of gears.

Notice that the second, very descriptive sentence appears next to a first, shorter and less descriptive one. Such a pattern creates a balance and prevents the reader from feeling there is too much.

Arranging Detail

If your descriptive essay includes a thesis, that thesis can state what you are describing and the impression you have formed about what you are describing. A suitable thesis for a descriptive essay could be something like this:

> As a child, and now as an adult, I have always been drawn to Grandma's attic because it is filled with reminders of the past.

The above thesis indicates that what will be described is Grandma's attic, and the impression is that it is filled with reminders of the past.

When you form your thesis, strive to express your impression in specific language. Impressions expressed in words like *nice, great, wonderful, awful, terrible,* and *bad* are vague and do not tell the reader much. However, words like *relaxing, scenic, cheerful, depressing, congested,* and *unnerving* are specific and give the reader a clearer understanding of how you feel about what you are describing.

You can also let your introduction state what it is you are describing *without* specifying your impression. When you use this technique, the reader gathers the impression from the details in the body, so that by the time the conclusion is reached, the reader knows how the writer feels about his or her subject.

It is, of course, your body paragraphs that form the heart of your essay. In these paragraphs you will provide the descriptive details that bear out your impression of your subject. A writer can approach the arrangement of descriptive details in body paragraphs in many ways. If you are describing a place, *spatial order* is useful. You can move from left to right, top to bottom, near to far, the center to the periphery, or the inside to the outside. Often when you are describing a place, a *progressive order* is effective. You can arrange your details so they build to the features that most clearly or strikingly convey your impression. Or it is possible to begin with your most telling description and move to the least striking. It is also logical to begin with your second-most-telling description, move to your least, and then build progressively to your most significant description. When you are describing a place, *chronological order* can even be effective at times, as when you are describing what you see as you move through a place.

When you are describing a person, a progressive arrangement is often the most useful. You can move from the most to the least telling feature, or move from least to most, or begin with the second-most-important feature, move to the least, and on progressively to the next important features. Chronological arrangement is also possible. You can move from a description of past actions to more current ones, for example. It is also possible to move from a physical description to a description of character to a description of actions—or this pattern can be rearranged.

Exercise: Description

1. Assume you must write an essay describing either the teacher who had the greatest impact on you (positive or negative impact) or your bedroom. First decide which of the two subjects you will describe. Then settle on a dominant impression of that subject. If you wish, complete the sentences on p. 136 to find your impression.
2. Write a thesis statement for your essay that includes your subject and impression.
3. Establish a purpose for your essay. If you like, answer the questions on p. 134 to arrive at your purpose.
4. Identify the audience for your description and determine the nature of that audience. To do these, you can answer the two sets of audience questions on p. 135.
5. List four details you might include in your essay. Be sure these are compatible with your audience, purpose, and impression.
6. Would the four items in your list best be arranged chronologically, spatially, or progressively? Number your ideas in the order you could treat them in your essay.
7. Select two of the details from your list and write one descriptive sentence for each of them. Strive for concrete sensory detail that conveys a clear mental image.

Points to Remember about Description

1. Descriptive detail is chosen on the basis of the writer's impression of the subject, purpose, and audience.
2. The writer of description relies heavily on concrete sensory detail.
   a. Usually one sense is relied on more than the others, but all the pertinent senses should be appealed to.
   b. Too much concrete sensory detail is overwhelming, so it is important to balance highly descriptive sentences with less descriptive ones.
3. The thesis for a descriptive essay can be stated or implied. If stated, it usually presents what the writer is describing and what the writer's impression of that subject is.
4. Descriptive detail can be arranged in progressive, spatial, or chronological order.

Reading Description

Below are descriptive pieces written by professionals. Some of them describe places, and some describe people. As you read these descriptions, notice the author's impression of what is being described, how that impression is conveyed, what descriptive detail is used, how concrete sensory detail is used, and how details are arranged. Following each description, there are questions for you to answer about descriptive writing technique.

The Sounds of the City

James Tuite

New York is a city of sounds: muted sounds and shrill sounds; shattering sounds and soothing sounds; urgent sounds and aimless sounds. The cliff dwellers of Manhattan—who would be racked by the silence of the lonely woods—do not hear these sounds because they are constant and eternally urban.

The visitor to the city can hear them, though, just as some animals can hear a high-pitched whistle inaudible to humans. To the casual caller to *Thesis statement* Manhattan, lying restive and sleepless in a hotel twenty or thirty floors above the street, they tell a story as fascinating as life itself. And back of the sounds broods the silence.

Night in midtown is the noise of tinseled honky-tonk and violence. Thin strains of music, usually the firm beat of rock 'n' roll or the frenzied outbursts of the discotheque, rise from ground level. This is the cacophony, the discordance of youth, and it comes on strongest when nights are hot and young blood restless.

Somewhere in the canyons below there is shrill laughter or raucous shouting. A bottle shatters against concrete. The whine of a police siren slices through the night, moving ever closer, until an eerie Doppler effect* brings it to a guttural halt.

There are few sounds so exciting in Manhattan as those of fire apparatus dashing through the night. At the outset there is the tentative hint of the first-due company bullying his way through midtown traffic. Now a fire whistle from the opposite direction affirms that trouble is, indeed, afoot. In seconds, other sirens converging from other streets help the skytop listener focus on the scene of excitement.

But he can only hear and not see, and imagination takes flight. Are the flames and smoke gushing from windows not far away? Are victims trapped there, crying out for help? Is it a conflagration, or only a trash-basket fire? Or, perhaps, it is merely a false alarm.

The questions go unanswered and the urgency of the moment dissolves. Now the mind and the ear detect the snarling, arrogant bickering of automobile horns. People in a hurry. Taxicabs blaring, insisting on their checkered priority.

Even the taxi horns dwindle down to a precocious few in the gray and pink moments of dawn. Suddenly there is another sound, a morning sound that taunts the memory for recognition. The growl of a predatory monster? No, just garbage trucks that have begun a day of scavenging.

Trash cans rattle outside restaurants. Metallic jaws on sanitation trucks gulp and masticate the residue of daily living, then digest it with a satisfied

* The drop in pitch that occurs as a source of sound quickly passes by a listener.

groan of gears. The sounds of the new day are businesslike. The growl of buses, so scattered and distant at night, becomes a demanding part of the traffic bedlam. An occasional jet or helicopter injects an exclamation point from an unexpected quarter. When the wind is right, the vibrant bellow of an ocean liner can be heard.

The sounds of the day are as jarring as the glare of a sun that outlines the canyons of midtown in drab relief. A pneumatic drill frays countless nerves with its rat-a-tat-tat, for dig they must to perpetuate the city's dizzy motion. After each screech of brakes there is a moment of suspension, of waiting for the thud or crash that never seems to follow.

The whistles of traffic policemen and hotel doormen chirp from all sides, like birds calling for their mates across a frenzied aviary. And all of these sounds are adult sounds, for childish laughter has no place in these canyons.

Night falls again, the cycle is complete, but there is no surcease from sound. For the beautiful dreamers, perhaps, the "sounds of the rude world heard in the day, lulled by the moonlight have all passed away," but this is not so in the city.

Too many New Yorkers accept the sounds about them as bland parts of everyday existence. They seldom stop to listen to the sounds, to think about them, to be appalled or enchanted by them. In the big city, sounds are life.

Questions on Technique: "The Sounds of the City"

1. Paragraphs 1 and 2 of "The Sounds of the City" form the introduction. While the two-paragraph introduction varies from the one-paragraph format discussed in Chapter 2, this is not an uncommon technique. Although it is two paragraphs, this introduction still presents the subject of the essay and the writer's reaction to his subject (the impression). What is the subject and what is the impression?
2. How does Tuite arrange his descriptive details?
3. Most of Tuite's descriptive details appeal to our sense of sound. What do all these sounds have in common?
4. Because Tuite's essay is about sounds, his concrete sensory detail appeals to our sense of hearing. Nonetheless, this detail still creates some visual mental images. For example, "Taxicabs blaring, insisting on their checkered priority" is primarily auditory detail, but it conjures up a visual image of Manhattan traffic. Cite another example of concrete sensory detail that plays at once on the auditory and the visual.
5. The effectiveness of Tuite's description comes in large part from effective word choice. His verbs, for example, are simple, clear, and specific, as in "a police siren slices through the night." Cite four verbs that particularly appeal to you.
6. Tuite's nouns are well chosen and hence highly descriptive. Notice, for

example, *bickering* in "arrogant bickering of automobile horns." Cite two other nouns that are effective description due to simplicity, clarity, accuracy, and specificity.

7. Tuite's modifiers contribute to his effective description. They are simple, clear, accurate, and specific. Notice, for example, *frenzied* in "frenzied outbursts of the discotheque." Cite four other effective modifiers.

8. Cite two descriptions that particularly appeal to you and explain why you like them.

9. What approach is used for the conclusion?

A Garden That Welcomes Strangers

Allen Lacy

I do not know what became of her, and I never learned her name. But I feel that I knew her from the garden she had so lovingly made over many decades.

The house she lived in lies two miles from mine—a simple, two-story structure with the boxy plan, steeply-pitched roof and unadorned lines that are typical of houses built in the middle of the nineteenth century near the New Jersey shore.

Her garden was equally simple. She was not a conventional gardener who did everything by the book, following the common advice to vary her plantings so there would be something in bloom from the first crocus in the spring to the last chrysanthemum in the fall. She had no respect for the rule that says that tall-growing plants belong at the rear of a perennial border, low ones in the front and middle-sized ones in the middle, with occasional exceptions for dramatic accent.

In her garden, everything was accent, everything was tall, and the evidence was plain that she loved three kinds of plant and three only: roses, clematis and lilies, intermingled promiscuously to pleasant effect but no apparent design.

She grew a dozen sorts of clematis, perhaps 50 plants in all, trained and tied so that they clambered up metal rods, each rod crowned intermittently thoughout the summer by a rounded profusion of large blossoms of dark purple, rich crimson, pale lavender, light blue and gleaming white.

Her taste in roses was old-fashioned. There wasn't a single modern hybrid tea rose or floribunda in sight. Instead, she favored the roses of other ages—the York and Lancaster rose, the cabbage rose, the damask and the rugosa rose in several varieties. She propagated her roses herself from cuttings stuck directly in the ground and protected by upended gallon jugs.

Lilies, I believe, were her greatest love. Except for some Madonna lilies it is impossible to name them, since the wooden flats stood casually here and there in the flower bed, all thickly planted with dark green lily seedlings. The occasional paper tag fluttering from a seed pod with the date and record of a cross showed that she was an amateur hybridizer with some special fondness for lilies of a warm muskmelon shade or a pale lemon yellow.

She believed in sharing her garden. By her curb there was a sign: "This is my garden, and you are welcome here. Take whatever you wish with your eyes, but nothing with your hand."

Until five years ago, her garden was always immaculately tended, the lawn kept fertilized and mowed, the flower bed free of weeds, the tall lilies carefully staked. But then something happened. I don't know what it was, but the lawn was mowed less frequently, then not at all. Tall grass invaded the roses, the clematis, the lilies. The elm tree in her front yard sickened and died, and when a coastal gale struck, the branches that fell were never removed.

With every year, the neglect has grown worse. Wild honeysuckle and bittersweet run rampant in the garden. Sumac, ailanthus, poison ivy and other uninvited things threaten the few lilies and clematis and roses that still struggle for survival.

Last year the house itself went dead. The front door was padlocked and the windows covered with sheets of plywood. For many months there has been a for sale sign out front, replacing the sign inviting strangers to share her garden.

I drive by that house almost daily and have been tempted to load a shovel in my car trunk, stop at her curb and rescue a few lilies from the smothering thicket of weeds. The laws of trespass and the fact that her house sits across the street from a police station have given me the cowardice to resist temptation. But her garden has reminded me of mortality; gardeners and the gardens they make are fragile things, creatures of time, hostages to chance and to decay.

Last week, the for sale sign out front came down and the windows were unboarded. A crew of painters arrived and someone cut down the dead elm tree. This morning there was a moving van in the driveway unloading a swing set, a barbecue grill, a grand piano and a houseful of sensible furniture. A young family is moving into that house.

I hope that among their number is a gardener whose special fondness for old roses and clematis and lilies will see to it that all else is put aside until that flower bed is restored to something of its former self.

Questions on Technique: "A Garden That Welcomes Strangers"

1. No single thesis sentence notes what will be described and the author's impression, but this information can be found in the first three paragraphs. According to these paragraphs, what will be described, and what is the author's impression of what will be described?
2. Paragraphs 3 and 4 establish a contrast. What is that contrast?
3. There is a larger contrast in the essay. What is it?

4. How does Lacy arrange his details?
5. To what sense do most of Lacy's details appeal?
6. Although Lacy is describing a garden, he is also saying something about the gardener. What is he saying?
7. Cite one example each of an effective noun, verb, and modifier.
8. What is the purpose of Lacy's description?
9. Cite a mental image you particularly like.

My Friend, Albert Einstein

Banesh Hoffmann

He was one of the greatest scientists the world has ever known, yet if I had to convey the essence of Albert Einstein in a single word, I would choose *simplicity*. Perhaps an anecdote will help. Once, caught in a downpour, he took off his hat and held it under his coat. Asked why, he explained, with admirable logic, that the rain would damage the hat, but his hair would be none the worse for its wetting. This knack for going instinctively to the heart of a matter was the secret of his major scientific discoveries—this and his extraordinary feeling for beauty.

I first met Albert Einstein in 1935, at the famous Institute for Advanced Study in Princeton, N.J. He had been among the first to be invited to the Institute, and was offered *carte blanche* as to salary. To the director's dismay, Einstein asked for an impossible sum: it was far too *small*. The director had to plead with him to accept a larger salary.

I was in awe of Einstein, and hesitated before approaching him about some ideas I had been working on. When I finally knocked on his door, a gentle voice said, "Come"—with a rising inflection that made the single word both a welcome and a question. I entered his office and found him seated at the table, calculating and smoking his pipe. Dressed in ill-fitting clothes, his hair characteristically awry, he smiled a warm welcome. His utter naturalness at once set me at ease.

As I began to explain my ideas, he asked me to write the equations on the blackboard so he could see how they developed. Then came the staggering—and altogether endearing—request: "Please go slowly. I do not understand things quickly." This from Einstein! He said it gently, and I laughed. From then on, all vestiges of fear were gone.

Einstein was born in 1879 in the German city of Ulm. He had been no infant prodigy; indeed, he was so late in learning to speak that his parents feared he was a dullard. In school, though his teachers saw no special talent in him, the signs were already there. He taught himself calculus, for example, and his teachers seemed a little afraid of him because he asked questions they could not answer. At the age of 16, he asked himself whether a light wave would seem stationary if one ran abreast of it. From that innocent question would arise, ten years later, his theory of relativity.

Einstein failed his entrance examinations at the Swiss Federal Polytechnic School, in Zurich, but was admitted a year later. There he went beyond his regular work to study the masterworks of physics on his own. Rejected when he applied for academic positions, he ultimately found work, in 1902, as a patent examiner in Berne, and there in 1905 his genius burst into fabulous flower.

Among the extraordinary things he produced in that memorable year were his theory of relativity, with its famous offshoot, $E = mc^2$ (energy equals mass times the speed of light squared), and his quantum theory of light. These two theories were not only revolutionary, but seemingly contradictory: the former was intimately linked to the theory that light consists of waves, while the latter said it consists somehow of particles. Yet this unknown young man boldly proposed both at once—and he was right in both cases, though how he could have been is far too complex a story to tell here.

Collaborating with Einstein was an unforgettable experience. In 1937, the Polish physicist Leopold Infeld and I asked if we could work with him. He was pleased with the proposal, since he had an idea about gravitation waiting to be worked out in detail. Thus we got to know not merely the man and the friend, but also the professional.

The intensity and depth of his concentration were fantastic. When battling a recalcitrant problem, he worried it as an animal worries its prey. Often, when we found ourselves up against a seemingly insuperable difficulty, he would stand up, put his pipe on the table, and say in his quaint English, "I will a little tink" (he could not pronounce "th"). Then he would pace up and down, twirling a lock of his long, graying hair around his forefinger.

A dreamy, faraway and yet inward look would come over his face. There was no appearance of concentration, no furrowing of the brow—only a placid inner communion. The minutes would pass, and then suddenly Einstein would stop pacing as his face relaxed into a gentle smile. He had found the solution to the problem. Sometimes it was so simple that Infeld and I could have kicked ourselves for not having thought of it. But the magic had been performed invisibly in the depths of Einstein's mind, by a process we could not fathom.

Although Einstein felt no need for religious ritual and belonged to no formal religious group, he was the most deeply religious man I have known. He once said to me, "Ideas come from God," and one could hear the capital "G" in the reverence with which he pronounced the word. On the marble fireplace in the mathematics building at Princeton University is carved, in the original German, what one might call his scientific credo:

"God is subtle, but he is not malicious." By this Einstein meant that scientists could expect to find their task difficult, but not hopeless: the Universe was a Universe of law, and God was not confusing us with deliberate paradoxes and contradictions.

Einstein was an accomplished amateur musician. We used to play duets, he on the violin, I at the piano. One day he surprised me by saying Mozart was the greatest composer of all. Beethoven "created" his music, but the music of Mozart was of such purity and beauty one felt he had merely "found" it—that it had always existed as part of the inner beauty of the Universe, waiting to be revealed.

It was this very Mozartean simplicity that most characterized Einstein's methods. His 1905 theory of relativity, for example, was built on just two simple assumptions. One is the so-called principle of relativity, which means, roughly speaking, that we cannot tell whether we are at rest or moving smoothly. The other assumption is that the speed of light is the same no matter what the speed of the object that produces it. You can see how reasonable this is if you think of agitating a stick in a lake to create waves. Whether you wiggle the stick from a stationary pier, or from a rushing speedboat, the waves, once generated, are on their own, and their speed has nothing to do with that of the stick.

Each of these assumptions, by itself, was so plausible as to seem primitively obvious. But together they were in such violent conflict that a lesser man would have dropped one or the other and fled in panic. Einstein daringly kept both—and by so doing he revolutionized physics. For he demonstrated they could, after all, exist peacefully side by side, provided we gave up cherished beliefs about the nature of time.

Science is like a house of cards, with concepts like time and space at the lowest level. Tampering with time brought most of the house tumbling down, and it was this that made Einstein's work so important—and controversial. At a conference in Princeton in honor of his 70th birthday, one of the speakers, a Nobel Prize-winner, tried to convey the magical quality of Einstein's achievement. Words failed him, and with a shrug of helplessness he pointed to his wristwatch, and said in tones of awed amazement, "It all came from this." His very ineloquence made this the most eloquent tribute I have heard to Einstein's genius.

We think of Einstein as one concerned only with the deepest aspects of science. But he saw scientific principles in everyday things to which most of us would give barely a second thought. He once asked me if I had ever wondered why a man's feet will sink into either dry or completely submerged sand, while sand that is merely damp provides a firm surface. When I could not answer, he offered a simple explanation.

It depends, he pointed out, on *surface tension,* the elastic-skin effect of a liquid surface. This is what holds a drop together, or causes two small raindrops on a windowpane to pull into one big drop the moment their surfaces touch.

When sand is damp, Einstein explained, there are tiny amounts of water between grains. The surface tensions of these tiny amounts of water pull all the grains together, and friction then makes them hard to budge. When the sand is dry, there is obviously no water between grains. If the sand is fully immersed, there is water between grains, but no water *surface* to pull them together.

This is not as important as relativity; yet there is no telling what seeming trifle will lead an Einstein to a major discovery. And the puzzle of the sand does give us an inkling of the power and elegance of his mind.

Einstein's work, performed quietly with pencil and paper, seemed remote from the turmoil of everyday life: But his ideas were so revolutionary they caused violent controversy and irrational anger. Indeed, in order to be able to award him a belated Nobel Prize, the selection committee had to avoid mentioning relativity, and pretend the prize was awarded primarily for his work on the quantum theory.

Political events upset the serenity of his life even more. When the Nazis came to power in Germany, his theories were officially declared false because they had been formulated by a Jew. His property was confiscated, and it is said a price was put on his head.

When scientists in the United States, fearful that the Nazis might develop an atomic bomb, sought to alert American authorities to the danger, they were scarcely heeded. In desperation, they drafted a letter which Einstein signed and sent directly to President Roosevelt. It was this act that led to the fateful decision to go all-out on the production of an atomic bomb— an endeavor in which Einstein took no active part. When he heard of the agony and destruction that his $E = mc^2$ had wrought, he was dismayed beyond measure, and from then on there was a look of ineffable sadness in his eyes.

There was something elusively whimsical about Einstein. It is illustrated by my favorite anecdote about him. In his first year in Princeton, on Christmas Eve, so the story goes, some children sang carols outside his house. Having finished, they knocked on his door and explained they were collecting money to buy Christmas presents. Einstein listened, then said, "Wait a moment." He put on his scarf and overcoat, and took his violin from its case. Then, joining the children as they went from door to door, he accompanied their singing of "Silent Night" on his violin.

How shall I sum up what it meant to have known Einstein and his works? Like the Nobel Prize-winner who pointed helplessly at his watch, I can find no adequate words. It was akin to the revelation of great art that lets one see what was formerly hidden. And when, for example, I walk on the sand of a lonely beach, I am reminded of his ceaseless search for cosmic simplicity—and the scene takes on a deeper, sadder beauty.

Questions on Technique: "My Friend, Albert Einstein"

1. According to the thesis, what is the subject of "My Friend, Albert Einstein," and what is the writer's impression of that subject?

2. Does the introduction stimulate your interest? Explain. What approach does the author take to the introduction?

3. Why does Hoffmann spend so little time describing Einstein's physical appearance?

4. What major points does Hoffmann make about Einstein to demonstrate his simplicity?

5. How does Hoffmann arrange his detail?

6. At times Hoffmann's detail takes the form of brief anecdotes (stories) that reveal aspects of Einstein's character. Cite one example of such an anecdote.

7. What effect do the anecdotes have on the reader?

8. Because Hoffmann is describing inner character rather than outward appearance, he has less need for concrete sensory detail to create mental images. Still, the author does rely on this descriptive technique to some extent. In paragraph 3, for example, there is "a gentle voice said, 'Come'—with a rising inflection that made the single word both a welcome and a question." Cite one other example of concrete sensory detail used to create a mental image.

9. Hoffmann's description of Einstein's simplicity includes some surprising facts, some aspects of Einstein's character that seem to contradict what we might assume about a person of such genius. For example, it is surprising to learn that Einstein did "not understand things quickly." What other surprising, seemingly contradictory details does Hoffman include?

10. When Hoffmann describes the simplicity of a man the reader might automatically think of as complex, and when he describes aspects of character that surprise the reader and contradict what the reader might assume, what effect is created in the mind of the reader?

11. Cite three examples of effective sentences due to specific yet simple word choice.

12. What approach does Hoffman take to the conclusion?

The Most Unforgettable Character I've Met

Leslie Roberts

The first time I saw Stephen Leacock at close quarters he came swinging into a classroom in Moyse Hall, the serenely ugly old Arts Building of McGill University in Montreal. The room was packed with undergraduates like me who had come with huge curiosity to listen to their first lecture on political science by a man whose humorous writing had rocked the English-

Leslie Roberts, "The Most Unforgettable Character I've Met." Reprinted with permission from the June 1961 *Reader's Digest*. Copyright © by The Reader's Digest Association, Inc.

speaking world with laughter, but who was a campus character for very different reasons.

Leacock enjoyed a reputation for eccentricity and for an impish individualism that expressed itself in blunt speech on every subject. Naturally we looked him over carefully.

What we saw was a shock of graying hair crowning a rugged face that wore a friendly smile, emphasized by crinkles of mirth about the eyes. I remember thinking, "He could use a haircut." His necktie had slipped its moorings, and his tweedy suit looked slept-in. Across his vest his watch chain had come apart in the middle and had been put together with a safety pin. The effect was of a man who gave no thought to his appearance. But his manner was far too buoyant to suggest the absent-minded professor.

His apparel was topped by one of those loose, black gowns professors wore in those days. Leacock's had been acquired about the time he received his Ph.D. from the University of Chicago in 1903. Even though the garment was showing signs of wear in 1914, it was still one of the essential properties of his play-acting. At least a dozen times during every lecture it would slip off his shoulders and seize him by the crook of his elbows. Without pause in the flow of talk and motion—he was a walking lecturer—a great shrug of the shoulders would hoist the gown part way into place.

Leacock was tremendously proud of his Chicago Ph.D., but it was inescapably in character that he must spoof it. "The meaning of this degree," he quipped in a lecture, "is that the recipient has been examined for the last time in his life and pronounced full. After this, no new ideas can be imparted to him."

In similar vein, after returning from a holiday abroad he told his class, "I was sitting quietly in my cabin when a steward knocked and, after making sure I am called Doctor, asked if I would come and look at the stewardess's knee. I was off like a shot, but another fellow got there ahead of me. He was a Doctor of Divinity."

What came through to me, even in the first lecture, was Leacock's warmth and humanness. I knew I was listening to a man who loved young people and was determined to give them as much wisdom as he could. His teaching methods were unconventional. He couldn't resist the temptation to explore bypaths. In discussing the days of Queen Victoria, he mentioned Disraeli, and this set him off to talk about the man rather than the Prime Minister—his way of living, his quick mind, his dilettantism, his great love affair with his wife. The digression lifted the great statesman into a framework of his own and, when Leacock returned to the main line of his subject, the listener understood, in a way no textbook could inform him, how such a man could bring off the coup which gave Britain control of the Suez Canal and made the Empire impregnable for decades to come.

His classroom methods were often the target of men who taught by the book. To those who complained that he was too unorthodox, Leacock retorted scornfully, "Economics isn't a rule-book business. Any theory which fails to recognize human aspirations is pure nonsense. People aren't statistics. Hell's bells! They're alive!" His critics, who related all teaching to exams, could never understand that by his methods he was fulfilling the purpose for which any university exists: he was teaching his students to think. "College," he once said, "is to teach the mind, not the thumb."

The humorous writing which brought him international fame and five times the income his job paid was an avocation which, to quote him, "played hell" with his workday and his sleep. But there is where his heart lay. "I would sooner have written *Alice in Wonderland* than the whole *Encyclopaedia Britannica*," he once remarked.

A direct line of laughter runs from Mark Twain through Leacock to such successors as Robert Benchley. The cord which ties them together is the feeling each had of the ridiculous nature of many of life's little complexities and of their own professed inability to cope with them. Critics and scholars have written that the essence of this brand of humor is its lack of malice. My own opinion is that many of the situations at which Leacock poked fun actually infuriated him. He simply set out to slay them with the light rapier of ridicule, instead of the heavy cudgels of wrath.

Teaching, writing and long hours of good talk were still not enough for this man of remarkable nervous energy. He plunged intermittently into Canadian politics with boiling enthusiasm. He could have had cabinet posts in two Conservative ministries, but he turned them down. "I can't picture myself as a professional stuffed shirt," he used to say to his cronies, "or as being in agreement with my Prime Minister for four consecutive years." What he meant was that he would allow nothing to sever him from teaching.

His students all knew vaguely that Leacock was a devoted husband and father, but on the campus he lived for them. And because he loved his profession, it was in his nature to deride it affectionately. "A teacher has more time to think than a businessman," he once told a business audience, "or, better still, time to stop thinking altogether for months." Again, on being appointed to head his department at McGill, he could not resist remarking wryly that he had "now reached an eminence so high that the emolument places me distinctly above policemen, postmen and streetcar conductors, and I am even able to mingle with poorer businessmen on terms of something like equality."

Leacock was every student's friend. He liked undergraduate talk and company. To the student with a serious financial problem he was the softest touch on the campus. He was the only senior faculty member I ever saw around the Student's Union on any but official occasions. He dropped in as casually as any sophomore, usually in search of a game of billiards, a favorite pastime, which, he always maintained, "stimulates conversation."

Indirectly this was my own introduction to a firm friendship with Stephen Leacock. His favorite opponent was a convivial campus character named William Ewart Gladstone Murray, later chairman of the Canadian

Broadcasting Corporation. By some preposterous device of their own invention, this happy-go-lucky pair became involved in a billiard match for 20,000 points, which was still in progress when Stephen died in 1944. The score then stood 18,975 for the retired professor and 16,793 for his ex-student. The marathon had been staged at various times in Montreal, Toronto, New York, Vancouver, London, Birmingham, Biarritz and Monte Carlo.

Once, after a long absence from Montreal, I ran into Murray as he was heading for the University Club to see Leacock. I went along, and kept going back. Leacock soon became a combination of friend and critic-of-manuscripts. At times when my economic problems were severe the telephone was likely to ring and a voice from an advertising agency would say, "Dr. Leacock suggested you might be willing to write a brochure for a client of ours." Any attempt to thank Stephen would be waved aside with a quip: "I hope you had the good sense to put a high price on your talents. The trick with these advertising fellows is to find out how much money they have—and don't take a cent more!"

He would push everything aside to help a former student, or any young person fighting his way up the steep ladder of the lively arts. He wrote a book for one young woman illustrator to fit drawings she had already made, thereby turning normal publishing processes upside down.

Leacock was probably the first Canadian to qualify as a "pro-American British imperialist." A colleague, Prof. John Culliton, said of him, "Long before Winston Churchill, Leacock was saving the Empire every Monday, Wednesday and Friday at 3P.M. in Room 20." He was also ahead of his time in prodding Americans and Britons toward greater friendship and understanding.

His feeling for both sides of the Atlantic came naturally. He was born on the isle of Wight in 1869, and emigrated to Canada as a six-year-old. On his retirement from McGill, influential English friends urged him to return to live in the land of his birth. He refused, saying, "I'd hate to be so far away from the United States. It's second nature, part of our lives, to be near them. Every Sunday morning we read the New York funny papers. All week we hear about politics in Alabama and Louisiana, and whether they caught the bandits who stole the vault of the National Bank—well, you know American news. There's no other like it."

In the eight years of his retirement, Stephen produced the work he believed most likely to endure. It was far removed from the kind of wit which had made him famous. He described his history, *Montreal: Seaport and City,* as "the best job I've done." Unlike most historical works it bubbles with the author's laughter. In his foreword, after thanking two former colleagues for checking the manuscript, he added that any errors which remained obviously must be theirs. "Acknowledging these debts," he concluded, "I also feel that I owe a good deal of this book to my own industry and effort."

Midway through World War II, I asked Stephen if he would write a foreword for a book I had written on the Canadian navy and its gallant role in convoy escort. He agreed. Some time later he handed me more than 20,000 words, in which he had told the whole fascinating background story of Canada's lifelong relationship to the sea. His research was staggering to a reporter who had simply described events and engagements to which he had been an eyewitness.

"I got interested in the subject," he explained. "If you don't like it, throw it way and I'll write something shorter."

Not a word was changed. To my joy, the book appeared under our joint by-lines. Soon after, throat cancer took Stephen from the thousands of Old McGillers who loved him.

Leacock loved human beings for their little vanities and pretensions—and laughed at his own. The fictional town of Mariposa of his famous "Sunshine Sketches" is obviously Orillia, Ontario, where Leacock built a summer home and developed a farm, which, he said, "used to lose a few dollars a year, but by dint of hard work and modernization, I have contrived to turn that into a loss of thousands." The citizens of Orillia had little difficulty in self-identification when the book reached town, but they soon realized that Leacock had ribbed his own idiosyncrasies more sharply than he had pinpointed theirs. Today's Orillians speak of him with the awe given to any community's adopted son, though it was he who adopted Mariposa-Orillia.

Stephen Leacock was so honestly simple that to many men he seemed to be a mass of complexities. To the world he remains the man of laughter. His greatest achievement, however, was that he taught thousands of young men and women to want to know. By example he proved one simple fact to all of us who attended his classes, certainly to that numerous crew who came to enjoy his friendship—that the right of outspoken dissent is the free man's most precious heritage. Such men do not often pass this way.

Questions on Technique: "The Most Unforgettable Character I've Met"

1. The first four paragraphs of Roberts' essay contain a physical description of Leacock. What effect does this description have?
2. Following the physical description, there are two paragraphs that contain Leacock's words. What do these contribute to the description?
3. Like Hoffmann (p. 144), Roberts makes clear what is special about the person he is describing. To do this, Roberts describes Leacock in a number of different roles. One of these roles is teacher. In what other roles is Leacock described?
4. Roberts has no introduction with a statement of dominant impression. Yet there is a place in the essay that conveys just what is so unforgettable about Leacock. What is that place?
5. Like Hoffmann, Roberts uses anecdotes to convey part of his description. Cite two of these anecdotes.

6. What do these anecdotes contribute to the effectiveness of the description?
7. Cite two examples of concrete sensory detail that creates vivid mental images.
8. Leacock is described as a man of energy and vitality. And Roberts' description is energetic and vital because of the author's effective word choice. Cite three sentences that have this vitality and analyze what makes for the effectiveness and vitality. (Hint: consider the principles for writing effective sentences discussed in Chapter 4.)
9. While both "My Friend, Albert Einstein" and "The Most Unforgettable Character I've Met" are strong descriptions of people, you may enjoy one piece more than the other. Which one do you prefer and why?

Student Writings to Read and Evaluate

Below are descriptive essays written by students. Two of the essays describe places, and two describe people. You will notice that some of the pieces are better than others, but each essay has definite strengths as well as some areas that could be improved with revision. As you read these essays, consider what the strengths and weaknesses of each are.

Following the student writings, there is an evaluation for you to apply to the essays to give you practice analyzing writing. This practice is valuable because you can learn successful techniques to include in your own writing as well as less successful ones to avoid. Also, this practice will help you develop your sense of what does and does not succeed in writing so you can develop a sharp critical ability. And once you become a reliable critic—a critic whose judgments are accurate—you can make determinations about your own writing that are trustworthy.

The Destruction Zone

If there is one thing I've learned from my college experience, it's that places where athletes party are nice to visit, but you don't want to live there. Like most good lessons, I learned this one the hard way. I made the mistake of throwing a party last April and inviting many members of the Youngstown State University Football team; luckily, it was my friend who made the mistake of letting me have the party at *her* apartment.

When I was first making out my guest list, I thought nothing of inviting the players. I'm friends with most of them, and who do you invite to parties but your friends? Having gone to many of their parties, I knew that there would be a mess, but I was sure the clean-up wouldn't be any phenomenal task that I would have trouble handling. Well, I was wrong! I found that out the morning after the party.

I spent the night at the tiny one-bedroom apartment with hopes of sleeping in, but at 6:30 A.M. I was awakened by the rousing bellows of an exalted video-evangelist delivering his soul-saving sermon. Someone had left the television on in the living room. I stumbled sleepily out of the bedroom to put an end to the roars of Oral Roberts before they woke up my more-than-generous friend. That was when I entered the destruction zone.

My first impulse was to call in the National Guard and declare the living room a disaster area. I stood in awe under an archway carefully constructed of half-empty Little Kings beer bottles and topped with a grease-spotted, empty Domino's pizza box. The thought of having to trudge through this catastrophe to turn off the T.V. made me cringe. I cautiously dodged through the maze of crumpled aluminum cans and garnet-colored bottles that lay on the floor. Potato chips and pretzels that were haphazardly scattered across the blue plush carpeting crunched under my feet. Just as I hit the off button on the T.V. set, something hit *me* on the head and left me startled. I looked down to find a very hard and weighty piece of pizza at my feet. Looking up, I found three more slices of cheese pizza dangling from the tomato-sauce–and–french-onion-dip–stained ceiling.

By now I had become overwhelmed by the stifling stench of stale cigarettes, warm beer, yesterday's pizza and spoiled french onion dip. I reached over to the wall and flipped the switch for the ceiling fan to get the air circulating. Suddenly, underwear began flying everywhere. I turned around just in time to have a large pair of unidentified jockey shorts hit me square in the face. Apparently several owners of men's underwear mistook the wooden ceiling fan for a clothes line. I quickly turned the fan off and hurtled to the window hoping in desperation for a crisp, clean breeze to penetrate the stagnant air. I strained to push up the ill-fitting wooden framed window, and I heard a moan. Reassuring myself it was just the window, I continued to press on it, but a loud snore accompanied another moan. I spun around to find a dozing 6-foot, 4-inch, 265-pound football player curled up in the fireplace and affectionately holding his empty bottle of Mad Dog like a teddy bear. That was the last straw.

I realized this shambles was more than I could handle on my own and stumbled back to the bedroom. Deciding to wait until my more-than-generous friend woke up, I scraped the grunge off my bare feet and crawled back into bed.

Never Intrude

It was early morning, and I was diving just off the shores of Grand Cayman Island when I swam through an opening in the coral. At first I could only hear the intermittent gurgle of exhaust air, but as my eyes adjusted to the dim light, I was astonished by the assortment of life in what appeared to be a coral room.

There in the middle of the floor, caught by surprise, a crab shuttled from side to side unable to decide which way to go, yet unbothered nearby a rust-red starfish worried at a clam it was trying to pry open. Deadman's fingers, a well-named rubbery sponge that was dangling from the ceiling, brushed my back. As I hung suspended just above the floor careful to avoid touching the few black sea urchins below. Fascinated, I watched as thousands of shrimp fry floated by like dust on a ray of sunlight, while hundreds of small fish, called neons, flitted in and out of the walls, their iridescent bodies giving the room a psychedelic effect. I looked at the wall on my right. There in a cubbyhole a porcupine fish had puffed itself up at least twice his normal size and was wedged tightly into his hole.

Bothered by my intrusion, a spotted jewfish loomed from the shadows to assert his territorial rights; when he swam towards me, lime-green anemones popped shut as if from fear. I could understand their concern, for he must have weighed over 100 pounds. When I raised my prod-rod, he seemed to reconsider his approach. With things at an impasse I had time to think of the position that I was in. Here in a room with jagged walls of blush pink, their white tips announcing it was fire coral. If he rammed me that coral would cut right through my wet suit and at best leave me with a nasty infection. Since I was the intruder, I carefully backed out into the open. Glad to be out of the confines of the coral room.

The Man

I stepped out of my family's mobile home and saw him, a man sitting on the end of a peninsula-shaped piece of rock which jutted out into the middle of the Grand Canyon. The spindling stone scarcely seemed strong enough to hold its own weight let alone the weight of the man. As I moved closer, I could see he was playing a guitar and singing. He looked as if he were serenading the huge crevice in a manner one might use while courting a sweetheart.

He was a young man of Indian descent. His long black hair was tied into a ponytail that ran the length of his back. The noonday sun made his denim jeans and blue cotton shirt blend in with the cloudless sky as if they were part of it. His feet in a pair of knee-high moccasins swung freely from the rock. The mile-deep canyon presented no danger to the man, for the only thing his hands held on to was the guitar. Even his reckless smile had a hint of defiance to it. Then he looked up at me and I quickly turned away. But before I did, I caught a glimpse of his dark brown eyes. They were open wide from taking in all the beauty that surrounded him, the beauty I had somehow missed while looking at the man.

Sadie

Of all the unforgettable characters I have met in my lifetime (and for some reason it seems I've encountered quite a few), my very dear friend, Sadie, is definitely a standout. In any ordinary day she would spend all-in-all at least 3 hours cleaning her dentures with Chlorox Bleach. The remaining time she devoted exclusively to the making and consuming of pizza.

Using Efferdent or Polident was much too conventional for Sadie and, according to her, infinitely inferior. Chlorox, she said, whitened her teeth as white as they could be. What it did not whiten, I think, it just disintegrated. It was a sure bet that once in the morning, once in the afternoon, and of course once at night, Sadie would be in her bathroom waiting for the Chlorox to go to work. For really stubborn stains, she would dip her red-handled toothbrush in a small yogurt carton she kept near her sink filled with Chlorox. Then she would begin to scrub—either the stain or enamel was sure to come off. She never used Scope; after all, how many germs can live in bleach? Certs or Chlorets were also out of the question. She didn't want any masking of that freshly laundered aroma that exuded from her whitened lips.

She probably would not have spent so much time cleaning her teeth if she had not had such an unearthly love of pizza. This is not to say that she was a glutton, for she enjoyed making pizza as much as eating it. Her eyes would shine as she mixed the flour, salt, and sugar together with the water and yeast into a tasty dough. While she waited for the dough to rise, she would reminisce on some of her past luscious creations. After the dough had risen, she would gingerly spread it out with just the tips of her fingers to the edges of the generously oiled pan. Skillfully she added each topping: first the tomato sauce, next the cheese, thirdly the pepperoni or sausage, and lastly the green pepper or mushrooms. Then, into the oven it went. Finally the long-awaited moment arrived. Out of the oven and into her mouth the masterpiece went. She truly enjoyed every succulent bite.

Although Sadie died three years ago at the age of 81, the memory of her is still very much alive in my mind. For every bottle of Chlorox or pizza that I see, reminds me of my dear friend, Sadie.

Evaluating Writing: Answering Questions in a Group

This book aims in part at helping you become a reliable critic, someone who can make accurate judgments about writing. It is important for you to become a reliable critic so you can make decisions about your own writing with confidence. To that end, the activity in this section gives you practice evaluating writing and supporting the decisions you make.

For this exercise, you will answer questions about the previous descriptive pieces written by students. You will work in groups of three. Each group should read all the previous essays written by students and then decide on one essay to evaluate (or evaluate the essay your instructor assigns).

The members of each group will make decisions about this essay by answering the evaluation questions that follow. One member should be designated the recorder. That person's job is to record the answers the group settles on. If group members disagree, they should discuss the areas of disagreement until they are of one mind. If no agreement is reached, the recorder should note the differing views and reasons for them.

Once each group has finished its evaluation, one member should report the group's findings to the rest of the class. If any class members disagree with some or all of a group's evaluation, the areas of disagreement should be noted and discussed.

This activity will give you experience making, supporting, and discussing assessments about writing. And all of this will give you improved awareness of reader reactions and of what does and does not succeed in writing—awarenesses you can bring to the next essay you write.

Evaluation Questions

1. Is it clear who or what is being described and what the writer's impression of the subject is?
2. Is the impression specific enough?
3. Is the detail adequate? Are all generalizations supported? If not, where is detail needed?
4. Is the detail relevant? If not, where is there a relevance problem?
5. Are there any points you do not understand? If so, which ones?
6. Does the description have an introduction and stated thesis? If it does, are they well handled? If it does not, is this a problem?
7. Is the conclusion satisfying?
8. By what organizational principle are the details arranged? Is this arrangement logical and effective? If not, what changes should be made?
9. Are the relationships among ideas clearly and logically expressed? If not, what problems are there?
10. In general, is the word choice specific yet simple and economical?
11. Are there any clichés that should be revised for fresh expression?
12. Is there adequate sentence variety? If not, where is sentence variety needed?
13. Does the writer use enough concrete sensory detail to create effective mental images? Are there any places where concrete sensory detail is needed? Are there any places where there is too much concrete sensory detail?
14. Is the essay carefully edited?

Essay Topics

Here are some suggestions for descriptive essay topics. They will require some shaping and narrowing, but any one of them can be turned into a suitable topic. If none of these appeals to you, perhaps they will suggest other, related topics that you would like to write about.

1. In "The Sounds of the City" (p. 140) Tuite captures the flavor of big-city life by recording the sounds heard in a 24-hour period. Try capturing the essence of some locale by relying predominantly on one sense.

2. In "My Friend, Albert Einstein" (p. 144) Hoffmann relies heavily on anecdotes to convey his impression of Einstein. Describe a person and convey a dominant impression by using anecdotes.

3. When Hoffmann describes Einstein as a simple man, he presents him as different from what most people might think. In fact, when he describes Einstein as a simple man despite his genius, he describes something that distinguishes Einstein from most others. Describe a person and convey what sets that person apart from many others.

4. When Roberts describes Leacock (p. 148), he shows the man in several different roles. Convey your impression of someone by showing that person in several roles.

5. In "A Garden That Welcomes Strangers" (p. 142) Lacy describes a garden before and after a major change. Like Lacy, describe some place before and after a change.

6. Like Roberts, write a piece describing the most unforgettable character you've met.

7. Describe your favorite (or most hated or feared) teacher.

8. Describe the most popular student in your high school.

9. Describe the place you go when you are seeking solitude.

10. Describe a room where you live.

11. Describe the student cafeteria during the rush hour.

12. Describe your favorite outdoor spot on campus.

13. Describe the view from a rooftop or window.

14. Describe a place or scene where you work.

15. Describe a person you admire greatly (or one you have little respect for).

16. Describe your campus library's reference room.

17. Describe a child busy at play.

18. Describe an employer or someone you work with.

19. Describe a bus, air, or train terminal.

20. Describe a schoolyard at recess, before school, or after school.

21. Describe your favorite night spot.

22. Describe someone you know who is eccentric (or daring or shy).

23. Describe a person who has had a lasting impact on you.

24. Describe your living room after you have thrown a big party.

Writing Strategies

Developing an approach to writing that is both effective and efficient involves experimentation. As explained earlier, you must first identify what you currently do when you write, and then you must determine which facets of your process need to be improved. Finally, you must try alternative approaches to the less successful features of your process, evaluate their effectiveness, and then go on to experiment further if necessary.

Chapters 1–3 and the exercise on p. 139 suggest techniques you can experiment with. In addition, the following strategies for generating a descriptive topic and supporting detail include techniques you can try.

Topic Selection

To decide on a person or place to describe and on your impression of your subject, fill in the blanks in the following sentence: _____ is the most _____ I know. Fill in the first blank with a person or place (your subject), and fill in the second blank with a characteristic (your impression). You will get something like "The student cafeteria at noon is the most hectic place I know," which will lead to a description of the hectic nature of the cafeteria at 12:00. Or you might get something like "Uncle Nathan is the most eccentric person I know," which will lead to a description of Uncle Nathan's eccentricity. Be careful to use specific words to fill in your blanks and to pick manageable subjects, so you do not end up with something too broad or vague, something like "Wichita is the most interesting city I know." All of *Wichita* is too much to handle in one essay, and *interesting* is too vague to be useful to the reader.

If you are describing a place, select one that you can visit and observe. If this is not possible, select one that is fresh and detailed in your memory. Otherwise, you may not have at hand enough detail to write an adequately developed essay.

If you have trouble settling on the dominant impression your description will convey about your subject, complete the sentences on p. 136.

Idea Generation

1. List writing can be an effective idea-generation technique for a descriptive essay. Listing is easiest to do when describing a place if you make your list at that place. If you are describing a person, you may wish to view the person before describing physical appearance and mannerisms. As you write your list, do not worry about effective sentences, mental images, organization, mechanics, and such; simply get down as best you can and as quickly as you can the details you believe should be included in your description. Try to select details that convey your impression. You would not, for example, list your grandmother's sparkling eyes if you wished to show her as intimidating. But you might want to list her hands gnarled with arthritis.

2. When you write your list, you may wish to avoid describing and instead just note the points you will cover, with a reminder of the approach you will take to the description. For example, a list for an essay about your intimidating grandmother might read, in part, like this:

gnarled hands
wrinkled, scary face
powerful voice
won't take no for an answer
pinches my shoulder when angry
fearsome eyes

Later, when you draft and revise, you can decide how to express these details descriptively.

A Postwriting Evaluation of Your Process

The following questions should be answered after you have written your descriptive essay. They are meant to help you evaluate the effectiveness of the process you used and help you decide what changes to experiment with the next time you write. Because other writers can suggest strategies that may work well for you, discuss your responses with your classmates and instructor.

1. When you wrote your description, what stages of the process went smoothly? (Remember, *smoothly* does not necessarily mean *quickly*.)
2. Did anything work well enough to repeat in the future? If so, what?
3. Was there anything about writing the essay that was unreasonably difficult and/or time-consuming? If so, what was it, and why do you think it was a problem? Has this been a problem in the past?
4. What stage(s) of your process will you handle differently next time? What will you do? Why?
5. Are you more comfortable writing now than you have been in the past? Why or why not?

6
Narration

"So tell me what happened." When someone says that, we respond by telling a story—by relating the events that occurred, where they occurred, when they occurred, and who was involved. In writing, such a story is called a *narration* or *narrative essay*.

Detail

Let's say two friends run into each other on campus and one says to the other, "What happened? You look terrible." Then the second friend replies, "I just went through the worst registration ever." The conversation that might follow reveals much about what it means to tell a story.

   John: What happened? You look terrible.

Marsha: I just went through the worst registration ever.

   John: Why? What happened?

Marsha: Well, I stood in line for 20 minutes, and when it was my turn I got turned away because I hadn't paid a library fine. So I went to the library and paid my $1.50, went back to registration, and stood in line for 20 minutes again, except this time when it was my turn the woman at the desk gave me a hard time.

John: Why? What did she say?

Marsha: She told me I needed the biology chairman's permission to take this biology course I wanted. I told her he already said it was OK, but she made a big deal about how I needed his signature on my schedule card. I got ticked and told her off.

John: Why so angry?

Marsha: Well, I'd already wasted over a half hour and didn't have one class scheduled, and I wasn't crazy about trying to run down Dr. Ingles all over again. Anyhow, I went to the biology department and got Ingles' signature. By the way, I saw Lorenzo there and he's leaving for Florida on break.

John: Forget Lorenzo and finish the story.

Marsha: Yeah, well I went back to registration, stood in line again, for 10 minutes this time, and you won't believe what happened when it was my turn.

John: I give up, what?

Marsha: The same woman was there and she told me to wait a minute—oh I forgot to tell you, this woman told me before that I better straighten out my act or I'd be in trouble.

John: Wait a minute—when? The first or second time? You're losing me.

Marsha: The second time, when I told her off. Anyway, when I got to her desk . . .

John: The third time?

Marsha: Yeah. When I got to her desk, she told me to wait—like I hadn't already done enough of that, you know. So I waited, and next thing I know, she's dragging some security guard over to me. And you know what he says?

John: Will you tell the story already?

Marsha: He tells me that unless I can act like an adult, I won't be allowed to register.

John: Why did he say that?

Marsha: I guess because when she made me get Ingles' signature, I called her a dumb broad.

John: Why didn't you tell me that before? Sounds to me like you got what you deserved.

Marsha: Yeah, I suppose.

This conversation between John and Marsha raises several points about effective narration. First, a good narration must include all the significant events. When Marsha neglects to tell John why she was angry, he asks her to supply this information. When she neglects to say that she called the woman a dumb broad, John is annoyed.

Second, an effective narration does not bring up insignificant points. When Marsha starts to speak of Lorenzo, John tells her to get back to the matter at hand.

Third, good narration follows a logical time sequence. When Marsha confuses the time she was told to straighten out her act and the time she got to the desk, John has to ask a question to get things clear.

Fourth, interesting narration does not drag on; its pace is brisk. When Marsha begins to bog down, John tells her to move the story along.

Finally, good narration usually has a point that can be drawn from the story. John and Marsha both conclude that she acted badly and deserved to be chastised by the security guard.

The dialogue between John and Marsha illustrates the following points about narration:

1. All the significant details must be supplied.
2. Insignificant or irrelevant details should be left out.
3. The story should be presented in a logical, understandable time sequence.
4. The story should be paced so it does not drag.
5. The story should make a point or lead to a conclusion the reader/listener can draw.

Selecting Detail

The five points made so far about narration, the ones in the box above, really pertain to the selection of details to include in your story and the order to present these details in.

Let's start with what details to include. When deciding what to include in your narration, you can answer the standard journalistic questions: *who? what? when? where? why? how?* Most readers will want to know what happened, when it happened, where it happened, why it happened, how it happened, and who was involved. If you are careful to respond to each of these questions, then you are likely to include all the significant information.

Be careful, however, that as you provide all the significant details, you do not get carried away and include insignificant ideas that are not really pertinent to the who, what, when, where, why, and how of your narration. If you do, your reader will surely grow impatient. We have all seen movies that seem to drag because of unnecessary detail, action, explanation, or dialogue. Such movies are boring. To avoid boring your reader, maintain a brisk pace by including only the significant details.

In addition to determining your significant details, you must determine which of these details require major emphasis, which require minor emphasis, and which need something in between. For some narrations, the who and where may deserve extended treatment, while the why, when, and how merit less development. Yet other narrations may dictate detailed discussion of the why. Which details you emphasize will be determined by the purpose of your narration and your audience.

Purpose

The detail you include and the journalistic questions you emphasize will be influenced by your purpose. Remember, a narrative essay can do more than tell a story. It can make a point with that story for a particular purpose. Let's say you plan to tell the story of the time your psychology teacher was unfair to you. If your purpose is to vent your anger, you may focus on yourself and your feelings. If your purpose is to convince your reader that students need a grievance procedure, you might focus more on what happened. If your purpose is to inform your reader that even the best of profs have their bad moments, you might emphasize the what and why of the event and the instructor involved. For this purpose, you might also describe the instructor as a typically fair one, which is something you would not do for the first two purposes.

To establish a purpose for your narration, try asking yourself the following questions:

1. What points can I make with my narration?
2. Of these points, which one point (or two closely related points) do I want to make?
3. Of these points, which will interest, inform, or persuade a reader?
   Note: The above questions can help you discover what point(s) your narration can make. The following questions can help you define your purpose for making your point.
4. Does my point allow me to share part of my experience with a reader?
5. Does my point allow me to inform my reader? If so, of what?
6. Does my point allow me to persuade my reader? If so, of what?

Audience

Like your purpose, your audience will influence the detail you include and the journalistic questions you emphasize. Let's return to the story of the psychology professor who was unfair to you to illustrate this. If your reader knows little about the workings of a college classroom, you might include more explanatory detail than if your reader is currently attending the university. If your audience is a classmate who witnessed the incident, you might emphasize what happened less than if your audience is someone who did not witness the event.

To settle on an audience for your narration, you can ask yourself the following questions:

1. Who would be interested in my story?
2. Who could learn something from my story?
3. Who could be influenced by my story?
4. Who would I like to share my experience with?

Once you have identified your audience, you must assess the nature of that audience so you know what kind of detail your reader requires. The following questions can help you here:

1. Are there any of the who, what, when, where, why, how questions my reader already knows the answers to?
2. Does my reader have any strong feelings that will influence reaction to my narration?
3. What must my reader know to appreciate my point?
4. Has my reader had an experience similar to the one I am narrating?

Arranging Detail

Narrative writers must settle on an appropriate, effective arrangement for their details. Because you are telling a story, your details will follow a certain time sequence—that is, they will have a certain *chronology*.

You might be thinking that detail arrangement is handled in a rather obvious way: simply start with what happened first, move to what happened next, and so forth. Well, you are right; often this is precisely the time sequence followed. However, this is not the only chronology available to the writer of narration. It is also possible to begin at the end and flash back to the first event and proceed in chronological order from there. Similarly, the writer can begin somewhere in the middle of a story and then flash back to the beginning.

Let's say I want to narrate the trauma of preparing for and taking a final exam. If I want to begin with the first event and move chronologically, I might begin this way:

> I filled the kettle with water enough to keep me in coffee for the rest of the night, put two fresh packs of Marlboro's on the desk next to my butane lighter, opened a 16-ounce bag of Fritos, arranged my statistics notes next to my text, and I was ready to make sense of T-scores and chi-squares.

After this opening sentence, I would describe the night of study, explaining events in the order they occurred. Then I would move on to the next morning and how I felt on the way to the exam. From there I would narrate the events of the exam.

But I could follow a different time sequence: I could begin in the middle.

> The alarm jarred me from a fitful 3 hours' sleep, and I knew the time for preparation was gone. In just 2 hours I would be sweating over my statistics exam. "Well, old girl,"

> I tried to reassure myself, "you certainly studied hard enough." Yes, I put in some kind of night preparing for the test.

From here I could flash back to narrate the night of study, return to the time I woke up, and move through the events up to and including the exam.

Or I could start at the end in this fashion:

> As I left the classroom, I knew I would be lucky to get a C− on my stat exam. Anything higher would call for divine intervention. Yet, it wasn't like I hadn't prepared for the test.

From this point I could flash back to the night of study and detail the events chronologically up to and including the exam.

The fact that narration has a logical chronology that is readily recognized by the reader can greatly influence the organization of a narrative piece. It is possible, for example, to omit topic sentences. Topic sentences are devices the writer uses to help the reader recognize the logical grouping of ideas. These organizational features give details an understandable, logical presentation. With narration, however, it is not always necessary or desirable to use topic sentences because the chronology is often enough to hold details together and give them a logical presentation. Once the reader grasps the time sequence at work, he or she easily understands why ideas are grouped and presented in the order that they are: they follow the governing chronology.

It is also possible to write a narrative essay without traditional paragraphs of introduction and conclusion. This is particularly true when the events in the narration speak so well for themselves that no formal working up to them (introduction) or tying off of them (conclusion) is necessary. Often, however, writers of narration feel the need for an introductory remark, so they precede their narration with a one- or two-sentence introduction before presenting the first chronological event. Sometimes this preliminary material presents the point of the narration.

Similarly, instead of a concluding paragraph, writers may tie things off with a brief one- or two-sentence closing, which may draw a conclusion from the narration or present something that occurred after the events narrated.

This is not to say that narration cannot have an introduction with thesis and a concluding paragraph. In fact, there are several narrative pieces in this chapter that follow that form successfully. For an example of narration that does have a formal introduction, stated thesis, and conclusion, read "My Not-So-Brilliant Debut," on p. 178.

Finally, narrative writers sometimes comment on the significance of aspects of their narrations. Sometimes an event, person, location, or time holds a significance that is not obvious from the story, or a writer may wish to underscore something in the story. This can be handled a number of ways. The writer can state the significance in the thesis, in the introductory remarks, or in the conclusion. Or the writer can state the significance at a logical point in the narration. "Shame" on p. 173 includes several comments on the significance of aspects of the narration.

Using Conversation

In a narrative essay, what people had to say can be important to the advancement and meaning of the story. For this reason, you should know how to punctuate conversation.

There is another reason writers use conversation: it can add vitality to an essay. To appreciate this, consider the following two sentences:

The coach shouted that we should get in there and hustle.
The coach shouted at us, "Get in there and hustle!"

The second sentence has more power than the first because the coach's exact words appear. As a result, this sentence will have greater impact on the reader and create more interest.

Typically, sentences that contain conversation have two parts: a part that notes what was said, and a part that indicates who did the speaking. If the spoken words come before the statement of who spoke, the sentence looks like this:

"Get out of here while you have the chance," the stranger warned.

1. Spoken words are enclosed in quotation marks.
2. Spoken words are followed by a comma, which appears before the final quotation marks. If a question is asked, then a question mark is used:

   "What chance do I have?" Joyce wondered.

3. The first of the words showing who spoke begins with a lower-case letter unless it is a proper noun (such as *Ed*) or a word always capitalized (such as *I*).

If the statement of who spoke comes before the words spoken, the sentence looks like this:

Alex responded quietly, "My sister is the one to blame."

1. The statement of who spoke is followed by a comma.
2. The spoken words appear in quotation marks.
3. The first of the spoken words is capitalized.
4. The spoken words are followed by a period, which appears before the final quotation marks.

If the spoken words come both before and after the statement of who spoke, the sentence will look like one of the following:

"I wish I knew," Paulette sighed, "why I always end up doing most of the work."
"Please be here by 8:00," Dad cautioned. "We don't want to get a late start."

1. The first and second groups of spoken words appear inside separate sets of quotation marks.
2. The first group of spoken words is followed by a comma.
3. If the first group of spoken words is not a sentence, a comma appears after the statement of who spoke.
4. If the first group of spoken words is not a sentence, the second group of spoken words does not begin with a capital letter.
5. If the first group of spoken words forms a sentence, the statement of who spoke is followed by a period, and the second group of spoken words begins with a capital letter.
6. The second group of spoken words is followed by a period, which appears inside the final quotation marks.

When the spoken words form a question, a question mark is used instead of the period or comma after the spoken words.

Malcolm asked, "Where did you park my van?"
"When is the last day of the book sale?" Carla questioned.
"Can we go now," Sis asked, "or do we still have to wait for Joe?"

1. In each case above, the question mark replaces the period or comma because the spoken words form a question.
2. The question mark appears inside the quotation marks.

When the entire sentence, rather than just the spoken words, is forming the question, the question mark appears outside of the quotation marks.

Can you believe that Professor Golden said, "If you want, we will postpone the test until Monday"?

The question mark is outside the quotation marks because the entire sentence, not the spoken words, forms the question.

When you use quotation marks to signal the use of conversation, be careful that you really do have spoken words. Notice the two sentences below.

Diane announced that she was quitting her job to attend school full-time.
Diane announced, "I'm quitting my job to attend school full-time."

1. While it is tempting to use quotation marks in the first sentence, no spoken words appear there.
2. The second sentence does have spoken words, so quotation marks are necessary.

There are two other points to make about using conversation. First, avoid using the vague *said* or *asked* in the statement of who spoke unless these words are the logical choice. Instead be more precise to increase the vitality of your writing. Below is a list of some substitutions for *said* and *asked*.

responded	whispered	explained
replied	whimpered	questioned
shouted	announced	inquired
cried	blurted out	wondered
snapped		

Finally, a person's thoughts are often punctuated the same way as spoken words.

Joshua thought to himself, "I'm sure I can win this event if I get a fast start."

Points to Remember about Narration
1. Your narration should make a specific point that is stated or strongly implied.
2. Detail selection is based on the answers to the who, what, when, where, why, how questions. Which details are emphasized is determined by the nature of the story, the writer's purpose, and the audience.
3. To hold interest, the story should be well paced and free of extraneous detail.
4. Detail is arranged chronologically, with or without flashbacks.
5. A formal introduction, stated thesis, topic sentences, and/or a concluding paragraph may or may not appear.
6. When necessary for emphasis or clarity, the writer can interrupt the narration to comment on the significance of a part of the narrative.
7. Narrative writers frequently use conversation to advance the story, bring out an important point, and/or add liveliness.

Exercise: Narration

1. Decide on a story you would like to tell. If you have trouble thinking of a story, consider the following subject areas:
   a. an embarrassing moment
   b. a surprising occurrence
   c. an incident in school
   d. an unusual evening out
   e. a frightening event
   f. a time you learned an important lesson
   g. a memorable family gathering

   2 pages
   don't allow others anxiety to inhibit yourself

2. What point could your narration make?
3. Decide on a purpose for your narration. You can do this by answering the questions on p. 164.
4. Establish an audience for your narration and assess the nature of that audience. You can do this by answering the two sets of questions on p. 165.
5. Which of the journalistic questions should receive major emphasis?
6. Write correctly punctuated sentences using conversation, according to the guidelines given:
   a. Write a sentence you have heard spoken on campus this week. Place the exact words first and the person who did the speaking second.
   b. Rewrite the sentence you wrote for (a) above, but this time place the exact words after the mention of the person who did the speaking.
   c. Write a sentence you have heard in a restaurant. Place exact words before and after the mention of who did the speaking.

Reading Narration

Below are three very different narrations by professional authors. As you read them, observe what detail is selected, what detail is emphasized, and how the detail is arranged. Also, determine what point or points can be drawn from each narration. After each selection, there are questions that raise points about narrative technique.

Coping with Santa Claus

Delia Ephron

Julie had turned 8 in October and as Christmas approached, Santa Claus was more and more on her mind. During the week before Christmas, every night she announced to her father, "I know who really brings the presents. You do!" Then, waiting a moment, she added, "Right?"

Jerry didn't answer. Neither he nor I, her stepmother, was sure she really wanted the truth. We suspected she did, but couldn't bring ourselves to admit it to her. And we both felt uncomfortable saying something hedgy. Something pretentious. Something like, "But Santa does exist, dear. He exists in spirit—in the spirit of giving in all of us." That sounded like some other parents in some other house with some other child.

I actually resented Julie for putting us on the spot. Wasn't the truth about Santa something one learned from a classmate? The same classmate who knows a screwed-up version of the facts of life. Or else from a know-it-all older sister—as I did. Mine sneaked into my room on Christmas Eve, woke me and said, "Go into the hall and look. You'll see who really puts out the presents."

There was another problem. Jerry and I were reluctant to give up Santa Claus ourselves. We got to tell Julie and her younger brother, Adam, to put out the cookies in case Santa was hungry. We made a fuss about the fire being out in the fireplace so he wouldn't get burned. We issued a few threats about his list of good children and bad. It was all part of the tension and thrill of Christmas Eve—the night the fantasy comes true. And that fantasy of a fat jolly man who flies through the sky in a sleigh drawn by reindeer and arrives via chimney with presents—that single belief says everything about the innocence of children. How unbearable to lose it. For them and for us. So Jerry and I said nothing. And the next night Julie announced it again.

Christmas Eve Julie appeared with a sheet of yellow, lined paper. At the top she had written, "If you are real, sign here." It was, she said, a letter to Santa. She insisted that on this letter each of us—her father, Adam and I—write the words "Santa Claus," so if Santa were to sign it, she could compare our handwriting with his. Then she would know she had not been tricked.

Jerry signed. I signed. Adam, who was 5 and couldn't write, gave up after the letter "S." Julie folded the paper into quarters, wrote "Santa Claus" on the outside and stuck it on a ledge inside the chimney along with two Christmas cookies.

After much fuss, Julie and Adam were tucked into bed. Jerry and I put out the presents. We were not sure what to do about the letter.

After a short discussion, and mostly because we couldn't resist, we opted for deceit. Jerry took the note and, in the squiggliest printing imaginable, wrote "Merry Christmas, Santa Claus." He put the note back in the fireplace and ate the cookies.

The next morning, very early, about 6, we heard Julie and Adam tear down the hall. Jerry and I, in bed, listened for the first ecstatic reactions to the presents. Suddenly, we heard a shriek. "He's real! He's real! He's really real!!!!" The door to our room flew open. "He's REAL!!!" she shouted. Julie showed us the paper with the squiggly writing.

Somehow, this was not what we had bargained for. I had expected some modicum of disbelief—at least a "Dad, is this for real?"

Julie clasped the note to her chest. Then she dashed back to the presents.

That afternoon, our friend Deena came over to exchange gifts. "Santa Claus is real," said Julie.

"Oh," said Deena.

"I know for sure, for really, really sure. Look!" And Julie produced the proof.

Just then the phone rang. Knowing it was a relative calling with Christmas greetings, Julie rushed to answer it. "Santa Claus is real," I heard her say to my sister Nora, the same sister who had broken the bad news about Santa Claus to me 30 years ago. Julie handed me the phone.

"What is this about?" asked Nora.

I told her the story, trying to make it as funny as possible, hoping she wouldn't notice how badly Jerry and I had handled what I was beginning to think of as "the Santa issue." It didn't work.

"We may have made a mistake here," said Nora, diplomatically including herself in the mess.

"You're telling me!" I said. "Do you think there's any chance Julie will forget all this?" That was what I really wanted, of course—for the whole thing to go away.

"I doubt it," said Nora.

We had a wonderful day—good food, good presents, lots of visitors. Then it was bedtime.

"Dad?" said Julie, as he tucked her in.

"What?"

"If Santa's real, then Rudolph must be real, too."

"What!"

"If Santa's real—"

"I heard," said Jerry. He sat down on her bed and took a deep breath. "You know, Julie," and then he stopped. I could see he was trying to think of a way, any way, to explain our behavior so it wouldn't sound quite as deceptive, wrong and stupid as it was. But he was stumped.

"Yeah," said Julie.

"I wrote the note," said Jerry.

She burst into tears.

Jerry apologized. He apologized over and over while Julie sobbed into her pillow. He said he was wrong, that he shouldn't have tricked her, that he should have answered her questions about Santa Claus the week before.

Julie sat up in bed. "I thought he was real," she said reproachfully. Then suddenly she leaned over the bed, pulled out a comic from underneath and sat up again. "Can I read for five minutes?" she said.

"Sure," said Jerry.

And that was it. One minute of grief at Santa's death, and life went on.

Jerry and I left Julie's room terribly relieved. I immediately got a craving for leftover turkey and headed for the kitchen. I was putting the bird back in the refrigerator when I heard Adam crying. I went down the hall. The door to his room was open and I heard Julie, very disgusted, say: "Oh, Adam, you don't have to cry! Only babies believe in Santa Claus."

Questions on Technique: "Coping with Santa Claus"

1. "Coping with Santa Claus" does not have an introduction with stated thesis, nor does it have a sentence that states the point of the narration. Still, the point of the narration can be determined from the events and author's commentary. What is that point?
2. Which of the who, what, when, where, why, how questions does Ephron emphasize?
3. Does the narration have a separate introduction and a separate conclusion? How does the author begin and end?
4. In which paragraphs does Ephron explain an event? In which paragraphs does Ephron comment on the significance of an event?
5. Ephron uses conversation in her essay. What does this conversation contribute to the narration?
6. What chronology does Ephron use?
7. What do you judge to be the purpose of Ephron's narration?
8. "Coping with Santa Claus" first appeared in the *New York Times Magazine*. How would you describe her original audience? Why is this audience appropriate for her narration?

Shame

Dick Gregory

I never learned hate at home, or shame. I had to go to school for that. I was about seven years old when I got my first big lesson. I was in love with a little girl named Helene Tucker, a light-complected little girl with pigtails and nice manners. She was always clean and she was smart in school. I think I went to school mostly to look at her. I brushed my hair and even got me a little old handkerchief. It was a lady's handkerchief, but I didn't want Helene to see me wipe my nose on my hand. The pipes were frozen again, there was no water in the house, but I washed my socks and shirt every night. I'd get a pot, and go over to Mr. Ben's grocery store, and stick my pot down into his soda machine. Scoop out some chopped ice. By evening the ice melted to water for washing. I got sick a lot that winter because the fire would go out at night before the clothes were dry. In the morning I'd put them on, wet or dry, because they were the only clothes I had.

Everybody's got a Helene Tucker, a symbol of everything you want. I loved her for her goodness, her cleanliness, her popularity. She'd walk down my street and my brothers and sisters would yell, "Here comes Helene," and I'd rub my tennis sneakers on the back of my pants and wish my hair wasn't so nappy and the white folks' shirt fit me better. I'd run out on the street. If I knew my place and didn't come too close, she'd wink at me and say hello. That was a good feeling. Sometimes I'd follow her all the way home, and shovel the snow off her walk and try to make friends with her

Momma and her aunts. I'd drop money on her stoop late at night on my way back from shining shoes in the taverns. And she had a Daddy, and he had a good job. He was a paper hanger.

I guess I would have gotten over Helene by summertime, but something happened in that classroom that made her face hang in front of me for the next twenty-two years. When I played the drums in high school it was for Helene and when I broke track records in college it was for Helene and when I started standing behind microphones and heard applause I wished Helene could hear it, too. It wasn't until I was twenty-nine years old and married and making money that I really got her out of my system. Helene was sitting in that classroom when I learned to be ashamed of myself.

It was on a Thursday. I was sitting in the back of the room, in a seat with a chalk circle drawn around it. The idiot's seat, the troublemaker's seat.

The teacher thought I was stupid. Couldn't spell, couldn't read, couldn't do arithmetic. Just stupid. Teachers were never interested in finding out that you couldn't concentrate because you were so hungry, because you hadn't had any breakfast. All you could think about was noontime, would it ever come? Maybe you could sneak into the cloakroom and steal a bite of some kid's lunch out of a coat pocket. A bite of something. Paste. You can't really make a meal out of paste, or put it on bread for a sandwich, but sometimes I'd scoop a few spoonfuls out of the paste jar in the back of the room. Pregnant people get strange tastes. I was pregnant with poverty. Pregnant with dirt and pregnant with smells that made people turn away, pregnant with cold and pregnant with shoes that were never bought for me, pregnant with five other people in my bed and no Daddy in the next room, and pregnant with hunger. Paste doesn't taste too bad when you're hungry.

The teacher thought I was a troublemaker. All she saw from the front of the room was a little black boy who squirmed in his idiot's seat and made noises and poked the kids around him. I guess she couldn't see a kid who mades noises because he wanted someone to know he was there.

It was on a Thursday, the day before the Negro payday. The eagle always flew on Friday. The teacher was asking each student how much his father would give to the Community Chest. On Friday night, each kid would get the money from his father, and on Monday he would bring it to the school. I decided I was going to buy me a Daddy right then. I had money in my pocket from shining shoes and selling papers and whatever Helene Tucker pledged for her Daddy I was going to top it. And I'd hand the money right in. I wasn't going to wait until Monday to buy me a Daddy.

I was shaking, scared to death. The teacher opened her book and started calling our names alphabetically.

"Helene Tucker?"

"My Daddy said he'd give two dollars and fifty cents."

"That's very nice, Helene. Very, very nice indeed."

That made me feel pretty good. It wouldn't take too much to top that.

I had almost three dollars in dimes and quarters in my pocket. I stuck my hand in my pocket and held onto the money, waiting for her to call my name. But the teacher closed her book after she called everybody else in the class.

I stood up and raised my hand.

"What is it now?"

"You forgot me."

She turned toward the blackboard. "I don't have time to be playing with you, Richard."

"My Daddy said he'd . . ."

"Sit down, Richard, you're disturbing the class."

"My Daddy said he'd give . . . fifteen dollars."

She turned around and looked mad. "We are collecting this money for you and your kind, Richard Gregory. If your Daddy can give fifteen dollars you have no business being on relief."

"I got it right now, I got it right now, my Daddy gave it to me to turn in today, my Daddy said . . ."

"And furthermore," she said, looking right at me, her nostrils getting big and her lips getting thin and her eyes opening wide, "we know you don't have a Daddy."

Helene Tucker turned around, her eyes full of tears. She felt sorry for me. Then I couldn't see her too well because I was crying, too.

"Sit down, Richard."

And I always thought the teacher kind of liked me. She always picked me to wash the blackboard on Friday, after school. That was a big thrill, it made me feel important. If I didn't wash it, come Monday the school might not function right.

"Where are you going, Richard?"

I walked out of school that day, and for a long time I didn't go back very often. There was shame there.

Now there was shame everywhere. It seemed like the whole world had been inside that classroom, everyone had heard what the teacher had said, everyone had turned around and felt sorry for me. There was shame in going to the Worthy Boys Annual Christmas Dinner for you and your kind, because everybody knew what a worthy boy was. Why couldn't they just call it the Boys Annual Dinner, why'd they have to give it a name? There was shame in wearing the brown and orange and white plaid mackinaw the welfare gave to 3,000 boys. Why'd it have to be the same for everybody so when you walked down the street the people could see you were on relief? It was a nice warm mackinaw and it had a hood, and my Momma beat me and called me a little rat when she found out I stuffed it in the bottom of a pail full of garbage way over on Cottage Street. There was shame in running over to Mister Ben's at the end of the day and asking for his rotten peaches, there was shame in asking Mrs. Simmons for a spoonful of sugar, there was shame in running out to meet the relief truck. I hated that truck, full of food for you and your kind. I ran into the house and hid when it came. And then I started to sneak through alleys, to take the long way home so people going into White's Eat Shop wouldn't see me. Yeah, the whole world heard the teacher that day, we all know you don't have a Daddy.

Questions on Technique: "Shame"

1. What sentence begins the actual narration?
2. What two purposes does the material before the opening of the narration serve? *subject & setting*
3. This narration includes explanatory detail. For example, the author departs from his narration to explain why he ate paste and how he managed to wash his clothes. What other examples of such explanation can you find?
4. What purpose do the explanations that depart from the narrative serve?
5. The author at times comments on the significance of certain aspects of his narration. For example, he says, "Everybody's got a Helene Tucker, a symbol of everything you want." What other such commentary appears in the piece?
6. This narration has conversation in it. Why is this an effective technique?
7. What points is the author making with this narration? Are the points stated or implied?
8. What kind of conclusion is used? Is it effective? Why?
9. In "Shame" we are not told why the teacher humiliated Gregory. How do you account for this? Is this a strength or a weakness in the narration? Why?
10. What would you judge to be the purpose of Gregory's narration?

From "University Days"

James Thurber

I passed all the other courses that I took at my university, but I could never pass botany. This was because all botany students had to spend several hours a week in a laboratory looking through a microscope at plant cells, and I could never see through a microscope. I never once saw a cell through a microscope. This used to enrage my instructor. He would wander around the laboratory pleased with the progress all the students were making in drawing the involved and, so I am told, interesting structure of flower cells, until he came to me. I would just be standing there. "I can't see anything," I would say. He would begin patiently enough, explaining how anybody can see through a microscope, but he would always end up in a fury, claiming that I could *too* see through a microscope but just pretended that I couldn't. "It takes away from the beauty of flowers anyway," I used to tell him. "We are not concerned with beauty in this course," he would say. "We are concerned solely with what I may call the *mechanics* of flars." "Well," I'd say, "I can't see anything." "Try it just once again," he'd say, and I would put my eye to the microscope and see nothing at all, except now and again a nebulous milky substance—a phenomenon of maladjustment. You were supposed to see a vivid, restless clockwork of sharply defined plant cells. "I see what looks like a lot of milk," I would tell him. This, he claimed, was the result of my not having adjusted the microscope properly, so he would readjust it for me, or rather, for himself. And I would look again and see milk.

I finally took a deferred pass, as they called it, and waited a year and tried again. (You had to pass one of the biological sciences or you couldn't graduate.) The professor had come back from vacation brown as a berry, bright-eyed, and eager to explain cell-structure again to his classes. "Well," he said to me, cheerily, when we met in the first laboratory hour of the semester, "we're going to see cells this time, aren't we?" "Yes, sir," I said. Students to right of me and to left of me and in front of me were seeing cells; what's more, they were quietly drawing pictures of them in their notebooks. Of course, I didn't see anything.

"We'll try it," the professor said to me, grimly, "with every adjustment of the microscope known to man. As God is my witness, I'll arrange this glass so that you see cells through it or I'll give up teaching. In twenty-two years of botany, I—" He cut off abruptly for he was beginning to quiver all over, like Lionel Barrymore,[1] and he genuinely wished to hold onto his temper; his scenes with me had taken a great deal out of him.

So we tried it with every adjustment of the microscope known to man. With only one of them did I see anything but blackness or the familiar lacteal opacity, and that time I saw, to my pleasure and amazement, a variegated constellation of flecks, specks, and dots. These I hastily drew. The instructor, noting my activity, came back from an adjoining desk, a smile on his lips and his eyebrows high in hope. He looked at my cell drawing. "What's that?" he demanded, with a hint of a squeal in his voice. "That's what I saw," I said. "You didn't, you didn't, you *didn't!*" he screamed, losing control of his temper instantly, and he bent over and squinted into the microscope. His head snapped up. "That's your eye!" he shouted. "You've fixed the lens so that it reflects! You've drawn your eye!"

Questions on Technique: From "University Days"

1. What sentence begins the actual narration?
2. In the first paragraph, Thurber does not narrate one specific happening. Instead he recounts what would always happen when he tried to view plant cells under a microscope. It is not until paragraph 2 that the author relates a

---

[1] A noted American stage, radio, and screen actor (1878–1954).

single, specific occurrence. What is the effect of paragraph 1 and how does it contribute to the narration?

3. Describe the chronology of this narration.
4. Thurber makes effective use of conversation. Comment on the purpose the conversation serves and why it is so effective.
5. Thurber's narration is humorous and entertaining. Do you believe that amusement is the sole purpose of the piece? Explain.
6. Is Thurber's message stated or implied?
7. Which of the who, what, when, where, why, and how questions are emphasized most?
8. In "Shame" we are told the thoughts and feelings of the young Gregory, and the effect is poignant and powerful. In "University Days" we are shown the frustrations and absurdity that are part of college life. How is the effect achieved?
9. Both Gregory and Thurber tell stories about difficulties they experienced in the classroom. Why do you suppose Thurber chose a humorous approach, while Gregory selected a serious one?

Student Writings to Read and Evaluate

Below are several narrative essays written by students. While the quality of these pieces varies, each of them has some real strengths, and each has some weaknesses.

As you read each essay, ask yourself what features appeal to you and try to determine why these aspects work well. Also ask yourself which features are not succeeding and try to determine why there is a problem and how that problem can be solved. If you pay attention to the ways other student writers handle their writing tasks, you can discover techniques to incorporate into your writing and pitfalls to avoid.

In addition, your careful evaluation of these writings will force you to make many judgments about what you read, and it will require you to back up your judgments with specific evidence from the essays. This is of the highest importance, for once you can make accurate judgments about other people's writing, you will find it easier to make the same kinds of decisions about your *own* writing. That is, once you have become a reliable critic, you can feel confident in your ability to determine accurately what is and is not working in your own essays.

My Not-So-Brilliant Debut

It was summer, and like a lot of 14-year-olds I was playing baseball. This particular game was going on like most of our games that year, with me sitting on the bench and my team losing in the field. Our coach, Mr. Hornsby, asked the pitching coach, Mr. Mostoy, "What happened? In practice those guys were throwing good curve balls and now nothing." Nervously, Mr. Mostoy shrugged his shoulders and peered at the bench, looking for a relief pitcher.

When our pitcher, John, gave up yet another home run, Mr. Mostoy went to the mound and yanked him. When he returned to the dugout and saw that I was the only eligible pitcher left, he let out a deep, painful sigh and barked, "Jefferson, warm up. I'm putting you in." He turned and jammed his hands into his pockets as I jumped eagerly to my feet and said, "Thanks, Coach!" He grumbled over his shoulder, "Don't thank me; you're all I've got left."

Slightly shaken by that remark but still enthusiastic about the assignment, I went out to the mound. I threw a few practice balls which sliced the air with speed and accuracy. Then the batter approached the plate, and things began to change.

I could feel the nervousness begin in my stomach and slowly spread through my body until it reached my pitching arm. My palms began to sweat, which made the ball slippery and hard to handle. The first ball got away from me and hit the batter on the wrist. Angrily, he threw the bat on the ground and advanced to first, massaging his wrist all the way. The next batter met a similar fate, and before long the crowd began to yell, "Throw the bum out." Luckily for me, the coach didn't get a chance to throw me out after only two pitches. The umpire came to my rescue and declared, "A whitewash has been achieved, and the continuation of this game is pointless."

Back in the dugout, the coach leered at me and snapped, "Jefferson, sit down and shut up." Even though I think I set a record for the shortest pitching career in history, my moments on the mound were among the most exciting in my adolescent life.

Lots of Locks

I was 12 years old at the time. It was the summer before I was to enter junior high school. I sat in the beautician's chair, awaiting the first haircut of my life. I stared at my long braided hair stretching down the middle of my back, the tip making a relaxed curl at my waist. As far back as I could remember, my hair had always been that long. Even old photographs of me at the age of 3 or 4, showed long locks of hair cascading over my shoulders and covering most of me. What a hastle those locks had been over the years. Most people had nightmares of assailants coming at them with a knife or gun. In my nightmares, I saw my mom coming at me with a wide-tooth comb.

Combing my hair was always such a huge task. I remember my mom standing me on an old wooden kitchen chair. Then she'd start combing. She'd angle the comb at the top of my head, ever so gently, then pull, tug, and yank until the comb made a jerky exit at the ends of my long strands.

"Ow," I'd holler. "That hurts!" "Use the brush," I'd plead.

"Now honey," she'd say calmly, "you know that brush won't get the tangles out."

"I don't care!", I'd start crying, hoping to change her mind.

Of course my whining didn't do a bit of good. My sisters, the brats that they were, hung around just to tease me.

"Whiney Caroliney, Whiney Caroliney," they'd taunt in unison and almost perfect harmony.

I'd cry even harder, and my mom would take a quick swat at them. She'd try to shut me up by cooing.

"Look honey at this big rats' nest I got out of your hair. You know that's what these tangles really are, don't you? If we don't get those buggers out of your hair today, there'll be twice as many in there tomorrow."

I would look at the knotted ball of hair wrapped around the teeth of the comb, with its stragley ends sticking out all over, and my childlike gullibility would lead me to believe her fabrication. When she finished, I imagined what a chicken might feel like after having all its feathers plucked.

I thought about other times when having long hair was a real pain (in a different sense of the word). Some mornings my mom would fix my hair into two long braids. Not only would family and friends give them a tug, but even an occasional stranger could not resist the urge to pull on my braids. It was as impossible as trying to resist the urge to, "squeeze the Charmin." Another hairdo she liked to deck me out in, was the crisscrossing of the two braids on the top of my head. I hated my hair like that. I felt I looked like the old woman in the T.V. series, *I Remember Momma,* (popular in the 50's). Since I was a tomboy, most of the time I just wore my hair in a ponytail. Still my hair would fly around and slap me in the face while playing kick the can, or homerun derby, like a horse's tail swatting flies. I would be glad to get rid of the nuisance. Who wouldn't be? My long locks were way overdue for a trimming.

Finally, the beautician entered the room. She picked up a pair of scissors larger than any I had ever seen. I felt one last, long tug on my hair and heard the muffled cutting sounds of the scissors. My long lifeless braid fell limp to the floor.

"Free at last!", I thought. "No more long tangle sessions," I sighed to myself. "No one would pull on my hair now," I mused. "How happy could any one person be?" I wondered.

At that moment, I felt a tear forming in the corner of my eye and I wondered why.

Seniors in the Night

As we go through life, few of us give much thought to what will become of us should we not be able to care for ourselves in our golden years. I, for one, would not mind living in a boarding home that had the atmosphere of Kay's Boarding Home for the Elderly. I worked for Kay, and I'll never forget the childlike innocence that engulfed the elderly who lived there.

I had the opportunity to work both day and night shifts at Kay's. Day turn consisted of basic care, giving baths, changing beds, light housekeeping, preparation and serving the meals, and making sure nobody slipped out the door to "go home." The patients were pretty much the typical vaguely senile senior citizens. A challenge to the workers' nerves at times, too. As the sun set, the patients would begin to scurry around and slip into PJs and beds. Everyone would be in bed by 9:00 p.m., donning their chameleon skins and waiting for me, the sole employee of midnight turn.

As I clocked in at 11:00 p.m., I knew the night would hold plenty of action for me before the sun would rise up in the morning. The intercom throughout the house let me hear every sound made by any of my 14 charges. Each patient had their own night time sound, so as I would go about my duties I could keep audio tabs on all.

Running up and down the basement stairs doing laundry, I would stop at intervals to listen for the slow, deep rasp of Bertha's snore—the night wouldn't be complete without it.

Working in the kitchen, I would hear the familiar squeak-creak, squeak-creak of the floor boards at the end of the hall indicating that I was right on schedule because Jr. met me each night around midnight to check on the time. "It's 12:15, Jr.," I'd tell him, but still hour by hour Jr. would be up throughout the night checking on the time. He had a phobia of missing breakfast—fat chance. After promising Jr. to wake him first in the morning, I'd give him a hug and tuck him back into bed, for the first of many times of the night.

About a half-hour later I'd see an awkward, eerily shaped shadow coming toward me—it's Uncle Alf taking his bihourly trip to the john. He'd do this all night, I think, so that he could fuss and holler all the next day that he didn't sleep well.

Upon completion of my hourly checks (making sure that no one "checked out" since the previous hour), a slow moving shadow is again making it's way down the hall, only this time it would be Pappy. Always fully attired in overalls, flannel shirt, boots, and a hunter's cap. Pappy was up and at 'em at 4:30 a.m. like clockwork ready for chores. After 5 or 10 minutes of persuasive arguments that there are no farms within hollering distance, he would finally go back to bed. Okay, so I promised that "the eggs had been gathered and the cows had been milked"; they had been—many years ago.

As 7:00 a.m. rolled around I would prepare to leave my little darlings, but not until I'd seen the twinkle in each of their eyes. Most of them would refer to me as "The Girl in the Night," just as if it was my name. Whatever they chose to call me, I can only hope that those who are capable of any memory at all are able to recall me with half the fondness as I have of them. Each of the night stalkers was me—yet to come.

I Learned to March

I can still see it clearly even after all these years. A bright cheerful fourth-grade room filled with thirty eager children of all varieties of body and mind. I can also hear it as if it enveloped me. The music of John Philip Sousa stays with me even today.

She played the records every day, that staunch old woman. Miss

Thompson was a matriarch. She was close to retirement that year, and feared by every third-grader walking the halls of Walker Elementary School. The summer before my fourth school year was one of great anticipation. Miss Thompson was a legend with a bifurcated image. She was feared due to her demanding nature, and respected for her strength. Miss Thompson was crippled. She had survived polio as a child and as a result walked with the aid of a cane and was marked with a deformed left foot and leg. The day those fourth-grade room assignments arrived the phone lines were jammed. Mary called Cindy, Cindy called Susie, and Susie called me. I alone, of all my friends, had been placed in Miss Thompson's class.

I wanted to cry, to scream of the injustice of it all. I knew what lay ahead. I could feel it in every nerve cell of my body. It was not the homework; it was not her demand to perform with above-average capabilities; it was that damned marching!

Everyday through the small glass window of Room 11, the students of Miss Thompson could be seen marching round the room, knees up high, heads back, chests out, marching to the music of "Stars and Stripes Forever." Worse, though, was the fact that the students of Room 11 could see the jeering faces of the crowds in the hallway. They laughed and snickered and even pointed! I could feel the shame even then, reading that small card with her name so stately printed upon it. I knew how I would look to them!

Yet, deep inside of me, slowly nurturing, was a slight sense of titillation. I was an extremely shy child. Having no brothers or sisters and an introverted mother, I too became quiet and reserved. Still, I was curious about this new twist in my life.

I survived the remainder of the summer by doing deep-breathing exercises, and arrived at school on the first day of fourth grade a total nervous wreck. I seated myself in the back of the room, unable at any time to remove my gaze from this silver-haired woman sitting perfectly erect at her desk.

How I learned that first day. I learned of consistent demand topped with a dollop of love; I learned to respect the grace of a woman who had midmorning tea brewed in a cup with a strange heating coil; I learned that indeed my back did feel better if I sat erect in my chair; and I learned to march—with my knees high, my head back, and my chest out, to John Philip Sousa's classic piece, "Stars and Stripes Forever."

Evaluating Writing: Answering Questions

Select one of the previous student writings that you find interesting for its technique, content, and/or potential. Or perhaps your instructor will suggest the piece you should study. Read the essay closely and then answer the evaluation questions that appear below. These questions will help you focus on some of the individual elements that comprise the whole. They will help you appreciate how each aspect of an essay contributes to or detracts from its overall quality. Finally, this close look will expose you to successful techniques you may wish to bring to your own writing and to some less successful techniques to avoid.

1. Are the who, what, where, when, why, and how questions answered adequately? If not, which questions require more attention? Are any points given too much development? Which ones?
2. Is there a clearly stated or implied message to be drawn from the narration?
3. Does the writer interrupt the narration to comment or explain? If so, is this effective? If the writer did not do this, should he or she have? Where and why?
4. Are there any points that you do not understand? If so, which ones?
5. Is conversation used in the narrative? If so, is it appropriate and well handled? If not enough conversation is used, where should it be added?
6. Does the writer use (or omit) an introduction, stated thesis, topic sentences, and concluding paragraph effectively? If not, what problems exist?
7. What chronology is followed? Is it logical and effective? If not, why?
8. Do all the details belong in the paragraphs they appear in? If not, which details do not belong?
9. Are the relationships among ideas logically and clearly expressed? If not, what problems exist?
10. In general, is the word choice specific, economical, and simple? What words, if any, would you revise?
11. Does the writer use concrete sensory detail to create effective mental images? If not, should the writer have done so, and where in the essay is this needed?
12. Are there any clichés that should be revised for fresh expression? If so, which ones?
13. Does the essay have adequate sentence variety? If not, where is sentence variety needed?
14. Is the essay carefully edited?

Essay Topics

Below are ideas for narrative essay topics. If none of them appeals to you, perhaps you can use them as a springboard to a topic you *are* interested in.

1. Relate an occurrence that caused you to change your view of someone or something. Make sure it is clear what your view was both before and after the event. You might also want to indicate why the occurrence caused you to change your view.
2. Tell of an event that had a significant impact on you. Be sure it is clear what the impact was/is. You might also want to tell why the event affected you as it did.
3. Tell a story that describes a single, specific school experience. While it is

not necessary, you may want to use a humorous approach, as Thurber (p. 176) does.

4. Narrate an event or moment that was embarrassing, amusing, distressing, or puzzling to you or someone else.
5. Tell of a time when things did not go as you, or another, expected them to. Be sure it is clear what the expectation was. Comment on why things didn't go as planned.
6. Write a narrative essay about a single, specific job experience you have had.
7. Narrate a childhood memory.
8. Tell the story of your best (or worst) date.
9. Narrate a moment or event that marked a turning point in your life.
10. Tell of a time when you (or another) were treated unjustly.
11. Write an account of the time you were the angriest you have ever been.
12. Tell of an event that caused you to feel regret.
13. Narrate the happiest moment you have had with a friend or member of your family.
14. Relate an incident that caused you to realize something for the first time. Explain what the effect of that realization has been.
15. Tell a story of a time you witnessed (or displayed) courage.
16. Relate a memorable experience you have had in a sports competition.
17. Tell the story of some first-time experience.
18. Write of a time when a friend or relative disappointed you.
19. Write an account of your happiest birthday.
20. Narrate your proudest moment.

Writing Strategies

As you write your narrative essay, continue experimenting to improve your writing process. Chapters 1–3 describe techniques you can try, as does the exercise on p. 170. In addition, the following procedures may prove useful.

Topic Selection

If you are having trouble settling on the story you want to tell, fill in the blanks in one of the following sentences:

1. I'll never forget the time I _____ .

2. I was never so embarrassed as when _____ .

3. The first time I _____ I learned _____ .

Idea Generation

To generate ideas, answer the following questions:

1. Who was involved?
2. What happened?

3. When did it happen?
4. Where did it happen?
5. Why did it happen?
6. What was the effect?
7. Who was affected?
8. How did it happen?
9. Could it happen again?
10. Why is it important?
11. What was learned?
12. Was it expected to happen?

Write out in essay form what happened first, second, third, and so on. Simply begin at the beginning and write through to the last element of the story. Do not worry about grammar, spelling, punctuation, sentence effectiveness, or anything else except getting every occurrence in chronological order. Comment on and/or explain points if it occurs to you to do so, and use conversation when this comes naturally and seems fitting. Do not worry at this point about an introduction, thesis, or conclusion. **First Draft**

After distancing yourself for a time, reread your first draft and consider the following points: **Evaluating the First Draft**

1. Are the who, what, when, where, why, and how questions answered? If any of these have been left out, be sure it is appropriate to leave them out. If the omission is not appropriate, write in the margin of your draft "add where" (or whatever needs to be added).
2. What point or points does your narration make? Across the top of your draft write out the point or points.
3. Once you know what point the narration makes, you are ready to decide which of the who, what, when, where, why, and how questions require major emphasis and which require less detailed treatment. In the margin of your draft, list the questions that deserve special emphasis.
4. If you used conversation in your draft, is it appropriate? Is there enough of it to add vitality, facilitate the narration, or establish character? If you judge you need more conversation, place check marks on your draft at the places conversation should be added.
5. Do you need any comment on or explanations of aspects of your narration beyond what appears in the draft? If so, write "comment" or "explain" at the appropriate points on your draft.
6. The chronology of your draft runs from beginning to end, first event to last. Decide whether this is the chronology you wish to follow. If it is not, on your draft number the elements of your narration in the order you wish them to appear. Be sure the chronology you use is a logical one.

1. Write a second draft from the first, this time making the adjustments you noted on the first draft. Emphasize the points you decided warranted special treatment, add conversation where you designated it was desirable, com- **Revision**

ment and explain where you indicated these were in order, and adjust the chronology, if necessary. Again, do not worry about refinements, grammar, spelling, and so on. Just concentrate on adequate, relevant detail.

2. Read your second draft and decide whether it would benefit from a formal introduction with lead-in and thesis. In part, you can base your decision on whether the point(s) you wrote at the top of the first draft come across clearly. If the point of the narration is not implied strongly enough, you may wish to state the point in a thesis. If you sense a need for an overt statement of the point, or if you feel the need to emphasize an implied message, or if you sense the need for some preliminary sentences before the actual narrative begins, write a formal introduction or an introductory sentence or sentences, whichever seems appropriate.

3. Once again, read your second draft and determine whether you need a formal conclusion. In part, you can base your decision on whether you need to interpret the events of the narration or state a conclusion not previously noted. If you need to interpret or emphasize or draw a conclusion, or if you sense that the last event in the narration does not provide adequate closure, write a conclusion, in sentence or paragraph form—whichever seems better.

4. Now you are ready to polish your prose, supply necessary transitions, check for sentence variety, shape effective sentences, and generally smooth out the rough spots. Before you do this you would be wise to leave your work for a time to clear your head and restore objectivity. When you return to your essay, check the pace—you do not want your narration to drag. One way to avoid this is to eliminate unnecessary detail; another way is to strive for vivid, specific word choice.

5. Many times, writers of narration rely heavily on descriptive writing techniques, particularly when they want to convey a clear sense of where something happened, what the people involved were like, and/or how people felt. If you wish your reader to appreciate any of these points, apply the principles of descriptive writing you learned in the previous chapter.

A Postwriting Evaluation of Your Process

After writing your narrative essay, answer the following questions. They will help you determine the effectiveness of your process and which aspects to retain. In addition, they will help you decide how to experiment the next time you write to discover techniques to replace any unsuccessful ones you used. Share your responses with your teacher and classmates because these writers may have suggestions to offer.

1. When you wrote your narration, what stages of your process went smoothly? (Remember, *smoothly* does not necessarily mean *quickly*.)

2. Did anything work well enough to repeat in the future? If so, what?

3. Was there anything about writing the essay that was unreasonably difficult and/or time-consuming? If so, what was it, and why do you think it was a problem? Has this been a problem in the past?

4. What stage(s) of your process will you handle differently next time? What will you do? Why?

5. Are you more comfortable writing now than you have been in the past? Why or why not?

7
Illustration

An illustration is an example—and nothing can help a reader understand a writer's point better than an example.

Think about a time when you were reading an explanation and feeling unsure that you really understood what the writer meant. Just when you were feeling the most uncertain, you may have come across the words, "for example." Remember how hopeful you felt when you read those words, knowing they were introducing an illustration that would clarify things? And remember how much better you understood the writer's point after you read the example? That is because a well-chosen illustration can crystallize meaning. In short, one carefully selected example can be worth hundreds of words of explanation.

Detail

Illustration is a vital component of clear expression, whether it is written or verbal. Even our most routine communications rely heavily on examples to make their point. Let's say a friend asked you who to take for geology and you replied, "Take Cooper; he's the most reasonable." Well, your friend would probably want you to clarify why Cooper is the most reasonable, and you might explain by providing examples of his reasonableness: "His tests are graded on the curve, he only requires one research paper, and he's always in his office to

Illustration **189**

help students." Even the question "What do you want to do tonight?" can prompt the use of examples. If you replied, "Something relaxing," you would not be as clear as if you added examples: "Something relaxing like a movie or a quiet dinner at Alonzo's."

Illustration provides clarity because it makes the general more specific; it allows the writer to nail down a generalization by providing specific instances of how that generalization is true. Consider, for example, the following four sentences.

> It is not easy today for a young married couple to get off to a good start. Mortgage rates are high, making home ownership almost impossible, so the couple may spend many years in a cramped apartment. Unemployment is high, so many couples cannot find the jobs they need to secure their income. And perhaps most significantly, young marrieds find that financial worries cause significant tensions that strain the marriage bond.

In the above example, the first sentence expresses a generalization. The three sentences after that provide illustrations of the difficulties young married couples can encounter. The examples provide clarification by specifying instances that bear out the generalization. In Chapter 2, when supporting detail was discussed, you were cautioned to *show* rather than *tell* (see p. 41). Very often, illustrations help you show by providing instances to make generalizations concrete.

In addition to providing clarity and concreteness, illustrations add interest to writing. Writing that never goes beyond generalizations is often vague and dull. Yet some carefully chosen examples can lend vitality and create reader interest by bringing things down from the abstract level to a more specific, easily understood one.

Because illustrations add clarity, concreteness, and interest, they are a frequent component of writing, regardless of the dominant method of development. Essays developed primarily with description, narration, comparison and contrast, or any other method can make liberal use of examples. In this chapter, however, our concern will be with using illustration as the primary method of development.

Purpose

The writer's purpose will influence the illustrations used. Say you plan to write an essay that explains the psychological benefits of running. There are a number of reasons you might want to do this. Perhaps you want to influence your reader to take up running, or maybe you want your reader to understand why running is such an important part of your life, or perhaps you wish to make your reader aware that running provides more than physical exercise, or maybe you want your reader to understand what distinguishes running from other forms of exercise.

One way to get at the purpose you want to establish for your writing is to ask yourself the following questions:

1. Do I want to share my reaction to or feeling about my subject?
2. Do I want to help my reader understand why I respond to my subject as I do?
3. Do I want to clarify the nature of my subject?
4. Do I want to convince my reader of something?

Let's return to the essay about the psychological benefits of running to see how these questions can help a writer establish purpose. Say I run 4 miles every day, regardless of the weather, and many of my friends have considered me odd for this. I might want to help my friends understand my dedication to running so they will alter their view of me. Thus, my purpose (as a result of answering question 2 above) could be to illustrate what motivates me by giving examples of the psychological benefits I get from running. This I would do in hopes of earning my friends' understanding.

Now let's assume I have a friend who is depressed and tense much of the time. After answering question 4, I might decide to illustrate the ways running can decrease depression and tension. This I could do in an effort to convince my friend to begin running to improve his state of mind.

My purpose will partly dictate what illustrations I use. For the first essay I would provide examples of all the benefits important to me, but in the second I would provide examples only of ways running combats depression and tension.

Audience

Audience, too, is an important consideration because it affects the examples used. To determine your audience, you can answer the following questions:

1. With whom do I want to share? (Or whom do I want to inform, or convince?)
2. Who would benefit from reading about my subject?
3. Who does not know enough about my subject?
4. Who sees my subject differently than I do?
5. Who would be influenced by reading about my subject?

Once audience is identified, the writer of illustration should determine the nature of that audience by answering questions like the following:

1. How much does my reader know about my subject?
2. Is my reader's knowledge of my subject first-hand?
3. Does my reader have any strong feelings about my subject?
4. Does my reader have an interest in my subject?
5. Is my subject important to my reader?

To appreciate how audience influences the choice of examples, assume you are writing a piece about why your college is a good one and in it you plan

Illustration **191**

to have examples to illustrate some of your school's strengths. If you are writing for an academically oriented audience that didn't care much for sports, it would not be very effective to cite as an example that your football team is the conference champion. Similarly, a paper aimed at parents of prospective freshmen probably should not cite as example the wild dorm parties on Saturday nights. Thus, when you select your examples, keep your reader in mind.

The Nature and Number of Illustrations

When you develop an essay with illustrations, you must decide how many examples to use. This is a key decision, because it is possible to undermine the effectiveness of your essay by using too few examples or too many. With too few examples you may fail to clarify your generalization and provide the necessary concreteness. With too many examples, you may be guilty of overkill. In general, writers of illustration have four options. They can provide just a few examples, say two or three, and develop each one in great detail. Or they can provide quite a few examples, say six or more, and develop each one in far less detail. Or they can provide a moderate number of examples, each developed to a degree somewhere between the other two extremes. Finally, it is possible to have quite a few examples, some of which are highly detailed and some of which receive far less development.

As you make your decisions about the number of illustrations and degree of development, keep in mind the principle of adequate detail discussed in Chapter 2. This principle can be your guide because it dictates that whatever number of examples you have, it must be enough to explain and support your generalization adequately. And to whatever degree you develop an illustration, there must be enough detail that your reader appreciates the point it makes.

The examples you use can come from a variety of sources. Often your illustrations will be drawn from your own experiences and observations. Other times you may draw them from class readings and lectures, personal reading, or television viewing. Notice below how each generalization is followed by an illustration taken from a different source.

generalization: Too often, young children believe that what they see on television is an accurate representation of reality.
example from personal reading: I recall many years ago reading of a young child who died after jumping from a window and trying to fly like the Superman character he had seen on TV.
generalization: Of all the television comedies that have enjoyed wide popularity, *MASH* is the most unusual.
example from observation: It is the only successful show I have watched that uses humor to convey a serious message.
generalization: It is quite trying to be a salesperson, especially at Christmastime.

example from experience: Last Christmas I worked at the jewelry counter of a local department store. Although it is supposed to be a season of goodwill, I found that Christmas made ordinarily pleasant people pushy and demanding. Once, an elderly woman insisted that I bring out every watch in the stockroom just so she could verify that all the styles were on display.

generalization: Few of the early immigrants to this country found life easier here than it was in their homeland.

example from class reading or lecture: My history instructor, for example, explained that many of those who survived the Atlantic crossing spent their lives in sweatshops, working for slave wages.

generalization: It is possible for people in high-pressure jobs to reduce their risk of heart attack.

example from television viewing: A recent television documentary explained that executives could strengthen their hearts by parking a mile from their office and walking to work with a heavy briefcase.

You may find yourself using narration to illustrate your point because a story can be an excellent way to achieve clarity and concreteness. Description, too, can be highly illustrative, so there will be times when some of your examples take this form. For example, part of an essay developing the thesis or generalization "It's quite trying to be a salesperson, especially at Christmastime" could have a paragraph telling the story of the time the elderly woman demanded to see all the watches in the stockroom. Similarly, an essay developing the thesis or generalization "Few of the early immigrants to this country found life easier here than it was in their homeland" could have a paragraph describing what it was like to work in the sweatshops.

Arranging Detail

In an illustration essay it is possible to express the generalization in the thesis. The body paragraphs, then, can present and develop the various illustrations of that generalization.

When just a few illustrations are used, each one can be presented and developed in its own body paragraph. Or if an illustration is an extended example, it may require more than one body paragraph for adequate development. When quite a few illustrations are used and each one gets less extensive development, it is often desirable to group several related examples together in the same body paragraph.

It is important for writers to consider what order their illustrations should appear in. Often, a progressive order is used. If some of your examples are more telling than others, you may want to save your most compelling example for last in order to build to a big finish. You could begin with your least powerful example, or your second-best example can appear first to help im-

Illustration **193**

press your reader right off with the validity of your generalization. This would sandwich your less telling illustrations in the middle, where they get less emphasis. It can also be effective to begin with your best example to impress your reader initially, while reserving your second-most-effective example for last to ensure a strong final body paragraph.

When you have quite a few examples and some get extended treatment and some do not, you can begin with the illustrations that get less development and move on to the ones that are more detailed. Or you can do the reverse.

Sometimes you can arrange your illustrations in a chronological or spatial order. Say you write a thesis with a generalization that says the fans at local high school basketball games are rowdy. You could arrange your illustrations chronologically by giving first some examples of rowdyism before the game begins, then some examples of rowdyism during halftime, and finally some examples of rowdyism after the game. It is also possible to sequence your examples in a spatial order. If you are writing an essay developing the generalization that the playground in the city park was not really designed with children in mind, you could begin at one end of the playground and work your way around, ordering your examples to correspond with this movement through space.

Other logical arrangements are also possible. If some of your examples come from your own, first-hand experience, some from your own observation, and some from the experience of others, you can group together the examples from the same source.

Points to Remember about Illustration
1. Illustrations should be selected to provide clarity, concreteness, and interest.
2. Illustrations should be appropriate to the audience and purpose.
3. Use enough illustrations to clarify the generalization, but not so many that you belabor the point.
4. In general, the fewer illustrations used, the more detailed each one is.
5. Illustrations can be drawn from personal experience, observation, course work and lectures, reading, television viewing, and the like.
6. Illustrations can be narrations and descriptions as well as explanations.
7. The thesis can present the generalization, with the body paragraphs presenting the illustrations.
8. Illustrations are often arranged progressively, but other arrangements, such as spatial or chronological order, can be effective.

Exercise: Illustration

1. Write three different generalizations about childhood. Each generalization can be expressed in one or two sentences.
2. Select one of the generalizations you wrote for number 1 above, assume it will

eventually be the thesis for an illustration essay, and establish a possible purpose for this essay. To do this you may want to answer the purpose questions on p. 190.

3. Establish a possible audience for the illustration essay. If you wish, answer the audience questions on p. 190 to arrive at an audience.

4. Generate as many examples as you can to support the generalization by answering the following questions:
   a. What have I experienced first-hand that supports the generalization?
   b. What have I observed that supports the generalization?
   c. What have I heard or read that supports the generalization?

5. Which of the examples you generated for number 4 are suited to the audience and purpose you established?

6. Will any of your examples be developed with descriptions or narrations?

7. Arrange the examples suited to your audience and purpose in a progressive order. Are any other orders logical? If so, what are they?

Reading Illustration

The selections that follow, all written by professional authors, are developed with illustrations. As you read these pieces, notice how the authors employ the principles for selecting and arranging detail discussed in this chapter. Following each selection, there are questions for you to answer which point out several aspects of the illustrative technique.

The Honest Repairman—A Vanishing American?

Ken W. Purdy

A few weeks ago I took a Minox camera into a New York shop for repairs. The trouble seemed simple enough: I couldn't load it, the film cassette wouldn't go in. The clerk told me it needed cleaning and lubrication, one week, $6.50. When I came back the camera was taken out of a drawer in an elaborately wrapped, stamped, tagged package. I paid the $6.50. It didn't *look* any cleaner than it had been, but I thought the important work had been done on the inside.

I bought a cassette of film. It wouldn't go in. Amazement and bafflement were registered by the clerk. He tried to load it. Another clerk tried. Another. No use, it would have to "go back to the shop." Ten days. Right.

Next time, when the Minox was taken out of its official-looking wrapping, I realized I was being hustled: when I told the clerk I wanted to *see* if it would take film there was a pregnant pause. I pointed to an open cassette on a nearby shelf. It was "new" and I couldn't use it. . . . I used it anyway. It wouldn't go in, as everybody in the shop had known it would not.

I raised the roof. I made a phone call to a famous New York pho-

Illustration 195

tographer who knew the president of the Minox importing company. Unpleasantness followed, and by next day I could prove that the camera had been nowhere near the repair shop and that it had not even been dusted off, much less cleaned and lubricated. The store returned my $6.50 without a word of argument or defense. The Minox company cleaned, lubricated and practically rebuilt the camera for me without charge, entirely as a courtesy, since the company itself had been in no way involved. But this happy ending came about only because I knew whom to call. Most customers being deliberately cheated are helpless.

Unless he's lucky the cheated customer may never find out. I took my daughter's expensive watch, made by an internationally known company, to a shop displaying the company's dealership sign. The watch had been running badly. It needed, the man said, a complete cleaning and adjustment, $20. He was an old-world-craftsman-type, with just a trace of accent, probably fake Swiss, and he looked as trustworthy as your grandmother. When I came back for the watch he said he needed "another three days for checking, just to be sure." I returned, gave him the $20 and took the watch. It stopped dead four days later. Even in my rage, I had to admire the subtlety of his technique. Who could suspect a man who wanted three extra days just to be sure he'd done a great job?

I went to the U.S. headquarters of the company. A woman clerk in the elaborate and luxurious repair department took the watch away, brought it back and told me it needed a complete cleaning and adjustment, $30, ready in 12 weeks.

I told her that since the watch had just come from one of its dealerships, I required to know its precise condition.

"We don't give out that information," she said.

I explained the position more fully: somebody, I said, was a liar and a cheat. After a considerable discussion, and one more trip to consult with the technicians in the back room, she was able to say that the work did in fact need to be done, and that, yes, that indicated pretty clearly that it certainly had not been done by the little old watchmaker with the winning ways.

I entered a complaint with an official of the company, but he chose to make no comment.

It used to be that occasionally one would find repair work had been badly done. Now it seems to me that more and more one finds it hasn't been done at all. I suspected that a garage was cheating me. I took a car in for gear-box adjustment, but I sealed the gear-box lid. It could be opened easily enough, but it would show. When the car came back, with a bill for over $30, the seal hadn't been broken. Nobody had even looked into the gear-box, much less adjusted anything. I screamed. I refused to pay. I let it come to suit and settled for 50 percent. So, after a great deal of trouble, I came out only half-cheated.

Legally to prove a case of non-service, Better Business Bureau officials say, the customer must be expert or sophisticated or lucky or all three.

Probably for this reason, and also because often the customer doesn't know he's been victimized, non-service complaints are uncommon. What is *not* uncommon are complaints about incompetent or careless service and repair, or fraudulent guarantees, or "hijacking," the technique of enticing a customer with a promise of a low-cost minor job, then hitting him with expensive, unnecessary work—which may or may not be done at all.

"We just don't have enough people to go out and thoroughly investigate non-service complaints," the Metropolitan New York Better Business Bureau says. "Often it's a case of one man's judgment or opinion. And it's very difficult to get people to testify. One mechanic bills a customer $189 for new transmission parts, let's say. A week later another mechanic, one whom the customer knows and trusts, tells him that no such work has been done. But will he make an affidavit, or testify in court? No, he won't. Almost never.

"All we can tell people is to deal with reputable stores and shops, and get written guarantees for work and parts clearly spelled out on the bill. Beware of come-ons, of big bargains. Today it's hard enough to get something for something; you certainly aren't going to get something for nothing."

There is no doubt that the standard of morality has dropped sharply in recent years (shoplifting and cheating by customers is booming, too) and there are probably many repairmen who consider themselves honest because they don't do anything worse than persuade a customer to buy something he doesn't need. After all, if the customer actually gets the part or the service he paid for, that's not stealing, is it?

The TV and radio field, which used to be rich ground for swindlers, has been notably cleaned up. Most manufacturers now maintain factory service or use authorized service agencies which are tightly checked and supervised. A service agency with a good company is lucrative, it's well worth having, and smart operators won't risk losing it for the sake of a couple of hundred dollars on the side. If a shop does start to cheat, the word soon gets out. The BBB recently took a Bronx repairman to court when he billed a customer $47.50 on a TV "repair." The set was a plant, in perfect order except for a $7 tube. It was taken straight from the crooked shop to a reputable one, where it was established that $40.50 of the bill was overcharge.

A current gold mine for crooked repairmen is the air-conditioner field. The BBB says that there are no authorized service agencies for air conditioners. A standard ploy begins with a baited offer to recondition your machine for $8.95 or so. The repairman arrives and goes into a well-rehearsed act: your freon is missing, the frattistat valve is completely shot, you could be asphyxiated in your sleep, the conditioner has to go into the shop. The next bulletin is that the bill won't be $8.95, it will be $34.95. You still want the $8.95 special? Well, there's a trucking charge of $7.50 and the conditioner is now all taken apart, it will have to be put together again . . . most people finally authorize the $34.95 overhaul.

Illustration **197**

Some mechanics find woman customers irresistible targets. Mrs. Anita Lemberg of Brooklyn went to a muffler shop for a while-you-wait replacement. When her car was on the hoist, the mechanic told her a horror story about the condition of her steering system, it was so dangerous she shouldn't drive another foot, and so on. In only two hours, he said, he could "replace all the bushings" and perform other wonders. The bill was $51. Her regular mechanic, doing a lube job a week later, showed her that the grease and grime on her steering system was a year old if it was a minute. She went back to the muffler shop, where she was told that her mechanic was a liar.

An Ellenville, N.Y., woman, Mrs. Marian Talken, had trouble with her clothes dryer. The repairman told her it needed a new drive-shaft and bearings. The bill was $72, and when the original trouble recurred, he wouldn't come back. Another repairman charged $13 to take the dryer apart and show Mrs. Talken that the same old drive-shaft was still in business at the same old spot. He would not, however, be her witness. "I don't want to get involved," he said. "You'll have to settle it yourself."

Doesn't anything *good* ever happen? Well, yes. A few months ago a friend of mine asked a jeweler how much he would charge to fix an old watch. The man said he didn't like to work on anything but brand-new watches. A second watchmaker said, reluctantly, that he'd do it, for around $150. My friend kept shopping around until he got a better price—$7.20— and a prompt, superb job. How? That part was a little tricky: he asked a friendly airline pilot to take it to a shop in London. But even that is not a guaranteed solution. A London jeweler charged me twice the list price for a wrist-watch crystal three years ago, probably because I had an American accent.

Maybe the answer is to do it yourelf, or forget it.

Questions on Technique: "The Honest Repairman— A Vanishing American?"

1. What generalization does Purdy illustrate in his essay? Is the generalization implied or stated in a thesis?
2. The first 10 paragraphs function as an introduction. What approach does the author take to this introduction?
3. What method of development does Purdy use for most of his illustrations?
4. What purpose does the example in paragraph 13 serve?
5. What is the topic sentence of paragraph 17? Of paragraph 18?
6. What is the purpose of the example in paragraph 20?
7. What is the purpose of the example in paragraph 35?
8. In what order does Purdy arrange his illustrations?
9. What approach does Purdy take to his conclusion?

This Is Progress?

Alan L. Otten

A couple I know checked into one of the new Detroit hotels a few months ago and, in due course, left a 7 a.m. wake-up call.

Being an early riser, however, the husband was up long before 7, and decided he'd go down to breakfast and let his wife sleep late. He dialed the hotel switchboard, explained the situation, and said he'd like to cancel the wake-up call.

"Sorry, sir," the answer came, "but we can't do that. It's in the computer, and there's no way to get it out now."

Consider another story. A while back, a reporter phoned a congressional committee and asked to speak to the staff director. Unfortunately, he was told, the staff director wouldn't be in that morning; there'd been a power failure at his home. Well, the reporter persisted, that was certainly too bad, but just why did a power failure prevent him from coming to work?

"He can't get his car out of the garage," the secretary explained. "The garage doors are electrically controlled."

As these two anecdotes suggest, this is a column in praise of progress: those wonderful advances in science and technology that leave the world only slightly more snafued than before.

The balance sheet will eschew such common complaints as the way the modern office grinds to a halt whenever the copying machine is out of order. Or the computerized magazine subscription lists that take only four times longer than formerly to effect changes of address and which start mailing renewal notices six months before the subscription expires and then continue at weekly intervals.

Or the form letters that provide The New Yorker with so many droll end-of-the-column items, like the letter that was sent to the "News Desk, Wall Street Journal," and led off, "Dear Mr. Desk. . . ." Or the new drugs, operations and health regimens that in due time are shown to be more dangerous than the illnesses.

Computers bulk centrally in many of the "this is progress?" stories. For instance, a friend recently went to make a deposit at her local bank in upstate New York. The deposit couldn't be accepted, she was informed, "because it's raining too hard." Seems that when the rain gets beyond a certain intensity, the wires transmitting the message from the branch banks to the computer at the main bank in Albany send jumbled signals—and so branch-bank operations have to be suspended temporarily.

Every newspaper person knows that each technological advance in the printing process somehow makes news deadlines earlier, rather than later as might logically be assumed. Computers, though, can foul things up in other ways, too. At a recent conference on press coverage of presidential campaigns, many participants suggested that the lengthy background stories

Illustration **199**

prepared early in the campaign by the wire services or such special news services as those of The New York Times and Washington Post might be saved by subscribing papers and then used late in the campaign, when the public was more in the mood to pay attention.

"Are you kidding?" demanded a publisher present. "That stuff now all comes in computerized, and it's erased at the end of the day. We don't save any copy anymore."

Computers aren't the only villains, to be sure. Everyone has observed bizarre scenes of a dozen people down on hands and knees searching the pavement or the grass or a tennis court for a lost contact lens. The other day, however, a colleague announced she was having trouble seeing out of one eye and was off to the optometrist's. About a half hour later, she was back, giggling. The night before, she had apparently put one contact lens on top of another in the case where she kept an extra lens, and had that morning unwittingly put two lenses in one eye.

During last winter's snow storms, the Amtrak Metroliners frequently had to be removed from service as snow clogged the motors so cleverly mounted underneath the new high-speed trains. (The cars are now beginning to be converted to a different motor-mounting scheme.) A number of high schools in this area have been built with windows that don't open; when the air conditioning fails on a hot spring or fall day, students are given the day off. Last fall, when the nation moved back to standard time, a young friend was appalled to find she was going to have to turn her time-and-date digital wristwatch ahead 30 days and 23 hours.

Still another acquaintance had his car battery go dead while his power windows were rolled down—and then the rains came and poured in while he was parked alongside the highway waiting for help.

Society's rush to credit cards has its convenient aspects—but also unpleasant ones. Just try to check into a hotel announcing that you prefer to pay cash rather than use a credit card. Scorn, suspicion, hostility, un-American, if not downright communistic.

Once upon a time, you could look up at the postmark on a letter and see exactly where and when it had been processed at the post office.

Now, not only does the postmark deny you some or all of this occasionally useful information, but it insists on selling you something instead: "National Guard Month—Gain Skills By Serving" or "Save Energy—Turn Off Lights."

And like most creations of American ingenuity, this, too, has been exported to less fortunate lands. A letter from Belgium, the other day carried the exhortatory postmark: *"Prévenez l'Hypertension. Evitez le Sel."** In case your French wasn't up to it, there was a drawing of a salt shaker.

In all likelihood, corrective measures are being developed for many of

---

*"Prevent high blood pressure. Avoid salt."

the problems described above, and helpful correspondents will be writing in to tell me all about it. Yet I remain confident that new examples will come along to fill the gap. After all, that's progress.

Questions on Technique: "This Is Progress?"

1. In "This Is Progress?" what generalization does Otten illustrate? (Hint: check the thesis.)
2. Some of Otten's examples are more detailed than others. How do you suppose the author determined which ones to develop more extensively?
3. Otten wrote his piece as an article for a large newspaper. Has the author selected his illustrations with his audience in mind? Explain.
4. What is the source of Otten's illustrations?
5. What methods of development does Otten use for his examples? For each method you note, cite one of Otten's illustrations as an example of the method.
6. How does Otten arrange his examples? That is, what is his organization principle?
7. What approach does Otten take to his introduction? Why is his introduction so long?
8. What approach does Otten take to his conclusion? Why is it effective?

Daddy Tucked the Blanket around Mama's Shoulders

Randall Williams   Implied Thesis: Poverty impairs relationships

About the time I turned 16, my folks began to wonder why I didn't stay home any more. I always had an excuse for them, but what I didn't say was that I found my freedom and I was getting out.

I went through four years of high school in semirural Alabama and became active in clubs and sports; I made a lot of friends and became a regular guy, if you know what I mean. But one thing was irregular about me: I managed these four years without ever having a friend visit at my house.

I was ashamed of where I lived. I had been ashamed for as long as I had been conscious of class.

We had a big family. There were several of us sleeping in one room, but that's not so bad if you get along, and we always did. As you get older, though, it gets worse.

Being poor is a humiliating experience for a young person trying hard to be accepted. Even now—several years removed—it is hard to talk about. And I resent the weakness of these words to make you feel what it was really like.

We lived in a lot of old houses. We moved a lot because we were al-

Illustration **201**

ways looking for something just a little better than what we had. You have to understand that my folks worked harder than most people. My mother was always at home, but for her that was a full-time job—and no fun, either. But my father worked his head off from the time I can remember in construction and shops. It was hard, physical work.

I tell you this to show that we weren't shiftless. No matter how much money Daddy made, we never made much progress up the social ladder. I got out thanks to a college scholarship and because I was a little more articulate than the average.

I have seen my Daddy wrap copper wire through the soles of his boots to keep them together in the wintertime. He couldn't buy new boots because he had used the money for food and shoes for us. We lived like hell, but we went to school well-clothed and with a full stomach.

It really is hell to live in a house that was in bad shape 10 years before you moved in. And a big family puts a lot of wear and tear on a new house, too, so you can imagine how one goes downhill if it is teetering when you move in. But we lived in houses that were sweltering in summer and freezing in winter. I woke up every morning for a year and a half with plaster on my face where it had fallen out of the ceiling during the night.

This wasn't during the Depression; this was in the late 60's and early 70's.

When we boys got old enough to learn trades in school, we would try to fix up the old houses we lived in. But have you ever tried to paint a wall that crumbled when the roller went across it? And bright paint emphasized the holes in the wall. You end up more frustrated than when you began, especially when you know that at best you might come up with only enough money to improve one of the six rooms in the house. And we might move out soon after, anyway.

The same goes for keeping a house like that clean. If you have a house full of kids and the house is deteriorating, you'll never keep it clean. Daddy used to yell at Mama about that, but she couldn't do anything. I think Daddy knew it inside, but he had to have an outlet for his rage somewhere, and at least yelling isn't as bad as hitting, which they never did to each other.

But you have a kitchen which has no counter space and no hot water, and you will have dirty dishes stacked up. That sounds like an excuse, but try it. You'll go mad from the sheer sense of futility. It's the same thing in a house with no closets. You can't keep clothes clean and rooms in order if they have to be stacked up with things.

Living in a bad house is generally worse on girls. For one thing, they traditionally help their mother with the housework. We boys could get outside and work in the field or cut wood or even play ball and forget about living conditions. The sky was still pretty.

But the girls got the pressure, and as they got older it became worse. Would they accept dates knowing they had to "receive" the young man in a dirty hallway with broken windows, peeling wallpaper and a cracked ceiling? You have to live it to understand it, but it creates a shame which drives the soul of a young person inward.

I'm thankful none of us ever blamed our parents for this, because it would have crippled our relationships. As it worked out, only the relationship between our parents was damaged. And I think the harshness which they expressed to each other was just an outlet to get rid of their anger at the trap their lives were in. It ruined their marriage because they had no one to yell at but each other. I knew other families where the kids got the abuse, but we were too much loved for that.

Once I was about 16 and Mama and Daddy had had a particularly violent argument about the washing machine, which had broken down. Daddy was on the back porch—that's where the only water faucet was—trying to fix it and Mamma had a washtub out there washing school clothes for the next day and they were screaming at each other.

Later that night everyone was in bed and I heard Daddy get up from the couch where he was reading. I looked out from my bed across the hall into their room. He was standing right over Mama and she was already asleep. He pulled the blanket up and tucked it around her shoulders and just stood there and tears were dropping off his cheeks and I thought I could faintly hear them splashing against the linoleum rug.

Now they're divorced.

I had courses in college where housing was discussed, but the sociologists never put enough emphasis on the impact living in substandard housing has on a person's psyche. Especially children's.

Small children have a hard time understanding poverty. They want the same things children from more affluent families have. They want the same things they see advertised on television, and they don't understand why they can't have them.

Other children can be incredibly cruel. I was in elementary school in Georgia—and this is interesting because it is the only thing I remember about that particular school—when I was about eight or nine.

After Christmas vacation had ended, my teacher made each student describe all his or her Christmas presents. I became more and more uncomfortable as the privilege passed around the room toward me. Other children were reciting the names of the dolls they had been given, the kinds of bicycles and the grandeur of their games and toys. Some had lists which seemed to go on and on for hours.

It took me only a few seconds to tell the class that I had gotten for Christmas a belt and a pair of gloves. And then I was laughed at—because I cried—by a roomful of children and a teacher. I never forgave them, and that night I made my mother cry when I told her about it.

In retrospect, I am grateful for that moment, but I remember wanting to die at the time.

Illustration **203**

Questions on Technique: "Daddy Tucked the Blanket around Mama's Shoulders"

1. Williams' thesis is more implied than stated. His thesis, which embodies the generalization he develops with illustrations, is that poverty had adverse effects on his family and their relationships. The symbol of this poverty and its impact is Williams' old houses. Below is a list of some of the points Williams makes to support his thesis. For each point, mention the illustrations Williams uses for support.
   a. Poverty causes shame and humiliation.
   b. Poverty causes discomfort.
   c. Poverty causes frustration.
   d. Poverty interferes with dating.
   e. Poverty causes arguments.
   f. Poverty ruins marriages.
   g. Poverty means painful sacrifices.
2. Williams' examples are drawn from his own experience and that of his family members. Would his piece have been more effective if he had drawn some examples from his observations of others or from his reading? Explain.
3. Williams is conveying the difficulties he and his family members suffered because of their poverty. If his purpose were different, if he were trying to convey the effects of poverty on people in general, would his illustrations be as effective? Explain your view.
4. Why do so many of Williams' examples pertain to the old houses he lived in, and why do these illustrations form the central core of the essay?
5. Like Otten's, Williams' piece appeared in a large daily newspaper. Are his examples well suited to the average reader of such a newspaper?
6. Williams develops the illustrations of his old houses the most. The illustrations of his relationships with his classmates and the relationship between his parents receive less development. Does the fact that these latter examples receive less development present a problem with adequate detail? Explain your view.
7. Why does Williams conclude his essay with the Christmas narration?
8. Williams' style is uncomplicated and compact. His vocabulary is simple and his paragraphs are short. Why is this an effective style for this particular essay?
9. Cite three examples of effective concrete sensory detail.

Student Writings to Read and Evaluate

The following essays, written by students, are developed with illustrations. All have strengths and weaknesses for you to notice as you read.

The evaluation questions after the essays will guide you through an examination of one student writing so that you can practice forming and supporting critical judgments. This evaluation of student writing will sharpen your critical skill so you are better able to assess your own writing. It will also increase your awareness of what does and does not work in writing.

Coming In Last Isn't All Bad

In every family each child must have his place. He may be the oldest, youngest, or somewhere in the middle. He may even be an only child. Regardless of the number of children, a child will fall into one of these categories. In my case, I fill the role of the youngest of three girls. After years of playing this part, I find there are two worthwhile advantages of coming in last place.

Since my parents decided to stop having children after me, I was automatically branded "the baby." Regardless of age, I am still referred to and often introduced this way. This may not sound like a desirable title, yet I find it usually works to my advantage.

For as far back as I can remember, the blame would be on someone else's shoulders. It was taken for granted that I simply didn't know any better. For example, once my sister Betty and I were caught red-handed throwing our goldfish into the toilet bowl. We figured they would love swimming around in the new environment. After a few minutes of watching them swish their fins, we decided to see what would happen when we flushed. Needless to say, that was the last we saw of our goldfish. In the midst of our screaming, Mom decided that it was Betty's fault, because I was "the baby," and she should know better.

Well into my teens, I was still "the baby." Betty and I would go out on weekend nights with strict orders not to break our midnight curfew. When we came dismally home at 12:30, we pushed the car quietly into the drive with the lights off. We then eased the key into the front door and tiptoed into the house. Through the living room we'd stumble in the dark, for fear of waking someone with the lights. But it was too late, we couldn't make the final steps to our bedroom for a safe getaway. Dad was sitting in the dark living room waiting for an explanation. Both of us, too startled to breathe, had no excuse. Betty once again was found guilty. For she was older and therefore should be more responsible. Unfortunate as this was for my sister, the system saved me countless weeks of being grounded.

Another advantage of coming in last is that rules can change by the time they get to "the baby." My sister Lorraine was not allowed to go away for vacation with her girlfriends until she was a senior in high school. Even after hours of pleading, begging, and giving her speech about how mature she was. My parents kept a firm upper lip and stuck to their answer. There was no way she could go until she was a senior. By the time I was 16, and casually asked if I could go away with Carrie and Meg for spring break, my parents' defenses were worn down. They easily agreed I could go as long as I promised to call. By the time they got to me, they were too tired to argue.

Illustration **205**

So being the youngest does not mean that all you get are hand-me-downs. It can mean many lucky breaks if you play your cards right.

Going Back

On a bright fall afternoon, my husband and I leisurely rode along city streets laden with colorful fallen leaves. Since I pay no attention to my whereabouts while riding, I was astonished to find the locale familiar. As I drove through my old neighborhood, I recalled several places associated with pleasant memories of my childhood. Oak Street, Garland Avenue, and finally Shehy Street.

One of these places was my old front yard underneath the gigantic, sentrylike buckeye tree where I spent my leisure hours. The tree occupied one-third of our front yard, which was shaped in a triangle. As I lounged in the summer, the huge spreading branches provided shade against the blistering sun and minimized the amount of rain that reached the ground. During fall, I vividly remember the many happy hours I spent perched on one of the exposed, clawlike roots busily stringing the fallen buckeyes into necklaces. Buckeyes, a species of horse chestnut, were gathered into piles, and holes were laboriously bored in each one to accommodate the elasticlike string. "Gosh," I thought, "those necklaces sure were heavy." Each one, however, represented a treasured item of jewelry.

Located approximately 1 mile from our home, going north on Shehy Street, was Oakland Field, the sandlot diamond where double-A amateur-league teams would compete. Being the tomboy in a family of five girls, I enjoyed the sport of baseball. My knowledge of and interest in baseball resulted from the early exposure provided by my dad. We would briskly walk from our house, over the bridge and up the highway just in time for the first pitch. Of course, as we passed the concession stand, Dad would ask, "Want some popcorn?" He knew I wouldn't refuse. Up the bleachers we went, hand in hand; we took our seats and as the game progressed, I got play-by-play explanations.

Memories are jewels of the past, which occupy special places in our minds. My most vivid one is snuggling close to my dad on those special days when I had him all to myself. By giving of myself to my children and now to my grandchildren, I hope to contribute in some small way to their memories.

Trees Are a Nuisance

All year round trees do nothing but cause me a lot of unnecessary work. It seems that each season brings never-ending problems.

In the winter the old trees that could not stand the cold die. If a big gust of wind does not blow the trees over, branches will break off all winter long. This leaves me with tedious, backbreaking, and time-consuming work. I can rid myself of this dilemma by cutting the trees down, but then I have to worry about the stumps.

Then rolls around what some people refer to as "the beautiful spring." Because of our lovely northern trees, messy birds fly up from the south to nest.

When they are not noisily chirping in the early morning, they are bombarding my walkways and car with their droppings. It seems as though I spend the entire season washing or hosing something down.

Summer comes around with the hot, bright sunshine I have been waiting for all year. However, the huge green trees block the welcomed rays. Also this season, I wax my car and wash my house down, only for sap to bleed all over them. The sap stains everything it touches, and nothing less than a putty knife will remove the awful goo.

Lastly arrives a tree's most vicious season of all, autumn. Every morning I wake to find tons of leaves covering every inch of my yard. I rake them daily, only to find just as many the following morning. It almost seems that the trees are challenging me, throwing their leaves down into my face.

I might be accused of being a nature-hater, but without our tall elms and maples my life would be much easier. Where's Paul Bunyan when you really need him?

In Trouble

All the students I knew seemed to get through their years in high school without getting into any trouble. Even the kids who smoked in the john seemed to escape without getting caught. I was not one of these kids. I always ended up in trouble when I cut a class.

I will never forget Senior Cut Day in my freshman year. Senior Cut Day was an illegal holiday designated for the seniors and underclassmen to skip classes for the day. In spite of the severe warning by the principal, attendance was very low that morning. Sitting in my first-period civics class with two other kids, I was bored and made up my mind to leave. Sneaking down the hall, I came to the door, pushed it open, and was pleasantly greeted by the beautiful spring morning. I noticed a group of my friends who were sitting under a tree, and decided to join them. I was not there 5 minutes when suddenly Mr. Snyder, a tall, heavy-jowled man who was the assistant principal, came storming out of the door. His face red with rage he yelled, "Why aren't you kids in your classes?" "Take off!" someone shouted, and we all ran in different directions. When I went to school the next day, I was summoned to the principal's office, and was handed a detention slip to be served for the remainder of the year.

As if I hadn't learned my lesson from that incident, I foolishly cut a class again one chilly October day, and ended up in a more frightening situation. My girlfriend and I decided to take a walk instead of returning to our classes that afternoon. While walking down a side street, three older men in a rusted blue Chevelle pulled along side us. "Hey, ya girls know where Camron Street is?" the glassy-eyed driver slurred. My girlfriend told them where it was, but they persisted, "Come on and show us." The driver stopped the car and one of them got out and started walking quickly towards us. I grabbed Debbie by the arm, and without looking back we ran screaming hysterically. The car came roaring down the street, and as it passed the occupants shouted obscenities at us.

Illustration **207**

I realized later that I had learned a valuable lesson. No matter what the other kids did, I just used my common sense and tried to stay out of trouble. I never cut a class again.

Evaluating Writing: Assessing Strengths and Weaknesses

The activity in this section gives you additional practice making critical judgments, so that when you evaluate your own work you can do so in a reliable way. By evaluating writing from a reader's perspective, you will become more sensitive to how readers react to writing and why they react as they do. This sensitivity should help condition you to the reader's orientation so you can revise your work successfully.

For this activity, break into groups of three. Select one of the previous student essays (or use one your instructor assigns). It would be effective if each group dealt with a different essay. As a group, decide first which features of the essay are strongest. Then decide which features are weak or not as strong as they could be. Decide, too, on the main revisions you would recommend to the writer of the essay. When the group has finished its evaluation, a report should be written for presentation to the rest of the class. The report should note what the group agrees are the dominant strengths of the essay. It should explain what elements the group determines are the significant weaknesses and why these features need improvement. Finally, the report should reveal what the group sees as the three most necessary revisions, with suggestions for how these revisions should be handled. At times, there may be disagreement among group members. If this disagreement cannot be resolved, it can be noted in the report for class discussion.

Your report should be as specific as possible. For example, if you note that a particular illustration is not effective, do not simply say that the example does not work. Instead, explain why (perhaps it is not sufficiently relevant to the generalization presented in the thesis). Also, when you recommend a revision, indicate an approach to that revision. For example, if you suggest clarifying a particular point, mention also how that can be done (perhaps with the addition of an explanatory sentence or a certain kind of detail). It is not necessary to write the revision; just indicate the nature of the revision recommended. When all the reports are complete, they can be shared with the class for discussion.

The evaluation questions below may help you review the essay your group studies.

Evaluation Questions

1. Is it clear what generalization the author is illustrating?
2. Are there enough examples to adequately illustrate the generalization? Are there too many examples?
3. Are any examples inadequately detailed?

4. Are there any illustrations that fail to clarify the generalization?
5. Are there any illustrations that are not sufficiently concrete?
6. From what sources are the illustrations drawn? Are these sources appropriate to the nature of the generalization?
7. Are there any points you do not understand because of inadequate detail or poor detail selection?
8. Does the essay have an introduction that is appropriate and interesting?
9. Does the introduction have a thesis that presents the generalization to be illustrated, or is the generalization strongly implied?
10. By what principle does the author arrange the illustrations? Is the arrangement logical and effective?
11. Do all the body paragraphs have a topic sentence? If not, should they have? If so, are the topic sentences relevant to the thesis? Are all the details relevant to their topic sentence?
12. Does the essay have a separate conclusion? If not, should it have? If so, does the conclusion bring the essay to a satisfying close?
13. In general, is the word choice specific, economical, and simple? What, if any, words would you revise?
14. Does the writer use concrete sensory detail effectively? If not, should the writer have done so, and where in the essay is this needed?
15. Are there any clichés that should be revised for fresh expression?
16. Is there adequate sentence variety? If not, where is it needed?
17. Are transitions used effectively? If not, where are they needed, or where should the transitions be changed?
18. Is the essay carefully edited?

Essay Topics

The following list of ideas may help you arrive at a topic for an illustration essay. As they are, these topics may require narrowing and shaping.

1. As Purdy does in "The Honest Repairman—A Vanishing American?" write an essay that illustrates that the consumer is taken advantage of.
2. Write an essay illustrating that sometimes an automobile can be more trouble than it is worth.
3. In "This Is Progress?" Otten says he is writing "in praise of progress," but in fact he is illustrating that science and technology can create problems that never before existed. Like Otten, write an essay illustrating that modern advances bring unexpected problems.
4. Select one modern device (video games, television, toasters, washing machines, alarm clocks, stereos, electric blankets, etc.) and write an essay illustrating the problems the device can cause.
5. In "Daddy Tucked the Blanket around Mama's Shoulders," Randall Williams writes of the effect poverty had on him. Write an essay illustrating

Illustration **209**

how some condition in your life affected you dramatically. You might write about being an only child (oldest child, middle child, etc.), about being the child of divorced parents, about being a member of a minority group, about being tall or short for your age, about being athletic (or musically inclined or artistic), about being the class clown, and so on.

6. Write an essay illustrating that high school did (or did not) adequately prepare you for college.
7. Write an essay illustrating the happy times you had with a childhood friend.
8. Illustrate the strengths of your favorite teacher or illustrate the weaknesses of your least favorite one.
9. Select one season of the year and illustrate why you like (or dislike) it.
0. Write an essay illustrating that things do not always go as planned.
1. Write an essay illustrating that advertising leads people to view certain luxuries as necessities.
12. Illustrate that people are at their worst when they are behind the wheel of a car.
13. Illustrate the frustrations (or joys) of college life.
14. Use examples to illustrate how some group (homemakers, working women, husbands, police officers, bachelors) is depicted on television.
15. Select a particular situation (such as the first day of school, moving to a new town, losing a job, having a friend move away, etc.) and illustrate the effect it has or had on you.
16. Select a person (or use yourself) and use examples to illustrate one of that person's personality traits.
17. Select a person you have been close to or have had many dealings with and use examples to illustrate the kind of relationship you have had with that person. You may wish to narrow this topic to one aspect of your relationship.
18. Select a circumstance or situation that makes you feel insecure or frightened or tense. Write an essay with examples to illustrate times when that circumstance or situation caused the feeling.
19. Write an essay illustrating the effect the women's movement has had on television commercials (or magazine ads).
20. Write an essay illustrating the fact that appearances can be deceiving.

Writing Strategies

Some of the following strategies may help as you experiment to discover your own effective, efficient writing process. Review them, along with the suggestions in Chapters 1–3 and those in the exercise on p. 193, to find alternatives to any unsuccessful or inefficient aspects of your process.

1. Topic selection for an illustration essay amounts to settling on a generalization you can support with examples. One way to arrive at such a generaliza- **Topic Selection**

tion is to fill in the blanks in the following sentence: _____ is the most _____ I know. This will give you something like ''Taking a 3-year-old on a long car trip is the trickiest thing I know.'' It is also possible to alter the words in the sentence to get something like ''Registration is the biggest hassle I know.'' With the blanks filled in, you have a topic that can be developed using examples.

2. Another way to arrive at a generalization/topic is to take a common saying and show that it is *not* true. For example, provide illustrations to show that a bird in the hand is *not* worth two in the bush, honesty is *not* the best policy, ignorance is *not* bliss, and so on.

Answering the questions below may help you discover examples for supporting your thesis.

Idea Generation

1. What have I done that illustrates my generalization?
2. What have I seen that illustrates my generalization?
3. What have I heard that illustrates my generalization?
4. What have I read that illustrates my generalization?
5. What have others experienced that illustrates my generalization?
6. What story can I tell to illustrate my generalization?
7. What can I describe that illustrates my generalization?

Outlining

1. List all the examples you will use and number them in the order they are to appear in your essay. This will give you an informal outline for your body paragraphs.
2. Note in your outline the approach you will take to your introduction and conclusion. If you plan on a specifically stated thesis, this can be a statement of your generalization. If you have trouble deciding on an approach to the rest of your introduction, try explaining why your topic is important. If you have trouble deciding on an approach to your conclusion, try a reaffirmation of your main point and/or drawing a conclusion from the generalization.

A Postwriting Evaluation of Your Process

Answering the questions below will help you become more aware of your writing process, which features of it are successful, and which features of it are not yet as successful as you would like. With this knowledge, you can make decisions about what to do differently the next time you write and what to keep the same.

After answering the questions, discuss your responses with your classmates and instructor. These writers may have ideas about techniques you can try in the future.

Illustration **211**

1. When you wrote your illustration essay, what stages of the process went smoothly for you? (Remember, *smoothly* does not necessarily mean *quickly*.)
2. Did you do anything that worked well enough for you to repeat in the future? If so, what? Why do you think the technique was successful?
3. Was there anything about writing the essay that was unreasonably difficult and/or time-consuming? If so, what was it, and why do you think it was a problem? Has this been a problem in the past?
4. What stage(s) of your process will you handle differently next time? What will you do? Why?
5. Are you more comfortable writing now than in the past? Why or why not?

8
Process Analysis

A *process analysis* explains how something is made or done. In fact, we encounter process analysis frequently. The directions that explain how to assemble the toy you bought your nephew for his birthday take the form of process analysis. The instructions in your biology lab manual explaining how to prepare a slide are also process analysis—so are the explanation for making simple repairs given in the owner's manual of your stereo, the magazine article that describes how to land the perfect job, and the directions for preparing a gourmet meal found in the cookbook on the kitchen counter. In short, anything that tells a reader how to do something (such as grow prize-winning roses) or how something is made (such as paper) is a process analysis.

Purpose

The obvious purpose of a process analysis is to inform a reader about how something is made or done. Often the process analysis is meant to help the reader learn to follow the process and make or do something. This would be the case with a process analysis that explains how to hang wallpaper. A person could read this process analysis to learn how to hang wallpaper and thus could avoid paying someone else to do it.

Sometimes the reader already knows how to make or do something. In this case, the purpose can be to make the reader aware of a better or faster way to perform the process. Perhaps your reader already knows how to take an essay examination, but you can describe a process that helps the student budget time better. If you explained this process, you would do so to help your reader learn a *better* way to do something.

A process analysis is often written even when it is most unlikely that the reader will perform the process. In this case the writer's purpose can be to increase the reader's knowledge about how something works or how it is made. For example, if you wrote a description of how computers work, your purpose would be to increase your reader's knowledge. This would also be the case if you explained how alligators hunt their prey.

Another reason to write a process analysis is to help your reader appreciate the difficulty, complexity, or beauty of a process. For example, if you think your reader does not sufficiently appreciate how hard it is to be a waiter, you could describe the process of waiting on tables to heighten your reader's appreciation.

Sometimes the purpose of a process analysis is not to inform but to persuade. You could, for example, describe a process in an effort to convince your reader that it is superior to another way of doing things. This would be the case if you wrote to your registrar to describe a registration process that you believe is less troublesome than the current process.

Sometimes the purpose of a process analysis is to entertain, as is the case with the humorous "Loafing Made Easy" on p. 218.

If you have trouble determining the purpose of your process analysis, answer these questions:

1. Do I want to describe a process so my reader can perform it?
2. Do I want to describe a process so my reader is aware of it?
3. Do I want to describe a process so my reader will appreciate it more?
4. Do I want to convince my reader that there is a better way to perform a process?
5. Do I want to entertain my reader by showing the humor in a process?

Audience

Your audience can affect the process you explain. For example, assume you will write about how to handle a job interview. If your audience is personnel officers, you may want to explain how to construct effective questions; however, if your audience is college students, you will focus on how to respond to questions effectively.

Audience will affect the detail you include even after you have decided on your specific approach. For example, if you are explaining how to use a particular word processing program for a reader who understands computer operation, you will not have to explain the computer parts (like disk drive) or define many terms (like format a disk). However, if your audience is someone who just bought a computer and knows little about it, you will need to identify the parts and define terms.

The nature of your audience will also affect whether you must explain the importance of the process, provide examples, and explain steps in detail.

Here are questions that can help you identify your audience:

1. Who does not know how to perform the process I am describing?
2. Who does not fully understand or appreciate the process?
3. Who should be convinced to perform the process?
4. Who would be entertained by reading about the process?

Here are questions that can help assess the nature of your audience:

1. Does my reader appreciate the importance of the process?
2. Has my reader had any experience with the process?
3. How interested is my reader in the process?
4. Does my reader need any terms defined?
5. Will any steps in the process prove difficult for my reader to perform or understand?

Selecting Detail

Obviously, the primary detail in a process analysis will be the steps performed in the process. Of course, the writer must be careful not to omit any steps, or the reader may not be able to understand or perform the process. However, providing the steps alone may not be enough; you will often need to explain just *how* the steps are performed. For example, if you are explaining how to discover ideas to include in an essay, don't just note that a writer can try freewriting. You also have to explain how that freewriting is done.

In addition to explaining how steps are performed, you may need to explain *why*, particularly if you suspect your reader will not appreciate the importance of a step and therefore perhaps skip it. For example, assume you are explaining how to land a perfect job. Also assume that you mention that the reader should send a thank-you note to the personnel director immediately after the interview. If you suspect your reader may not appreciate the importance of this step, explain that sending the note impresses the personnel director with your courtesy and follow-through.

Interestingly, you may sometimes find it necessary to explain what is *not* done, for instance, when you fear your reader will do something that is unnecessary or incorrect. Assume again that you are explaining how to land the perfect job. You may want to caution your reader *not* to smile too much, for too much smiling can create a frivolous or insincere image.

If some steps in the process can prove troublesome, you should point out the possible problem and how to avoid it. For example, let's say you are explaining how to choose a responsible baby-sitter, including asking friends who they use. You might want to note that this step will only work if you speak to friends whose judgment you trust.

If your reader needs to assemble materials to perform the process, be sure to mention everything that will be needed. Also, if your reader needs an understanding of special terms, be sure to provide the necessary definitions. For example, if you are explaining how to make the best-ever chocolate cake, tell your reader early on what ingredients to have on hand. And if the cake will be baked in a springform pan, explain what this is if your reader is not likely to know.

Illustrations and descriptions can also be included in a process analysis. Both of these methods of development can help a reader understand the nature and significance of steps in a process. Thus, you might want to describe a springform pan or give examples of questions to ask during an interview.

Finally, if your reader does not fully appreciate the importance of performing or understanding the process, include this detail as well. For example, if you are explaining how television advertisements persuade people to buy, you can mention that people should understand this process so they can recognize attempts to manipulate them.

Arranging Detail

Since the supporting detail for a process analysis is primarily the steps in the process, it is easy to see that chronological order (see p. 165) is the most common pattern of detail arrangement. Most often, a reader needs the steps presented in the order they are performed. At times, however, chronological order is not necessary. For example, if you are explaining how to dress for success, the order of steps may not be significant.

If you are explaining what is *not* done, you should do this near the step the caution is related to. For example, in a cake recipe, you would explain not to overbake at the point you mention baking time. If your process analysis includes several statements of what not to do, you might want to group all the cautions together in their own paragraph.

If you must define a term, do so the first time the term is used. If you explain a troublesome aspect of the process, do so just after presenting the step under consideration. And if you explain why a step is performed, do so just before or after your explanation of the step. If necessary materials are listed, group together this information in an early paragraph, perhaps even in the introduction.

The introduction of a process analysis can include a thesis that mentions the process that will be explained. In addition, the thesis can note the importance of understanding the process. Here are two thesis statements that could appear in process analysis essays:

1. Car owners can save a great deal of money if they learn to change their own points and plugs. (The process is changing points and plugs; understanding the process is important because it can save the reader money.)
2. There is only one efficient way to study for a final examination. (This thesis mentions the process without noting its importance.)

To create interest in your topic, you can explain in the introduction why understanding the process is important (if your thesis does not do this). You might also tell why you are qualified to explain the process, arouse the reader's curiosity about how the process is performed, or combine approaches.

The conclusion can be handled using any of the approaches given for the introduction. Sometimes summarizing the steps in the process is useful. At times a separate conclusion is unnecessary because the last step in the process provides sufficient closure.

Points to Remember about Process Analysis

1. A process analysis explains how something is made or done.
2. The purpose of a process analysis can be to
   a. show the reader how to make or do something
   b. make the reader aware of a better way to make or do something
   c. increase the reader's knowledge about how something works or how it is made
   d. increase the reader's appreciation of the difficulty, complexity, or beauty of a process
   e. persuade the reader that one process is better than another
   f. entertain the reader with the humorous aspects of a process
3. Detail for a process analysis can include
   a. the steps in the process and how they are performed
   b. why steps are performed
   c. what is *not* done
   d. explanations of troublesome aspects of the process
   e. materials needed
   f. clarifying definitions
   g. the significance of the process
   h. illustrations and description
4. Detail is usually arranged in chronological order.
5. The thesis can include the process to be explained and the significance of the process.
6. The introduction and conclusion can tell why it is important to understand the process and/or why the writer is qualified to describe the process. The introduction can also arouse curiosity about the process, and the conclusion can summarize the steps or present the last step in the process.

Exercise: Process Analysis

1. To find a process to explain, think of something you do well (shop for bargains, make friends, plan a party, buy used cars, study, babysit, and so forth).
2. Assume you will write a process analysis for the process you identified in number 1. What would be your purpose for writing the process analysis? Answer the questions on p. 213 if you need help identifying a purpose.
3. Who would be a suitable audience for the process analysis? Answer the audience identification questions on p. 214 if you need help establishing an audience.
4. List the steps in the process (in the order they are performed if chronological order is important).
5. To generate additional detail, review your list of steps and answer these questions:
   a. Is it necessary to explain *how* any steps are performed?
   b. Is it necessary to explain *why* any steps are performed?
   c. Will the reader understand better if I explain something that is *not* done?
   d. Are there troublesome aspects that should be explained?
   e. Are any materials needed?
   f. Should any terms be defined?
   g. Is it possible to describe anything?
   h. Is it possible to use illustrations?
6. What is the significance of the process?

Reading Process Analysis

The professional writings that follow are process analysis essays that illustrate many of the points made so far in this chapter. The questions at the end of each selection will help you identify some of the writings' chief features.

How to Build a Fire in a Fireplace
Bernard Gladstone

Though "experts" differ as to the best technique to follow when building a fire, one generally accepted method consists of first laying a generous amount of crumpled newspaper on the hearth between the andirons. Kindling wood is then spread generously over this layer of newspaper and one of the thickest logs is placed across the back of the andirons. This should be as close to the back of the fireplace as possible but not quite touching it. A second log is then placed an inch or so in front of this, and a few additional sticks of kindling are laid across these two. A third log is then placed on top to form a sort of pyramid with air space between all logs so that flames can lick freely up between them.

A mistake frequently made is in building the fire too far forward so that the rear wall of the fireplace does not get properly heated. A heated back wall helps increase the draft and tends to suck smoke and flames rearward with less chance of sparks or smoke spurting out into the room.

Another common mistake often made by the inexperienced fire-tender is to try to build a fire with only one or two logs, instead of using at least three. A single log is difficult to ignite properly, and even two logs do not provide an efficient bed with adequate fuel-burning capacity.

Use of too many logs, on the other hand, is also a common fault and can prove hazardous. Building too big a fire can create more smoke and draft than the chimney can safely handle, increasing the possibility of sparks or smoke being thrown out into the room. For best results, the homeowner should start with three medium-size logs as described above, then add additional logs as needed if the fire is to be kept burning.

Questions on Technique: "How to Build a Fire in a Fireplace"

1. What is the purpose of Gladstone's process analysis?
2. Who would you judge to be his intended audience?
3. Gladstone does not have a separate introduction with a thesis and material to engage reader interest. Is this a problem? Explain.
4. Where does Gladstone note the troublesome aspects of the process? What purpose does this information serve?
5. Would the essay benefit from a sentence or two early on that mentions the materials needed? Explain.
6. Would the essay benefit from the definition of *kindling wood* and *andirons*? Explain.
7. The essay has no separate conclusion. Is this a problem? Explain.

Loafing Made Easy

Sam Negri

The fabled season of the sun is upon us and it is once again time to hook our thumbs in our suspenders and talk about America's most treasured art form, loafing.

The purest form of loafing is practiced in Arizona, where summertime temperatures will often exceed 110 degrees. If we regard the Arizona loafer as a natural resource, as I've been doing for the last eight years, we will see that the art form has applications that go far beyond the business of surviving in hot weather.

When I came to Arizona, I was a mediocre loafer, displaying a definite need for a degree of mental reconditioning. I'd moved here from Connecticut, where people relax by putting aside their copy of Gray's "Anatomy" and picking up a novel by Dostoevsky. In Arizona, this is referred to as insanity.

Here is a better method:

To begin with, shut the damper on your fireplace, if you have one, and turn on your air-conditioner, if you have one. Otherwise, hang a wet sheet in the window and pray for a breeze.

Now you are ready to memorize a handful of important and useful phrases. Try these: "I don't know"; "I don't care"; "no"; and the old standby, "well . . ."

These phrases are extremely valuable when your jaws are sagging like deflated bicycle tubes and your mind has turned to wax.

For example, it is 106 degrees in the shade and your son comes racing in the house, shouting, "Hey, you seen those long-handled pliers anywhere?" With a minimum of effort you are free to say, "no."

His anger may mount and he'll insist: "But you were using them yesterday! Where'd you leave 'em?"

If you haven't passed out from the strain of this conversation, you can then reply, "I don't know."

"But I need those pliers to fix my skateboard," he will cry. Then you break out the ultimate weapon in the loafer's lexicon. Without any inflection whatsoever, you declare, "Well . . ."

You can now get back to some serious loafing, which means that you will try to prove that Benjamin Franklin was correct when he observed: "It is hard for an empty sack to stand upright." In short, empty your mind. Learn to ask questions like these: "Mail come yet?" and "Anything doin'?" The responses to these questions usually involve one word, and often they aren't debilitating.

There are a few additional rules to keep in mind for successful loafing.

First, never loaf near a pool or a lake because you might be tempted to go for a swim. Swimming frequently leaves a body feeling refreshed and may lead to a desire to do something.

Second, under no circumstances should you allow anyone to coax you into a camping trip in the mountains. Mountains tend to be lush, green and cool, and next thing you know you'll be wanting to split logs for a fire, go for a hike, or pump up your Coleman stove. Resist. "Patience is a necessary ingredient of genius," said Disraeli. If you want to be a fine loafer you have to make enemies.

Of course, it is impossible to get by in life if you don't do something, even in the summer. Household jobs are the easiest for a loafer to contend with, if he is selective and deliberate.

One satisfying and undemanding job involves a ball of twine. Find a ball of twine that a cat has unraveled so badly that you can't find the end. Get scissors and slowly cut it into small pieces, scrunch it into a smaller ball, and throw it away. Now look at all the extra space you have in your junk drawer.

Another relatively simple and useful job for summertime loafing centers on light bulbs. Limp through your house or apartment, removing the light bulbs from every lamp. Coat the very bottom of each bulb with petroleum jelly and put it back in the lampsocket. This will clean some of the crud off the contact point and solve the problems with flickering lightbulbs. For variety you can take the bulb that was in a living-room lamp and put it in a bedroom lamp. It helps to sigh and gaze wistfully at the base of the lightbulb as you are performing this function.

Last, if you have a dog, sit in your most comfortable chair and stare at your dog's eyes for five or 10 minutes. Every so often, mutter something incomprehensible. Your dog is certain to understand, and your family will not come near you for the rest of the afternoon.

Questions on Technique: "Loafing Made Easy"

1. What is the thesis of "Loafing Made Easy"? Does the thesis present just the process or the process and its significance?
2. A four-paragraph introduction precedes the explanation of the process. What purposes do these four paragraphs serve?
3. What do you judge to be the writer's purpose?
4. This essay first appeared in the *New York Times*. How does Negri address the needs of his audience?
5. Although used to achieve comic ends, Negri employs some standard process analysis techniques. For example, he explains what *not* to do. In which paragraph does he do this, and what purpose does it serve?
6. Negri also uses illustrations for comic effect. Which paragraphs include illustrations, and how do they contribute to the humor?
7. Which part of the essay relies heavily on chronological order? Why is chronological order less significant later in the essay?
8. Negri moves the reader smoothly from step to step with skillful use of transitions. Cite three sentences that include transitions to ease the reader into a new step or rule.
9. What approach does Negri take to his conclusion?

A Delicate Operation

Roy C. Selby, Jr.

In the autumn of 1973 a woman in her early fifties noticed, upon closing one eye while reading, that she was unable to see clearly. Her eyesight grew slowly worse. Changing her eyeglasses did not help. She saw an ophthalmologist, who found that her vision was seriously impaired in both eyes. She then saw a neurologist, who confirmed the finding and obtained X rays of the skull and an EMI scan—a photograph of the patient's head. The latter revealed a tumor growing between the optic nerves at the base of the brain. The woman was admitted to the hospital by a neurosurgeon.

Further diagnosis, based on angiography, a detailed X-ray study of the circulatory system, showed the tumor to be about two inches in diameter and supplied by many small blood vessels. It rested beneath the brain, just above the pituitary gland, stretching the optic nerves to either side and intimately close to the major blood vessels supplying the brain. Removing it would pose many technical problems. Probably benign and slow-growing, it may have been present for several years. If left alone it would continue to grow and produce blindness and might become impossible to remove completely. Removing it, however, might not improve the patient's vision and could make it worse. A major blood vessel could be damaged, causing a stroke. Damage to the undersurface of the brain could cause impairment of memory and changes in mood and personality. The hypothalamus, a most important structure of the brain, could be injured, causing coma, high fever, bleeding from the stomach, and death.

The neurosurgeon met with the patient and her husband and discussed the various possibilities. The common decision was to operate.

The patient's hair was shampooed for two nights before surgery. She was given a cortisonelike drug to reduce the risk of damage to the brain during surgery. Five units of blood were cross-matched, as a contingency against hemorrhage. At 1:00 P.M. the operation began. After the patient was anesthetized her hair was completely clipped and shaved from the scalp. Her head was prepped with an organic iodine solution for ten minutes. Drapes were placed over her, leaving exposed only the forehead and crown of the skull. All the routine instruments were brought up—the electrocautery used to coagulate areas of bleeding, bipolar coagulation forceps to arrest bleeding from individual blood vessels without damaging adjacent tissues, and small suction tubes to remove blood and cerebrospinal fluid from the head, thus giving the surgeon a better view of the tumor and surrounding areas.

A curved incision was made behind the hairline so it would be concealed when the hair grew back. It extended almost from ear to ear. Plastic clips were applied to the cut edges of the scalp to arrest bleeding. The scalp was folded back to the level of the eyebrows. Incisions were made in the muscle of the right temple, and three sets of holes were drilled near the temple and the top of the head because the tumor had to be approached from directly in front. The drill, powered by nitrogen, was replaced with a fluted steel blade, and the holes were connected. The incised piece of skull was pried loose and held out of the way by a large sponge.

Beneath the bone is a yellowish leatherlike membrane, the dura, that surrounds the brain. Down the middle of the head the dura carries a large vein, but in the area near the nose the vein is small. At that point the vein and dura were cut, and clips made of tantalum, a hard metal, were applied to arrest and prevent bleeding. Sutures were put into the dura and tied to the scalp to keep the dura open and retracted. A malleable silver retractor, resembling the blade of a butter knife, was inserted between the brain and skull. The anesthesiologist began to administer a drug to relax the brain by removing some of its water, making it easier for the surgeon to manipulate the retractor, hold the brain back, and see the tumor. The nerve tracts for smell were cut on both sides to provide additional room. The tumor was seen approximately two-and-one-half inches behind the base of the nose. It was pink in color. On touching it, it proved to be very fibrous and tough. A special retractor was attached to the skull, enabling the other retractor blades to be held automatically and freeing the surgeon's hands. With further displacement of the frontal lobes of the brain, the tumor could be seen better, but no normal structures—the carotid arteries, their branches, and the optic nerves—were visible. The tumor obscured them.

A surgical microscope was placed above the wound. The surgeon had selected the lenses and focal length prior to the operation. Looking through the microscope, he could see some of the small vessels supplying the tumor and he coagulated them. He incised the tumor to attempt to remove its core and thus collapse it, but the substance of the tumor was too firm to be removed in this fashion. He then began to slowly dissect the tumor from the adjacent brain tissue and from where he believed the normal structures to be.

Using small squares of cotton, he began to separate the tumor from very loose fibrous bands connecting it to the brain and to the right side of the part of the skull where the pituitary gland lies. The right optic nerve and carotid artery came into view, both displaced considerably to the right. The optic nerve had a normal appearance. He protected these structures with cotton compresses placed between them and the tumor. He began to raise the tumor from the skull and slowly to reach the point of its origin and attachment—just in front of the pituitary gland and medial to the left optic nerve, which still could not be seen. The small blood vessels entering the tumor were cauterized. The upper portion of the tumor was gradually separated from the brain, and the branches of the carotid arteries and the branches to the tumor were coagulated. The tumor was slowly and gently lifted from its bed, and for the first time the left carotid artery and optic nerve could be seen. Part of the tumor adhered to this nerve. The bulk of the tumor was amputated, leaving a small bit attached to the nerve. Very slowly and carefully the tumor fragment was resected.

The tumor now removed, a most impressive sight came into view—the pituitary gland and its stalk of attachment to the hypothalamus, the hypothalamus itself, and the brainstem, which conveys nerve impulses between the body and the brain. As far as could be determined, no damage had been done to these structures or other vital centers, but the left optic nerve, from chronic pressure of the tumor, appeared gray and thin. Probably it would not completely recover its function.

After making certain there was no bleeding, the surgeon closed the wounds and placed wire mesh over the holes in the skull to prevent dimpling of the scalp over the points that had been drilled. A gauze dressing was applied to the patient's head. She was awakened and sent to the recovery room.

Even with the microscope, damage might still have occurred to the cerebral cortex and hypothalamus. It would require at least a day to be reasonably certain there was none, and about seventy-two hours to monitor for the major postoperative dangers—swelling of the brain and blood clots forming over the surface of the brain. The surgeon explained this to the patient's husband, and both of them waited anxiously. The operation had required seven hours. A glass of orange juice had given the surgeon some additional energy during the closure of the wound. Though exhausted, he could not fall asleep until after two in the morning, momentarily expecting a call from the nurse in the intensive care unit announcing deterioration of the patient's condition.

At 8:00 A.M. the surgeon saw the patient in the intensive care unit. She was alert, oriented, and showed no sign of additional damage to the optic nerves or the brain. She appeared to be in better shape than the surgeon or her husband.

Questions on Technique: "A Delicate Operation"

1. The thesis of "A Delicate Operation" is implied rather than stated. What is the thesis? Where is it most strongly suggested?
2. The introduction is the first three paragraphs. What approach do these paragraphs take?
3. Who would you judge to be Selby's intended audience? What is his purpose?
4. In what order are the details arranged?
5. Selby frequently defines medical terms. Cite three terms that he defines. Why does he provide these definitions?
6. In which paragraphs does Selby explain why steps are performed? How do these explanations help Selby fulfill his purpose?
7. In which paragraph does Selby explain how a step is performed? How does this explanation help Selby fulfill his purpose?
8. Paragraph 6 includes description. What purpose does this description serve?
9. In which two paragraphs does Selby note troublesome aspects of the process? What does this contribute?
10. What approach does the author take to the conclusion?

Student Writings to Read and Evaluate

The essays that follow were written by students. Some of the essays are better than others, but each has strengths and weaknesses. As you read the pieces, identify their chief strengths and weaknesses. This practice will help you judge the effective and ineffective features of your own drafts. For further help, complete the evaluation exercise following the student writings.

Locating a Buck: The Key to Success

Every year I hear a different list of excuses from my hunting buddies. All of them telling me why they didn't get a buck. Some tell me there are not any deer. Others tell me that all they see are does. But I know the real reason for their failures. It is the fact that they never stepped foot in the woods until the opening day of the season. They didn't know whether there was a buck in the area they were hunting in or not. That is the reason 90 percent of the hunters do not bag a buck. If there is one thing I've learned from my hunting experiences, it is this: the key to successful buck hunting is locating a buck before the season. However, before you can locate a buck, you must know when and where to look for its signs.

During the fall of every year, the bucks begin to prepare for the mating season. Their first step is polishing their antlers. This is usually done by rubbing them on small saplings and trees. Finding one or more of these rubs indicates there is a buck in the vicinity. Some good areas to look for rubs are along fence rows or secluded roadways and also in dense, brushy fields or woodlands.

The buck's next step in preparing for the mating season is scraping. Scrapes provide another excellent source of locating a buck. Scrapes are very easily identified; they consist of a small area of ground approximately 2 feet by 2 feet which has been scraped clean of leaves and grass. Scrapes are usually found beneath a low-hanging limb. The reason for this is after making the scrape, the buck will chew the tip of the limb leaving a saliva deposit. He does this as a way of marking his territory. Scrapes can often be found in one of the following areas: along the edge of a field, on a remote trail or roadway, or possibly in a small clearing. One point to remember is scrapes are usually not found until sometime in October, whereas rubs can be found as early as August.

Once you have located a buck, the next step is determining his time schedule. By this I mean knowing approximately when he is traveling through a certain area on a specific trail. This is not a simple task; it can require a tremendous amount of time and patience. One possible method of determining this is to spend a few days watching the trail. This tends to get very boring and also very time-consuming because often a buck will travel a trail only every couple of days. Another problem occurs if the buck is traveling the trail at night. These two factors led me to create another method. This method consists of stretching a piece of thread across each of the trails you believe the buck is using. By examining the threads two or three times a day to see if they are broken, you can determine approximately when the deer is using each trail. This method also enables you to observe the trails at night. Knowing the schedule of the deer can eliminate many wasted hours in your stand during the season.

Aside from the importance of locating a buck before the season, you must remember that this is not something you are required to do. It is merely a suggestion, one that will put you a step ahead of 90 percent of the other hunters. And as I have found, it is something that leads to success.

Homemade Pizza

When I smell the unmistakable scent of the spicy, pungent sauce bubbling on the stove, I know there is only one thing that can possibly fill the void in my stomach—my mother's homemade pizza.

The most difficult and frustrating episode of the process is fighting with the dough on the pizza pans. My mother begins by retrieving six well-used pizza pans from the overcrowded cupboard. A little oil rubbed over each pan by well experienced hands makes the pans so slippery they are difficult to handle. With a keen eye, she then divides the dough into six precision-cut pieces. Now the real battle begins. It's woman against the yeast dough. She rolls the soft and slippery dough and pulls it out to the border of the pan. As she releases it, it snaps back into a little circle like a rubber band. Again and again she gently pulls, pushes, and rolls the dough back into its position. After several tries it finally ceases to retreat to the middle of the pan. By the time she has won the battle, she looks as though she hasn't the strength to continue. However, another smell of the fine aroma of the sauce revives her.

After spreading a tiny portion of oil onto the defeated dough, she begins the addition of all the ingredients that really make a fantastic pizza. As she spoons the red, bubbling sauce onto the shiny dough, I can distinctly smell the onion bits, oregano, garlic salt, and the salt and pepper that the sauce contained. The once-white dough is now painted a bright red. With her hand she crumbles the dark brown chunks of the cooked ground sausage and sprinkles it evenly over the six pizzas. Next comes the main item. The little, round, coarse pieces of pepperoni accurately sliced the right thickness bring out all the flavor of the heavy spices. With a careful touch, she tops it off with long, smooth slices of mozzarella cheese that taste as mild as they feel.

The oven is hot and she steps back a few steps to survey her fine sculptures. Carefully, so as not to destroy them, she inserts two of the pizzas into the oven. With an eager eye, she peers through the glass oven door. The crusts turn to a golden, nut brown, the sausage browns even darker, and the thin strips of cheese melt and cover the entire surface as though they were hot lava flowing over rough ground.

After what seems like eternity, the entire family gathers to gobble up every last crumb. When it is all over, I sit back and release a belch of satisfaction and realize the great taste was well worth the wait.

Brownnosing Your Way to Academic Success

This is for those misguided souls who are going through school the hard way, by studying. Listen up all you drudges because you're working too hard. And where does it get you? Lonely Saturday nights in the library. Sunday afternoons sweating over biology notes. Hours upon hours pouring over thick philosophy texts. Wise up, scholars; there's an easier way to earn that degree. With the proper effort and guidance, you too can brownnose your way to academic success.

The key to successful brownnosing is subtle technique. A successful brownnose is not the sniveling, apple-polishing, boot-licking, fawning sort. No indeed. The expert brownnose has finesse. He drops by Professor Boredom's office just before class to announce with just the right amount of awe that the last lecture really inspired him and would he mind recommending additional reading? An experienced brownnose will linger a moment after Dr. Confusion's class to mention that this is the first time he has ever understood quantum physics.

One of the most skilled brownnoses it has been my pleasure to know came up with this brilliant ploy. He wrote a letter to the dean singing the praises of his history teacher, a prof long known for giving impossible exams guaranteed to flunk two-thirds of the class. Well, aspiring brownnoses, take heed. My friend who knew about as much history as my 4-year-old nephew earned a respectable C in his history class.

So, if you're still going for your degree the hard way, consider the rewards of brownnosing. You too can party hearty and still keep from flunking out. Just learn the art of brownnosing.

How to Buy a Ski Boat

The spring season is upon us, and the number of people considering the purchase of a ski boat will increase in enormous proportions. These consumers will have many questions which must be answered carefully for a successful first-time purchase of a new ski boat.

First the consumer must decide on his or her budget capacity. Since showroom ski boats range from $8000 to $25,000, it would be very wise to set a price that can be afforded. With this decision made, purchasers will most likely avoid overspending, providing they hold firm to the price they set.

Since most buyers finance their new ski boat, a good word of warning is to avoid borrowing through the dealership, mainly for two reasons. First, the new boat dealership is usually affiliated with one particular loan company. The dealer will insist on borrowing from this company. The reason for this persistence is that the dealer will earn up to 2.5 percent interest on the amount borrowed for each time the percentage is compounded. In other words, the loan company gives a percentage to the dealer as a commission for making the loan. The net effect is usually an interest rate far over the typical lending rate. A second crucial concern of financing is finding out how often the interest is assessed on the principal. Many times the dealer will offer what seems to be a low rate of interest. But the catch is that the rate may be compounded semiannually or even quarterly. This means the buyer could end up paying two to four times the said rate on a yearly basis. The best advice for the borrowing consumer is to finance through an accredited banking institution that charges the lowest interest around.

After setting a price range, getting ideas on financing, and learning what to look for, the consumer is ready to shop around to see the various prices and models dealerships have to offer. Of course, one could look up dealerships in the classified section of the newspaper or in the phone book's yellow pages to find their location and travel all over to see these places. But the most convenient method of shopping is to attend an annual spring boat show, located in most major metropolitan areas. These shows are always advertised in outdoor publications, which give the time and place of the shows occurring in the area. Representatives from area dealerships bring at least one variety of each type of boat the dealer has to offer. Along with these boats, the representatives present will answer questions and even make a sale if the customer has found what he or she wants. If customers do not reach that decision, they may take home various brochures with a list of sale prices that are usually good for 30 days after the show.

If the consumer is not sure as to what would be most desirable, perhaps a few handy hints will help. The most appropriate boat for skiing is an outboard semi-V fiberglass hull of 16 to 20 feet in length, the length pending on the buyer's needs for capacity. A boat powered by an outboard motor is very economical and swift in the water. The motor should be rated for at least 100 horsepower. Motors rated over this would provide less economy but better performance. The second factor is the shape of the hull. A semi-V hull will perform quickly and lightly on the water for greater waterskiing pleasure. The last component of a ski boat and one of the most important for maintenance and care of your boat is to buy a fiberglass ski boat. A fiberglass hull is virtually maintenance free. A simple washing and waxing will keep the finish in top condition. Unlike aluminum and wood hulls, fiberglass will polish to a slick finish, allowing the craft to move through the water with ease and precision.

A boat is a major investment. The purchase of one should be carefully planned to avoid unnecessary anguish and expense.

Evaluating Writing: Assessing Strengths and Weaknesses

This activity will help you become a more reliable judge of writing. It provides experience in determining the successful and unsuccessful features of writing so you can better decide what changes to make in your own drafts.

To gain experience judging writing, break into groups of three. Select one of the previous student essays (or use one your instructor assigns). As a group choose the strongest features of the essay and the features that are most in need of revision. Then prepare a group report that explains the essay's chief strengths and weaknesses. Be sure the report notes the specific kinds of changes needed. For example, do not just say that more detail is needed in paragraph 3; state that paragraph 3 should explain how the step is performed. Also, if there is disagreement among your group members, be sure to note what points people disagree on. When your report is complete, present it to the rest of the class. The following evaluation questions can be used to guide you through your assessment of the essay.

Evaluation Questions

1. Does the essay include all the necessary steps in the process?
2. Where necessary, does the essay explain how the steps are performed?
3. Where necessary, does the essay explain why steps are performed?
4. Where necessary, does the essay explain what is *not* done?
5. Are troublesome aspects of the process explained?
6. If necessary, does the essay list needed materials?
7. Are necessary definitions provided?
8. Is the significance of the process clear?
9. Are any illustrations and/or description needed?
10. Does the essay have an appropriate, interesting introduction?
11. Does the thesis mention the process and, if appropriate, its significance?
12. If necessary, are the steps given in the order they are performed?
13. Do all the body paragraphs have a topic sentence? If not, is this a problem?
14. Do all the details in the body paragraphs belong where they are? Are there any relevance problems?
15. Does the essay have a separate conclusion that brings the essay to a satisfying end?
16. Is the word choice specific and economical? What, if anything, would you revise?
17. Are there any clichés that should be revised for fresh expression?
18. What, if anything, would you revise for clarity?
19. Is there adequate sentence variety?
20. Are transitions used effectively? Are additional transitions needed?
21. Is the essay carefully edited?

Essay Topics

As you work to discover a suitable topic for a process analysis, consider the following possibilities.

1. As Gladstone does in "How to Build a Fire in a Fireplace," select a process that you perform well and describe it so someone else can perform it. You can describe how to change the oil in a car, how to train for an athletic competition, how to build a campfire, how to serve a tennis ball, how to buy

a used car, how to plant a garden—anything you have had successful experience with.

2. As Negri does in "Loafing Made Easy," write a process analysis for comic effect. Possibilities include how to avoid working, how to make a rotten impression on a first date, how to fail an exam, wasting time made easy, and annoying a professor made easy.

3. As Selby does in "A Delicate Operation," describe a process to increase the reader's appreciation. Consider something such as how to write a poem, how to design clothing, how to raise show dogs, how to design scenery for a play, how legislation is passed in Congress, and how plants manufacture oxygen.

4. Help your reader give up a bad habit you have overcome by writing about how to quit smoking, how to lose weight, how to stop procrastinating, etc.

5. Write about any of these processes to help first-year students at your college:
   a. how to register
   b. how to select a major
   c. how to select an advisor
   d. how to find and check out a book from the campus library
   e. how to study for an exam
   f. how to meet people
   g. how to live with a roommate

6. Think of something that you know how to make, and describe the process so someone else can make it.

7. Some miscellaneous topics that might appeal to you are
   a. how to survive adolescence
   b. how to buy the perfect gift
   c. how to plan the perfect party
   d. how to make the perfect pizza (or some other food)
   e. how to buy the right running shoes
   f. how to choose the right college
   g. how to catch a bass
   h. how to form a band

Writing Strategies

In addition to the strategies you learned in chapters 1–3 and in the exercise on p. 217, the following suggestions may help you as you write your process analysis.

1. Think of your past experiences and activities. They may suggest processes **Topic Selection** you can describe. If you were involved in athletics, perhaps you can describe how to coach Little League, how to block a tackle, how to shoot a

foul shot, or how to prepare mentally for a game. If you were a scout, maybe you can explain how to prepare for a hike or how to survive in the wilderness. If you babysat, maybe you can explain how to sit for very young children, and so forth.

2. Think of what you have learned in your classes. Maybe as a result of what you have learned you can explain how to teach reading, how to prepare a slide to view under a microscope, how the Depression started, and so forth.

Generating and Ordering Ideas

1. List every step in the process in the order it is performed.
2. For each step you have listed, answer the following questions:
    a. Should I explain how the step is performed?
    b. Should I explain why the step is performed?
    c. Should I explain something that is *not* done?
    d. Should I explain a troublesome aspect of the step?
    e. Should I define a term?
    f. Should I describe something?
    g. Should I illustrate something?
3. For which of the following reasons will your process be of interest to a reader?
    a. It will show the reader how to do or make something.
    b. It will make the reader aware of a better way to perform the process.
    c. It will increase the reader's knowledge.
    d. It will help the reader appreciate the beauty, difficulty, or complexity of the process.
    e. It will persuade the reader that your way is better.
    f. It will entertain the reader.

Now shape a preliminary thesis that mentions the process and suggests why it will be of interest to the reader.

A Postwriting Evaluation of Your Process

The questions below will help you discover which aspects of your writing process work well so that you can make decisions about how to alter your process. Remember, your goal is to discover a set of effective, efficient procedures. In addition to answering these questions, talk to your instructor and classmates to learn procedures to try.

1. When you wrote your process analysis, what stages of the process went smoothly for you? (Remember, *smoothly* does not necessarily mean *quickly*.)
2. Did anything you did this time work well enough to repeat in the future? If so, what? Why do you think the technique was successful?

3. Was there anything about writing the process analysis that was unreasonably difficult and/or time-consuming? If so, what was it, and why do you think it was a problem? Has this been a problem in the past?
4. What stage(s) of your process will you handle differently next time? What will you do? Why?
5. Are you more comfortable writing now than in the past? Why or why not?

9

Comparison and Contrast

When we compare and contrast two or more things, we are identifying and examining their similarities and differences. We are placing two or more things side by side to determine in what ways they are alike and in what ways they are different. While *comparison* refers to similarity and *contrast* refers to difference, in common usage an essay that looks at both likenesses and differences is known as a *comparison essay*. In this chapter, too, comparison will refer to the study of both similarities and differences.

One way to develop a thesis for a comparison or contrast essay is to state the subjects you are considering and indicate whether you are comparing or contrasting or doing both. Below are three possible thesis statements developed this way.

1. I expected college to be vastly different from high school, but I soon discovered they are not much different at all. (High school and college will be compared.)
2. After a month in my own apartment, I realized that living on my own was not what I imagined it to be. (The reality of and the author's expectation for living alone will be contrasted.)
3. The movie and television versions of *MASH* are alike in several important ways, but they differ significantly as well. (The movie and TV versions of *MASH* will be compared and contrasted.)

Selecting Subjects

A writer developing an essay using comparison and contrast must give careful thought to topic selection. For one thing, the items must have enough in common to warrant their side-by-side consideration. Usually this means that the subjects being compared must belong to the same category. It is possible, for example, to sensibly compare or contrast a Camaro with a Firebird because both of these belong to the same category—cars (or more specifically, high-performance cars). It is possible to compare or contrast two jobs, two teachers, two forms of government, two ways to study, two kinds of dates, two ways to celebrate Christmas, two cities you have lived in, and so on. These comparisons and contrasts are possible and sensible because the items viewed next to each other share enough features to make their comparison or contrast logical and meaningful. It would be silly, however, to compare learning to use a personal computer and learning to roller skate. Even if you could manage some corresponding statements about both of these activities, the comparison would be strained, probably more clever than valid. And the contrasts would be so obvious, they could really go without saying. As a result, such an essay would serve no useful purpose.

Purpose

A comparison or contrast essay can serve a variety of purposes. Sometimes it serves to clarify the unknown by placing it next to something more familiar to determine in what ways the two are alike and in what ways they are different. For example, an essay comparing rugby (less understood) with football (well known) could serve this purpose. Once the lesser-known rugby is explained in light of how it is like and unlike the better-known football, rugby can be better understood.

Sometimes the purpose of a comparison of contrast is to lend a fresh insight into something familiar. This can be achieved when similarities are drawn between things typically viewed as dissimilar or when differences are noted in things usually seen as comparable. Love and hate, for example, are usually seen as opposites, but an essay that explains their similarities by pointing out that both emotions are highly motivating, potentially self-destructive, and sometimes irrational can lead to new awarenesses about these familiar feelings.

A comparison or contrast can sometimes serve to bring things into sharper focus. For example, while we may understand what Catholicism and Protestantism are, an essay comparing and contrasting their basic tenets may lead to a clearer understanding of the nature of each religion.

Finally, a comparison or contrast essay can demonstrate that one thing is superior to another. When the features of one thing are compared or contrasted with the features of another, it is possible to judge which one is superior on the basis of the similarities and differences noted. If, for example, the platforms of two mayoral candidates are compared, it is possible to determine which of the two candidates would make the better mayor. When comparison or contrast is used to indicate that one thing is better than another, the paper is persuasive.

Your purpose will largely determine the details you select to develop your essay. Say, for example, that you decide to note the differences between dating practices today and those of 30 years ago. If your purpose is to demonstrate that women are more assertive now, you might note that they can take the initiative today, but 30 years ago they seldom asked men out or picked up bar tabs. If your purpose is to argue that dating was easier 30 years ago, you might mention that relationships were simpler before the sexual revolution. If you wish to clarify how prescribed codes of conduct have relaxed and blurred, you might explain the expected ways men and women behaved on a date 30 years ago and then explain the less predictable ways they behave now. In short, it is seldom possible—or desirable—to point out every similarity and difference. Instead, a writer selects detail on the basis of the purpose for the comparison.

To determine the purpose for your essay, you can ask yourself these questions:

1. Do I want to clarify the nature of one unfamiliar subject by placing it next to another, more familiar subject?
2. Do I want to lend a fresh insight into one subject by placing it next to another?
3. Do I want to bring one or both of my subjects into sharper focus?
4. Do I want to show that one of my subjects is superior to the other?

Audience

Like purpose, audience will affect the detail you include in your essay. How much your reader knows about your subjects, how your reader feels about your subjects, and how strong these feelings are—these influence the details you select. For example, let's return to the essay that contrasts dating practices today with those of 30 years ago, and let's say your purpose is to convince the reader that dating was more fun 30 years ago. If your reader is a feminist, you will not want to note that 30 years ago men and women had more prescribed roles and hence were more certain how to act. However, if your reader is a teenager who finds the sexual revolution frightening, you might note that there was less sexual pressure for teens who dated 30 years ago.

To determine your audience, you can ask yourself these questions:

1. Who could learn something by reading my essay?
2. Who could be influenced to share my point of view?
3. Who does not currently know much about one of my subjects?
4. Who would enjoy reading my essay?

Once you have targeted your audience, you can determine the nature of that audience by answering these questions:

1. How much does my reader know about my subjects?
2. How much interest does my reader have in my subjects?
3. How does my reader feel about my subjects?
4. How strongly does my reader feel about my subjects?

Selecting Detail

Comparison and contrast detail can be developed a number of ways. It is quite possible that you will rely on some or all of the methods of development discussed so far in this book: description, narration, process analysis, and illustration. Comparing cars could involve you in a description of interiors and options. Comparing ways to celebrate Christmas could involve you in narrations of two different Christmas celebrations you were part of. Comparing teachers could involve you in illustrations of the methods of each. Comparing study techniques could involve explaining how each one works. Sometimes you may find yourself combining all or some of these methods within the same essay.

Regardless of the methods of development you use, there is one thing to keep in mind: there must be balance among the points you discuss. This means that any point you discuss for one subject should also be mentioned for the other. Let's say, for example, you are comparing your family life before your parents divorced with your family life after they divorced, for the purpose of explaining that children can be better off if their parents end an unhappy marriage. If in this essay you describe mealtime before the divorce as a time of squabbling that made you tense and afraid, then you should say something about what mealtime was like after the divorce.

This need for balance does not mean that you must treat a point with exactly the same degree of development for each subject. You may, for example, find it appropriate to describe extensively the mealtime squabbling that occurred before the divorce to give your reader a clear picture of its nature and effect on you. However, you may find that you can note the peaceful nature of meals after the divorce in just two or three sentences. Similarly, you may find that some individual points get more development than others, that either the comparison or the contrast is more detailed, or that one of the subjects gets more development than the other. This is fine. As long as everything treated is developed *adequately*, there is no need to ensure that everything is developed *equally*.

As you select your detail, there is another thing you should keep in mind: be careful that you do not point to comparisons and contrasts that are so obvious they do not need to be mentioned. If, for example, you were comparing the Camaro and the Firebird, it would be silly to note that they both have engines.

Arranging Detail

Whether your essay points just to similarities, just to differences, or to both, there are several organizational strategies available to you. One common arrangement is *subject-by-subject*. In this scheme you make all your points about your first subject, and then you go on to make all your points about your second subject. Say, for example, you are comparing and contrasting living in a dorm with living at home. If you organized your essay following the subject-by-subject pattern, then first you would provide all your details about living in a dorm (in one or more paragraphs), and then you would provide all your details about living at home (in one or more paragraphs). Or you could reverse this order. An outline for this essay, following the subject-by-subject pattern, could look like this:

I. Living in a dorm
    A. Amount of privacy
    B. Amount of freedom
    C. Climate for studying
    D. Degree of comfort

II. Living at home
    A. Amount of privacy
    B. Amount of freedom
    C. Climate for studying
    D. Degree of comfort

Notice that the outline is balanced. The points that are discussed for the first subject are also discussed for the second. While it is not necessary to develop each point equally for each subject, it is a good idea to deal with the same issues for each subject. Otherwise you do not have a comparison, but an assortment of details on two subjects—an assortment that does not hang together in any way.

The subject-by-subject organization can be used for essays that show just similarities, for ones that show just differences, or for ones that show both. However, this organization generally works best for an essay that is not long, complex, or developed with a great many points. Otherwise, the reader working through your points on the second subject must keep too many points about the first subject in mind.

Longer, more complex essays can be organized following the *point-by-point* arrangement. With this pattern you make a point about your first subject and then treat the corresponding point about your second subject. Then you treat the next point about your first subject and follow it with the corresponding point about your second subject. You continue in this alternating fashion until all your points have been presented and developed. Say, for example, that you are contrasting your high school history teacher with your college history teacher. And assume you plan to discuss the way each presents material, the way each interacts with students, and the way each tests students' knowledge. An outline for your paper could look like this:

I. Presentation of material
  A. High school teacher
    1. Long, boring lectures
    2. No class participation
  B. College teacher
    1. Brief, stimulating lectures
    2. A great deal of class participation

II. Interaction with students
  A. High school teacher
    1. Standoffish
    2. Acts superior to students
  B. College teacher
    1. Interacts with students often
    2. Acts as though students are her equal

III. Tests of student knowledge
  A. High school teacher
    1. Gives only two tests each term
    2. Gives objective tests
    3. Asks trick questions
  B. College teacher
    1. Gives four tests each term
    2. Gives essay tests
    3. Never asks trick questions

You can tell from the outline that balance is important in point-by-point development. It is necessary to treat the same points for both subjects under consideration, although it is not required that you give the same degree of development to each point for each subject.

Although the point-by-point organization is useful for more complex essays, it can be used successfully for any comparison or contrast piece. Also, this pattern will work for essays that just compare, just contrast, or do both.

For essays that show both similarities and differences, a third method of organization is possible. You can first discuss all the similarities between your subjects and then go on to discuss all the differences. Or you can reverse this order. Say you wanted to show how Las Vegas and Atlantic City compare and contrast as vacation spots. An outline that deals first with similarities and then with differences could look like this:

I. Similarities
  A. Gambling
  B. Top-level entertainment
  C. High-class hotels

II. Differences
   A. Gambling
      1. More casinos in Vegas
      2. Cheaper gambling available in Vegas
      3. Gambling 24 hours a day, 7 days a week in Vegas

   B. Top-level entertainment
      1. More big-name entertainers in Vegas
      2. More free entertainment in Vegas

   C. High-class hotels
      1. More hotels in Vegas
      2. Greater variety of accommodations in Vegas
      3. Lower room rates available in Vegas

In the above outline, first the similarities are noted, using a point-by-point development, and then the differences are cited, again using a point-by-point pattern. However, it is also possible to develop the similarities with a point-by-point pattern and the differences with a subject-by-subject pattern. With this organization the outline would look like this:

I. Similarities
   A. Gambling
   B. Top-level entertainment
   C. High-class hotels

II. Differences
   A. Atlantic City
      1. Gambling
      2. Entertainment
      3. Hotels
   B. Las Vegas
      1. Gambling
      2. Entertainment
      3. Hotels

Notice the balance in this outline. The same aspects (gambling, entertainment, hotels) are discussed for the similarities and for the differences. While this balance is frequently possible and desirable, it is not necessary. You can discuss some features of similarity between both subjects and then go on to discuss different features of contrast. Of course, it will still be necessary to achieve balance within the discussion of similarities by treating the same points for both subjects. And it is necessary to achieve balance within the discussion of differences by dealing with the same points for both subjects. Whether you discuss the similarities first or the differences first will depend on which you want to emphasize more. Those points treated second typically get the greater emphasis because the closer to the end, the more emphatic the position.

You have no doubt gathered that the arrangement of details for a comparison or contrast essay requires careful planning. Often it involves making a decision about which of several possible arrangements will be the most effective, and this means that you will probably want to do some careful outlining. Even if you do not ordinarily do much outlining, you will find that a comparison or contrast paper comes together better when you take some time with this step. Without an outline it can be tricky to arrange details logically and effectively while achieving the necessary balance.

Points to Remember about Comparison and Contrast

1. A comparison essay notes either similarities or similarities and differences; a contrast essay notes differences.
2. There should be a logical basis for the comparison or contrast of two subjects.
3. The comparison or contrast should make some point or serve some purpose. Often such essays do one of the following:
   a. Clarify something unknown or not well understood
   b. Lead to a fresh insight or new way of viewing something
   c. Bring one or both of the subjects into sharper focus
   d. Show that one subject is better than the other
4. The thesis can present the subjects and indicate whether they will be compared, contrasted, or both.
5. Detail selection is in large measure determined by the purpose of and the audience for the essay.
6. Comparison and contrast detail can be in the form of narration, description, illustration, process analysis, and/or explanation.
7. The same points should be discussed for both subjects; it is not necessary, however, to give both subjects the same degree of development.
8. The following detail arrangements are possible:
   a. subject-by-subject
   b. point-by-point
   c. comparisons followed by contrasts (or the reverse)
   d. a combination of the above patterns
9. Outlines facilitate the organization of comparison or contrast essays.

Exercise: Comparison and Contrast

1. Assume you plan to write an essay showing similarities, differences, or both. Your subjects are your current writing process and the one you used at some point in the past (say, before this term began or when you wrote your first essay of the term). Make one list of all the similarities you can think of and one of all the differences.
2. Decide on a purpose for your essay by asking yourself the following questions:

a. Do I want to clarify the nature of one or both of the processes?
b. Do I want to achieve a fresh insight into one or both of the processes (or writing in general)?
c. Do I want to bring the act of writing (or one or both of my processes) into sharper focus?
d. Do I want to show my reader that one approach to writing is superior to the other?
e. Do I want to help my reader understand the way my writing process has changed (or stayed the same)?
3. Decide on an audience for your essay by asking yourself these questions:
a. Who would be interested in my essay?
b. Who would learn something from my essay?
c. Who would be influenced by my essay?
d. Who would enjoy reading my essay?
e. Who does not currently know much about my subjects?
4. Identify the nature of your audience by asking yourself the following questions:
a. How much does my reader know about my subjects?
b. How much interest does my reader have in my subjects?
c. How does my reader feel about my subjects?
d. How strongly does my reader feel about my subjects?
5. With your audience and purpose in mind, review your list of similarities and differences and decide whether you will treat likenesses, differences, or both.
6. Circle the points in your list(s) that you would treat because they are suited to your audience and purpose. Do you think you will need to generate any additional details?
7. As far as you can tell now, what method of organization (subject-by-subject, point-by-point, comparisons followed by contrasts, contrasts followed by comparisons, or a combination) would be most effective for your essay? Why?

Reading Comparison and Contrast

The following professional writings represent some of the range of comparison and contrast. One piece shows only similarities, two show only differences, and one shows both. One of the selections is organized in subject-by-subject fashion, two are organized in point-by-point fashion, and one shows first the similarities and then the differences. As you read these pieces, keep in mind the guidelines for selecting and arranging detail for comparison and contrast. Also, after each selection, there are some questions for you to answer to raise points about each author's technique.

A Fable for Tomorrow
Rachel Carson

There was once a town in the heart of America where all life seemed to live in harmony with its surroundings. The town lay in the midst of a checkerboard of prosperous farms, with fields of grain and hillsides of orchards where, in spring, white clouds of bloom drifted above the green fields. In autumn, oak and maple and birch set up a blaze of color that flamed and flickered across a backdrop of pines. Then foxes barked in the hills and deer silently crossed the fields, half hidden in the mists of the fall mornings.

Along the roads, laurel, viburnum and alder, great ferns and wildflowers delighted the traveler's eye through much of the year. Even in winter the roadsides were places of beauty, where countless birds came to feed on the berries and on the seed heads of the dried weeds rising above the snow. The countryside was, in fact, famous for the abundance and variety of its bird life, and when the flood of migrants was pouring through in spring and fall people traveled from great distances to observe them. Others came to fish the streams, which flowed clear and cold out of the hills and contained shady pools where trout lay. So it had been from the days many years ago when the first settlers raised their houses, sank their wells, and built their barns.

Then a strange blight crept over the area and everything began to change. Some evil spell had settled on the community: mysterious maladies swept the flocks of chickens; the cattle and sheep sickened and died. Everywhere was a shadow of death. The farmers spoke of much illness among their families. In the town the doctors had become more and more puzzled by new kinds of sickness appearing among their patients. There had been several sudden and unexplained deaths not only among adults but even among children, who would be stricken suddenly while at play and die within a few hours.

There was a strange stillness. The birds, for example—where had they gone? Many people spoke of them, puzzled and disturbed. The feeding stations in the backyards were deserted. The few birds seen anywhere were moribund; they trembled violently and could not fly. It was a spring without voices. On the mornings that had once throbbed with the dawn chorus of robins, catbirds, doves, jays, wrens, and scores of other bird voices there was now no sound; only silence lay over the fields and woods and marsh.

On the farms the hens brooded, but no chicks hatched. The farmers complained that they were unable to raise any pigs—the litters were small and the young survived only a few days. The apple trees were coming into bloom but no bees droned among the blossoms, so there was no pollination and there would be no fruit.

The roadsides, once so attractive, were now lined with browned and withered vegetation as though swept by fire. These, too, were silent, deserted by all living things. Even the streams were now lifeless. Anglers no longer visited them, for all the fish had died.

In the gutters under the eaves and between the shingles of the roofs, a white granular powder still showed a few patches; some weeks before it had fallen like snow upon the roofs and the lawns, the fields and streams.

No witchcraft, no enemy action had silenced the rebirth of new life in the stricken world. The people had done it themselves.

This town does not actually exist, but it might easily have a thousand counterparts in America or elsewhere in the world. I know of no community that has experienced all the misfortunes I describe. Yet every one of these disasters has actually happened somewhere, and many real communities have already suffered a substantial number of them. A grim specter has crept upon us almost unnoticed, and this imagined tragedy may easily become a stark reality we all shall know.

Questions on Technique: "A Fable for Tomorrow"

1. Is Carson comparing, contrasting, or doing both?
2. What are the subjects placed next to each other in Carson's essay?
3. What pattern does Carson use for the arrangement of her details?
4. Is the treatment of both subjects balanced? Explain.
5. Carson develops her discussion of the town after the blight in greater detail than she does her discussion of the town before the blight. Is this a problem? What effect does this have on the reader?
6. "A Fable for Tomorrow" is a contrast piece with elements of narration and description. How does the narration function? The description?
7. How does Carson effect the transition from her first subject to her second?
8. What is the purpose of Carson's essay? That is, what point does her contrast make?
9. Where in the essay does Carson make her point known?
10. Carson does not use a formal introduction, yet this is not a problem. Why?
11. What kind of conclusion does Carson use? Why is it effective?

Columbus and the Moon

Tom Wolfe

The National Aeronautics and Space Administration's moon landing 10 years ago today was a Government project, but then so was Columbus's voyage to America in 1492. The Government, in Columbus's case, was the Spanish Court of Ferdinand and Isabella. Spain was engaged in a sea race with Portugal in much the same way that the United States would be caught up in a space race with the Soviet Union four and a half centuries later.

The race in 1492 was to create the first shipping lane to Asia. The Portuguese expeditions had always sailed east, around the southern tip of Africa. Columbus decided to head due west, across open ocean, a scheme that was feasible only thanks to a recent invention—the magnetic ship's compass. Until then ships had stayed close to the great land masses even for the longest voyages. Likewise, it was only thanks to an invention of the

1940's and early 1950's, the high-speed electronic computer, that NASA would even consider propelling astronauts out of the Earth's orbit and toward the moon.

Both NASA and Columbus made not one but a series of voyages. NASA landed men on six different parts of the moon. Columbus made four voyages to different parts of what he remained convinced was the east coast of Asia. As a result both NASA and Columbus had to keep coming back to the Government with their hands out, pleading for refinancing. In each case the reply of the Government became, after a few years: "This is all very impressive, but what earthly good is it to anyone back home?"

Columbus was reduced to making the most desperate claims. When he first reached land in 1492 at San Salvador, off Cuba, he expected to find gold, or at least spices. The Arawak Indians were awed by the strangers and their ships, which they believed had descended from the sky, and they presented them with their most prized possessions, live parrots and balls of cotton. Columbus soon set them digging for gold, which didn't exist. So he brought back reports of fabulous riches in the form of manpower; which is to say, slaves. He was not speaking of the Arawaks, however. With the exception of criminals and prisoners of war, he was supposed to civilize all natives and convert them to Christianity. He was talking about the Carib Indians, who were cannibals and therefore qualified as criminals. The Caribs would fight down to the last unbroken bone rather than endure captivity, and few ever survived the voyages back to Spain. By the end of Columbus's second voyage, in 1496, the Government was becoming testy. A great deal of wealth was going into voyages to Asia, and very little was coming back. Columbus made his men swear to return to Spain saying that they had not only reached the Asian mainland, they had heard Japanese spoken.

Likewise by the early 1970's, it was clear that the moon was in economic terms pretty much what it looked like from Earth, a gray rock. NASA, in the quest for appropriations, was reduced to publicizing the "spinoffs" of the space program. These included Teflon-coated frying pans, a ballpoint pen that would write in a weightless environment, and a computerized biosensor system that would enable doctors to treat heart patients without making house calls. On the whole, not a giant step for mankind.

In 1493, after his first voyage, Columbus had ridden through Barcelona at the side of King Ferdinand in the position once occupied by Ferdinand's late son, Juan. By 1500, the bad-mouthing of Columbus had reached the point where he was put in chains at the conclusion of his third voyage and returned to Spain in disgrace. NASA suffered no such ignominy, of course, but by July 20, 1974, the fifth anniversary of the landing of Apollo 11, things were grim enough. The public had become gloriously bored by space exploration. The fifth anniversary celebration consisted mainly of about 200 souls, mostly NASA people, sitting on folding chairs underneath a camp meeting canopy on the marble prairie outside the old Smithsonian Air Museum in

Washington listening to speeches by Neil Armstrong, Michael Collins, and Buzz Aldrin and watching the caloric waves ripple.

Extraordinary rumors had begun to circulate about the astronauts. The most lurid said that trips to the moon, and even into earth orbit, had so traumatized the men, they had fallen victim to religious and spiritualist manias or plain madness. (Of the total 73 astronauts chosen, one, Aldrin, is known to have suffered from depression, rooted, as his own memoir makes clear, in matters that had nothing to do with space flight. Two teamed up in an evangelical organization, and one set up a foundation for the scientific study of psychic phenomena—interests the three of them had developed long before they flew in space.) The NASA budget, meanwhile, had been reduced to the lightbill level.

Columbus died in 1509, nearly broke and stripped of most of his honors as Spain's Admiral of the Ocean, a title he preferred. It was only later that history began to look upon him not as an adventurer who had tried and failed to bring home gold—but as a man with a supernatural sense of destiny, whose true glory was his willingness to plunge into the unknown, including the remotest parts of the universe he could hope to reach.

NASA still lives, albeit in reduced circumstances, and whether or not history will treat NASA like the admiral is hard to say.

The idea that the exploration of the rest of the universe is its own reward is not very popular, and NASA is forced to keep talking about things such as bigger communications satellites that will enable live television transmission of European soccer games at a fraction of the current cost. Such notions as "building a bridge to the stars for mankind" do not light up the sky today—but may yet.

Questions on Technique: "Columbus and the Moon"

1. What subjects does Wolfe bring together in his essay? Are these subjects compared, contrasted, or both?
2. In what pattern does Wolfe arrange his details—subject-by-subject or point-by-point?
3. What do you judge to be the purpose of Wolfe's comparison?
4. Wolfe's comparison has balance for the most part, but one point is made about Columbus that is not made about NASA. What is that point? Why is the corresponding point not made about NASA?
5. Although Wolfe does not compare the value of Columbus' voyages across time and NASA's worth in the future, what comparison can be drawn by the reader?
6. Which paragraphs make use of illustration?
7. What approach does Wolfe take to his conclusion?

That Lean and Hungry Look
Suzanne Britt Jordan

Caesar was right. Thin people need watching. I've been watching them for most of my adult life, and I don't like what I see. When these narrow fellows spring at me, I quiver to my toes. Thin people come in all personalities, most of them menacing. You've got your "together" thin person, your mechanical thin person, your condescending thin person, your tsk-tsk thin person, your efficiency-expert thin person. All of them are dangerous.

In the first place, thin people aren't fun. They don't know how to goof off, at least in the best, fat sense of the word. They've always got to be adoing. Give them a coffee break; and they'll jog around the block. Supply them with a quiet evening at home, and they'll fix the screen door and lick S & H green stamps. They say things like "there aren't enough hours in the day." Fat people never say that. Fat people think the day is too damn long already.

Thin people make me tired. They've got speedy little metabolisms that cause them to bustle briskly. They're forever rubbing their bony hands together and eying new problems to "tackle." I like to surround myself with sluggish, inert, easygoing fat people, the kind who believe that you clean it up today, it'll just get dirty again tomorrow.

Some people say the business about the jolly fat person is a myth, that all of us chubbies are neurotic, sick, sad people. I disagree. Fat people may not be chortling all day long, but they're a hell of a lot *nicer* than the wizened and shriveled. Thin people turn surly, mean and hard at a young age because they never learn the value of a hot-fudge sundae for easing tension. Thin people don't like gooey soft things because they themselves are neither gooey nor soft. They are crunchy and dull, like carrots. They go straight to the heart of the matter while fat people let things stay all blurry and hazy and vague, the way things actually are. Thin people want to face the truth. Fat people know there is no truth. One of my thin friends is always staring at complex, unsolvable problems and saying, "The key thing is . . ." Fat people never say that. They know there isn't any such thing as the key thing about anything.

Thin people believe in logic. Fat people see all sides. The sides fat people see are rounded blobs, usually gray, always nebulous and truly not worth worrying about. But the thin person persists. "If you consume more calories than you burn," says one of my thin friends, "you will gain weight.

It's that simple." Fat people always grin when they hear statements like that. They know better.

Fat people realize that life is illogical and unfair. They know very well that God is not in his heaven and all is not right with the world. If God was up there, fat people could have two doughnuts and a big orange drink anytime they wanted it.

Thin people have a long list of logical things they are always spouting off to me. They hold up one finger at a time as they reel off these things, so I won't lose track. They speak slowly as if to a young child. The list is long and full of holes. It contains tidbits like "get a grip on yourself," "cigarettes kill," "cholesterol clogs," "fit as a fiddle," "ducks in a row," "organize" and "sound fiscal management." Phrases like that.

They think these 2,000-point plans lead to happiness. Fat people know happiness is elusive at best and even if they could get the kind thin people talk about, they wouldn't want it. Wisely, fat people see that such programs are too dull, too hard, too off the mark. They are never better than a whole cheesecake.

Fat people know all about the mystery of life. They are the ones acquainted with the night, with luck, with fate, with playing it by ear. One thin person I know once suggested that we arrange all the parts of a jigsaw puzzle into groups according to size, shape and color. He figured this would cut the time needed to complete the puzzle by at least 50 per cent. I said I wouldn't do it. One, I like to muddle through. Two, what good would it do to finish early? Three, the jigsaw puzzle isn't the important thing. The important thing is the fun of four people (one thin person included) sitting around a card table, working a jigsaw puzzle. My thin friend had no use for my list. Instead of joining us, he went outside and mulched the boxwoods. The three remaining fat people finished the puzzle and made chocolate, double-fudged brownies to celebrate.

The main problem with thin people is they oppress. Their good intentions, bony torsos, tight ships, neat corners, cerebral machinations and pat solutions loom like dark clouds over the loose, comfortable, spread-out, soft world of the fat. Long after fat people have removed their coats and shoes and put their feet up on the coffee table, thin people are still sitting on the edge of the sofa, looking neat as a pin, discussing rutabagas. Fat people are heavily into fits of laughter, slapping their thighs and whooping it up, while thin people are still politely waiting for the punch line.

Thin people are downers. They like math and morality and reasoned evaluation of the limitations of human beings. They have their skinny little acts together. They expound, prognose, probe and prick.

Fat people are convivial. They will like you even if you're irregular and have acne. They will come up with a good reason why you never wrote the great American novel. They will cry in your beer with you. They will put your name in the pot. They will let you off the hook. Fat people will gab, giggle, guffaw, gallumph, gyrate and gossip. They are generous, giving and gallant. They are gluttonous and goodly and great. What you want when you're down is soft and jiggly, not muscled and stable. Fat people know this. Fat people have plenty of room. Fat people will take you in.

Questions on Technique: "That Lean and Hungry Look"

1. What subjects is Jordan bringing together in the essay? Are these subjects compared, contrasted, or both?
2. By what pattern of development does Jordan organize her details? Why is this pattern more suitable than the alternative?
3. What is the purpose of Jordan's essay?
4. Is Jordan's purpose stated in a thesis or implied?
5. What points are developed to support Jordan's contention that fat people are better than thin people? Where are these points first presented?
6. Is the treatment of both subjects balanced? Explain.
7. The subject of thin people is developed in a bit more detail than the subject of fat people. What is the effect of this?
8. In paragraph 4 and paragraph 9 Jordan refers to a thin person she knows. What is the function of this detail?
9. What kind of conclusion does Jordan use?
10. What kind of transition does Jordan use most frequently to move from one subject to the next?

Bing and Elvis

Russell Baker

The grieving for Elvis Presley and the commercial exploitation of his death were still not ended when we heard of Bing Crosby's death the other day. Here is a generational puzzle. Those of an age to mourn Elvis must marvel that their elders could really have cared about Bing, just as the Crosby generation a few weeks ago wondered what all the to-do was about when Elvis died.

Each man was a mass culture hero to his generation, but it tells us something of the difference between generations that each man's admirers would be hard-pressed to understand why the other could mean very much to his devotees.

There were similarities that ought to tell us something. Both came from obscurity to national recognition while quite young and became very rich. Both lacked formal music education and went on to movie careers despite lack of acting skills. Both developed distinctive musical styles which were originally scorned by critics and subsequently studied as pioneer developments in the art of popular song.

In short, each man's career followed the mythic rags-to-triumph pattern in which adversity is conquered, detractors are given their comeuppance and estates, fancy cars and world tours become the reward of perseverance. Traditionally this was supposed to be the history of the American business striver, but in our era of committee capitalism it occurs most often in the mass entertainment field, and so we look less and less to the board room for our heroes and more and more to the microphone.

Both Crosby and Presley were creations of the microphone. It made it possible for people with frail voices not only to be heard beyond the third row but also to caress millions. Crosby was among the first to understand that the microphone made it possible to sing to multitudes by singing to a single person in a small room.

Presley cuddled his microphone like a lover. With Crosby the microphone was usually concealed, but Presley brought it out on stage, detached it from its fitting, stroked it, pressed it to his mouth. It was a surrogate for his listener, and he made love to it unashamedly.

The difference between Presley and Crosby, however, reflected generational differences which spoke of changing values in American life. Crosby's music was soothing; Presley's was disturbing. It is too easy to be glib about this, to say that Crosby was singing to, first, Depression America and, then, to wartime America, and that his audience had all the disturbance they could handle in their daily lives without buying more at the record shop and movie theater.

Crosby's fans talk about how "relaxed" he was, how "natural," how "casual and easy going." By the time Presley began causing sensations, the entire country had become relaxed, casual and easy going, and its younger people seemed to be tired of it, for Elvis's act was anything but soothing and scarcely what a parent of that placid age would have called "natural" for a young man.

Elvis was unseemly, loud, gaudy, sexual—that gyrating pelvis!—in short, disturbing. He not only disturbed parents who thought music by Crosby was soothing but also reminded their young that they were full of the turmoil of youth and an appetite for excitement. At a time when the country had a population coming of age with no memory of troubled times, Presley spoke to a yearning for disturbance.

It probably helped that Elvis's music made Mom and Dad climb the wall. In any case, people who admired Elvis never talk about how relaxed and easy going he made them feel. They are more likely to tell you he introduced them to something new and exciting.

To explain each man in terms of changes in economic and political life probably oversimplifies the matter. Something in the culture was also changing. Crosby's music, for example, paid great attention to the importance of lyrics. The "message" of the song was as essential to the audience as the tune. The words were usually inane and witless, but Crosby—like Sinatra a little later—made them vital. People remembered them, sang them. Words still had meaning.

Although many of Presley's songs were highly lyrical, in most it wasn't the words that moved audiences; it was the "sound." Rock 'n' roll, of which he was the great popularizer, was a "sound" event. Song stopped being song and turned into "sound," at least until the Beatles came along and solved the problem of making words sing to the new beat.

Thus a group like the Rolling Stones, whose lyrics are often elaborate, seems to the Crosby-tuned ear to be shouting only gibberish, a sort of accompanying background noise in a "sound" experience. The Crosby generation has trouble hearing rock because it makes the mistake of trying to understand the words. The Presley generation has trouble with Crosby because it finds the sound unstimulating and cannot be touched by the inanity of the words. The mutual deafness may be a measure of how far we have come from really troubled times and of how deeply we have come to mistrust the value of words.

Questions on Technique: "Bing and Elvis"

1. What subjects does Baker place side by side in his essay? Are these subjects compared, contrasted, or both?
2. What pattern does Baker use for the arrangement of his details?
3. Baker discusses similarities first and then moves on to differences. Are the details in the paragraphs about similarities and the details in the paragraphs about differences organized subject-by-subject or point-by-point?
4. What is the purpose of Baker's comparison and contrast?
5. Baker's essay has a thesis, but it is not in the first paragraph. What is that thesis?
6. Baker's thesis is a general statement of what his essay is about. However, in his conclusion the author makes a more specific statement of the point to be drawn from his comparison and contrast. Which sentence makes that more specific statement?
7. The comparisons that make up the first part of Baker's essay lead to two conclusions about American culture in the Crosby era that hold true for the Presley era. What are these conclusions?
8. Why does Baker devote more detail to his discussion of differences than to his discussion of similarities? And why does he consider the similarities first?

Student Writings to Read and Evaluate

The comparison-and-contrast essays that follow were written by students. Some of the essays are stronger than others, but each has strengths and weaknesses. Each essay can teach us something about what works well in writing (and why) and what is less successful (and why). As you react to these student writings, you can learn about strategies to try and techniques to avoid. Furthermore, you will sharpen your critical ability so that the assessments you make about your own writing will become more reliable. After the student writings, there are evaluation questions you can apply to the student essays to arrive at conclusions about the quality of the selections.

Two Styles of Karate

When selecting a martial art, you should be aware that there are many different styles with differences in techniques and fighting philosophies. Even though there are many different styles, all of them evolved from only two styles, Japanese Shoto Kan and Korean Tae Kwon Do. When you select an art, you should be aware of the differences in these two styles.

A major difference in these two styles is how each uses the stance and punch to eliminate an opponent. The Koreans believe that speed is the most important aspect of fighting. They believe speed is power. The swiftest, quickest way to the target is the most effective means of overcoming an opponent according to the Koreans. In contrast, the Japanese sacrifice the speed to generate enormous amounts of power to overcome an opponent. They focus their strength, not on the target, but past the striking zone.

The stance is a primary focal point in both styles. The way a Karatá (a practitioner of karate) stands is important to his defense. The Japanese use a stance that is long and wide. Weight is evenly distributed. The back is at a 90-degree angle, and the front foot is straight forward; the back foot is at a 60-degree angle. When the Japanese move, the head does not bob at all.

In contrast, the Koreans believe that most of the weight should be forward. Seventy percent of the karatá's weight is leaning forward at a 70- to 80-degree angle. The head does not bob.

Power is another difference between the two styles. While power starts in the stance, it is finally demonstrated in the punch. A Korean punch is designed with speed in mind. Speed is generated by the hips and shoulders working in the opposite directions, like when cracking a whip. In contrast, the Japanese punch is designed to generate power. The Japanese believe that the target is past the striking surface. For example, when the target is the sternum, the strike is centered 2 inches past the back bone. The idea is to deliver the punch with a great force and drive through the target.

Although these two styles demonstrate different methods of eliminating the opponent, they are both very effective. When you choose an art, you should consider whether you are a slow-moving person or a quick, agile one. With this in mind, you will be able to adapt well to one of the karate styles.

Togetherness: Before Children and After

When I was sweet sixteen, getting married and having three children was the progression a young woman's life was supposed to take. Older women made motherhood look totally satisfying. These same women said that having children brought husbands and wives closer together. Well, I don't want to call the older generation mentally deficient, but I do think they fibbed just a little. I genuinely love being a parent, but the truth of the matter is that after a child enters into a marriage, a couple becomes a trio and togetherness takes on a new and sometimes frustrating meaning.

For instance, after a child is born those regular Friday-night candlelight dinners for two that were followed by dancing until 1:00 in the morning suddenly become reserved for anniversaries and birthdays. McDonalds is now the "in" place to go on Friday nights. And what all-American family isn't glued to their television sets at 8:00 p.m. to watch Bo and Luke Duke have another horrendous crash?

Saturday mornings used to be routinely slept through, that is, before two became three. Our day would start around 1:00 p.m. and end with going to the theater and seeing a wicked R-rated movie. But now that we have a child, we reluctantly roll out of bed at 8:00 a.m. to the sound of the Roadrunner's beep-beep. And to make Saturday an absolutely perfect "family day," we will go see *Star Wars* for the tenth time. Instead of husband and wife holding hands through a sizzling love story, mother and father now hold their son's popcorn and pop during a G-rated space adventure.

Vacations—what romantic, intimate times they once were. A week in the lush Pocono Mountains with afternoons spent in a heart-shaped bathtub sipping wine certainly promoted togetherness. Now our vacations are spent with the three of us standing in an hour-long line waiting to ride on Space Mountain in Disneyworld. Somehow it's just not the same!

Raising a child is a wonderful responsibility, but it's very hard to stay lovers after becoming parents. When that little bundle of joy sits in the middle at the movies, succumbs to Ronald McDonald's advertising messages, and voices his opinion as to where vacations should be spent, things certainly do change.

Like Mother Like Daughter

My mother died of cancer when I was 19 years old. She suffered a slow, painful death, and the final five years of her life were devastating to me. Having been the youngest of her four children, it was I who remained at home to do the housekeeping chores, plan and prepare meals, and just give her care and support when necessary. I felt resentful that my teenage years were marred by that feeling of being trapped at home. On the other hand, I never questioned the fact that it was my responsibility to be there when she needed me. The feelings of sadness, guilt, and denial completely overshadowed any fond, happy memories I had for my mother during the years I was growing up and she was healthy. It was not until seven years following her death that my attitude toward my mother changed.

By this time I was married and the mother of two sons. I was hosting a family reunion—my brother and his family came from California, and my two sisters and their families arrived from New York and New Jersey. There were fourteen of us living together at my house for two whole weeks, and although chaos prevailed, I loved being together.

To prevent the children from becoming bored, we kept busy picnicking, swimming, playing tennis, and visiting relatives. Then one evening, my brother and I were alone. We were reminiscing about the fact that I was only 6 years old when he left home for college and that he never really knew me. He looked at me and said, ''I want you to know that you are more like Mom than Ruth and Rose will ever be.'' He pointed out that I was functioning as a mother and a homemaker exactly as she did. It was like opening a door to my past, and the more we talked, the more I realized that my mother gave me more love and direction than I could ever give back.

I began to remember the lessons I learned. She was the daughter of Italian immigrants and had a total preoccupation with food. I was constantly at her side licking cake batter, rolling pie dough, stirring spaghetti sauce. When family or company visited, we seldom sat in her immaculate parlor; she ordered everyone to sit at the old chrome kitchen table while she perked fresh, steaming coffee. How remarkable that our friends today seem to gather in the kitchen rather than the family room. Could it be that I lead them there?

To my mother, food was the symbol of life. We were healthy to her because we were fat! I too push food in front of my family; if company arrives, I head for the refrigerator. How I envy my skinny friends who can fast all day while I have to eat breakfast by 8:30.

My mother taught me respect for food. I can still hear her preach, ''Eat, eat . . . think of those poor children in India who don't have food!'' How ironic that I have repeated those same words to my sons as they rush from the table with plates half-full. To this day, I cannot bear to see food wasted.

Thrift was a profound lesson that I learned. She managed my father's paycheck from the mill better than any banker. She took me to sales and clearances and taught me to bargain-hunt. How remarkable that I rarely pay full retail price for clothing or merchandise today.

Finally, the most important trait my mother shared with me was a warmth and loyalty to family. Her only job in life was to keep house and care for her family. And even though I am pursuing an education and career now, I will never regret staying home with my family when they were babies and young children. Although my children never knew their grandmother, I have kept her memory alive without being consciously aware that I did.

Running the Distance

My daughters, Laura and Jennifer, ran with the Columbiana High School Cross Country Team. Although they both had determination and devotion, their training techniques, running styles, and attitudes toward spectators were quite different.

During training, Laura developed a vigorous stretching routine which she used before each meet. She made adjustments in her running position to help increase her speed, such as leaning forward when running uphill. Since she wore out easily, she went to bed earlier and watched her diet. She ate balanced meals and believed that a steak dinner was the best meal to have the evening before a meet.

Laura's running style was a pleasure to watch. Her short frame seemed to be made for running. She looked like a thoroughbred horse gracefully running the course. Her legs stretched out as she made strong, even strides. She paced herself so she could, at just the right moment, begin to speed up for her big sprint to the finish. Since she never seemed to sweat, she appeared to still have energy after crossing the finish line.

Laura thrived on the spectators' cheers. The encouragement she received from the crowd motivated her to try harder. She always wanted people positioned along the course to cheer for her and to give her instructions. The coach would run back and forth across the course to give her tips during the race. Her best running time was when the entire boy's team went from point to point along the course and cheered for her from start to finish.

Jennifer's approach to running was totally different. While she was training, her stretching routine was kept at the bare minimum, and she made few adjustments in her running position. She never went to bed early. When she was hungry, her stomach came before her runner's diet. For example, when a county meet was delayed because of rain, she filled her empty stomach with greasy french fries. Spaghetti was her ideal meal the night before a meet.

Since Jennifer had runner's knee, her running style was far from graceful. Her entire body seemed to be fighting her determination to run. The agonizing pain of each step could be seen in her distorted face. She wore a sweat band around her head to keep the perspiration from streaming into her eyes. With each stride of her long, slender legs, her feet appeared to plop heavily to the ground. Jennifer's speed only varied slightly during a race. Although she was never able to sprint, it was evident that she gave all she had to the race. After she crossed the finish line, her body would collapse to the ground in gruelling pain. When describing her running, her younger brother Kurt jokingly commented, "When Jennifer runs, she looks like a dog with two legs. And those two legs have cement blocks on them."

Since the cheering spectators interfered with Jennifer's concentration, she preferred to run without onlookers. She made me aware of this preference at her first cross-country meet. As she ran past me, I cheered, "Come on Jennifer!" While still running, she turned and looked at me with glaring eyes. She snapped, "You get out here and try it!" After the meet, she informed me that I could continue to come to the meets if I promised never to cheer for her.

Although their training techniques, running styles, and attitudes toward spectators differed, each daughter received awards and trophies for her efforts. Along with acknowledgments for devotion, Laura was recognized for her speed and Jennifer for her determination.

Look Out! Here Comes a New York Driver!

New York with its traffic lights, four-lane streets, traffic jams, and wild drivers. Warren and its stop signs, single-lane roads, smooth-flowing traffic, and relaxed drivers. A big city and a rural community are separate worlds with a multitude of differences, including driving habits. Though Warrenites are more dependent on driving, since it is their only practical method of transportation, New Yorkers seem to have developed driving into more of a sport than a way to get from one place to another. The major differences between New York driving and Warren driving lie in driving strategies, parking, and obeying traffic rules.

Due to the hectic nature of city driving, a New York driver must adopt a different driving strategy than a Warren driver. Darwin's theory that only the strong survive can well be applied to city driving, since a New York driver must be extremely offensive and be able to bully his way through traffic with sharp driving skills. He will cut other drivers off and be as rude as he has to be to get to his destination. In Warren, driving is not nearly as competitive as in New York. The main issues in rural driving seem to be politeness and driving etiquette instead of aggressiveness. Most drivers in Warren are willing to let others enter their lane or pass first at a stop sign. There is no need to be assertive at the wheel in Warren because other drivers are usually courteous to you.

Another major difference between New York driving and Warren driving is the aspect of parking. New Yorkers do not have the luxury that Warrenites have with their large parking lots, wide driveways, and individual garages. A New Yorker must either spend a lot of time looking for a space or spend a lot of money to park in a parking lot. Even when a New Yorker does find a parking space, he must go through the struggle of parallel parking on a busy street. Warrenites should appreciate the fact that they can usually find a parking space when they go out, and that there is always a parking space waiting for them when they return.

Following traffic rules is another comparable aspect of New York and Warren driving. Since city people always seem to be in a big rush, traffic rules seem to become optional in New York. Even common courtesy, such as using directional signals, is not always common practice in New York. It would be unthinkable for a Warren driver to go through a red light or not follow the arrows in a mall parking lot! Since Warren drivers follow traffic rules more diligently and are more courteous to other drivers than New Yorkers, Warren is a much safer and easier place to drive in.

New York is a great city with a lot to offer, but it is no place for an insecure driver. City drivers have totally different driving strategies, parking conditions, and attitudes toward obeying traffic rules than rural drivers. A New Yorker driving through Warren would stick out like a punk rocker at a tea party. A Warren driver might never get out of an intersection in New York. Warrenites may complain about how dull their lives are, but they should be thankful that their excitement does not have to come from the challenge of driving through a city like New York.

Evaluating Writing: Comparing Strengths and Weaknesses

The purpose of evaluating student writing is to sharpen your critical sense so you can judge the successful and unsuccessful features of your drafts. For this chapter's evaluation, select one of the previous student writings (or use the one your instructor selects) and identify its major strengths and its most disturbing weaknesses. To aid you with these identifications, the next section contains evaluation questions you can apply to the essay you have selected.

Once you have decided on the essay's strengths and weaknesses, write an evaluation of the essay in several paragraphs. In your introduction, explain your overall reaction to the piece. In your first body paragraph (or paragraphs), detail the primary strengths of the essay, and in the next body paragraph (or paragraphs) detail the major weaknesses. By way of conclusion, summarize your most significant findings, discuss what conclusions about writing you reached as a result of your evaluation, and/or mention the best way to approach a revision of the piece.

When you write your evaluation, you need not discuss every strength and weakness. Instead focus on the ones that most significantly affect the overall quality of the piece. This means that in addition to judging strengths and weaknesses, you will be assessing which features contribute the most to the overall impression the writing makes. Also, to avoid writing unsupported generalizations, back up your conclusions with specific references to the essay you are evaluating. In other words, use examples.

Evaluation Questions

1. Is there a logical basis for the selection of subjects compared or contrasted?
2. Does the comparison or contrast make a point or serve a purpose? If so, what is that point or purpose?
3. Is the essay balanced so the same points are discussed for both subjects?
4. Are there enough details to develop the thesis (stated or implied) and topic sentences adequately? If not, what kind of detail is needed? Where?
5. Are all the topic sentences and details relevant to the thesis?
6. Are there any points you do not understand?
7. Does the essay have an introduction? If so, is it appropriate and interest-holding? If it does not have an introduction, should it have one?
8. Is there a clear thesis, either stated or strongly implied?
9. Is there a formal conclusion? If not, should there be? If there is a conclusion, does it bring the essay to a satisfying close?
10. How is the detail arranged? Is this the best organization to use?
11. Do all the details belong in the paragraphs they appear in? If not, which details do not belong where they are? Why?
12. Does the writer use transitions effectively to move from subject to subject and from point to point?

13. In general, is the word choice specific, economical, and simple? What, if anything, would you revise?
14. Are there any clichés that should be revised for fresh expression?
15. Does the essay flow well because of adequate sentence variety? If not, where is sentence variety needed?
16. Is the essay carefully edited?

Essay Topics

Below are pairs of subjects that can be treated in comparison-and-contrast essays. In some cases you will need to decide whether to treat similarities, differences, or both.

1. Write an essay that compares and/or contrasts two books, television shows, or movies that have similar themes.
2. In "That Lean and Hungry Look" Jordan writes that fat people are better than thin people. In the same tone that Jordan uses, write a response using contrast to explain that thin people are better than fat people.
3. In "Bing and Elvis" Baker uses comparison and contrast to show that the popularity of each singer reflects the sociological climate of different generations. Select two entertainers, movies, television shows, or songs and use comparison and/or contrast to reveal how they reflect the values of two different groups of people or the climates of two periods of time.
4. A fable is a story, written in a simple style, that has a moral or lesson to be taken from it. Write a fable in the style of Carson's "A Fable for Tomorrow" in which you compare and/or contrast life as it is today with life as it would be if population growth continued unchecked or if the unemployment rate continued to climb. Begin your fable, as Carson does, with "There was once." Be sure some moral or lesson is apparent.
5. Compare and/or contrast life as it is today with life as it would be without some modern fact of life, such as the car, the telephone, antibiotics, professional or collegiate football, airplanes, computers, alarm clocks, etc. Be careful not to dwell on the obvious.
6. Compare and/or contrast the way you view something or someone now with the way you did when you were a child.
7. Compare and/or contrast two magazine ads or two television commercials for the same kind of product (wine, cigarettes, cars, jeans, cold remedies, etc.).
8. Compare and/or contrast the skill and technique of two athletes who play the same sport.
9. Compare and/or contrast two celebrations of the same holiday (Halloween, Thanksgiving, New Year's Eve, etc.).
10. Compare and/or contrast your feelings and behavior while anticipating an important event (graduation, a final exam, a big date, entering college, the

first day of a job, a big game, etc.) with your feelings and behavior after the event was over.

11. Compare and/or contrast two people you enjoy who have very different outlooks on life. Try to determine why both people appeal to you.
12. Compare and/or contrast two ways to do something difficult (diet, quit smoking, save money, raise your grades, offer criticism, etc.).
13. Compare and/or contrast two people you admire for their success.
14. Compare and/or contrast the way some group of people (working women, teachers, doctors, fathers, police officers, children, etc.) is depicted on television with the way that group is in reality.
15. Compare and/or contrast two restaurants that you have eaten at.
16. Compare and/or contrast two vacations you have had. Be sure to find a focus. You cannot discuss everything about both vacations.
17. Compare and/or contrast two cities you have spent time in. Be sure to find a focus; you cannot discuss everything about both cities.
18. Compare and/or contrast the way you thought something would be with the way it actually turned out to be.
19. Compare and/or contrast what advertisements tell you some products will be like and what they will do with the way these products actually are and the way they actually perform. For example, does using a certain toothpaste really guarantee white teeth and romance?
20. Compare and/or contrast the way problems are solved on soap operas with the way they are solved in real life. (Or compare and/or contrast some other feature of soap operas with the same feature in real life.)

Writing Strategies

As you write your comparison-and-contrast essay and experiment to improve your writing process, you may find some of the following strategies helpful. In addition, you may wish to try some of the techniques described in chapters 1–3 and in the exercise on p. 239.

Topic Selection

If you are having trouble arriving at a topic, consider discussing the similarities between two things generally thought of as different or the contrasts between two things generally viewed as similar. For example, an essay noting the differences between getting a degree and getting an education could clarify the real essence of education, despite the fact that "getting a degree" is commonly equated with "getting an education." Similarly, an essay discussing the similarities between eccentricity and genius, two very different states in many ways, could foster greater understanding of one or both of these. If you use this approach, be sure that the comparisons or contrasts you draw are valid and useful. While is it possible to compare studying for an exam with preparing for war, this would have little use beyond an exercise in ingenuity.

1. List writing can be particularly helpful for generating ideas. Make two lists. One can include every similarity you can think of, and the second can include every difference. At this point, write everything that occurs to you without evaluating the worth of anything.
2. When you have completed your lists, look them over. Circle each comparison that you find particularly meaningful or interesting, and do the same for the contrasts.
3. If you are not certain whether to treat similarities, differences, or both, some consideration of the ideas in your lists may help you decide. However, do not think that if you have circled more similarities than differences that it is obviously similarities you should deal with. Take some time to consider whether the differences, although fewer, are more telling because they lead to the more significant conclusion.

A Postwriting Evaluation of Your Process

To develop a successful writing process, you must become aware of the techniques you currently employ, and you must evaluate their effectiveness. In addition, you should experiment to determine how you can improve the aspects of your process that are not as successful as you would like. The questions below are meant to help you evaluate your process and decide what changes to make. Because other writers can suggest strategies that might be right for you, discuss your answers with your instructor and classmates.

1. When you wrote your comparison-and-contrast essay, what stages of the process went smoothly (not necessarily quickly)?
2. Did you do anything that worked well enough to repeat in the future? If so, what? Why do you think the technique was successful?
3. Was there anything about writing the essay that was unreasonably difficult and/or time-consuming? If so, what was it, and why do you think it was a problem? Has this been a problem in the past?
4. What stage(s) of your process will you handle differently next time? What will you do? Why?
5. Are you more comfortable writing now than in the past? Why or why not?

10

Cause-and-Effect Analysis

A cause-and-effect analysis examines why an event or action occurred (the causes), what resulted from the event or action (the effects), or both. People engage in cause-and-effect analysis regularly because we always want to know why something happened and what its effects were. In short, cause-and-effect analysis helps us make sense of the world. Cause-and-effect analysis is common in efforts to understand the past, for example, when we identify the causes of the stock market crash in 1929 and go on to determine how that event affected our country and its people. Cause-and-effect analysis is also common when we look to the future. For example, we might predict the effects of the current air pollution rate on the quality of life 20 years from now.

Purpose and Audience

The purpose of a cause-and-effect analysis can be to inform, persuade, or share. Say, for example, you wrote an essay explaining what causes leaves to change color and fall from the trees in autumn. This examination of cause can inform a reader. Similarly, if you wrote an essay explaining what happens to teenagers when their parents divorce, your purpose could also be to inform your reader.

Often a cause-and-effect analysis serves to persuade a reader. For exam-

259

ple, you could explain the effects of teenage alcoholism in persuading your reader to do something to solve the problem. Also, you could explain the effects of too much television viewing among preschool children to persuade your readers to limit the amount of television their children watch.

Sometimes the writer of a cause-and-effect analysis wishes to share. If you wrote about how your parents' divorce affected you, your purpose could be to share your feelings and experiences. Similarly, if you wrote about what caused you to join the nuclear disarmament movement, your purpose might also be to share feelings and experiences.

To establish a purpose for your cause-and-effect analysis, answer these questions:

1. Can I inform my reader of something?
2. Can I persuade my reader to think or act a certain way?
3. Can I share my feelings or experiences with a reader?

The audience for your cause-and-effect analysis will be very much tied to your purpose. If you want to inform your reader, your audience must not currently know the cause-and-effect information you are providing. If you want to persuade your reader to think or act a certain way, your audience must not currently hold your view. And, of course, if you want to share, your audience should be someone you wish to share with.

To identify an audience for your cause-and-effect analysis, answer these questions:

1. Who would be interested in my cause-and-effect analysis?
2. Who could learn something from my cause-and-effect analysis?
3. Who could the cause-and-effect analysis persuade to think or act a certain way?
4. Who would I like to share my feelings or experiences with?

Selecting Detail

When you select detail for a cause-and-effect analysis, remember that in addition to the obvious ones, *underlying* causes and effects are likely. For example, if you are examining the causes of the high divorce rate, you might note the increase in two-career marriages. This would be an obvious cause. However, a closer examination of this cause would reveal underlying causes: Two-career marriages mean less clearly defined roles, less clearly defined divisions of labor, added job-related stress, and increased competition between partners. If you are discussing effects, then you should be on the lookout for underlying effects. For example, let's say you are examining the effects of being the youngest child in a family. An obvious effect to report is that the youngest is considered "the baby." Look beyond that obvious effect, and you can discover underlying effects: The youngest can come to view himself or herself as the baby and hence less capable, less mature, and less strong; the youngest, viewed as a baby, may not be taken seriously by other family members. When you develop detail for your cause-and-effect analysis, be sure to report the underlying causes and effects as well as the obvious ones.

Many cause-and-effect relationships are part of causal chains. A *causal chain* occurs when a cause leads to an effect and that effect becomes a cause which leads to another effect and that effect becomes a cause leading to another effect, and so on. To understand causal chains, consider the effects of the portrayal of the father on *The Bill Cosby Show*.

The father on *The Bill Cosby Show* (Cliff Huxtable) is portrayed as good-natured all the time, wise all the time, loving all the time, and happy all the time; he has the solutions to all his children's problems, a better-than-average income, looks, brains, and talent. What is the effect of this portrayal? First, children may feel their fathers are not as good as Cliff Huxtable. That's the first effect. This effect becomes a cause: it causes children to be disappointed in their fathers. This effect becomes a cause: It causes fathers to feel inadequate because their children are disappointed in them. When you develop detail for a cause-and-effect analysis, you should be careful to identify and report causal chains.

One way to develop detail for a cause-and-effect analysis is to think of each cause and effect as a generalization that must be supported with adequate detail (see p. 41 for a discussion of supporting generalizations). Sometimes an illustration will do this. For example, say you are explaining the effects of moving to a new town when you were in seventh grade, and one of those effects was that you felt like an outsider. You could illustrate this point by telling of the time no one wanted to sit with you at lunch.

Description is another technique used in cause-and-effect analysis. For example, if you were discussing the effects of dumping industrial waste into rivers, you could describe the appearance of a river that has had industrial waste dumped into it.

Narration can also appear in a cause-and-effect analysis. Say you are explaining why more women than men suffer from math anxiety. One cause you offer is that female students are often told that they are not as good at math as males. To support this point, you could tell the story of the time your seventh-grade guidance counselor told you not to take algebra because you were a girl.

Another way to support a cause or effect generalization is with process analysis. For example, assume you are explaining the long-term effects of using pesticides, and you mention that pesticides work their way into the food chain. To support this point, you could describe the process whereby the pesticide goes from soil to plant to animal to human.

Explaining why or how something is a cause or effect can also be helpful. For example, assume you are explaining that one effect of divorce on young children is to make them feel responsible for the breakup of their parents' marriage. You should go on to explain why: Young children think that if they behaved better, their parents would not have fought as much and would have stayed married.

Sometimes a cause-and-effect analysis explains something that is *not* a cause or effect, as when dispelling mistaken notions that something is a cause or effect that really is not. For example, say you are explaining the causes of math anxiety among women. If many people believe women are genetically incapable of excelling in math and you know this is not the case, then you can note this fact. You may also go on to explain why this is not true: No studies to date have proven anyone is genetically good or bad at mathematics.

When you are generating ideas for a cause-and-effect analysis, remember that something that happens before an event cannot always be taken as the cause of that event. For example, if you wash the car and then it rains, assuming that washing a car causes rain would be ridiculous.

Arranging Detail

The detail for a cause-and-effect analysis can be arranged a number of ways. Very often a progressive order is used. In this case, the most significant or obvious causes or effects are given first, and the writer works progressively to the least significant or obvious causes or effects. Or it is possible to move from the least significant or obvious to the most significant or obvious.

A chronological arrangement is possible if the causes or effects occur in a particular time order. If you are reproducing causal chains, a chronological order is likely since one cause will lead to effects and causes that occur in a particular time sequence. When reproducing causal chains, get the sequence of causes and effects in the correct order.

Sometimes you will group causes and effects in particular categories. For example, say you are explaining what causes high school students to drop out of school. You could group together all the causes related to home life, then group together all the causes related to peer pressure, and then group together all the causes related to academic environment.

The introduction of a cause-and-effect analysis can be handled in any of the ways described in Chapter 2 (see p. 32). In addition, you may want to explain why an understanding of the cause-and-effect relationship is important. For example, if you want to provide reasons for adolescent drug abuse, your introduction could note that understanding the reasons for the problem is an important first step toward solving the problem.

If your essay will treat the causes of a problem, your introduction can provide a summary of the chief effects. For example, say you will explain why fewer people are entering the teaching profession. Your introduction can note some of the chief effects of this phenomenon: fewer qualified teachers, a decline in the quality of education, larger class sizes. Similarly, if your essay will explain the effects of something, your introduction can note the chief causes. For example, if your essay will discuss the effects of increased tuition fees at your school, your introduction can briefly explain the causes of the increase: lower enrollment generating less income, higher operating costs, an expensive building program.

A suitable thesis for a cause-and-effect analysis can indicate the relationship that will be analyzed. It can also note whether causes, effects, or both will be treated. Here are some examples:

If we are to solve the problem of teenage drug abuse, we must first understand what leads teenagers to take drugs. (This thesis notes that the essay will analyze the causes of drug use among teenagers.)

Not everyone realizes the subtle yet devastating effects unemployment has on a person's self-image. (This thesis notes that the essay will analyze the effects of unemployment on self-image.)

The reasons Congress is cutting aid to the homeless are clear, but the effects of this action are less well understood. (This thesis notes that the essay will treat both the causes and effects of cuts in aid to the homeless.)

The conclusion of a cause-and-effect analysis can be handled in any of the ways described in Chapter 2. Often a cause-and-effect analysis ends with a conclusion drawn from the cause-and-effect relationship. For example, if your essay has shown what the causes of teenage drug abuse are, your essay could end with a conclusion drawn about the best way to combat the problem. A summary can also be an effective way to end. If the cause-and-effect relationship is complex, with several causal chains, your reader may appreciate a final reminder.

Points to Remember about Cause-and-Effect Analysis

1. A cause-and-effect analysis can analyze causes, effects, or both.
2. A cause-and-effect analysis can inform, persuade, or share.
3. Detail should
   a. include obvious *and* underlying causes and/or effects
   b. include a faithful reproduction of causal chains
4. Each cause and effect should be considered a generalization that must be supported with adequate detail. Support can include
   a. illustration
   b. description
   c. narration
   d. process analysis
   e. an explanation of why or how something is a cause or effect
5. Sometimes a cause-and-effect analysis explains what is *not* a cause or effect.
6. Detail is often arranged in a progressive order, chronological order, or categorical order.

7. Approaches to the introduction include
   a. explaining why an understanding of the cause-and-effect relationship is important
   b. explaining causes if the essay will discuss effects
   c. explaining effects if the essay will discuss causes
8. The thesis can indicate the cause-and-effect relationship to be analyzed and whether causes, effects, or both will be treated.
9. A cause-and-effect analysis can conclude in a number of ways, including
   a. drawing a conclusion from the cause-and-effect relationship
   b. summarizing, if the causes and/or effects are many and complex

Exercise: Cause-and-Effect Analysis

1. To find a topic for a cause-and-effect analysis, pick an important decision you made sometime in your life. Possibilities include your decision to quit the football team, your choice of college, your decision to join the army, your decision to major in a particular field, your decision to move away from home, your decision to break up with a boyfriend or girlfriend, your decision to marry.
2. Decide whether you want to analyze what caused you to reach your particular decision, the effects of that decision, or both causes and effects.
3. Select an audience and purpose for your analysis by answering the questions on p. 260.
4. Pick one cause or effect that could appear in the essay and answer these questions:
   a. Can I develop the cause or effect generalization with illustration?
   b. Can I develop the cause or effect generalization with description?
   c. Can I develop the cause or effect generalization with narration?
   d. Can I develop the cause or effect generalization with process analysis?
   e. Can I develop the cause or effect generalization with an explanation of why or how?
5. Should any causal chains be reproduced? If so, list every cause and effect in one such chain.

Reading Cause-and-Effect Analysis

The professional essays that follow illustrate many of the points made so far in this chapter. The questions at the end of each selection will help you identify the chief features of the writings.

Man of Wisdom

Robert Jastrow

Starting about one million years ago, the fossil record shows an accelerating growth of the human brain. It expanded at first at the rate of one cubic inch[1]

---

[1] One cubic inch is a heaping tablespoonful. [Author's footnote.]

of additional gray matter every hundred thousand years; then the growth rate doubled; it doubled again; and finally it doubled once more. Five hundred thousand years ago the rate of growth hit its peak. At that time the brain was expanding at a phenomenal rate of ten cubic inches every hundred thousand years. No other organ in the history of life is known to have grown as fast as this.[2]

What pressures generated the explosive growth of the human brain? A change of climate that set in about two million years ago may supply part of the answer. At that time the world began its descent into a great Ice Age, the first to afflict the planet in hundreds of millions of years. The trend toward colder weather set in slowly at first, but after a million years patches of ice began to form in the north. The ice patches thickened into glaciers as more snow fell, and then the glaciers merged into great sheets of ice, as much as two miles thick. When the ice sheets reached their maximum extent, they covered two-thirds of the North American continent, all of Britain and a large part of Europe. Many mountain ranges were buried entirely. So much water was locked up on the land in the form of ice that the level of the earth's oceans dropped by three hundred feet.

These events coincided precisely with the period of most rapid expansion of the human brain. Is the coincidence significant, or is it happenstance?

The story of human migrations in the last million years provides a clue to the answer. At the beginning of the Ice Age Homo[3] lived near the equator, where the climate was mild and pleasant. Later he moved northward. From his birthplace in Africa[4] he migrated up across the Arabian peninsula and then turned to the north and west into Europe, as well as eastward into Asia.

When these early migrations took place, the ice was still confined to the lands in the far north; but eight hundred thousand years ago, when man was already established in the temperate latitudes, the ice moved southward until it covered large parts of Europe and Asia. Now, for the first time, men encountered the bone-chilling blasts of freezing winds that blew off the cakes of ice to the north. The climate in southern Europe had a Siberian harshness then, and summers were nearly as cold as European winters are today.

In those difficult times, the traits of resourcefulness and ingenuity must have been of premium value. Which individual first thought of stripping the pelt from the slaughtered beast to wrap around his shivering limbs? Only by such inventive flights of the imagination could the naked animal survive a harsh climate. In every generation, the individuals endowed with the at-

---

[2] If the brain had continued to expand at the same rate, men would be far brainier today than they actually are. But after several hundred thousand years of very rapid growth the expansion of the brain slowed down and in the last one hundred thousand years it has not changed in size at all. [Author's footnote.]

[3] Latin for "man."

[4] Until recently, the consensus among anthropologists placed the origin of man in Africa. However, some recent evidence suggests that Asia may have been his birthplace. [Author's footnote.]

tributes of strength, courage, and improvisation were the ones more likely to survive the rigors of the Ice Age; those who were less resourceful, and lacked the vision of their fellows, fell victims to the climate and their numbers were reduced.

The Ice Age winter was the most devastating challenge that Homo had ever faced. He was naked and defenseless against the cold, as the little mammals had been defenseless against the dinosaurs one hundred million years ago. Vulnerable to the pressures of a hostile world, both animals were forced to live by their wits; and both became, in their time, the brainiest animals of the day.

The tool-making industry of early man also stimulated the growth of the brain. The possession of a good brain had been one of the factors that enabled Homo to make tools at the start. But the use of tools became, in turn, a driving force toward the evolution of an even better brain. The characteristics of good memory, foresight, and innovativeness that were needed for tool-making varied in strength from one individual to another. Those who possessed them in the greatest degree were the practical heroes of their day; they were likely to survive and prosper, while the individuals who lacked them were more likely to succumb to the pressures of the environment. Again these circumstances pruned the human stock, expanding the centers of the brain in which past experiences were recorded, future actions were contemplated, and new ideas were conceived. As a result, from generation to generation the brain grew larger.

The evolution of speech may have been the most important factor of all. When early man mastered the loom of language, his progress accelerated dramatically. Through the spoken word a new invention in tool-making, for example, could be communicated to everyone; in this way the innovativeness of the individual enhanced the survival prospects of his fellows, and the creative strength of one became the strength of all. More important, through language the ideas of one generation could be passed on to the next, so that each generation inherited not only the genes of its ancestors but also their collective wisdom, transmitted through the magic of speech.

A million years ago, when this magic was not yet perfected, and language was a cruder art, those bands of men who possessed the new gift in the highest degree were strongly favored in the struggle for existence. But the fabric of speech is woven out of many threads. The physical attributes of a voice box, lips, and tongue were among the necessary traits; but a good brain was also essential, to frame an abstract thought or represent an object by a word.

Now the law of the survival of the fittest began to work on the population of early men. Steadily, the physical apparatus for speech improved. At the same time, the centers of the brain devoted to speech grew in size and complexity, and in the course of many generations the whole brain grew with them. Once more, as with the use of tools, reciprocal forces came into play in which speech stimulated better brains, and brains improved the art of speech, and the curve of brain growth spiraled upward.

Which factor played the most important role in the evolution of human intelligence? Was it the pressure of the Ice-Age climate? Or tools? Or language? No one can tell; all worked together, through Darwin's[5] law of natural selection, to produce the dramatic increase in the size of the brain that has been recorded in the fossil record in the last million years. The brain reached its present size about one hundred thousand years ago, and its growth ceased. Man's body had been shaped into its modern form several hundred thousand years before that. Now brain and body were complete. Together they made a new and marvelous creature, charged with power, intelligence, and creative energy. His wits had been honed by the fight against hunger, cold, and the natural enemy; his form had been molded in the crucible of adversity. In the annals of anthropology his arrival is celebrated by a change in name, from Homo erectus—the Man who stands erect—to Homo sapiens—the Man of wisdom.

The story of man's creation nears an end. In the beginning there was light; then a dark cloud appeared, and made the sun and earth. The earth grew warmer; its body exhaled moisture and gases; water collected on the surface; soon the first molecules struggled across the threshold of life. Some survived; others perished; and the law of Darwin began its work. The pressures of the environment acted ceaselessly, and the forms of life improved.

The changes were imperceptible from one generation to the next. No creature was aware of its role in the larger drama; all felt only the pleasure and pain of existence; and life and death were devoid of a greater meaning.

But to the human observer, looking back on the history of life from the perspective of many eons, a meaning becomes evident. He sees that through the struggle against the forces of adversity, each generation molds the shapes of its descendants. Adversity and struggle lie at the root of evolutionary progress. Without adversity there is no pressure; without pressure there is no change.

These circumstances, so painful to the individual, create the great currents that carry life forward from the simple to the complex. Finally, man stands on the earth, more perfect than any other. Intelligent, self-aware, he alone among all creatures has the curiosity to ask: How did I come into being? What forces have created me? And, guided by his scientific knowledge, he comes to the realization that he was created by all who came before him, through their struggle against adversity.

Questions on Technique: "Man of Wisdom"

1. Does Jastrow treat causes, effects, or both?
2. What approach does Jastrow take to the introduction?
3. Although the essay has no stated thesis with a topic and view, which sentence indicates what the essay is about?

---

[5] British naturalist Charles Darwin (1809–1882) theorized that all species of life evolved from lower forms through "natural selection."

4. Which paragraphs include process analysis? What purpose does the analysis serve?
5. Which paragraphs include description?
6. What causes are given for the development of the human brain?
7. What causal chains are reproduced in the essay?
8. In what order are the details arranged? What words indicate that this is the order used?
9. What is the purpose of paragraph 15?
10. What approach does Jastrow take to the conclusion?
11. What do you judge to be the intended audience and purpose of "Man of Wisdom"?

The Best Years of My Life

Betty Rollin

I am about to celebrate an anniversary. Not that there will be a party with funny hats. Nor do I expect any greetings in the mail. Hallmark, with its infinite variety of occasions about which to fashion a 50-cent card, has skipped this one. This, you see, is my cancer anniversary. Five years ago tomorrow, at Beth Israel Hospital in New York City, a malignant tumor was removed from my left breast and, along with the tumor, my left breast. To be alive five years later means something in cancer circles. There is nothing intrinsically magical about the figure five, but the numbers show that if you have survived that many years after cancer has been diagnosed, you have an 80 percent shot at living out a normal life span.

Still, you probably think Hallmark is right not to sell a card, and that it's weird to "celebrate" such a terrible thing as cancer. It's even weirder than you imagine. Because not only do I feel good about (probably) having escaped a recurrence of cancer, I also feel good about having gotten cancer in the first place. Here is the paradox: although cancer was the worst thing that ever happened to me, it was also the best. Cancer (the kind I had, with no spread and no need of chemotherapy, with its often harrowing side effects) enriched my life, made me wiser, made me happier. Another paradox: although I would do everything possible to avoid getting cancer again, I am glad I had it.

There is a theory about people who have had a life-and-death scare that goes something like this: for about six months after surviving the scare, you feel shaken and grateful. Armed with a keen sense of what was almost The End, you begin to live your life differently. You pause during the race to notice the foliage, you pay more attention to the people you love—maybe you even move to Vermont. You have gained, as they say, a "new perspective." But then, according to this theory, when the six months are over, the "new perspective" fades, you sell the house in Vermont and go back to the same craziness that was your life before the car crash or whatever it was. What has happened is that you've stopped feeling afraid. The crash is in the past. The it-can't-happen-to-me feelings that were dashed by the accident re-emerge, after six months, as it-can't-happen-to-me-*again*.

It's different for people whose crash is cancer. You can stay off the freeways, but you can't do much about preventing whatever went wrong in your own body from going wrong again. Unless your head is buried deep in the sand, you know damn well it *can* happen again. Even though, in my case, the doctors say it isn't likely, the possibility of recurrence is very real to me. Passing the five-year mark is reassuring, but I know I will be a little bit afraid for the rest of my life. But—ready for another paradox?—certain poisons are medicinal in small doses. To be a little bit afraid of dying can do wonders for your life. It has done wonders for mine. That's because, unlike the way most people feel, my sense of death is not an intellectual concept. It's a lively presence in my gut. It affects me daily—for the better.

First, when you're even slightly afraid of death, you're less afraid of other things—e.g., bosses, spouses, plumbers, rape, bankruptcy, failure, not being liked, the flu, aging. Next to the Grim Reaper, how ferocious can even the most ferocious boss be? How dire the direst household calamity? In my own professional life, I have lost not only some big fears, but most of the small ones. I used to be nervous in front of television cameras. That kind of nervousness was a fear of not being thought attractive, smart and winning. It still pleases me greatly if someone besides my husband and mother thinks I'm attractive, smart and winning; but I am no longer afraid that someone won't. Cancer made me less worried about what people think of me, both professionally and socially. I am less concerned about where my career is going. I don't know where it's going. I don't think about that. I think about where I am and what I'm doing and whether I like it. The result is that these days I continually seem to be doing what I like. And probably I'm more successful than when I aimed to please.

My book *First, You Cry,* which has given me more pleasure than anything else in my professional life, is a good example of this. As a career move, leaving television for six months to write a book about a cancer operation seemed less than sensible. But as soon as I got cancer, I stopped being "sensible." I wanted to write the book. And, just in case I croaked, I wanted to write it the way that was right for me, not necessarily for the market. So I turned down the publisher who wanted it to be a "how-to" book. I like to think I would have done that, cancer or not, but had it not been for cancer, I probably wouldn't have written a book at all, because I would have been too afraid to drop out of television even for six months. And if I had written a book, I doubt that I would have been so open about my life and honest about my less-than-heroic feelings. But, as I wrote, I remember thinking, "I might die, so what does it matter what anyone thinks of me?" A lot of people write honestly and openly without having had a disease, but I don't think I would have. I hadn't done it before.

A touch of cancer turns you into a hypochondriac. You get a sore throat and you think you've got cancer of the throat; you get a corn from a pair of shoes that are too tight and you're sure it's a malignant tumor. But— here's the bright side—cancer hypochondria is so compelling it never occurs to you that you could get anything *else*. And, when you do, you're so glad it's not cancer that you feel like celebrating. "Goody, it's the flu!" I heard myself say to myself a couple of weeks ago.

Some physicians are more sensitive than others to cancer anxiety. My gynecologist prattled on once about some menstrual irregularity without noticing that, as he spoke, I had turned to stone. "Is it cancer?" I finally whispered. He looked dumbfounded and said, "Of course not!" As if to say, "How could you think such a thing?" But an orthopedist I saw about a knee problem took an X-ray and, before saying a word about what it was (a torn cartilage), told me what it wasn't. I limped home joyously.

I never went to Vermont because I can't stand that much fresh air; but in my own fashion, I sop up pleasure where and when I can, sometimes at the risk of professional advancement and sometimes at the risk of bankruptcy. An exaggeration, perhaps, but there's no question about it: since cancer, I spend more money than I used to. (True, I have more to spend, but that's mostly because of the book, which is also thanks to cancer.) I had always been parsimonious—some would say cheap—and I'm not anymore. The thinking is, "Just in case I do get a recurrence, won't I feel like a fool for having flown coach to Seattle?" (I like to think I'm more generous with others as well. It seems to me that, since having cancer, I give better presents.)

Cancer kills guilt. You not only take a vacation now because next year you might be dead, but you take a *better* vacation because, even if you don't die soon, after what you've been through, you feel you deserve it. In my own case, I wouldn't have expected that feeling to survive six months because, once those months passed, I realized that, compared to some people, I had not been through much at all. But my hedonism continues to flourish. Maybe it was just a question of changing a habit.

My girlish masochism didn't resurface, either. Most women I know go through at least a phase of needing punishment from men. Not physical punishment, just all the rest: indifference, harshness, coldness, rudeness or some neat combination. In the past, my own appetite for this sort of treatment was voracious. Conversely, if I happened to connect with a man who was nice to me, I felt like that song: "This can't be love because I feel so well." The difference was that, in the song, it really *was* love, and with me, it really *wasn't*. Only when I was miserable did I know I really cared.

The minute I got cancer, my taste in men improved. It's not that my first husband was a beast. I'm fond of him, but even he would admit he was very hard on me. Maybe I asked for it. Well, once you've been deftly kicked in the pants by God (or whoever distributes cancer), you stop wanting kicks from mortals. Everyone who knows the man I married a year ago thinks I'm lucky—even my mother!—and I do, too. But I know it wasn't only luck. It was that cancer made me want someone wonderful. I wasn't ready for him before. I was so struck by this apparent change in me that I checked it out with a psychoanalyst, who assured me that I was not imagining things—that the damage to my body had, indeed, done wonders for my head.

Happiness is probably something that shouldn't be talked about too much, but I can't help it. Anyway, I find the more I carry on about it, the better it gets. A big part of happiness is noticing it. It's trite to say, but if you've never been ill, you don't notice—or enjoy—not being ill. I even notice my husband's good health. (He doesn't, but how could he?)

I haven't mentioned losing that breast, have I? That's because, in spite of the fuss I made about it five years ago, that loss now seems almost not worth mentioning. Five years ago, I felt sorry for myself that I could no longer keep a strapless dress up. Today I feel that losing a breast saved my life, and wasn't I lucky. And when I think of all the other good things that have come from that loss, I just look at that flat place on my body and think: small price.

Most of my friends who are past 40 shudder on their birthdays. Not me. They feel a year closer to death, I suppose. I feel a year further from it.

O.K., what if I get a recurrence? I'm not so jolly all the time that I haven't given this some serious thought. If it happens, I'm sure I won't be a good sport about it—especially if my life is cut short. But even if it is, I will look back at the years since the surgery and know I got the best from them. And I will be forced to admit that the disease that is ending my life is the very thing that made it so good.

Questions on Technique: "The Best Years of My Life"

1. What approach does Rollin take to the introduction? What is her thesis?
2. Does the essay treat causes, effects, or both?
3. What do you judge to be the author's intended audience and purpose?
4. What does Rollin give as the effects of her cancer?
5. Where does Rollin explain what is *not* an effect?
6. Which paragraph includes process analysis? What is the purpose of this analysis?
7. Where does the author use examples?
8. Where does the author explain how or why something is an effect?
9. What causal chain does the author reproduce?
10. Cite two topic sentences that present an effect to be explained in the body paragraph.
11. What approach does Rollin take to the conclusion?

When Bright Girls Decide That Math Is "A Waste of Time"

Susan Jacoby

Susannah, a 16-year-old who has always been an A student in every subject from algebra to English, recently informed her parents that she intended to drop physics and calculus in her senior year of high school and replace them with a drama seminar and a work-study program. She expects a major in art or history in college, she explained, and "any more science or math will just be a waste of my time."

Her parents were neither concerned by nor opposed to her decision. "Fine, dear," they said. Their daughter is, after all, an outstanding student. What does it matter if, at age 16, she has taken a step that may limit her understanding of both machines and the natural world for the rest of her life?

This kind of decision, in which girls turn away from studies that would give them a sure footing in the world of science and technology, is a self-inflicted female disability that is, regrettably, almost as common today as it was when I was in high school. If Susannah had announced that she had decided to stop taking English in her senior year, her mother and father would have been horrified. I also think they would have been a good deal less sanguine about her decision if she were a boy.

In saying that scientific and mathematical ignorance is a self-inflicted female wound, I do not, obviously, mean that cultural expectations play no role in the process. But the world does not conspire to deprive modern women of access to science as it did in the 1930's, when Rosalyn S. Yalow, the Nobel Prize-winning physicist, graduated from Hunter College and was advised to go to work as a secretary because no graduate school would admit her to its physics department. The current generation of adolescent girls—and their parents, bred on old expectations about women's interests—are active conspirators in limiting their own intellectual development.

It is true that the proportion of young women in science-related graduate and professional schools, most notably medical schools, has increased significantly in the past decade. It is also true that so few women were studying advanced science and mathematics before the early 1970's that the percentage increase in female enrollment does not yet translate into large numbers of women actually working in science.

The real problem is that so many girls eliminate themselves from any serious possibility of studying science as a result of decisions made during the vulnerable period of midadolescence, when they are most likely to be influenced—on both conscious and subconscious levels—by the traditional belief that math and science are "masculine" subjects.

During the teen-age years the well-documented phenomenon of "math anxiety" strikes girls who never had any problem handling numbers during earlier schooling. Some men, too, experience this syndrome—a form of panic, akin to a phobia, at any task involving numbers—but women constitute the overwhelming majority of sufferers. The onset of acute math anxiety during the teen-age years is, as Stalin was fond of saying, "not by accident."

In adolescence girls begin to fear that they will be unattractive to boys if they are typed as "brains." Science and math epitomize unfeminine braininess in a way that, say, foreign languages do not. High-school girls who pursue an advanced interest in science and math (unless they are students at special institutions like the Bronx High School of Science where everyone is a brain) usually find that they are greatly outnumbered by boys in their classes. They are, therefore, intruding on male turf at a time when their sexual confidence, as well as that of the boys, is most fragile.

A 1981 assessment of female achievement in mathematics, based on research conducted under a National Institute for Education grant, found significant differences in the mathematical achievements of 9th and 12th graders. At age 13 girls were equal to or slightly better than boys in tests involving algebra, problem solving and spatial ability; four years later the boys had outstripped the girls.

It is not mysterious that some very bright high-school girls suddenly decide that math is "too hard" and "a waste of time." In my experience, self-sabotage of mathematical and scientific ability is often a conscious process. I remember deliberately pretending to be puzzled by geometry problems in my sophomore year in high school. A male teacher called me in after class and said, in a baffled tone, "I don't see how you can be having so much trouble when you got straight A's last year in my algebra class."

The decision to avoid advanced biology, chemistry, physics and calculus in high school automatically restricts academic and professional choices that ought to be wide open to anyone beginning college. At all coeducational universities women are overwhelmingly concentrated in the fine arts, social sciences and traditionally female departments like education. Courses leading to degrees in science- and technology-related fields are filled mainly by men.

In my generation, the practical consequences of mathematical and scientific illiteracy are visible in the large number of special programs to help professional women overcome the anxiety they feel when they are promoted into jobs that require them to handle statistics.

The consequences of this syndrome should not, however, be viewed in narrowly professional terms. Competence in science and math does not mean one is going to become a scientist or mathematician any more than competence in writing English means one is going to become a professional writer. Scientific and mathematical illiteracy—which has been cited in several recent critiques by panels studying American education from kindergarten through college—produces an incalculably impoverished vision of human experience.

Scientific illiteracy is not, of course, the exclusive province of women. In certain intellectual circles it has become fashionable to proclaim a willed, aggressive ignorance about science and technology. Some female writers specialize in ominous, uninformed diatribes against genetic research as a plot to remove control of childbearing from women, while some well-known men of letters proudly announce that they understand absolutely nothing about computers, or, for that matter, about electricity. This lack of understanding is nothing in which women or men ought to take pride.

Failure to comprehend either computers or chromosomes leads to a terrible sense of helplessness, because the profound impact of science on everyday life is evident even to those who insist they don't, won't, can't understand why the changes are taking place. At this stage of history women are more prone to such feelings of helplessness than men because the culture judges their ignorance less harshly and because women themselves acquiesce in that indulgence.

Since there is ample evidence of such feelings in adolescence, it is up to parents to see that their daughters do not accede to the old stereotypes about "masculine" and "feminine" knowledge. Unless we want our daughters to share our intellectual handicaps, we had better tell them no, they can't stop taking mathematics and science at the ripe old age of 16.

Questions on Technique: "When Bright Girls Decide That Math Is 'A Waste of Time'"

1. What paragraphs form Jacoby's introduction? What is the thesis of the essay?
2. The introduction includes narration and illustration. What does each of these methods of development contribute?
3. Does the essay treat causes, effects, or both?
4. What does Jacoby offer as the *obvious* cause of females' turning from math and science? What does she offer as the *underlying* causes?
5. Where does the explanation of effects begin? What does the author present as the effects of females' avoiding math and science?
6. What approach does Jacoby take to the conclusion?
7. What do you judge to be the intended audience and purpose of this essay?

Student Writings to Read and Evaluate

The cause-and-effect analyses here were written by students. They are of varying quality, but all have some strengths and weaknesses. As you read these essays, identify their chief strong and weak points. This will help you become a better judge of writing so you can better decide what to include in your writing and what to avoid. An evaluation exercise follows the student essays.

Athletes on Drugs: It's Not So Hard to Understand

On June 17, 1986, Len Bias, a basketball star from the University of Maryland, was the second pick in the National Basketball Association amateur draft. Bias had everything going for him; he was a 22-year-old kid about to become a millionaire and superstar. He was on top of the world (or so it seemed). Forty hours later Len Bias was dead—from an overdose of drugs. The Len Bias story is tragic, but it is just one of the many cases that have surfaced recently. Just 8 days following the Bias tragedy, Cleveland Browns all-pro safety Don Rogers, then 23, died of a drug overdose. Steve Howe, once a dazzling pitcher in the early 1980s, now finds himself out of baseball because of his drug problems. And the list goes on. Why? Why are professional athletes, people who have money, success, fame, and power, destroying their lives with drugs?

To most people the life of professional athletes is filled with glamour. All they see are the sports cars, the million-dollar contracts, and the adoring fans. People do not realize the mental anguish that is involved with being a professional athlete. The loneliness, the fear of failure, and the insecurities of their jobs are just a few of the pressures that athletes have to deal with every day. In some sports, such as baseball, basketball, and hockey, the teams play five to seven games a week, so the athletes must travel to two or three different cities. This constant travel has an adverse effect on athletes' ability to cope with daily pressures. They begin to miss family and friends, often becoming lonely and depressed. As an alternative to this depression, they turn to drugs.

In most cases, professional athletes of today have been the best in their sports since childhood. They have won honors and awards for their talents all through their lives. They have seldom been failures, and fear of becoming one is their worst nightmare. The athletes are surrounded by family, friends, and coaches who tell them they are the best. These people attempt to make the athletes feel flawless, incapable of making a mistake. Therefore, when players do have a bad day, they not only let themselves down but those people too. Again, in order to deal with the pressure, drugs become a solution.

For most of today's professional athletes, sports is all they know. Many do not have a college education, and, more than likely, without sports they would not have a career. Athletes must remain above the competition to keep their jobs. In some cases, when the God-given ability is not enough, the player uses drugs for improvement. Athletes have found that some drugs, such as amphetamines, can increase their physical abilities. These drugs help the athlete to perform better, therefore giving her or him a greater chance of success. For example, steroids have almost become a norm in some sports. Bodybuilders and football players have discovered that these drugs speed up the development of strength and muscles. In professional football, large numbers of offensive and defensive linemen claim to have used steroids at least once in their careers. Those professional athletes who refuse to use amphetamines and steroids are no doubt at a disadvantage.

In today's sports athletes are bigger, stronger, and faster; therefore, more injuries are occurring. Injuries are part of the game, and all players have suffered at least one in their careers. The most discomforting fact about injuries for professional athletes of today is not the pain but the drugs that are used to ease their discomfort. In many cases, coaches and trainers strongly encourage the use of such drugs. In the high-priced world of sports, time is money. Athletes cannot afford to sit out and allow their injuries to heal properly. They often turn to drugs to help speed up the healing process. Often these drugs are illegal; sometimes they are more dangerous than the injury itself, but for the athlete the use of the drug appears to be the only choice. Without the drugs, the players face the loss of thousands of dollars as well as their livelihoods.

The professional athlete has to deal with a great deal of pressure. As the mental struggles begin to mount and the aches and pains begin to multiply, the athlete becomes more susceptible to drug use. Drug use should never be accepted, but in the case of the professional athlete, condemning the problem will not solve it. The fans, owners, and especially the players themselves must reexamine the pressures and stop the drug problem before it destroys more people's lives.

The Distribution of Student Loan Funds

On the first day of classes, students who applied for guaranteed student loans were inconvenienced by a lack of funds. The need for the loans to be distributed in advance was evident.

When I applied for my loan at the bank, I was informed that some legal changes were made. The loan would be paid in two payments, and the check would be made out to me and to my college. At this time, the loan officer was not sure where I would pick up the first check, at the bank or at the college. About a month before college classes were to begin, I received a form noting the approval of my loan, the amount approved, the amount of each check, and when the checks would be disbursed. There was no information as to where the checks would be sent. When I located my check at the college, I was informed that the new law stated that no disbursement of funds could be made until the first day of school.

My need for the loan increased as the first day of classes grew nearer. Since my daughter is a freshman at another university, she too was not disbursed her guaranteed student loan money. Our budget was stretched to the limit. For my daughter to begin classes, it was necessary to pay for her apartment, to put a deposit on her utilities, and to transport her belongings to Columbus. I just prayed my two bald tires would make it to Columbus and would not need to be replaced before I picked up my loan check. When I wrote the check for my 14-year-old son's school shoes, I had to go home and scrape up the money to cover it.

On the first day of classes, I became aware that I was not the only one that was inconvenienced. Since I was finished with my classes and drop-add at

10:30 a.m., I had the opportunity to talk with other students while waiting until 2:00 to pick up my loan. There were complaints about the hassle at drop-add because fees were not paid, about the waste of study time because students couldn't buy books, about the problem of finding time to wait in lines to receive the checks, and about the waste of time spent going back and forth across campus between classes trying to pick up the loan money. Some students were scheduled to get their loans at 10:00 and were told to come back at 2:00, and some were not scheduled to get their loans until Friday. Another widespread complaint developed when the computer system went down, creating a delay that lasted an hour.

It is hard to understand the reason for delaying the distribution of loan checks that are supposed to help pay for fees, books, room and board, and transportation. But the effects of the delay are clear: students are hassled unnecessarily.

Friends at Work

You may have had experience with or heard statements about the disadvantages of having friends who suddenly become coworkers. Trust me; what you heard is correct.

Last spring I worked at a small but heavily trafficked truck stop. My boss decided to hire some new employees to increase the efficiency of the afternoon shift, so I recommended my friend Robert. Dreading the process of taking in numerous applications and granting endless interviews, my boss agreed to hire Robert. I was sure Robert was a good choice, so I was not anticipating any problems.

The first day with Robert started out smoothly. I discovered that he was a very hard worker and that he possessed the strength to unload delivery trucks and scrub the fuel islands, which I was unable to do. I knew the boss would be pleased. When the time arrived for Robert to work at the cashier's counter, however, his incompetency in that area overwhelmed me. At first, a few difficulties were to be expected until he became familiar with the routines. As the weeks passed, though, his progress was minimal, and I found myself answering his same questions over and over again. I stressed firmly but politely that he would have to concentrate harder and to interrupt my own customer relations less often. His efforts thereafter were admirable, but the more Robert worked on his own, the more mistakes he made; the situation was going out of control.

Robert was fired after the boss realized his incompatibility with the job. I felt sorry for Robert, but because of his mistakes (and the mistake of hiring him at all), I knew it would take awhile for me to redeem myself in the eyes of my employer. After all, I persuaded him to have the utmost confidence in Robert.

The opportunity to redeem myself came a few weeks later after more attempts to find competent help failed. I then discovered that my friend Joyce, who was presently working at a truck stop, would consider leaving her position for the higher-paying job on my shift. I convinced the supervisor that she would be much better for the job than Robert was since she was already familiar with truck stop procedures. To my surprise, my boss decided to take another chance with my recommendation.

Joyce and I worked well together and had fun doing our jobs. Our problems, however, started when we learned that the assistant manager was leaving and his position would be filled using one of the five cashiers. I assumed that I would be considered because of my seniority over the others and my unblemished work record. To my extreme shock and dismay, I learned from Joyce that she was appointed to the job. "That's great," I muttered sarcastically. Apparently, she had developed a "relationship" with one of the regional supervisors, who requested the store manager to give her the promotion. I could not believe she accepted it—she knew that promotions were always granted on the basis of seniority. She certainly did not exhibit any special skills above and beyond mine, except of course with the regional supervisor.

When I confronted my boss about the unfair situation, he seemed not to be concerned and figured that I would "get over it." He did not even satisfy me with an explanation of how the decision was made. I had difficulty understanding such callous disregard for my abilities and feelings. The following day, my letter of resignation was delivered.

The causes are not always the same, but the effects usually are: friends who work together do not stay friends for long. I regret the strain on the friendships I had with two people, and I regret having to give up my job. But I should have known better.

Fear of College

I didn't go to college right after high school graduation because I was afraid. And I stayed afraid for years to come.

When my wife graduated from college, my fear became even more pronounced. Oh, I kept hinting that one of these days I would enroll, but I always found an excuse not to. So many times my wife would ask when I planned to start, but I just waved her off with a vague "one of these days."

The real reason for my fear was that I did poorly in high school. Even though my counselors informed me that I did well on the so-called I.Q. tests, I refused to apply myself. To me, high school was a playground, not a place to receive an education. Needless to say, I did not finish high in my class at graduation. My grade point average was a mere 1.62, and I was 247th of 305 seniors. I thought of myself as dumb, and I knew I would flunk out of college. So I didn't go.

By the time I was 27, my wife had graduated, and I had another reason to fear college: I was too old. I was sure I couldn't compete with younger, smarter kids fresh out of high school. Now I had two reasons not to go.

Without realizing it, I came to resent my wife's education. She couldn't make a comment on important or everyday subjects because of my inferiority complex. Whenever she said something, I accused her of showing off because she had a college degree. Naturally she would defend herself, and then the arguments would start.

Eventually, I decided my wife looked down on me, and I moved out, thinking that she felt I wasn't good enough for her. I demanded a divorce, and she demanded counseling.

The marriage counselor said all the problems were the result of the feelings of inferiority I had because my wife had a college education and I didn't. He encouraged me to enroll in school on a part-time basis.

I have completed 16 hours now, and I have a high C average. My wife and I are back together, and I feel better about myself than I ever have. Who knows? I may even go on to graduate school.

Evaluating Writing: Assessing Cause and Effect

Evaluating the previous student essays can sharpen your awareness of effective and ineffective writing so you can better judge your own writing and make wise revision decisions.

Since this chapter deals with cause-and-effect writing, you will evaluate an essay by writing a cause-and-effect analysis. First select one of the student essays (or use one your instructor assigns). Reread the essay, and make notes about how you react to the piece—what effects the essay has on you. Try to be specific; note such things like "the introduction bores me," "the first body paragraph made me smile," "I could really relate to the example in the third paragraph."

Then go back through the essay and try to find specific reasons for your reactions. These reasons will be the causes. For example, if the introduction bored you, recheck the introduction and maybe you will see that all it does is state the obvious.

When you finish going back through the essay, write a 1- or 2-page cause-and-effect analysis. Cite your reactions as the effects, and as the causes cite what the writer has done to elicit these reactions. The following evaluation questions can serve as a guide for your analysis.

Evaluation Questions

1. Are both obvious and underlying causes and/or effects given?
2. Is there a faithful reproduction of all causal chains?
3. Is each cause-and-effect generalization supported with adequate detail?
4. If necessary, has the author explained what is *not* a cause or effect?
5. Are there enough details to develop the thesis adequately?
6. Are all topic sentences and details relevant to the thesis?
7. Are there any points you do not understand?

8. If any description, illustration, narration, or process analysis appears, is it handled appropriately?
9. Does the essay have an introduction? If so, is it appropriate and interest-holding?
10. Is there a clear thesis, either stated or strongly implied?
11. Is there a formal conclusion? If not, should there be? If there is a conclusion, does it bring the essay to a satisfying close?
12. Are all the details in an easy-to-follow, logical order?
13. Are there any relevance problems?
14. In general, is the word choice specific, economical, and simple?
15. Are there any clichés that should be revised for fresh expression?
16. Does the essay flow well because of adequate sentence variety?
17. Are transitions used effectively?
18. Is the essay carefully edited?

Essay Topics

As you work to develop a topic for a cause-and-effect analysis, consider the possibilities given here.

1. As did Betty Rollin in "The Best Years of My Life," consider the effects of an illness or handicap on you or someone you know.
2. If you avoided math and science in the way described by Susan Jacoby, consider the causes and effects of your avoidance. Or consider the causes and effects of avoiding some subject such as composition.
3. Think back to your earlier school days and recall a traumatic event (not making the baseball team, losing a class election, breaking up with a girl or boyfriend, failing a course, the death of a loved one, and so forth). Write an essay that analyzes the causes and/or effects of this event.
4. Analyze the effects of some recent innovation or invention such as the videocassette recorder (VCR), the compact disc player, word processors, or video games.
5. Analyze the causes and/or effects of a current fad or trend such as interest in fitness, Yuppie living, the current popular music trends.
6. Analyze the effects of your association with a religious group, sorority or fraternity, ethnic group, theater group, etc.
7. Analyze the causes and effects of a long-term friendship you have had.
8. Identify a problem on your campus (inadequate housing, crowded classes, outdated requirements, high tuition, etc.) and analyze its causes and/or effects.
9. Explain why some college students drop out of school.
10. Analyze the causes and/or effects of a fear you have now or have had.

11. Analyze the causes and/or effects of one of your bad habits.
12. Explain the effects attending college has had on your life.
13. Analyze the effects of television portrayals of some group (women, police officers, fathers, teenagers, doctors, etc.).
14. Explain the causes or effects of either racial or religious prejudice.
15. Explain how someone other than a family member (a teacher, scout leader, coach, neighbor, friend, etc.) has influenced your life.
16. Explain the long-term effects of a childhood experience.
17. If you or a family member has been unemployed, explain the effects of this unemployment.
18. Where we grow up has an enormous effect on who and what we become. How did where you grew up (big city, small town, farm, poor neighborhood, affluent suburb, etc.) affect you?
19. Explain how the way we dress affects how people perceive us.
20. Explain how television influences our view of the world.

Writing Strategies

In addition to the suggestions in Chapters 1–3 and in the exercise on p. 264, some of the following strategies may help with your cause-and-effect analysis.

Topic Selection

1. If you are having trouble finding a topic, think of something you do particularly well or particularly badly (run track, do math, make friends, play the piano, paint, etc.). Then consider why you do the thing well or badly and how your ability or lack of it has affected you.
2. Identify something about your personality, environment, or circumstances, and assess how this factor has affected you. You could analyze the effects of poverty, shyness, a large family, moving, and so forth.

Idea Generation

1. To generate ideas, list every cause and/or effect you can think of. Do not censor yourself; write down everything that occurs to you.
2. To get at underlying causes and effects, ask *why?* and *then what?* after every cause and effect in your list. For example, if you listed difficulty making friends as an effect of shyness, ask *then what?*, and you may get the answer "I was lonely." This answer could be an underlying effect of your shyness. If you listed strong legs as a reason for your success at running track, ask *why?*, and you may get the answer "I lifted weights to increase leg strength." This would give you an underlying cause. Asking *then what?* will also help you discover causal chains.
3. Ask yourself why an understanding of the cause-and-effect relationship is important. The answer to this question can appear in your introduction or conclusion.

A Postwriting Evaluation of Your Process

Becoming a better writer requires that you be aware of what you do when you write and how successful your procedures are. Then you must experiment to find procedures to replace the ones that are not working well for you. The questions here will help you decide how to alter your process. In addition, talk to your instructor and classmates to discover what they do when they write.

1. When you wrote your cause-and-effect analysis, what stages of the process went smoothly (not necessarily quickly)?
2. Did you do anything differently this time that worked well enough to repeat in the future? If so, what?
3. Was there anything about writing the essay that was unreasonably difficult and/or time-consuming? If so, why do you think it was a problem? Has it been a problem in the past?
4. What stage(s) of your process will you handle differently next time? What will you do? Why?
5. Are you more comfortable writing now than in the past? Why or why not?

11
Definition

If you want to discover what a word means, you go to the dictionary, right? Well, yes—sometimes. But sometimes the dictionary is not enough. Sure, you can check a dictionary to learn the meaning of a word like *fun*, but what's fun to you may not be fun to someone else, so the full meaning of that word will vary among individuals to an extent. Some words symbolize abstractions, the subtleties of which cannot all be taken in by an inch or so of space in a dictionary. What, for example, does *justice* mean? Certainly it is a concept with complexities far beyond its neat dictionary definition. And, of course, there are words with meanings so complex that a dictionary definition can only hit the high points, leaving quite a bit unexplained. *Democracy* is such a word. Not only is its meaning complex, but it varies greatly according to which country's democracy is referred to. Furthermore, its meaning goes beyond politics to have significance in many facets of our lives.

So while dictionary definitions can tell us much, when it comes to the controversial, abstract, or complex, something more may be needed. And this something can be an extended definition. An *extended definition* goes far beyond the concise, formal definition that appears in a dictionary. The extended definition explores the *nature* of something, including the aspects, significances, nuances, or complexities that are not part of what a dictionary takes in.

Purpose

Definition can clarify. Many concepts—ones like wisdom, courage, freedom, hate, and so on—are multifaceted and difficult to grapple with. In fact, there is not always agreement on what these concepts mean. An extended definition of such a term can provide clarification.

A second purpose of an extended definition can be to bring to the reader's attention something that is taken for granted. For example, an extended definition of a free press can lead the reader (and the writer) to a fresh appreciation for something so much a part of daily life that it is undervalued.

Another purpose of an extended definition can be to bring the reader to a sharper awareness of something familiar but only vaguely understood. An essay defining the microchip might serve this purpose. Or an extended definition can explain the meaning and nature of something not at all understood by the reader, say, a token economy. It is even possible to inform the reader of something new by defining the commonplace. An extended definition of senior citizen might lead to a new knowledge of what it means to grow old in this country. Or a definition of something commonplace, such as neighborhood bars, can be written to entertain at the same time it is pointing out some truths. Sometimes definition is used to make a statement about some issue that goes beyond the subject actually defined. An essay that defines rock music can at the same time comment on the orientation, values, and thinking of young people. That is, because musical preferences among youth are often an index to the prevailing needs and attitudes of young people, a definition of one makes significant statements about the other.

Thus, an extended definition can clarify, inform, or increase awareness of the nature of something. It can force a study of something taken for granted or only casually understood, and it can provide fresh appreciation for the commonplace. It can even make statements that have significance to issues beyond the idea or thing being defined.

To determine your purpose, answer the following:

1. Do I want to clarify the nature of a familiar subject?
2. Do I want my reader to become more aware of something taken for granted?
3. Do I want my reader to better understand an unfamiliar subject?
4. Do I want to give my reader a fresh outlook on my subject?
5. Do I want to make a statement about an issue that goes beyond (but is related to) the subject defined?
6. Do I want my reader to appreciate my subject more?

The purpose you establish for your definition will influence the detail included. Let's say you decide to define *fear* and you wish to give your reader a fresh outlook on this feeling by helping him or her see that fear is really a positive emotion. Such a purpose might lead you to note that fear is adaptive because it ensures our survival. You might also note instances when we would endanger ourselves needlessly were it not for fear. If, however, your purpose were something different, then your detail would be different. Say you want your definition to show that fear keeps us from realizing our potential. Then you might instead include detail that relates lack of achievement to fear of failure and fear of taking risks.

Audience

Your reader will affect the detail you include in your definition. Answers to questions such as these will influence what you include in your essay.

1. How much does my reader know about my subject?
2. Does my reader feel as I do about my subject?
3. How much interest does my reader have in my subject?
4. How receptive to my point of view will my reader be?

To see how audience affects detail selection, assume you are writing an essay defining *teenager* and your purpose is to make your reader aware of how difficult the teen years are. If your reader is 25 and likely to remember adolescence, you will have to explain less than if your audience is much further removed from those years and needs to be reminded of a few things. Similarly, if your audience is a neighbor who has been expressing concern over "what the youth in this country have come to," you may want to explain why teenagers behave as they do in order to address and discharge your reader's negative feelings. However, if your audience is a teenager, there will be no ill will to overcome, so you might instead include detail to reassure the teen that he or she is not alone in the struggle.

To target a specific audience, you can answer the following questions:

1. With whom would I like to share my view?
2. Who would be influenced by my essay?
3. Who sees my subject differently than I do?
4. Who does not fully understand my subject?
5. Who takes my subject for granted?
6. Who would enjoy reading my definition?

Selecting Detail

A piece developed with extended definition can include any other methods of development—description, narration, illustration, comparison and contrast, and so on. Part of your definition may be a description of the characteristics of what you are defining. Sometimes you may provide examples to explain the nature or function of something. Other times you may find yourself comparing and contrasting what you are defining with something else in order to sharpen the definition. It is even possible that narrating a story will aid your definition by providing a telling instance.

In addition to these methods for presenting detail, you can also explain the various characteristics of what you are defining. In other words, if you are defining Christmas spirit, you can cite and explain the characteristics that make up Christmas spirit.

It can also be useful to include some statements of what your subject is *not*. For example, if you are defining freedom, you may want to say that freedom is *not* doing anything you want, it is *not* a privilege, and it is *not* necessarily guaranteed to everyone in this country. From here you could go on to explain what freedom *is*. This technique can be useful when you wish to make important distinctions or dispel common misunderstandings.

As you can see, the writer of extended definition has many decisions to make about detail. If you are defining Christmas spirit, you could tell a story that reveals what Christmas spirit is, or you could compare and contrast Christmas spirit with the feelings people get on other holidays in order to clarify the nature of the spirit. You could provide a number of examples to illustrate the nature of Christmas spirit, or you could describe how it makes people feel and what it makes people do. It is possible to mention what Christmas spirit is not, and it is possible to list and explain the distinguishing characteristics of Christmas spirit. And, of course, you can combine two or more of these techniques to form your definition. So how do you decide what detail to use and which of these methods of development to employ?

The detail you select and the way you present it will partly depend upon how you know what you know. If your understanding of Christmas spirit comes from your own experience with the feeling, you might describe your feelings or tell stories of times you witnessed or displayed the spirit. If your knowledge comes from reading or what others report about the feeling, you may prefer to explain the distinguishing characteristics. If your own observation has shown that Christmas spirit differs markedly from what many think it is, you might want to indicate what Christmas spirit is not. If over the years, the feeling has come to have certain personal associations for you, you may want to illustrate these with examples.

There is another point to keep in mind when you select detail for an extended definition: you should avoid stating the obvious. For example, if you are defining Christmas spirit, and you state that it is a mood that occurs at Christmastime, you run the risk of insulting your reader, who does not need to be reminded of such an obvious point. Also, although you are writing a definition, it is best to avoid the style found in dictionaries. Such a style lacks the vitality that is essential to a good essay. If you write that "Christmas spirit is that seasonal mood of ebullience and feeling of goodwill and generosity characteristic of and emanating from the yearly celebration of the birth of Jesus," you will surely fail to hold your reader's interest.

Arranging Detail

There are not many generalizations that can be made about arranging detail for extended definition, although some points hold true often enough to be worth noting. First, it often makes sense to indicate in the thesis what is being defined and what point can be drawn from the definition or what point of view the writer has. Such a thesis might be "Christmas spirit is not what it used to be," or "Christmas spirit is a natural high."

If your body paragraphs have aspects of narration, description, illustration, and/or comparison and contrast, you will want to follow the organization principles that govern these techniques. Otherwise, a progressive arrangement is frequently effective, perhaps beginning and ending with your strongest points.

Interesting introductions can be crafted in a variety of ways. You can explain what many people believe your subject means if you plan to show it means something else. Or you can explain why it is important to arrive at a definition of your subject. Often an anecdote about your subject can pave the way nicely for a definition of that subject. It can also be interesting to explain what your subject used to mean if your essay will go on to show how that meaning has changed. However, it is probably best to avoid including a dictionary definition in your introduction. While this can be effective at times, usually it is not. Your reader will know, at least approximately, how your subject is defined in Webster's, so a formal definition will probably annoy or bore a reader.

The conclusion of an extended definition very often elaborates on the significance of the definition—the points to be drawn from it. This approach is particularly effective when the thesis is only a broad statement of the writer's point of view (as are the two sample theses about Christmas spirit given at the beginning of this discussion of detail arrangement).

Points to Remember about Definition

1. An extended definition explains the meaning and nature of something. It goes beyond a dictionary definition to treat subtleties, abstractions, significances, implications, and/or personal associations.
2. The following can form the purposes of definition:
   a. clarifying a complex subject
   b. creating appreciation for or fresh awareness of something taken for granted
   c. informing about something not understood or only partially understood
   d. providing a new understanding of a familiar subject
   e. making a statement about an issue related to the subject defined
3. An extended definition can include narration, description, illustration, com-

parison and contrast, or any other method of development or combination of methods. It is also possible to note and explain the distinguishing characteristics of the subject and explain what the subject is not.

4. Detail selection and methods of development are usually determined by
   a. what you know about your subject
   b. the source of your knowledge about your subject
   c. the purpose of and audience for the definition
5. Avoid dictionary-type definitions and statements of the obvious.
6. The thesis can indicate the purpose of the definition or your point of view.
7. Possible approaches to the introduction include
   a. stating what many people believe your subject means if you will show it means something different
   b. explaining what your subject used to mean if you will show that it now means something different
   c. explaining why it is important to arrive at a definition of your subject
   d. telling a story about your subject
8. It should be clearly stated or strongly implied just what conclusion can be drawn from your definition or what significance your definition has. Often the conclusion is a good place for this.

Exercise: Definition

1. Select a subject you might like to write an extended definition of. If you have trouble deciding on a subject, page through a dictionary for some ideas.
2. Settle on a purpose for this essay by asking yourself the questions that appear on p. 284. Then write a possible thesis that presents your subject and indicates your purpose or point of view.
3. Establish an audience for this essay by answering questions 1–6 on p. 285.
4. Determine the nature of your audience by answering questions 1–4 on p. 285.
5. Generate four points suited to your audience and purpose that could be included in your essay. To stimulate your thinking, answer the following questions.
   a. What is the most distinguishing characteristic of my subject? The second-most distinguishing characteristic?
   b. What story can I tell that would help define my subject?
   c. What features of my subject can I describe?
   d. What illustrations would help define my subject?
   e. What can I compare my subject to? What can I contrast it with?
   f. What is my subject *not?*

Reading Definition

The following professional writings are extended definitions. As you read them, consider how they exemplify the principles discussed so far in this chapter. The questions that follow each selection are meant to raise several of these points.

What Is Freedom?

Jerald M. Jellison and John H. Harvey

The pipe under your kitchen sink springs a leak and you call in a plumber. A few days later you get a bill for $40. At the bottom is a note saying that if you don't pay within 30 days, there'll be a 10 percent service charge of $4. You feel trapped, with no desirable alternative. You pay $40 now or $44 later.

Now make two small changes in the script. The plumber sends you a bill for $44, but the note says that if you pay within 30 days you'll get a special $4 discount. Now you feel pretty good. You have two alternatives, one of which will save you $4.

In fact, your choices are the same in both cases—pay $40 now or $44 later—but your feelings about them are different. This illustrates a subject we've been studying for several years: What makes people feel free and why does feeling free make them happy? One factor we've studied is that individuals feel freer when they can choose between positive alternatives (delaying payment or saving $4) rather than between negative ones (paying immediately or paying $4 more).

Choosing between negative alternatives often seems like no choice at all. Take the case of a woman trying to decide whether to stay married to her inconsiderate, incompetent husband, or get a divorce. She doesn't want to stay with him, but she feels divorce is a sign of failure and will stigmatize her socially. Or think of the decision faced by many young men a few years ago, when they were forced to choose between leaving their country and family or being sent to Vietnam.

When we face decisions involving only alternatives we see as negatives, we feel so little freedom that we twist and turn searching for another choice with some positive characteristics.

Freedom is a popular word. Individuals talk about how they feel free with one person and not with another, or how their bosses encourage or discourage freedom on the job. We hear about civil wars and revolutions being fought for greater freedom, with both sides righteously making the claim. The feeling of freedom is so important that people say they're ready to die for it, and supposedly have.

Still, most people have trouble coming up with a precise definition of freedom. They give answers describing specific situations—"Freedom means doing what I want to do, not what the Government wants me to do;"

Jerald M. Jellison and John H. Harvey, "What Is Freedom?" Reprinted with permission from *Psychology Today Magazine*. Copyright © 1976 American Psychological Association.

or "Freedom means not having my mother tell me when to come home from a party"—rather than a general definition covering many situations. The idea they seem to be expressing is that freedom is associated with making decisions, and that other people sometimes limit the number of alternatives from which they can select.

Questions on Technique: "What Is Freedom?"

1. What would you judge to be the purpose of Jellison and Harvey's definition?
2. Why do the authors believe a definition of their subject is important? Where in the essay do they make this statement of import?
3. How do the authors use narration as part of their definition?
4. How do Jellison and Harvey use illustration to develop their definition?
5. In addition to using narration and illustration, Jellison and Harvey also develop their definition by indicating what their subject is not. At what point in the essay do the authors do this?
6. How do you think the authors arrived at their definition of freedom? That is, how do they know what they know?
7. How does the source of the authors' knowledge affect their detail selection?
8. What approach do Jellison and Harvey take to their introduction?
9. Where does the thesis appear?
10. What approach do the authors take to their conclusion?
11. Why is it that Jellison and Harvey's definition of such a complex, abstract subject seems so clear and simple?

Why I Want a Wife

Judy Syfers

I belong to that classification of people known as wives. I am A Wife. And, not altogether incidentally, I am a mother.

Not too long ago a male friend of mine appeared on the scene fresh from a recent divorce. He had one child, who is, of course, with his ex-wife. He is obviously looking for another wife. As I thought about him while I was ironing one evening, it suddenly occurred to me that I, too, would like to have a wife. Why do I want a wife?

I would like to go back to school so that I can become economically independent, support myself, and, if need be, support those dependent upon me. I want a wife who will work and send me to school. And while I am going to school I want a wife to take care of my children. I want a wife to keep track of the children's doctor and dentist appointments. And to keep track of mine, too. I want a wife to make sure my children eat properly and are kept clean. I want a wife who will wash the children's clothes and keep them mended. I want a wife who is a good nurturant attendant to my children, who arranges for their schooling, makes sure that they have an adequate social life with their peers, takes them to the park, the zoo, etc. I want a wife who takes care of the children when they are sick, a wife who arranges to be around when the children need special care, because, of course, I cannot miss classes at school. My wife must arrange to lose time at work, and not lose the job. It may mean a small cut in my wife's income from time to time, but I guess I can tolerate that. Needless to say, my wife will arrange and pay for the care of the children while my wife is working.

I want a wife who will take care of *my* physical needs. I want a wife who will keep my house clean. A wife who will pick up after me. I want a wife who will keep my clothes clean, ironed, mended, replaced when need be, and who will see to it that my personal things are kept in their proper place so that I can find what I need the minute I need it. I want a wife who cooks the meals, a wife who is a *good* cook. I want a wife who will plan the menus, do the necessary grocery shopping, prepare the meals, serve them pleasantly, and then do the cleaning up while I do my studying. I want a wife who will care for me when I am sick and sympathize with my pain and loss of time from school. I want a wife to go along when our family takes a vacation so that someone can continue to care for me and my children when I need a rest and change of scene.

I want a wife who will not bother me with rambling complaints about a wife's duties. But I want a wife who will listen to me when I feel the need to explain a rather difficult point I have come across in my course of studies. And I want a wife who will type my papers for me when I have written them.

I want a wife who will take care of the details of my social life. When my wife and I are invited out by my friends, I want a wife who will take care of the babysitting arrangements. When I meet people at school that I like and want to entertain, I want a wife who will have the house clean, will prepare a special meal, serve it to me and my friends, and not interrupt when I talk about the things that interest me and my friends. I want a wife who will have arranged that the children are fed and ready for bed before my guests arrive so that the children do not bother us. I want a wife who takes care of the needs of my guests so that they feel comfortable, who makes sure that they have an ashtray, that they are passed the hors d'oeuvres, that they are offered a second helping of the food, that their wine glasses are replenished when necessary, that their coffee is served to them as they like it. And I want a wife who knows that sometimes I need a night out by myself.

I want a wife who is sensitive to my sexual needs, a wife who makes love passionately and eagerly when I feel like it, a wife who makes sure that I am satisfied. And, of course, I want a wife who will not demand sexual attention when I am not in the mood for it. I want a wife who assumes the complete responsibility for birth control, because I do not want more children. I want a wife who will remain sexually faithful to me so that I do not have to clutter up my intellectual life with jealousies. And I want a wife who understands that *my* sexual needs may entail more than strict adherence to monogamy. I must, after all, be able to relate to people as fully as possible.

If, by chance, I find another person more suitable as a wife than the wife I already have, I want the liberty to replace my present wife with another one. Naturally I will expect a fresh, new life; my wife will take the children and be solely responsible for them so that I am left free.

When I am through with school and have a job, I want my wife to quit working and remain at home so that my wife can more fully and completely take care of a wife's duties.

My God, who *wouldn't* want a wife?

Questions on Technique: "Why I Want a Wife"

1. Syfers' essay first appeared in *Ms.* magazine. How would you describe her audience?
2. What do you judge to be Syfers' purpose? Is her audience likely to be sympathetic with her purpose and in agreement with her definition of a wife?
3. Syfers' thesis is implied. What is that thesis?
4. How does Syfers develop her definition? Is her detail exaggerated or balanced and fair?
5. Syfers defines a wife by classifying and listing her duties. What classifications of duties are given?
6. What is the source of Syfers' details?
7. Paragraphs 1 and 2 form the introduction. What approach does Syfers take to her introduction?
8. What approach does Syfers take to her conclusion?

The Egalitarian Error

Margaret Mead and Rhoda Metraux

Almost all Americans want to be democratic, but many Americans are confused about what, exactly, democracy means. How do you know when someone is acting in a democratic—or an undemocratic—way? Recently several groups have spoken out with particular bitterness against the kind of democracy that means equal opportunity for all, regardless of race or national origin. They act as if all human beings did not belong to one species, as if some races of mankind were inferior to others in their capacity to learn what members of other races know and have invented. Other extremists attack religious groups—Jews or Catholics—or deny the right of an individual to be an agnostic. One reason that these extremists, who explicitly do not want to be democratic, can get a hearing even though their views run counter to the Constitution and our traditional values is that the people who *do* want to be democratic are frequently so muddled.

For many Americans, democratic behavior necessitates an outright denial of any significant differences among human beings. In their eyes it is undemocratic for anyone to refer, in the presence of any other person, to differences in skin color, manners or religious beliefs. Whatever one's private thoughts may be, it is necessary to act as if everyone were exactly alike.

Behavior of this kind developed partly as a reaction to those who discriminated against or actively abused members of other groups. But it is artificial, often hypocritical behavior, nonetheless, and it dulls and flattens human relationships. If two people can't talk easily and comfortably but must forever guard against some slip of the tongue, some admission of what is in both persons' minds, they are likely to talk as little as possible. This embarrassment about differences reaches a final absurdity when a Methodist feels that he cannot take a guest on a tour of his garden because he might have to identify a wild plant with a blue flower, called the wandering Jew, or when a white lecturer feels he ought not to mention the name of Conrad's beautiful story *The Nigger of the "Narcissus."* But it is no less absurd when well-meaning people, speaking of the physically handicapped, tell prospective employers: "They don't want special consideration. Ask as much of them as you do of everyone else, and fire them if they don't give satisfaction!"

Another version of false democracy is the need to deny the existence of personal advantages. Inherited wealth, famous parents, a first-class mind, a rare voice, a beautiful face, an exceptional physical skill—any advantage has to be minimized or denied. Continually watched and measured, the man or woman who is rich or talented or well educated is likely to be called "undemocratic" whenever he does anything out of the ordinary—more or less of something than others do. If he wants acceptance, the person with a "superior" attribute, like the person with an "inferior" attribute, often feels obliged to take on a protective disguise, to act as if he were just like everybody else. One denies difference; the other minimizes it. And both believe, as they conform to these false standards, that they act in the name of democracy.

For many Americans, a related source of confusion is success. As a people we Americans greatly prize success. And in our eyes success all too often means simply outdoing other people by virtue of achievement judged by some single scale—income or honors or headlines or trophies—and coming out at "the top." Only one person, as we see it, can be the best—can get the highest grades, be voted the most attractive girl or the boy most likely to succeed. Though we often rejoice in the success of people far removed from ourselves—in another profession, another community, or endowed with a talent that we do not covet—we tend to regard the success of people close at hand, within our own small group, as a threat. We fail to realize that there are many kinds of success, including the kind of success that lies within a person. We do not realize, for example, that there could be in the same class one hundred boys and girls—each of them a "success" in a different kind of way. Individuality is again lost in a refusal to recognize and cherish the differences among people.

The attitude that measures success by a single yardstick and isolates the *one* winner and the kind of "democracy" that denies or minimizes differences among people are both deeply destructive. Imagine for a moment a family with two sons, one of whom is brilliant, attractive and athletic while the other is dull, unattractive and clumsy. Both boys attend the same high school. In the interest of the slower boy, the parents would want the school to set equally low standards for everyone. Lessons should be easy; no one should be forced to study dead languages or advanced mathematics in order to graduate. Athletics should be noncompetitive; every boy should have a chance to enjoy playing games. Everyone should be invited to all the parties. As for special attention to gifted children, this is not fair to the other children. An all-around education should be geared to the average normal child.

But in the interest of the other boy, these same parents would have quite opposite goals. After all, we need highly trained people; the school should do the most it can for its best students. Funds should be made available for advanced classes and special teachers, for the best possible coach, the best athletic equipment. Young people should be allowed to choose friends on their own level. The aim of education should be to produce top-flight students.

This is an extreme example, but it illustrates the completely incompatible aims that can arise in this kind of "democracy." Must our country shut its eyes to the needs of either its gifted or its less gifted sons? It would be a good deal more sensible to admit, as some schools do today, that children differ widely from one another, that all successes cannot be ranged on one single scale, that there is room in a real democracy to help each child find his own level and develop to his fullest potential.

Moving now to a wider scene, before World War I Americans thought of themselves as occupying a unique place in the world—and there was no question in most minds that this country was a "success." True, Europeans might look down on us for our lack of culture, but with a few notable, local exceptions, we simply refused to compete on European terms. There was no country in the world remotely like the one we were building. But since World War II we have felt the impact of a country whose size and strength and emphasis on national achievement more closely parallel our own. Today we are ahead of Russia, or Russia is ahead of us. Nothing else matters. Instead of valuing and developing the extraordinary assets and potential of our country for their own sake, we are involved in a simple set of competitions for wealth and power and dominance.

These are expensive and dangerous attitudes. When democracy ceases to be a cherished way of life and becomes instead the name of one team, we are using the word democracy to describe behavior that places us and all other men in jeopardy.

Individually, nationally and, today, internationally, the misreading of the phrase "all men are created equal," exacts a heavy price. The attitudes that follow from our misconceptions may be compatible with life in a country where land and rank and prestige are severely limited and the roads to success are few. But they are inappropriate in a land as rich, as filled with opportunities as our own. They are the price we pay for being *less* democratic than we claim to be.

"All men are created equal" does not mean that all men are the same. What it does mean is that each should be accorded full respect and full rights as a unique human being—full respect for his humanity *and* for his differences from other people.

Questions on Technique: "The Egalitarian Error"

1. What is the purpose of the authors' definition?
2. Where in the essay do Mead and Metraux present their purpose?
3. What technique do Mead and Metraux rely on most heavily to develop their definition? Why is this technique a logical choice?
4. What other methods of development do the authors use, and where in the essay are these found?
5. Where in the essay do the authors explain the significance of their definition?
6. What approach do Mead and Metraux take to their introduction?
7. What approach do Mead and Metraux take to their conclusion?

Student Writings to Read and Evaluate

The definition essays that follow were written by students. Some are stronger than others, but each has something to recommend it. As you read these pieces, you will be working to improve your ability to assess strengths and weaknesses so you can better judge your own work. In addition, exposure to the writing of other students will make you aware of successful techniques to incorporate into your own work and unsuccessful techniques to avoid. Following the student writings, there is a formal evaluation exercise for you to work on.

The Spirit of Prepdom

The fall of the hippie era of the sixties has paved the way for a new trend which has swept the nation. The preppy look is no longer restricted to New England, but can now be found anywhere in the United States.

The grooming of a preppy does not occur overnight. Like everything else, preppiness begins at home. At the moment of birth, Mummy and Daddy carefully select first and middle names for the newborn which often correspond to the names of dormitories at their prep alma maters. Aside from the given names bestowed upon preps by their parents, numerous nicknames can be a sure indication of a true prep. Missy, Buffy, Bitsy, and Kiki are common among female preppies, while Skip, Bink, Kip, and Win are well-known male preps.

Perhaps the most obvious trait of a preppy is their manner of dress. Although the preppy look can be imitated, nonpreps can easily be spotted by their ignorance of a few unspoken standards. Preppy clothes can be worn for many years without becoming outdated. The fabrics, the cuts, and the colors are the same, year after year. The preppy woman can be seen sporting shirts such as cotton turtlenecks covered with small prints of whales, ducks, and turtles, oxford-cloth buttondowns, and the famed Chemise Lacoste. Any shirt is worn tucked in—always. Whenever possible, collars are turned up.

Skirts are another must to the wardrobe of a female prep. Khaki A-lines, jean skirts, and tartan-plaid kilts have a sacred place in every female prep's closet. Skirts tend to disguise the female figure with modest length and the absence of cinched waists, high slits, and tightness around the derriere.

The male prep counterpart, when not wearing sailing or tennis gear, is almost always seen clad in oxford buttondowns, Lacoste sport shirts, and Shetland sweaters. Many times, the look is completed by the addition of a tweed blazer or a navy-blue jacket with a college or club insignia embroidered on the breast pocket.

There is only one cut for prep men's trousers—straight leg. Ideally, side pockets open along the side seam of the pants. All pants should be cuffed. The cuffs are about 1½ inches wide. A preppy man wears his trousers a little on the short side.

Many aspects of prep dress are common to both men and women. Sperry top-siders (always worn sockless), Gucci loafers, and Tretorn sneakers are the most popular prep footwear and shared by both sexes. Neither sex sports an abundance of jewelry. A school ring or family signet ring is the favored and very often the lone adornment of prep men and women. Although preppies are not interested in designer items, they do put their own monograms on everything from clothes to doorknobs, to wastebaskets.

Certain colors can also be attributed to the prep look. These colors are universal, and frequently appear in the closets of men and women alike. The most popular of these "special" schemes is the hot-pink and lime-green combination. This combination is a sure and quick way to identify a prep because it extends to all attire from shirts, to pants, to belts, to shoes. Brilliant yellow and Windex blue are also a major part of a prep's color scheme.

Outward appearances are not the only distinguishing feature of a preppy. They are also set apart by their speech, actions and forms of recreation.

If during the course of conversation, phrases such as "completely cube," "Mummy and Daddy," "divine," and "unreal" frequently pop up, it is safe to assume that the person to whom you are speaking is a member of the prep set.

There are also several activities, while not solely limited to preps, which are representative of their lifestyles. During a preppy's childhood, he or she is repeatedly exposed to activities such as piano lessons, summer camp, riding lessons, and dancing school. Tennis, skiing, and sailing, which are introduced to all prep children at an early age, continue to be a major source of enjoyment through a prep's entire life.

It is the inalienable right of every man, woman, and child to wear alligators. Looking, acting, and being prep is not restricted to an elite few lucky enough to attend prestigious private schools. In a true democracy, everyone can be upper-class, summer at Martha's Vineyard, wear lime green, and talk with clenched teeth. Possessing only one of the mentioned characteristics does not deem one a true preppy. All aspects, including dress, speech, and lifestyle, must be equally combined to capture the essence of a true preppy.

What It Means to Be a Friend

Although I feel that it is not extremely difficult for two people to begin establishing a relationship, maintaining that relationship may not be quite as easy. Undoubtedly, we all have our faults and flaws, our marks of imperfection, and as two people come to know more about one another, these flaws become more and more evident. It is the degree of emphasis placed on these flaws that determines whether or not a relationship blossoms into a true friendship. If a person is truly your friend, then even after he has come to know a lot about you, he will still care very much for you. A true friend is fun to be with, trustworthy, and reliable.

As I vividly recollect the past, I can recall the attempts that a certain young fellow and I made at establishing a true friendship. We tried to be courteous, respectful, and even witty. Yet our efforts were made in vain because we could never overlook one another's faults. I viewed him as being boisterous and cocky, and he often told me that I was extremely stubborn. Our relationship never really developed, for we constantly focused on the negative aspects of one another's characters. Eventually, we lost hope, and the relationship sort of faded out.

For some time after this experience, I didn't really try to make any new friends. Then one day, I met a certain individual, and after a while, he and I began associating on a regular basis. Fortunately, we were able to accept those flaws that we had detected, and we focused on the better characteristics we had also spotted. As a result of our efforts, our relationship grew stronger, and it developed into what I feel is truly a friendship.

As far as my true friend is concerned, I would have to say that he is a guy with whom I have been able to share fun times. We've gone to ball games, to parks, and to movies. We've enjoyed playing basketball and football. We've shared countless jelly donuts, bags of potato chips, and candy bars. Over the years, we have really enjoyed one another's company.

In addition to being a joy to be around, my friend is also someone whom I have come to trust. We could have never grown as close as we are had we not shared secrets, and we would have never shared secrets had we not trusted one another. Now in the early stages of our relationship, we were both tentative about relaying too much information about ourselves. However, gradually, we became more open, and we began sharing some of those deeper, inner feelings. For instance, once I was scared to go to school because I knew that this big, hulking fellow wanted to beat me up; yet, the only one to whom I was able to admit fear was my true friend. Somehow, I knew that he wouldn't brand me a coward, and just being able to tell someone what I was undergoing did wonders for my ego. Because he could be trusted, I could tell him that I was afraid, and I could rest assured that no one else would know of my fear. Because of trust, we were able to open up and thus come closer to one another.

Perhaps that which best exemplifies my true friend is his being available in times of need. Once, I was really in dire need of assistance. As I recall, I was playing football up the street from where I live. Suddenly, this band of ten-speed-bike-riding desperadoes came roaring up the street. Overcome with fright, I desperately sought to flee from the scene because I immediately remembered angering the forerunner of the gang the day before. Now, since they were rambling up the street and I lived down the street, my chances of getting home didn't look very good. Meanwhile, the other guys who were playing football had the luxury of living nearby, and they promptly ran home. However, my true friend remained, and though he also could have run home like the others, he first grabbed hold of me, and then together, we ran to his house. No doubt he saved me from considerable bodily injury, and my folks from outrageous hospital bills. For his act of valor, I will always be indebted, as I am for the times when I have needed someone to talk to, to console me, to encourage me, and to advise me, and he has been there.

As I recollect the various experiences that our relationship has undergone, I must say that my friend and I have come to know one another very well, and I believe that we have come to care about each other very much. To me, he has truly been fun to be with, trustworthy, and reliable, and I hope and pray that to some degree, I have been the same to him.

What Is Christmas Spirit?

A winter night, a brilliant star, and a tiny stable. A manger, straw, swaddling clothes, and a newborn infant. The crisp peal of church bells. The hustle and bustle of shoppers, the gaily decorated store windows. Holly on the door, candles in the windows, the fragrance of pine boughs, the sparkle of tinsel and mistletoe. Red and green, blue and silver. White. Fresh snowflakes, drifting in the starlight. Cards and ribbon, and tissue paper. A trip home, an open latch, and hugs from loved ones. Turkey and giblets. Cranberries and mincemeat pie. Christmas is the cold and warmth, forgiveness and love. Christmas is a prayer expressing the age-old hope: Peace on earth and goodwill towards men.

When people think of Christmas, reflections of the Christmas Spirit, like these, come to mind. Christmas, the word itself, is derived from the Old English *Cristes maesse,* "Christ's mass," a festival both secular and religious commemorating the birth of Jesus Christ. Spirit is defined as an animating or vital force giving life to otherwise inanimate organisms. In the composite—the Christmas Spirit—is the total of the Christmas season, that attitude, pervading feeling, that belief, that mood that permeates the community of those celebrating one of the greatest of Christian holidays.

There have been many variations in the personal and social manifestation of this mood since its origin. But it is a belief that can be experienced where other sociocultural intersects may be lacking: a Greek, a Mexican, and a Scandinavian all thrust together on December 25 and unable to communicate, having very different cultural backgrounds, can still be in a communion of spirit, sharing a common bond of festivity.

The spirit has its origins in the belief that on one day some 2,000 years ago, a God-Man came to redeem all men. This is a concept so magnificent in its nature that if believed, it is without parallel as a cause for celebration. There are many cross-links between specific cultures and ethnic groups with their particular social customs that give a special flavor to the celebration. Though many and varied, they each share oneness in spirit.

Though in the modern age materialism and commercialism may often outweigh the initial Christmas meaning, nevertheless there is usually that unsuppressible wish of all mankind to enjoy spiritual release from material things to those things pure and eternal. Perhaps it is best experienced by those who have known better times, by those who are alone, lonely, or forgotten, or perhaps by the individual who has negligible worldly worth, but nonetheless immense value by virtue of the coming of a personal savior, Jesus Christ. Therein lies the wellspring of the festivity. The lights, the song, the merrymaking are only exterior raiments of man's inner jubilation. Christmas, as a celebration, is recorded as early as the third century and has been celebrated on December 25 since the fourth century. Christmas has been commingled with the pagan solar and agricultural observances of midwinter, the Roman time of merrymaking and gift-giving, Saturnalia, plus a mixture of Teutonic and Celtic Yule rites with their fir trees, cakes, greenery, gifts, and comradery.

Reflections from ages past burst then each year anew in the eyes, hearts, and minds of modern man in the wonderful Spirit of Christmas.

The Final Stage

She has white hair, cloudy eyes, and a mind that wanders. Her voice crackles when she speaks. Her teeth are gone, for they were pulled many years ago. She's deaf. Her shoulders are stooped, her back hunched. She has brittle bones, wrinkled skin, and gnarled hands. She no longer recognizes her bowel urges. Her legs are weak. She's skinny. Because she dressed herself, her dress is on backward. She wears two pair of underwear and no shoes. She's not hungry. She never is. Fits of depression and crying jags are a usual occurrence. She is moody. She's confused and disoriented. Some days she is mean and nasty, uttering cruel words and spouting prejudices. She's disheveled and messy. She's tired. She's alone. She needs love, kindness, and patience. She is old.

This shell of a person used to be a productive human being. She was a mother, sister, wife, and daughter. She has lived, loved, and dealt with tragedy in her lifetime, and now she is walking her final miles. She remains in her own world completely dependent upon others for her care and personal safety.

This need for care and supervision leads her to a nursing home, where she will spend her remaining days enclosed in a building with very little mental stimulation. Consequently, she will become more confused and disoriented. Once in a while a family member may come to visit, send a card, or send some flowers. Rarer still, someone will come to take her out for the day.

Abandoned and alone, she looses sight of what little reality she has left. Loneliness and fear will be magnified as the darkness of night engulfs her, which in turn will set off a series of unfounded fears. As she cries out from her bed, she will accept little in the way of comfort and reassurance, for she is sure in her mind that the nurse or aide is there to harm her.

For many people, this is the final stage. Healthy limbs will atrophy. Intelligent minds will no longer function. A nimble step will become a shuffle. This is the final stage of life. This is old age.

Evaluating Writing: Assessing Strengths and Weaknesses

Pair up with a classmate and select one of the student definition essays, or use one your instructor assigns. Take three sheets of paper, and label one sheet *Introduction,* label one sheet *Body,* and label one sheet *Conclusion.* Go back through the essay and on the appropriate sheets record what you agree are the strengths and weaknesses. Also record an explanation for why each noted feature is strong or weak. You need not record *every* strength and weakness— just the major ones. If you and your partner disagree on some points, note this disagreement on your sheet. As you work through this evaluation, you may wish to refer to some or all of the evaluation questions that follow.

Evaluation Questions

1. Does the definition have some purpose that goes beyond a simple dictionary definition? Is this purpose clearly stated or strongly implied?
2. Has the author avoided a dictionary-style definition?
3. Has the author avoided obvious statements that can annoy the reader? If not, which points are too obvious to be included?

4. Is there enough detail in enough body paragraphs to adequately develop the definition? If not, where is additional detail needed?
5. Are there any points you do not understand? If so, what are they?
6. Does the essay have a clear thesis, stated or implied?
7. Do all the body paragraphs have a relevant topic sentence? If not, is this a problem?
8. Are there any relevance problems?
9. Is the detail ordered logically and effectively? If not, explain why.
10. Does the essay have a separate conclusion? If not, should it have? If there is a conclusion, does it bring the essay to a satisfying close?
11. In general, is the word choice specific, economical, and simple?
12. Are there any clichés that should be revised for fresh expression?
13. Is there adequate sentence variety?
14. Are transitions used effectively?
15. Is the essay carefully edited?

Essay Topics

The following list of topics for a definition essay may include something that appeals to you or something that can serve as a springboard to a desirable topic.

1. What is a freshman (or senior or some other campus "type," such as a jock, fraternity guy/sorority gal, egghead, etc.)?
2. Define male chauvinism (or male liberation or feminism).
3. Define frustration.
4. Define excitement.
5. Define anticipation (or dread).
6. Define maturity.
7. Define adolescence.
8. Define defeat.
9. Define greed.
10. Define satisfaction.
11. What is a bureaucrat?
12. Define the nature of a superhero or hero (Wonder Woman, Superman, John Wayne, etc.).
13. What is education?
14. What is inner strength?
15. Define the current trend in popular music.
16. Define tacky.
17. What is patriotism?
18. Define an ethnic term (chutzpah, gringo, etc.) that is not generally understood in all its connotations.

19. Define ambition.
20. Define the nature of a successful (*popular,* not necessarily *good*) television show.
21. Define jealousy.
22. What is hospitality?
23. What is runner's high?
24. Define cynicism.
25. Define writer's block.

Writing Strategies

In addition to the strategies noted in Chapters 1–3 and in the exercise on p. 283, the following suggestions for topic selection and idea generation may help you as you write your definition essay and experiment to improve aspects of your writing process.

1. What better way to explore topics for a definition essay than to browse through a dictionary? Simply leaf through the pages and consider the various entries. Make a list of words you might like to define and then choose one subject from this list. **Topic Selection**

2. If you have difficulty settling on a topic, consider your own experience. What moods or emotions have you known lately? Depression, anger, surprise, love—these can all be defined using narrations and illustrations from your own life. Or what people have you observed recently? Coaches, teachers, salespeople, doctors—these can be defined on the basis of your own observation.

1. Letter writing can be a productive idea-generation technique for a definition essay. Write a letter to someone you are comfortable with, and begin the letter in this way: "I'd like to explain what _____ means to me." (Fill in the blank with the subject you are defining.) **Idea Generation**

2. In addition to writing a letter, you can make lists to bring ideas forth. Make one list that notes narrations you can tell that help define your subject; make a second list that includes illustrations; make a third that notes comparisons and contrasts; make a fourth that describes your subject; and make a fifth that details what your subject is not. Between your letter and your lists, you will probably come up with quite a few details for developing your definition.

A Postwriting Evaluation of Your Process

Your answers to the questions below should point out techniques that are successful for you and ones that are not, so you can determine what to change in your writing process and what to keep the same. If you discuss your answers with your instructor and classmates, you can exchange ideas and learn helpful strategies to try.

1. When you wrote your definition essay, what stages of the process went smoothly for you? (Remember, *smoothly* does not necessarily mean *quickly*.)
2. Did anything work well enough to repeat in the future? If so, what? Why do you think the technique was successful?
3. Was there anything about writing the essay that was unreasonably difficult and/or time-consuming? If so, what was it, and why do you think it was a problem? Has this been a problem in the past?
4. What stage(s) of your process will you handle differently next time? What will you do? Why?
5. Are you more comfortable writing now than in the past? Why or why not?

12

Persuasion

Persuasion is everywhere. The friend who tries to convince you to skip class and catch an afternoon movie is engaging in persuasion—so too is the politician who delivers a speech to win your vote, the newspaper editor who writes an editorial to convince you of the dangers of a large national debt, and the advertising executive who creates an ad to make you believe that the surest path to popularity is using the right deodorant soap.

The fact that persuasion makes up a significant part of our lives is really not surprising, for as thinking, feeling creatures we are bound to form strong opinions on a broad range of issues. And it is only natural that we would want others to share our views. After all, the more people who agree with us, the likelier it is that the desired actions will occur—and the more comfortable we feel with our views.

To encourage others to adopt our views, we can write a persuasive essay. More than just an explanation of a subject, a persuasive essay attempts to win people over to a particular point of view or convince them to take a particular course of action.

Topic Selection

A persuasive topic must be controversial. That is, the issue at hand must be debatable; it must have at least two sides to it. It would serve no purpose, for example, to write an essay arguing that everyone needs some relaxation. No one would disagree with you. It *would* be purposeful, however, to argue that places of business should have recreation areas to allow employees to relax during lunch and break periods. Similarly, it would be pointless to write a persuasive essay on an issue that is a matter of individual taste. To argue that it is more pleasant to listen to Mozart than Bach makes little sense because the issue is strictly a matter of personal preference.

As a student writer you may want to avoid some of the standard persuasive topics. Most instructors are weary of reading about abortion, capital punishment, legalizing marijuana, lowering the drinking age, and the like. Unless you can find a fresh approach to topics like these, it is probably wise to avoid them.

One reason so many papers have been written on these standard topics may be that students feel that to be significant, their persuasive essays must be on topics of global importance. Yet this is not so. Many smaller-scale issues matter, and can be written about. Campus issues, work matters, and community issues can suggest persuasive topics. You *can,* however, write on matters of larger concern; just try to select something fresh. For example, a persuasive paper arguing that the elderly should be cared for at home rather than in institutions is significant yet not overworked. At the same time, it is also appropriate to treat something of narrower concern. You could, for example, write a fine paper arguing that your school should offer a major in hospital administration.

Audience and Purpose

Your audience and purpose significantly affect what you do. You might think that establishing audience and determining purpose are simple: the purpose is to convince the reader, and the reader is someone who disagrees. But that is only part of the picture. Let's consider audience first.

Certainly your audience will be someone who disagrees with you to some extent, for why bother trying to persuade someone who already agrees with you? But it is important to establish how great the disagreement is. Let's say you are writing an essay in opposition to birth control for teenagers. If your audience is a member of Planned Parenthood, you will need to be far more persuasive than you would be if your reader is someone who believes something closer to what you do.

When considering audience, you will also have to determine how much your reader knows about your issue. Let's say you are writing an essay in support of the legislative veto. If your audience is knowledgeable about the workings of the federal government, you will need to supply less background information than if your reader has only limited knowledge in this area.

Your purpose also deserves careful consideration. Sure, you want to convince your reader to see things just as you do, but that may be an unreasonable expectation. If you favor gun control and are writing to a member of the National Rifle Association, it would be realistic to set your purpose as convincing the reader we need stricter enforcement of existing laws. It might be unrealistic to expect you can convince your reader that handguns should be banned.

Sometimes a particular audience is so opposed to your view that the best you can hope for is that the reader will consider your points and agree that they have some merit. For example, if you are writing to the president of the local teachers' union about the hardships of teachers' strikes, you cannot expect your reader to come out against such strikes. However, if you present a good enough case, your reader can come to understand something he or she never realized before, and perhaps this new understanding will influence the reader's thinking and actions in the future.

To decide on your audience, you can ask yourself the following questions.

1. Who disagrees with me?
2. Of those who disagree, who might be influenced by my writing?
3. Of those who might be influenced, who has the power to act in accordance with my point of view?

After answering the third question, you will have your audience. Then you can answer the following questions to arrive at your purpose.

1. What can I reasonably expect my audience to think or do after reading my essay?
2. Of these things, which are the most important to me?

Detail

When you write persuasively, your purpose is to alter the reader's thinking or to convince the reader to take a particular course of action. Unfortunately, readers will not think or act a certain way just because you ask them to. Instead your reader must be given good reasons to share your beliefs. And it is these reasons that will form your supporting detail.

Above all, your persuasive detail must be firmly rooted in reason. If a thoughtful reader is to adopt your view, that person must see the wisdom of your stand. This means that your reader requires a carefully thought out argument—one that presents well-reasoned points in support of your view.

Otherwise your reader will not conclude that your view is the best one. When you write persuasively, think of yourself as a lawyer presenting a case to a jury in an effort to persuade that body to recognize the validity of your case.

However, as any successful attorney knows, sound logic and compelling facts are not all that can influence a person. Emotion, too, plays a role. After all, when we make up our minds about something, how we *feel* about the issue can determine our decision along with what we *think* about it. For this reason, a writer trying to persuade may work to move the reader's emotions as well as his or her intellect. This is why the writer of a toothpaste ad may emphasize fewer cavities *and* a brighter smile. Our intellect makes us understand the virtue of fewer cavities, but our emotional desire to be attractive makes us want a bright smile.

However, a writer must be careful with emotional appeals. Usually, they should not form the major portion of the essay, but should be used sparingly and with restraint. It is fine to call upon the reader's patriotism to earn support for the draft, but it is unfair, inflammatory, and illogical to whip up emotions by saying that anyone who does not support the draft is un-American. Thus, persuasive writers should rely on reason for the most part. They should be careful of emotional appeals, using them only to enhance their logical argument.

As a persuasive writer, then, you will strive to move your reader's intellect by providing sound reasons why your view should be adopted. You will state your case in the most compelling way you can to impress your reader with the reasonableness of your stand. This means that you will draw on some or all of the methods of development you have learned so far. Narration, description, illustration, comparison and contrast, cause-and-effect analysis, definition—some combination of these may appear in your persuasive essay.

Say, for example, that you wish to persuade your reader to vote for Chris Politician. You might *narrate* an episode that reveals Politician's integrity. You might also *describe* the various personality traits that identify Politician as the best candidate, or *illustrate* Politician's strengths with several examples. You could *compare and contrast* Politician with one or more of the other candidates. Or you may explain the effects of electing Politician. You could even *define* what a good public official is and then show how Politician fits this definition.

In addition to the methods of development you have learned so far, you may also find yourself relying on explanation. That is, your persuasion may give the reasons Politician is the best candidate. For each reason, you would offer details to clarify and explain the reason. For example, if you state that Politician should be elected because she supports affirmative action, you could go on to explain why affirmative action is desirable and that Politician is the only candidate to take a positive stand on that issue.

Often it is effective to speculate about what would happen if your view were adopted (or what would happen if it were not adopted). You could say, for example, that if Politician were elected, a bigger budget would be allotted to the safety forces so that police and fire protection would improve. Or you could explain something negative that would happen if Politician were *not* elected: police and fire protection would continue at substandard levels.

Raising and Countering Objections

Regardless of what strategies you employ to persuade your reader, you must present yourself as objective and clear-thinking. Otherwise, your reader will not trust your judgment. And if your reader does not trust your judgment, you will never succeed in persuading that person. One way you present yourself in a desirable light is to rely on reason and use emotional appeal carefully. Another way is to *raise and counter objections*.

To raise and counter objections, you do two things. First you state what the opposition would say in response to your argument; this is *raising the objection*. Second, you make this objection less compelling in some way; this is *countering the objection*. There are three ways you can counter an objection: you can state that while the opposition's point is a good one, your point is also a good one; you can state that while the opposition's point is a good one, your point is better; you can state that the opposition's point is not true. Below are examples of each of these three ways to raise and counter objections.

Opposition's point is good, but so is yours: There are those who claim that Politician lacks experience in municipal government and hence cannot manage the city well [objection raised]. However, while Politician may not have actual experience in government, her 10 years as president of City Bank have provided her with all the managerial skills any mayor could need [objection countered].

Opposition's point is good, but yours is better: Although some contend that the increased safety forces budget that Politician supports is inflationary [objection raised], the fact remains that without adequate police and fire protection, we will never attract new industry to our city and revitalize our local economy [objection countered].

Opposition's point is untrue: It is puzzling that so many people feel a woman cannot run a city [objection raised]. Why, women have run whole countries successfully. Just look at Golda Meir and Margaret Thatcher [objection countered].

It is important to raise and counter objections because no matter what stand you take on an issue, there will be intelligent, reasonable people who disagree with you. By acknowledging and coming to terms with points counter to your view, you help incline your reader toward your position because you make it clear that you have examined all sides of your issue, considered them carefully, and concluded that your view is the best. This helps you present yourself as a reasonable, clear-thinking person rather than one who ignores important facts simply because they do not support the stand being advanced.

Selecting Detail

There are several things to keep in mind as you decide on persuasive detail. For one thing, audience must be carefully assessed. How much does your reader know about your subject? That is, should you provide background information on the issue and lots of explanation for each point? How receptive will your audience be to your stand? Some audiences are harder to persuade than others. For example, it would be easier to convince a principal that candy machines should be taken out of schools than it would be to convince the students. How much are you asking of your audience? It would be easier to convince people to donate $5 to the leukemia drive than it would be to get them to donate $50 to the Save the Caribou Fund. How knowledgeable your audience is, how inclined toward your view, and how difficult the desired response—these will affect the detail you use.

You will also have to make some thoughtful decisions about which objections to raise and counter. For the most part, you can base this decision on which objections will be the most compelling to your particular audience. This, of course, means that you will have to put yourself in your reader's place and decide which arguments against your stand are likely to interfere with the acceptance of your view.

Let's return to persuading a reader that candy machines should be removed from schools. If your audience is the principal, one objection that reader could have is that students would be angry about the removal and perhaps create problems. This objection could be countered with an explanation that annoyance would soon pass as students grew accustomed to not having the machines around.

If, however, your audience is the students themselves, a likely objection could be that removing the machines would eliminate one of the few pleasant aspects of school. Because it is unlikely that this audience would be appeased by being told they would get used to it, another approach to the counter is necessary. You could, for example, suggest that the money usually fed into the machines could be donated to finance a class trip. This stands a far better chance of winning your audience over to your view. Thus, persuasive writers must select carefully the objections to raise, and they must counter them with equal care.

If you are to persuade your reader, the logic behind your arguments must be flawless. Yet there are a few logical traps persuasive writers can fall into if they are not careful. Because these errors in reasoning can seriously detract from the persuasiveness of your argument, you should familiarize yourself with them. Below are some of the errors in reasoning that persuasive writers must avoid.

1. Do not defend or attack an idea on the basis of the people associated with that idea.

   example: Only liberals oppose balancing the federal budget, and we all know the mess they've gotten this country into.

   explanation: The groups of people who do or do not champion an idea or course of action have nothing to do with the validity of that idea or action.

2. Do not engage in name calling.

   example: The president of this college is an idiot if he thinks students will sit still for another tuition increase.

   explanation: It is legitimate to criticize what people do or think, but it is unfair and immature to attack the personalities of the people themselves.

3. Do not defend or attack an idea or action on the grounds that people have always believed that idea or performed that action.

   example: Children have always learned to read in first grade, so why should we begin teaching them any earlier now?

   explanation: It is not true that everything believed and done in the past and present is for the best. Perhaps new research in education indicates children are capable of reading before the first grade.

4. Do not make illogical comparisons.

   example: The voters in this city have not passed a school levy for seven years. It is unlikely they will vote for a teacher to become our next senator.

   explanation: How voters feel about school levies has nothing to do with how they feel about a political candidate who happens to be a teacher. The comparison is not logical.

5. Do not assume that what is true for one person will be true for everybody.

   example: When I was a child, my parents spanked me regularly, and I turned out just fine. Clearly, there is no harm in spanking as a form of punishment.

   explanation: It does not hold that because one person suffered no ill effects from spanking, no one will suffer ill effects from spanking.

6. Do not overgeneralize. Very little is true all of the time.

   example: We might as well return to the 70-mph speed limit; after all, everyone drives faster than 55 mph anyway.

   explanation: While *some* people surely exceed 55 mph, and perhaps *many* people do, it is an invalid and inflated generalization to claim that *everyone* does.

Persuasive detail can come from a variety of sources. Your argument can be based on what you have learned from your own experience and observation. Details can also come from your reading, television viewing, and class lectures.

You might even come up with support as a result of talking to people knowl-edgeable about your subject. If some of your support comes from library research, however, check with your instructor. He or she may want you to document these sources according to the conventions discussed in Chapter 13.

Arranging Detail

Organizing your points from the least to the most compelling can be effective because the potency of your argument gradually builds until it reaches the strongest possible conclusion. An effective alternative to this organization is to begin with your second-strongest point and then build from your least to most compelling reasons. This arrangement allows you to begin and end powerfully to create strong initial and final impressions.

Often the reasons you use to support a view have a relationship to each other which dictates a certain arrangement. For example, one supporting argument may be the result of or grow out of another. When this is the case, it will be necessary for you to arrange details so that the relationship between them is clear.

You must also decide where in the essay to raise and counter objections. Usually the most effective way is to raise and counter objections at the points in your essay where the objections logically emerge. This means that objections may be dealt with at various places where the discussion points to the objec-tions. For example, let's say you are arguing that children should not be allowed to play with toy guns, and you explain that violent play leads to violent behavior. It would make sense in that paragraph (or in a paragraph immediately after) to raise and counter the objection that gun play can vent violent tenden-cies harmlessly and thus reduce violent behavior.

Another way to handle objections to your view is to raise them all in your introduction or in your first body paragraph. The rest of the essay can be devoted to an extensive countering of the objections. This arrangement is most useful when your stand is unpopular and there are many objections to it. Then it can be effective to make your point by showing how the prevailing beliefs are mistaken. Such an approach would work if you were taking the unpopular stand that military service should be mandatory for all 18-year-olds. For this argument, you could first cite all the reasons people are opposed to this and then go on to show why these reasons are not good ones.

If the objections to your view are few and not very compelling, you may raise and counter all of these objections in one paragraph. Sometimes you do this in the introduction, sometimes in a single body paragraph (usually the first or the last), and sometimes in the conclusion.

When you are arranging your persuasive detail, keep in mind that you need a clear statement of the issue and your stand on the issue. Typically, this is the thesis statement in your introduction. The rest of your introduction can be handled in a variety of ways. You might want to explain why the issue is important; you might want to trace the history of the issue; you might want to raise and counter objections.

In the conclusion, it is often effective to reaffirm the position you have taken; or it can be effective to make a final appeal to the reader by summarizing your most compelling points. You might want to discuss what would happen if your view were adopted; you might prefer to raise and counter objections; or you might discuss your final and most persuasive point.

Points to Remember about Persuasion
1. The purpose of a persuasive essay is to encourage others to adopt a view or take a particular course of action.
2. The subject of a persuasive essay must be a debatable issue; matters of taste are not suitable subjects.
3. Persuasive detail should be rooted in logic, so be careful to avoid the logical traps; emotional appeals should be restrained and fair.
4. Persuasive essays can incorporate narration, description, illustration, comparison and contrast, definition, cause and effect, and/or explanation.
5. Persuasive writers can speculate about what would happen if their views were (or were not) adopted.
6. The most compelling objections should be raised and countered.
7. Persuasive detail is determined in part by the views and knowledge of the audience.
8. The arrangement of persuasive detail should be carefully thought out. Often, it is effective to move from the least to the most compelling points, or to begin with the second-most persuasive point and end with the most persuasive. Other times, reasons are arranged according to how they relate to each other.
9. It often works well to write a traditional thesis that states the issue and your stand.

Exercise: Persuasion

1. Which of the following thesis statements would not be suitable for a 500-word persuasive essay? Why not?
   a. Because the PG and R movie ratings are not accomplishing what they were designed to, a new ratings system should be devised.
   b. A 10-month school year would help return the United States to its previous level of educational excellence.
   c. There is no doubt about it; dogs make better pets than cats.
   d. If parents want their children to thrive, they should spend as much time with them as possible.
   e. The music young people listen to has no redeeming aesthetic qualities.

2. For each issue below, decide where you stand. Then answer the questions on p. 306 to arrive at a possible audience and purpose for a persuasive essay on each issue.
   a. Mandatory retirement at age 67
   b. Raising tuition $100 a term to finance construction of a new campus library
   c. Requiring 4 years of natural science, math, and English for all high school students
   d. Banning cigarette advertisements from print media
3. Assume you are in favor of raising the tax on whiskey to increase federal revenues, and you plan to write an essay on the subject. What reasonable purpose could you establish for your writing if your audience were a tavern owner? An occasional drinker? A nondrinker?
4. Assume you are opposed to a three-term composition requirement at your school because you feel three terms are too many. Also assume you plan to write an essay to that effect. Decide on one compelling detail to support your stand for each of the audiences listed below.
   a. The president of student government
   b. The chairperson of the English department
   c. The university's board of trustees
   d. The chairperson of the chemical engineering department (you are majoring in chemical engineering)
5. Decide on how you feel about each issue below. Then write a sentence (or more) to raise and counter an important objection to your stand.
   a. The right of adopted children to learn the identity of their natural mothers
   b. Raising the driving age to 18 in all states
   c. Graduating only those high school seniors who pass a proficiency exam

Reading Persuasion

As you read the following persuasive pieces, all of which have been published, notice what strategies the authors employ to convince the reader. After each selection, there are questions meant to point out various persuasive strategies.

I Wish They'd Do It Right

Jane Doe

My son and his wife are not married. They have lived together for seven years without benefit of license. Though occasionally marriage has been a subject of conjecture, it did not seem important until the day they announced, jubilantly, that they were going to have a child. It was happy news. I was ready and eager to become a grandmother. Now, I thought, they will take the final step and make their relationship legal.

I was apprised of the Lamaze method of natural childbirth. I was prepared by Leboyer for birth without violence. I admired the expectant mother's discipline. She ate only organic foods, abstained from alcohol, avoided insecticides, smog and trauma. Every precaution was taken to insure the arrival of a healthy, happy infant. No royal birth had been prepared for more auspiciously. All that was lacking was legitimacy.

Finally, when my grandson was two weeks old, I dared to question their intentions.

"We don't believe in marriage," was all that was volunteered.

"Not even for your son's sake?" I asked. "Maybe he will."

Their eyes were impenetrable, their faces stiffened to masks. "You wouldn't understand," I was told.

And I don't. Surely they cannot believe they are pioneering, making revolutionary changes in society. That frontier has long been tamed. Today marriage offers all the options. Books and talk shows have surfeited us with the freedom offered in open marriage. Lawyers, psychologists and marriage counselors are growing rich executing marriage contracts. And divorce, should it come to that, is in most states easy and inexpensive.

On the other hand, living together out of wedlock can be economically impractical as well as socially awkward. How do I present her—as my son's roommate? his spouse? his spice, as one facetious friend suggested? Even my son flounders in these waters. Recently, I heard him refer to her as his girl friend. I cannot believe that that description will be endearing to their son when he is able to understand.

I have resolved that problem for myself, bypassing their omission, introducing her as she is, as my daughter-in-law. But my son, in militant support of his ideology, refutes any assumption, however casual, that they have taken vows.

There are economic benefits which they are denying themselves. When they applied for housing in the married-students dormitory of the university where he is seeking his doctorate, they were asked for their marriage certificate. Not having one, they were forced to find other, more expensive quarters off campus. Her medical insurance, provided by the company where she was employed, was denied him. He is not her husband. There have been and will be other inconveniences they have elected to endure.

Their son will not enjoy the luxury of choice about the inconveniences and scurrility to which he will be subject from those of his peers and elders who dislike and fear society's nonconformists.

And if in the future, his parents should decide to separate, will he not suffer greater damage than the child of divorce, who may find comfort in the knowledge that his parents once believed they could live happily ever after, and committed themselves to that idea? The child of unwed parents has no sanctuary. His mother and father have assiduously avoided a pledge of permanency, leaving him drifting and insecure.

I know my son is motivated by idealism and honesty in his reluctance to concede to what he considers mere ceremony. But he is wise enough to know that no one individual can fight all of society's foibles and frauds. Why does he persist in this, a battle already lost? Because though he rejects marriage, California, his residence, has declared that while couples living together in imitation of marriage are no longer under the jurisdiction of the family court, their relationship is viewed by the state as an implicit contract somewhat like a business agreement. This position was mandated when equal property rights were granted a woman who had been abandoned by the man she had lived with for a number of years.

Finally, the couple's adamancy has been depriving to all the rest of the family. There has been no celebration of wedding or anniversaries. There has been concealment from certain family elders who could not cope with the situation. Its irregularity has put constraint on the grandparents, who are stifled by one another's possible embarrassment or hurt.

I hope that one day very soon my son and his wife will acknowledge their cohabitation with a license. The rest of us will not love them any more for it. We love and support them as much as possible now. But it will be easier and happier for us knowing that our grandson will be spared the continued explanation and harassment, the doubts and anxieties of being a child of unmarried parents.

Questions on Technique: "I Wish They'd Do It Right"

1. "I Wish They'd Do It Right" originally appeared in the *New York Times*. Its author wished to remain anonymous, and hence the name "Jane Doe." The author presents the issue and her stand in a thesis, but that thesis does not appear in paragraph 1. What is the thesis?
2. The seven brief paragraphs before the thesis form the introduction. What approach does the author take to this introduction?
3. Which reasons for her stand does the author develop with illustration? With explanation? Where does the author use narration?
4. How does the author raise and counter her son's objection to her stand?
5. To what extent does the author speculate about what will happen if her view is not adopted? Where does the author speculate about what will happen if her view *is* adopted?
6. What elements of emotional appeal appear in the essay? Are these controlled and fair or unrestrained and unfair? Explain.
7. Why does the author deal first with social awkwardness, next with economic issues, and then with the effect on loved ones?
8. What approach does the author take to her conclusion?

Why Gun Control Laws Don't Work

Barry Goldwater

Let me say immediately that if I thought more gun-control laws would help diminish the tragic incidence of robberies, muggings, rapes and murders in the United States, I would be the first to vote for them. But I am convinced that making more such laws approaches the problem from the wrong direction.

It is clear, I think, that gun legislation simply doesn't work. There are already some 20,000 state and local gun laws on the books, and they are no more effective than was the prohibition of alcoholic beverages in the 1920s. Our most recent attempt at federal gun legislation was the Gun Control Act of 1968, intended to control the interstate sale and transportation of firearms and the importation of uncertified firearms; it has done nothing to check the availability of weapons. It has been bolstered in every nook and cranny of the nation by local gun-control laws, yet the number of shooting homicides per year has climbed steadily since its enactment, while armed robberies have increased 60 percent.

Some people, even some law-enforcement officials, contend that "crimes of passion" occur because a gun just happens to be present at the scene. I don't buy that. I can't equate guns with the murder rate, because if a person is angry enough to kill, he will kill with the first thing that comes to hand—a gun, a knife, an ice pick, a baseball bat.

I believe our *only* hope of reducing crime in this country is to control not the weapon but the user. We must reverse the trend toward leniency and permissiveness in our courts—the plea bargaining, the pardons, the suspended sentences and unwarranted paroles—and make the lawbreaker pay for what he has done by spending time in jail. We have plenty of statutes against killing and maiming and threatening people with weapons. These can be made effective by strong enforcement and firm decisions from the bench. When a man knows that if he uses a potentially deadly object to rob or do harm to another person he is letting himself in for a mandatory, unparolable stretch behind bars, he will think twice about it.

Of course, no matter what gun-control laws are enacted—including national registration—the dedicated crook can always get a weapon. So, some people ask, even if national registration of guns isn't completely airtight, isn't it worth trying? Sure, it would cause a little inconvenience to law-abiding gun owners. And it certainly wouldn't stop all criminals from obtaining guns. But it might stop a few, maybe quite a few. What's wrong with that?

There are several answers. The first concerns enforcement. How are we going to persuade the bank robber or the street-corner stickup artist to register his means of criminal livelihood? Then there is the matter of expense. A study conducted eight years ago showed a cost to New York City of $72.87 to investigate and process one application for a pistol license. In mid-1970 dollars, the same procedure probably costs over $100. By extrapolation to the national scale, the cost to American taxpayers of investigating and registering the 40 to 50 million handguns might reach $4 billion or $5 billion. On top of that, keeping the process in operation year after year would require taxpayer financing of another sizable federal bureau. We ought to have far better prospects of success before we hobble ourselves with such appalling expenditures.

Finally, there are legal aspects based on the much-discussed Second Amendment to the Bill of Rights, which proclaims that "A well regulated Militia, being necessary to the security of a free State, the right of the people to keep and bear Arms, shall not be infringed." The anti-gun faction argues that this right made sense in the days of British oppression but that it has no application today. I contend, on the other hand, that the Founding Fathers conceived of an armed citizenry as a necessary hedge against tyranny from within as well as from without, that they saw the right to keep and bear arms as basic and perpetual, the one thing that could spell the difference between freedom and servitude. Thus I deem most forms of gun control unconstitutional in intent.

Well, then, I'm often asked, what kind of gun laws *are* you for? I reply that I am for laws of common sense. I am for laws that prohibit citizen access to machine guns, bazookas and other military devices. I am for laws that are educational in nature. I believe that before a person is permitted to buy a weapon he should be required to take a course that will teach him how to use it, to handle it safely, and keep it safely about the house.

Gun education, in fact, can actually reduce lawlessness in a community, as was demonstrated in an experiment conducted in Highland Park, Mich. City police launched a program to instruct merchants in the use of handguns. The idea was to help them protect themselves and their businesses from robbers, and it was given wide publicity. The store-robbery rate dropped from an average of 1.5 a day to none in four months.

Where do we go from here? My answer to this is based on the firm belief that we have a crime problem in this country, not a gun problem, and that we must meet the enemy on his own terms. We must start by making crime as unprofitable for him as we can. And we have to do this, I believe, by getting tough in the courts and corrections systems.

A recent news story in Washington, D.C., reports that, of 184 persons convicted of gun possession in a six-month period, only 14 received a jail sentence. Forty-six other cases involved persons who had previously been convicted of a felony or possession of a gun. Although the maximum penalty for such repeaters in the District of Columbia is ten years in prison, half of these were not jailed at all. A study last year revealed that in New York City, which has about the most prohibitive gun legislation in the country, only one out of six people convicted of crimes involving weapons went to jail.

This sorry state of affairs exists because too many judges and magistrates either don't know the law or are unwilling to apply it with appropriate vigor. It's time to demand either that they crack down on these criminals or be removed from office. It may even be time to review the whole system of judicial appointments, to stop weakening the cause of justice by putting men on the bench who may happen to be golfing partners of Congressmen and too often lack the brains and ability for the job. In Arizona today we elect our judges, and the system is working well, in part because we ask the American and local bar associations to consider candidates and make recommendations. In this way, over the last few years, we have replaced many weaklings with good jurists.

We have long had all the criminal statutes we need to turn the tide against the crime wave. There is, however, one piece of proposed legislation that I am watching with particular interest. Introduced by Sen. James McClure (R., Idaho), it requires that any person convicted of a federal crime in which a gun is used serve five to ten years in jail automatically on top of whatever penalty he receives for the crime itself. A second conviction would result in an extra ten-year-to-life sentence. These sentences would be mandatory and could not be suspended. It is, in short, a "tough" bill. I think that this bill would serve as an excellent model for state legislation.

And so it has in California which, last September, signed into law a similar bill requiring a mandatory jail sentence for any gun-related felony.

Finally, it's important to remember that this is an area of great confusion; an area in which statistics can be juggled and distorted to support legislation that is liable to be expensive, counter-productive or useless. The issue touches upon the freedom and safety of all of us, whether we own firearms or not. The debate over gun control is an adjunct to the war against crime, and that war must be fought with all the intelligence and tenacity we can bring to it.

Questions on Technique: "Why Gun Control Laws Don't Work"

1. Goldwater presents the issue and his stand in his thesis. What is that thesis?
2. What reasons does Goldwater give for the view stated in his thesis?
3. To develop his stand, Goldwater employs explanation, comparison, and illustration. For the paragraphs cited below, state which method of development or combination of methods is used.
   paragraph 2
   paragraph 4
   paragraph 11
   paragraph 12
4. Which objections to his stand does Goldwater raise and counter?
5. To what extent does Goldwater appeal to emotions?

6. For the most part, Goldwater develops his reasons for his stand with adequate detail. There is, however, one generalization that goes unsupported by facts. What is that generalization? Why do you suppose Goldwater fails to support this generalization, and what is its effect on you?
7. Much of Goldwater's essay is devoted to presenting alternatives to national gun registration (education, stricter enforcement of existing laws, new criminal statutes, user education, mandatory sentences). What effect does this tactic have on the persuasive quality of the piece?
8. What approach does Goldwater take to his conclusion?

Parents Also Have Rights

Ronnie Gunnerson

"What's a parent to do?" is the punch line to many a joke on the perils of raising children. But what a parent does when a teenager gets pregnant is far from a joke; it's a soul-searching, heart-wrenching condition with responses as diverse as the families affected.

In an era besotted with concern for both the emotional and social welfare of teenage mothers and their babies, anger seems to be forbidden. Yet how many parents can deny anger when circumstances over which they have no control force them into untenable situations?

And untenable they are. What I discovered after my 16-year-old stepdaughter became pregnant shocked me. Parents have no rights. We could neither demand she give the baby up for adoption, nor insist on an abortion. The choice belongs to the teenage mother, who is still a child herself and far from capable of understanding the lifelong ramifications of whatever choice she makes.

At the same time, homes for unwed mothers, at least the two we checked in Los Angeles, where we live, will house the teenager at no cost to the family, but they will not admit her unless her parents sign a statement agreeing to pick up both her and her baby from a designated maternity hospital. Parents may sit out the pregnancy if they so desire, but when all is said and done, they're stuck with both mother and baby whether they like it or not.

In essence, then, the pregnant teenager can choose whether or not to have her baby and whether or not to keep it. The parents, who have the legal responsibility for both the teenage mother and her child, have no say in the matter. The costs of a teenage pregnancy are high; yes, the teenager's life is forever changed by her untimely pregnancy and childbirth. But life is forever changed for the rest of her family as well, and I am tired of the do-gooders who haven't walked a yard, let alone a mile, in my shoes shouting their sympathy for the "victimized" teen.

What about the victimized parents? Are we supposed to accept the popular notion that we failed this child and that therefore we are to blame for her lack of either scruples or responsibility? Not when we spend endless hours and thousands of dollars in therapy trying to help a girl whose behavior has been rebellious since the age of 13. Not when we have heart-to-heart talks until the wee hours of the morning which we learn are the butt of jokes between her and her friends. And not when we continually trust her only to think afterward that she's repeatedly lied to us about everything there is to lie about.

Yes, the teenager is a victim—a victim of illusions fostered by a society that gives her the right to decide whether or not to have an illegitimate baby, no matter what her parents say. Many believe it is feelings of rejection that motivate girls to have babies; they want human beings of their own to love and be loved by. I wouldn't disagree, but another motive may be at work as well: the ultimate rebellion. Parents are forced to cope with feelings more devastating than adolescent confusion. And I'm not talking about the superficial, what-will-the-Joneses-think attitudes. I mean gut-gripping questions that undermine brutally the self-confidence it can take adults years to develop.

We can all write off to immaturity mistakes made in adolescence. To what do we attribute our perceived parental failures at 40 or 50? Even as I proclaim our innocence in my stepdaughter's folly, I will carry to my grave, as I know my husband will, the nagging fear that we could have prevented it *if only* we'd been *better* parents.

And I will carry forevermore the sad realization that I'm not the compassionate person I'd tried so hard to be and actually thought I was. My reaction to my stepdaughter's pregnancy horrified me. I was consumed with hatred and anger. Any concern I felt for her was overridden by the feeling that I'd been had. I'd befriended this child, housed her and counseled her for years, and what did I get in return? Not knowing her whereabouts that culminated in her getting pregnant with a boy we didn't even know. At first I felt like a fool. When I discovered how blatantly society's rules favor the rule breaker, I felt like a raving maniac.

Resentment and rage: It took more hours of counseling for me to accept my anger than it did for my stepdaughter to deal with her pregnancy. But then, she had the support of a teenage subculture that reveres motherhood among its own and a news-media culture that fusses and frets over adolescent mothers. Few ears were willing to hear what my husband and I were feeling. While I can't speak for my husband, I can say that today, a year after the baby's birth, he still turns to ice when his daughter is around. Smitten as he is with his first grandchild, he hasn't forgotten that the joy of the boy's birth was overshadowed by resentment and rage.

Fortunately, my stepdaughter recently married a young man who loves her son as his own, although he is not the father. Together, the three of them are a family who, like many a young family, are struggling to make ends meet. Neither my stepdaughter nor her husband has yet finished high school, but they are not a drain on society as many teenage parents are. She and her husband seem to be honest, hard workers, and I really think they will make it. Their story will have a happy ending.

My stepdaughter says she can't even understand the person she used to be, and I believe her. Unfortunately, the minds of adults are not quite as malleable as those of constantly changing adolescents. My husband and I haven't forgotten—and I'm not sure we've forgiven—either our daughter or ourselves. We're still writing the ending to our own story, and I believe it's time for society to write an ending of its own. If a pregnant teenager's parents are ultimately responsible for the teenager and her baby, then give those parents the right to decide whether or not the teenager keeps her baby. Taking the decision away from the teen mother would eliminate her power over her parents and could give pause to her reckless pursuit of the ''in'' thing.

Questions on Technique: "Parents Also Have Rights"

1. The most direct statement of Gunnerson's issue and stand does not appear in the introduction but in the conclusion. What sentence provides this statement?
2. What approach does Gunnerson take to her introduction?
3. What purpose do paragraphs 2 and 3 serve?
4. Does Gunnerson rely more heavily on emotional appeal or logical argument?
5. ''Parents Also Have Rights'' first appeared in *Newsweek*. Is the strong emotional appeal in the essay likely to move the author's intended audience? Explain.
6. In what paragraphs does Gunnerson raise and counter objections? How does she counter each objection?
7. What is Gunnerson's main reason for believing parents should decide the fate of their teenager's baby?
8. Does the fact that Gunnerson's stepdaughter ultimately married and made a life for herself (although a difficult one) detract from the author's argument?
9. If you strip away the emotional appeal, how much logical argument is left?
10. Where does Gunnerson speculate what would happen if her view were adopted?
11. What approach does Gunnerson take to her conclusion?

Student Writings to Read and Evaluate

The persuasive essays on the following pages were all written by students. You will notice that some are more effective than others but that each has strengths and weaknesses. Reading and evaluating these essays will make you a more knowing judge of your own writing. Also, by studying what others have done, you can discover successful techniques to incorporate into your own writing and less successful techniques to avoid.

The Old Ball Game

"For it's one, two, three strikes you're out at the old ball game." A catchy tune if you happen to be singing it, agonizing reality if you happen to be 6 or 7 years old and playing in an organized baseball league. Six- and seven-year-old children are simply not emotionally ready, and therefore should simply not be permitted, to play on an organized baseball team.

Consider this not-so-uncommon scene: The pitch is made. The bat and ball connect, and the grounder heads toward the $3\frac{1}{2}$-foot-tall first baseman. He opens his glove. He just has to pick up the ball, tag first base, and the runner will be out. He misses the ball. Hurriedly trying to retrieve it, the first baseman's attempt is futile, and the runner is safe. The manager, the father of one of the boys, stops the game, walks out halfway toward the first baseman, and yells, "What are you doing, Michael? You should have had that ball. Now settle down." There's nothing like public humiliation to damage a tender psyche.

Some people argue that just as much, if not more, yelling goes on during backyard neighborhood games. This is true, but the yelling there goes back and forth among the kids. In the organized leagues, the manager yells at, and sometimes even humiliates, his players. The player, of course, is not permitted to respond, and thus frustration and feelings of inadequacy can build. He can only try to cope with these feelings that have been heaped on him, which can be quite an emotional struggle for a child so young.

Even major league baseball players make mistakes on the field; can a 6- or 7-year-old player be expected to be any better? If a player misses the ball, no one feels worse than he does. Instead, why not praise the good plays made by the kids and ignore the mistakes? Unfortunately, this doesn't seem to be what happens in many cases.

I believe the goal of organized sports is for the children involved to have fun. Unfortunately, this frequently does not happen. Too much emphasis is placed on winning by both the managers and the parents. This inevitably leads to feelings of disappointment and failure in the children. Imagine being 6 years old and up to bat. One hit is all you need to win the ball game. This would create a lot of pressure for many adults. It is simply too much pressure for 6- and 7-year-olds. The pitch is made and you're out. Some might say that children must learn to deal with disappointment and failure. I also believe this is true, but certainly not at such a young age.

It has been said that organized sports are a good source of discipline. However, children should be learning discipline in the home, as well as in school. Further sources of discipline are unnecessary.

To me, there is nothing more heartbreaking than watching a 6- or 7-year-old baseball player crying because he just struck out, he missed the ball, or he just got yelled at by his manager. I guess I'm old fashioned—I prefer games that make children laugh and leave them smiling.

Ban Those Traps

American history reveals that one of the keys to survival in this country has been trapping such animals as beaver, otter, muskrat, mink, fox, coyote, bear, mountain lion, rabbit, and raccoon for their meat and hides. There is no longer a need for the meat of these animals, however, because humans have developed easier ways of getting food. Yet they remain victims of trappers because of the value of their pelts. Today trapping supports very few people, and most of those who do derive income from it have other sources of income. This fact alone should discourage trapping, but there are other, stronger reasons which should encourage action to prohibit it: The techniques of trapping animals are cruel; trapping can lead to the extinction of animal species; and above all, there is no longer a need to trap because modern technology has introduced better ways to secure food and pelts.

Trapping is death by torture for the animals who are its victims, for they are strangled, drowned, or starved to death, depending on the trapping device used. There are two types of steel traps which are commonly used. The Conibear trap is set in the water and grabs the animal behind the ears, cutting off the circulation. Sometimes this causes the animal to die instantly, but frequently it causes the animal to fall and drown. The leg-hold trap clamps down on the victim's leg or paw with bone-crushing force, causing painful entrapment. A victim may be left in the trap for days before the trapper arrives to release and kill it. The pain suffered by the animal is so intense that many times, although the trapper finds the animal still alive, it has gnawed its trapped leg or paw, broken its teeth from gnawing on the trap, or frozen its tongue to the cold steel trap. Often the animal is dead from loss of blood, gangrene, infection, or internal bleeding. If the victim was "fortunate" enough to escape, it managed to do so only by gnawing off the leg or paw, which then made the animal easy prey for predators. A third kind of trap, the snare, consists of a rope which is tied in a hangman's noose and cast over a tree or branch with a piece of bait attached. The bait is placed over a concealed hole in the ground. When the animal approaches the bait, it falls into the hole and is caught by the rope and consequently hanged. Other traps, such as the deadfall or pitfall, lure the animal with bait and then kill it by either striking it with a log or rock or forcing it to fall on sharp sticks. In every case, trapped animals are victims of cruel treatment because they cannot defend themselves as they would in natural conditions.

All of this suffering and destruction serves no real need. Modern technology meets the demands of fashion with human-made and ranch-grown furs. We now have human-made furs that look and feel like the real thing, but are better. They are moth-proof, they need no cold storage, and they do not crack with age. In addition, many people now breed and raise fur-bearing animals on ranches specifically for the use of their pelts. These animals are fed and cared for properly, and they are killed humanely.

Trapping, therefore, should be outlawed. It is cruel, it can cause extinction of valuable species, and it is unnecessary because modern technology has replaced the need for it with pelts of better quality which are acquired much more easily and humanely. Although trappers claim that their hobby provides a fantastic experience because it allows them to enjoy the solitude and beauty of the wilderness, they are really contributing to the destruction in that wilderness. That destruction must be stopped.

Mandatory Jocks

I'm a business major and I'd like to know what modern dance, fencing, and riflery have to do with a degree in business? Will modern dance help when I am making a sales presentation? Will fencing skills help me balance my books? Will riflery be necessary to me as a manager dealing with employees? The answer to all these questions is no! Yet these are three examples of physical activities required by the university for graduation.

The function of a college is to provide the skills necessary to get a job in your chosen field. College students have already been exposed to mandatory athletics and health classes in high school and do not need more of these. Some say the college is requiring these classes to make sure students continue to get enough exercise. While an incoming freshman of age 18 may not mind, I feel older students who work full-time and go to school should not be forced to waste their time and money in this way.

Requiring these classes amounts to nothing more than forcing all students to help support the athletic department. While some say that sports are an important part of college, I am paying to get my degree to better myself, not help some coach earn a paycheck.

A total of 6 hours of health and physical activities are required for my bachelor's degree. At $35 per hour, that comes to $210 that I have to pay for classes that have nothing to do with my degree. On top of the fee, classes like bicycling or scuba diving require me to bring my own equipment. This means even more expense.

If the financial part is not bad enough, the time factor is. Scheduling school around my work and home responsibilities is hard enough, without having to worry about fitting an archery class into my schedule. I feel that working six days a week and taking care of my home, along with going to school four nights a week, gives me more than enough exercise.

How many students have had to pass up job opportunities because these activity requirements kept them in school longer than necessary? "Gee Bill, I wish I could help you. You're in the top third of your class, but I just can't hold this job for three months while you finish your bowling and volleyball classes. Come back when you're done, and if you're lucky, maybe something else will have opened up."

The time has come for the university administration to reexamine its curriculum requirements. Students who work full-time should no longer be forced to waste their time and money on these health and physical education requirements. With state and federal governments cutting back on wasteful programs, the university should follow suit. By eliminating these unnecessary requirements, YSU could save money by letting go some of the people required to teach these classes. People in favor of athletics will complain and scream no, but it's time to get back to the basic idea of college—education.

Why Not Be a Secretary?

When the time comes to choose a career, care must be taken to make the best possible choice. Oh, there are many different careers. Some people decide to become doctors, some lawyers, others architects. The list seems endless. There is, however, only one choice for bright, level-headed individuals such as myself. I chose to become a secretary.

Because a secretary performs a number of varied duties, she is seldom bored; in fact, she can even gain experience that may later be of value to her. Making coffee that even Mrs. Olsen would be proud of can bring a great feeling of satisfaction; and there is no greater thrill to a secretary than being able to serve five cups of coffee—one black, two with sugar, one cream, one sugar and cream—without a drop spilled and with every cup to the proper person. A good secretary can recite at the drop of a yellowing leaf the best lighting and watering procedures for at least ten exotic household (rather, office) plants. Only inexperienced secretaries would complain about purchasing gifts for the boss's spouse. It should instead be considered a compliment: the boss obviously believes you have wonderful taste!

Secretaries enjoy excellent salaries. The average secretary can afford an unfurnished efficiency apartment. Experienced, higher-paid secretaries are even able to furnish their apartments. Raises are often given yearly. When the minimum wage goes up, so does a secretary's salary.

What could be more fun than daily contact with that wonderful group of people known as "the public"? Many lively, fun discussions with disgruntled customers add variety to a secretary's day. Defending policy made by someone "higher up," which even the boss seems unable to explain, can leave a secretary with a wonderful feeling of satisfaction. Once perfected, the ability to smile through gritted teeth is a great asset.

And how many jobs have an entire week set aside to honor its workers? Very few, I'm afraid. Secretaries have National Secretaries' Week—a week when bosses show their appreciation to their secretaries in the form of flowers, candy, perhaps even other small gifts. I'll never forget, back in '78, receiving a bouquet of fresh daisies from my boss. Not many people would take the time to jump out of their car at a red light to pick flowers on a vacant corner lot. It still gives me a warm feeling just thinking about it.

Yes, there are many jobs from which to choose. But for the really intelligent person, the choice will be clear: choose something other than secretarial work.

Evaluating Writing: Assessing Strengths and Weaknesses

To continue improving your critical abilities and to continue discovering what does and does not succeed in writing, pair off with a classmate and select one of the persuasive essays you find interesting for some reason—for the subject, for the potential, for the technique, or for the interesting mix of strengths and weaknesses. Next, each of you individually answer the evaluation questions below and compare your responses. If there is disagreement, discuss your reactions in an effort to resolve the disagreement.

After each pair has completed an evaluation and discussion, the findings should be reported to the class. Each report should present the major strengths of each essay, the chief areas that call for revision, and any significant disagreement. It is not necessary to report your every finding—just the most important ones. As each report is given, class members should comment when they have something to add.

Evaluation Questions

1. Is the writer's reasoning logical? Are there any points that fail to persuade because of faulty logic?
2. Are there any emotional appeals? If so, are they suitably restrained, appropriate, and fair?
3. Is there enough detail to adequately defend the writer's stand? Where, if anywhere, is more detail needed?
4. Does the writer raise and counter objections effectively? Are there any objections that should have been raised and countered but were not?
5. Are all generalizations adequately supported? If not, which generalizations require more support?
6. Is there a thesis that accurately presents the issue and the writer's stand? If not, should there be?
7. Is the arrangement of persuasive points logical? Does the arrangement contribute to the persuasive quality of the essay?
8. Are all the details relevant to the thesis and appropriate to the topic sentence? If not, which details create a relevance problem?
9. Does the essay have a conclusion that leaves the reader with a positive final impression?
10. In general, is the word choice specific, economical, and simple?

11. Are there any clichés that should be revised for fresh expression?
12. What, if anything, should be revised for clarity?
13. Is there adequate sentence variety?
14. Are transitions used effectively?
15. Is the essay carefully edited?

Essay Topics

If you are having trouble settling on a persuasive essay topic, the following list of ideas may help. These topics may require some shaping and narrowing, or they may prompt you to think of a different topic.

1. Write an essay to Jane Doe (see p. 313) from the point of view of her son and daughter-in-law, arguing that it is better to live together than to marry. While you may bring in any persuasive points you care to, be sure you address the most compelling of Jane Doe's reasons for her stand.
2. In response to Barry Goldwater's essay, write an essay entitled, "Why Gun Control Laws Would Work." Raise and counter some of Goldwater's most serious objections to gun control (or all of his objections, if you prefer).
3. Write an essay that argues against the point of view reflected in "Parents Also Have Rights." That is, argue that unwed teens, not their parents, should decide the fate of their babies.
4. Taking the point of view opposite that of the student who wrote "The Old Ball Game" (p. 322), write an essay defending organized baseball leagues for 6- and 7-year-olds.
5. Taking the point of view opposite that of the student who wrote "Mandatory Jocks" (p. 324), write a persuasive essay defending physical education requirements for all degree programs. (Or argue against some other degree requirement.)
6. Write an essay for or against allowing advertising in television programming aimed at children.
7. Write an essay advocating some specific change at your college or where you work.
8. Write a letter to the brother or sister of one of your friends in order to persuade that person to attend (or not to attend) your college.
9. Write an essay defending or attacking the following proposition: Professional athletes should be paid salaries equal to those of teachers.
10. Write an essay defending or attacking the following proposition: In order to graduate from high school, students should have to pass a proficiency examination.
11. Which would you rather be: extremely good looking but stupid, or ugly but very intelligent? Write an essay defending your choice.

12. If you had the power to draft one piece of legislation that would improve the quality of life in this country, what would it be? Write an essay that explains the legislation and argues for its passage.
13. Write a persuasive essay defending or attacking the practice of awarding athletes scholarships so they can play college ball.
14. Write an essay arguing for or against tax credits for those who send their children to private schools.
15. Write an essay arguing for or against a mandatory retirement age.
16. Pick one invention or technological advance and argue that it has done more harm than good.
17. Write an essay arguing for or against the open-admissions policy of many colleges.
18. Write an essay defending or attacking the following proposition: Cigarette, cigar, and pipe smoking should be illegal in all public places.

Writing Strategies

The following strategies are ways you can handle topic selection, idea generation, and determination of audience and purpose for a persuasive essay. These strategies, along with those presented in Chapters 1–3 and in the exercise on p. 000, may include some procedures you would like to try.

Topic Selection

1. Review the editorial pages and letters to the editor in your campus and community newspapers. They will present controversial issues, one of which may appeal to you as the topic for your persuasive essay.
2. Filling in the blank in the following sentence can lead to a persuasive topic: I think it is unfair that _____. If, for example, you complete the sentence to get "I think it is unfair that teachers' strikes hurt students," you can write an essay arguing that teachers should not be permitted to strike.
3. Other sentences with blanks that may lead you to a topic include:
   a. I have always been angry that _____. (Argue for a change in what angers you.)
   b. The worst feature of this university is _____. (Argue for a change that would improve the feature.)
   c. If I had the power, I would _____. (Argue for the advisability of what you would do.)
   d. I disagree with people who believe _____. (Show why these people are wrong and support your view.)

Idea Generation

1. To generate ideas to support your view, answer the following questions:
   a. Why is the issue I've chosen important?
   b. What would happen if my view were adopted?
   c. What would happen if my view were not adopted?

    d. If my fairy godmother appeared and said she would see to it that my view were adopted *if* I could give her three good reasons, what reasons would I give her?

    e. What are the two strongest objections to my view?

    f. How can these objections be countered?

2. To help generate ideas *and* determine methods of development, answer this set of questions:

    a. What story can I tell to support my view?

    b. Is there anything I can describe to support my view?

    c. What examples can I provide to support my view?

    d. Are there any comparisons I can make to support my view?

    e. Are there any contrasts I can draw to support my view?

    f. Do any aspects of my topic require definition?

    g. Do any cause-and-effect relationships support my view?

3. List every reason you can think of to support your stand. Do not evaluate the strength of these reasons; just get down everything that occurs to you. When you can think of no more reasons, take a second sheet and list every reason you can think of to oppose your view. This second list will be a source of ideas for raising and countering objections. Next to each opposition point, jot a few words to remind you of a way the objection can be countered.

Whether you establish audience first or purpose first is not of itself important. However, it is likely that the one you establish first will affect the determination of the other. Say, for example, you settle on an audience that is strongly opposed to your point of view. This may make it unrealistic to establish your purpose as changing the audience's mind. It may be more realistic to set your purpose as getting your audience to consider your view seriously and lessen its opposition as a result. Here is a chart of audience and purpose and some likely ways these can function together.

Establishing Audience and Purpose

If your audience . . .	*. . . a possible purpose is:*
1. is well informed and strongly opposed to your view,	1. to lessen the opposition by convincing the audience that some of your points are valid and worth consideration.
2. is poorly informed and opposed to your view,	2. to inform the audience and to change the audience's view.
3. would find it difficult to perform the desired action,	3. to convince the audience that it is worth the sacrifice or to convince the audience to do some part of what is desired.
4. would not find it difficult to perform the desired action,	4. to convince the audience to perform the action.
5. has no interest one way or the other in the issue,	5. to arouse interest and persuade the audience to your view.

A Postwriting Evaluation of Your Process

To continue working to become more aware of your writing process and ways to improve it, answer the questions below. They are designed to help you determine what is and is not working for you, so you can make informed choices about which aspects of your writing process to retain and which aspects to alter. It would be wise to discuss your answers with your classmates and instructor, for they can have valuable suggestions for procedures to try.

1. When you wrote your persuasive essay, what stages of the process went smoothly? (Remember, *smoothly* does not necessarily mean *quickly*.)
2. Did you do anything that worked well enough for you to repeat in the future? If so, what? Why do you think the technique was successful?
3. Was there anything about writing the essay that was unreasonably difficult and/or time-consuming? If so, what was it, and why do you think it was a problem? Has this been a problem for you in the past?
4. What stage(s) of your writing process will you handle differently next time? What will you do?
5. Are you more comfortable writing now than in the past? Why or why not?

13

Using Research to Develop Essays

You are probably familiar with the traditional research paper. Even if you have never written one, you have probably seen one or are aware that such a thing exists. In the traditional research paper the writer studies a narrow topic in depth by presenting and evaluating a great many facts found in books and articles in the library. These papers have many quotations and paraphrases. While this kind of research paper is useful, it is not the kind discussed here. Instead we will turn our attention to how writers can use research to supplement their own supporting detail.

Say you are writing a persuasive essay that argues against the elimination of the foreign language requirement for business majors at your school. You are a management student who has taken 6 years of Spanish, so you have a great many points you could make as a result of your own experience. It is likely that your essay will be most convincing; but consider for a moment how much more persuasive it could be if it included statements testifying to the importance of a second language for those in middle and upper management positions—statements made by respected authorities in the business world.

Now say you are writing a contrast piece to show the differences between public and private high school educations in order to explain why private school students score higher on college entrance exams. You have attended both kinds of schools, so your own experience offers much for supporting detail. In addition, you are an education major who just listened to a lecture on this topic, which will supply additional detail to write. As you develop your

331

essay, you begin to wonder whether private school students score higher because they are advised of test-taking strategies, while their public school counterparts are not. To learn whether this is the case, you go to the library and research the point. If you discover that private school students are told of certain strategies but public school students are not, you would have an important point to add to your essay.

Now say you are writing an extended definition of the teenager, and you realize that today's teenager is different from the teenager of the seventies, who was different from the teenager of the sixties, who was different from the teen of the fifties, and so on. While you realize there are differences, you are not sure of what all those differences are. Yet you would like to begin your definition with an overview of what the teenager has been over the last 30 years. Well, some library research could yield the material you desire.

An illustration essay, too, might be strengthened with some research material. Let's say you wish to supply several examples to illustrate the point that people are becoming desensitized to violence. You have three extended examples to write as a result of your own observation. However, you feel the need for an additional example, perhaps a dramatic one, to emphasize your point. No doubt, in the library you will find many such examples.

What's in the Library: Books and How to Find Them

A good academic library houses more material than anyone could get through in many lifetimes. In fact, once they become familiar with the way the library works, students could get along without instructors, for everything they would need for the best education possible would be readily available. That's really what makes library research so exciting: it affords us the opportunity to study independently any subjects we want, in whatever depth we desire.

For ease of discussion, it's possible to view the library as having two primary parts. There are the actual materials themselves (books, newspapers, journals, magazines, and so on) and the tools that give the library user access to these materials (the card catalog, bibliographies, and indexes).

Most of us are well aware that libraries have books—lots of them. And these books are on a variety of subjects so vast that listing them here would take considerable space. How then do users determine which of the library's many books are the ones of interest to them? The answer is the card catalog.

The card catalog gives the library user access to all the books in the library. That is, this catalog is a file of every book housed in the library. Card catalogs have two parts. First, there is the catalog file of books alphabetized according to author and title. In this section of the catalog, every book will have a card filed under its title and another card filed under its author's last name (books with two or more authors will have two or more author cards). Second, the card catalog has a subject file that arranges books alphabetically according to the subjects they treat. Thus, the book *Cholesterol and Heart Disease* could be listed in the subject portion of the card catalog under the following headings: ''Cholesterol,'' ''Health,'' ''Heart Disease,'' ''Medicine,'' ''Nutrition,'' and ''Physiology.''

Most often, researchers do not know the specific titles of books they are after. Instead, they know only that they want books on a certain subject. This means that researchers usually find themselves at the subject file of the card catalog, rather than at the author/title file. A person looking for material on whether or not cholesterol causes hardening of the arteries would go to the subject file of the card catalog, look up ''Cholesterol,'' and discover a number of book titles of possible interest.

In the upper-left corner of every card in the catalog is an identification number known as the ''call number.'' The call number (a Library of Congress or Dewey decimal number, depending on which system your library uses) will indicate where in the library a given book can be found.

The card catalog is a useful tool to the researcher because of its convenience. Without this file, the researcher would have to resort to the time-consuming, inefficient process of roaming the stacks looking for useful books.

The following is an example of a subject card that can be found in many card catalogs.

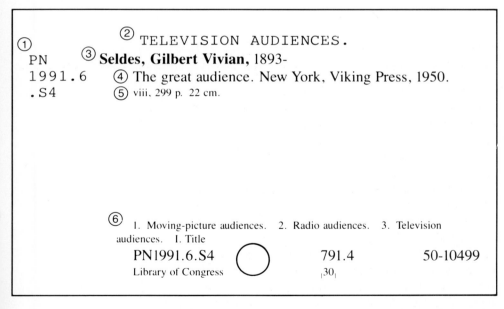

① call number

② subject card is filed under

③ author and date of birth (date of death often given as well)

④ title of book and publication data

⑤ pages before the first Arabic-numbered page, number of pages, height of book

⑥ tracings noting other headings this book is filed under

What's in the Library: Periodicals and How to Find Them

There is a wealth of information that is not in book form. Much of this material is in the form of *periodicals*. Periodicals are magazines, journals, and newspapers; they are printed forms that come out at regular intervals (that is, "periodically"). Periodicals can be of particular use to the researcher because often they contain the most current material available on a subject. This is because, unlike books, periodicals may be published as often as daily, weekly, monthly, or quarterly. Because periodicals contain the most up-to-date information, responsible researchers always investigate them.

Because libraries can house thousands of periodicals, researchers require some efficient way of locating these valuable tools. This access is provided by bibliographies and indexes, which give an alphabetical listing by subject of articles appearing in periodicals. Like the card catalog, bibliographies and indexes can be found in the library reference room.

Each type of periodical (magazine, journal, and newspaper) has bibliographies and indexes to help the researcher discover useful articles. For example, the following is a partial page from the *Humanities Index*, volume 9, which gives titles of journal articles.

---

1. subject
2. pertinent titles listed under headings below
3. title of article
4. author of article
5. abbreviated title of journal article appears in
6. volume number of journal
7. pages article spans
8. date of journal
9. article is *about* William Marshall, rather than written *by* him

① MARRIAGE
　② *See also*
　Endogamy and exogamy
　Married people
　Early feminist themes in French utopian socialism: the St-Simonians and Fourier. L. F. Goldstein. J. Hist Ideas 43:91-103 Ja/Mr '82
　　　　　Protestant churches
③ To preserve the marital state: the Basler Ehegericht. 1550-1592. T. M. Safley. bibl. J Fam Hist 7:162-79 Summ '82
　　④　　⑩　⑤ Ghana ⑥ ⑦　　⑧
　State and society, marriage and adultery: some considerations towards a social history of pre-colonial Asante. T. C. McCaskie. J Afric Hist 22 no4:477-94 '81
MARRIAGE (canon law)
　　See also
　Clandestinity (canon law)
MARRIAGE, Clandestine (canon law) See Clandestinity (canon law)
MARRIAGE and employment. See Married people – Employment
MARRIAGE in literature
　　See also
　Courtship in literature
　Of sex and the shrew, M. D. Perret. Ariel 13:3-20 Ja '82
　Thel. Thelyphthora, and the daughters of Albion. E. B. Murray. Stud Romant 20:275-97 Fall '81
　Third text of Sav me viit in be brom. O. S. Pickering. Eng Stud 63:20-2 F '82
MARRIAGE law

10. article
    contains a
    bibliography

Great Britain

Thel. Thelyphthora, and the daughters of Albion. E. B. Murray. Stud Romant 20:275-97 Fall '81

Switzerland

To preserve the marital state: the Basler Ehegericht. 1550-1592. T. M. Safley, bibl J Fam Hist 7:162-79 Summ '82

MARRIED people

Employment

'Til newsrooms do us part. B. Buresh. Colum Journalism R 21:43-6 My/Je '82

MARRS, Suzanne

Eudora Welty's snowy heron. Am Lit 53:723-5 Ja '82

MARSHALL, John

Hypothetical imperatives. Am Philos Q 19:105-14 Ja '82

MARSHALL, Peter

Nicole Oresme on the nature, reflection, and speed of light. Isis 72:357-74 S '81

MARSHALL, William, fl 1630-1650

about

⑨ Milton's Greek epigram. J. K. Hale. Il Milton Q 16:8-9 Mr '82

MARSHALS

See also

Montgomery of Alamein, Bernard Law Montgomery, 1st viscount

Ypres, John Denton Pinkstone French, 1st earl of

Magazines

To discover helpful magazine articles, the researcher can use the *Reader's Guide to Periodical Literature*, which is published once a month. The *Reader's Guide* indexes articles by subject from over 100 popular magazines, such as *Time, Newsweek, Saturday Evening Post, Ladies' Home Journal*, and *Harper's Bazaar*. Popular magazines are general-interest publications like those available on most newsstands. Such magazines contain much useful information, but it will not be of a scholarly nature.

Journals

When researchers are after more detailed, more scholarly information than that provided in magazines, they turn to journals. Journals are periodicals published by scholarly, professional organizations—groups like the American Psychological Association and the Modern Language Association. The treatment of subjects in journals is more detailed—aimed less at the general reader and more at the reader knowledgeable in the given field. However, this fact should not discourage you from using journal articles, because they can usually be understood by the college student. In fact, the more detailed, scholarly approach of the journal article often makes it a more satisfying choice than the magazine article.

To discover useful journal articles, researchers rely on bibliographies and indexes. There are actually many such bibliographies and indexes, one for almost every area of study. These tools of access list alphabetically, by subject, titles of articles in a number of journals. Below is a list of some of the most common of these bibliographies and indexes.

Applied Science and Technology Index
The Art Index
Basic Books and Periodicals of Home Economics
Bibliography of Modern History
*Bibliography on Women: With Special Emphasis on Their Roles in Science and
    Society*
Biological and Agricultural Index
Business Periodicals Index
Drama Bibliography
Education Index
Film Index
Health and Development: An Annotated Indexed Bibliography
Humanities Index
Index to Economic Journals
Index to Religious Periodical Literature
International Bibliography of Geography
International Bibliography of Political Science
International Computer Bibliography
*MLA International Bibliography of Books & Articles on the Modern Lan-
    guages & Literature*
The Music Index
Nursing Literature Index
Social Sciences and Humanities Index
Social Sciences Index
Women: A Bibliography

Newspaper Articles

Newspapers are often the best source of the most immediate information on subjects so current or so regional that books and other periodicals do not treat them much. However, newspapers also cover a wide variety of subjects also treated in books and other periodicals. Issues related to the arts, health and medicine, history, politics, travel, fashion, ecology, nuclear energy, economics, and more, are found in newspaper articles.

Newspaper articles are indexed alphabetically, by subject, in their own indexes. Three of the most useful indexes are *The New York Times Index, The Wall Street Journal Index,* and *The Washington Post Index.*

What's in the Library: Government Documents and How to Find Them

The United States government publishes more material than any other single publisher, and it publishes on a wide variety of subjects, including business and economics, domestic and foreign affairs, social sciences, education, and ecology. For this reason, researchers often turn to government publications for some of their information.

To find a U.S. document on a particular subject, the researcher can check the subject-index section of the *Monthly Catalog of U.S. Government Publications*. Also useful for locating helpful government documents are the *Congressional Information Service*, which indexes U.S. Congress publications, and *Public Affairs Information Service*, which indexes documents in the social sciences.

What's in the Library: Encyclopedias

There are two kinds of encyclopedias—general-knowledge encyclopedias and specialty encyclopedias—and both can be helpful to the researcher. You are probably familiar with general-knowledge encyclopedias, works such as *World Book, Encyclopaedia Britannica*, and *Encyclopedia Americana*. These encyclopedias, and others like them, provide excellent general information on a wide variety of topics.

The specialty encyclopedias, however, limit themselves to specific subject areas and treat them in more depth than do the general encyclopedias. There are a number of specialty encyclopedias, four of which are

Encyclopaedia Judaica
Encyclopedia of Education
Encyclopedia of Film and Television
Encyclopedia of World Art

Encyclopedias are useful to researchers for two reasons. First, the information they contain may be just what the researcher is after, particularly if an overview of the subject is what is needed. Second, encyclopedias can be excellent departure points for researchers. The overview these works provide helps researchers understand the scope of their subject and in what ways their subject can be narrowed.

Points to Remember about What's in the Library
1. The card catalog provides access to books in the library.
2. The card catalog has two parts: the author/title file and the subject file. Researchers can find books on their subject by checking the subject file.
3. The call number in the corner of the catalog card shows where the book is shelved.
4. Bibliographies and indexes provide access to articles in periodicals (magazines, journals, and newspapers).

5. There are bibliographies and indexes (located in the reference room) for almost every subject area.
6. *The New York Times Index, The Wall Street Journal Index,* and *The Washington Post Index* provide access to articles in the three newspapers.
7. Articles in bibliographies and indexes are alphabetized by subject.
8. Access to government publications can be gained through *Monthly Catalog of U.S. Government Publications, Congressional Information Service,* and *Public Affairs Information Service.*
9. General-knowledge and specialty encyclopedias can be useful to the researcher.

Gathering Information: Phase I, The Working Bibliography

Early on in their investigation, researchers must determine which of the many sources in the library might be of some use to them. To do this, researchers compile a *working bibliography*, which is a list of titles of works that may contain useful information.

A working bibliography is a time saver because it is a selective list of potentially helpful titles. Without this tool, the researcher would have to roam the library hoping to bump into useful material. To compile a working bibliography, follow these steps:

1. Look up your subject in the subject file of the card catalog. Make a bibliography card for any book that looks promising. (The form for bibliography cards will be discussed later.)
   a. If the catalog card indicates that the book contains a bibliography, make note of that fact so you can check that bibliography for other useful sources.
   b. Look at the bottom of each card for tracings, which are the other headings a book is filed under in the catalog (see the card on p. 333). A check under these headings can lead you to additional helpful titles.
2. Look up your subject in the appropriate bibliographies and indexes. Make a bibliography card for any journal or magazine article that looks promising.
3. Look up your subject in the newspaper indexes and make a card for any promising titles.
4. Check the *Essay and General Literature Index,* which references chapters of books on particular subjects. This tool is helpful because sometimes a book's title may not indicate that the work contains one or more chapters on your subject.
   Note: To save space, bibliographies and indexes are heavily abbreviated. To understand these abbreviations, refer to the key at the front of the work.

When deciding whether to make a bibliography card—that is, when determining whether a source holds promise—researchers must make a decision based on the title of the work. This is a judgment call, but it is not a difficult one. If there's even an outside chance that a work might be useful, make a card.

Whether you are dealing with a book or periodical material, any source you encounter will be one of two kinds: primary or secondary. A *primary source* is one that forms the subject of your essay. For example, if you were writing about the symbolism in *Moby Dick*, then *Moby Dick* would be a primary source. Similarly, if you were writing about the lives of pioneer women, a diary written by a pioneer woman would be a primary source. A *secondary source* is an author's commentary on your subject. A journal article about the symbolism in *Moby Dick* is a secondary source, as is a book written in 1976 that describes the lives of pioneer women. Both primary and secondary sources are important to a researcher, and whenever possible you should try to check both.

Bibliography Forms

Each time you discover a title that looks promising, you should record it so that later you can look it up for note taking. Your record of promising sources is your *working bibliography*. While a working bibliography can be written on scratch or note paper, many researchers and most instructors prefer that it be done on 3 × 5 index cards, one source per card. The form your sources should appear in on these cards is a standardized one. You should have your sources in these forms so that later, when you document your borrowings, you have all the necessary data and do not find yourself on an eleventh-hour search for missing publication dates and such.

Below is a sample bibliography card for a book written by one person. Notice the indentation, punctuation, information included, and the call number. Be sure your cards have all the necessary information and that they are in the correct form.

```
                                        HQ
                                        7365
                                        .R32

     Gaston, E. Thayer.   Music in Therapy.

         New York:  Macmillan, 1968.
```

If you make a bibliography card each time you encounter a likely source of information, and if you make sure your cards are correct by modeling them after the forms below, you will leave nothing to chance.

Bibliography Form: Books

Author, One
>Gaston, E. Thayer. Music in Therapy. New York: Macmillan, 1968.

Authors, Two
>Fisher, Seymour, and Rhoda L. Fisher. What We Really Know about Child Rearing. New York: Basic Books, 1976.

Authors, Three
>Richardson, Charles E., Fred V. Hein, and Dana L. Farnsworth. Living: Health, Behavior, and Environment. 6th ed. Glenview, Ill.: Scott, Foresman, 1975.

Authors, More Than Three
>Shafer, Raymond P., and others. Marijuana: A Signal of Misunderstanding. New York: New American Library, 1972.

Edition, Other than the First
>Langacker, Ronald W. Language and Its Structure: Some Fundamental Linguistic Concepts. 2nd ed. New York: Harcourt Brace Jovanovich, 1973.

Editor
>Catanzaro, Ronald J., ed. Alcoholism: The Total Treatment Approach. Springfield, Ill.: Charles C. Thomas, 1977.

Encyclopedia
>"Lombard." The World Book Encyclopedia. 1973 ed.

Translator
>Medvedev, Zhores A. Nuclear Disaster in the Urals. Trans. George Sanders. New York: W. W. Norton, 1979.

Bibliography Form: Periodicals

Author, anonymous
>"Night of Horror." Sports Illustrated, 13 Oct. 1980, 29.

Journal
>Crumley, E. Frank. "The Adolescent Suicide Attempt: A Cardinal Symptom of a Serious Psychiatric Disorder." American Journal of Psychotherapy 26 (1982): 158–165.

Magazine, monthly
>"TV and Movies May Contribute to Crime." Ebony, Aug. 1979, 88.

Magazine, weekly
>Kanfer, Stefan. "Doing Violence to Sport." Time, 31 May 1976, 64–65.

Newspaper article
>Farrell, William E. "Ex-Soviet Scientist, Now in Israel, Tells of Nuclear Disaster." New York Times, 9 Dec. 1976, 8.

Gathering Information: Phase II, Taking Notes

After your working bibliography is complete, you are ready to examine your promising sources. As you look at them, you will discover some material you wish to take notes on. To make note taking as efficient as possible, keep the following principles in mind:

1. Take your notes on index cards, but avoid the temptation to fill each card with data. Instead, write only one piece of information on each card. This will allow you to shuffle your note cards into a suitable order later when you experiment with possible organizations.
2. Be sure that you indicate on each note card the source and page number the note is taken from so that you can document the material in your paper. If you forget to do this, you will find yourself scurrying around at the last minute to locate the source of your information.
3. Most of the time your notes should be *paraphrases*. That is, they should be restatements of the author's ideas in your own words. However, when you encounter ideas that are expressed in a way that is particularly effective or in a way that is difficult to paraphrase, you may use direct quotation. Discussions of paraphrasing and quoting appear after number 5 below.
4. As you work through source material, ideas of your own may occur to you. You may think of an effective way to handle your introduction, or you may have an idea in response to what you have read, or you may think of a piece of information you should look up. When these ideas strike you, write them on note cards too, so you do not forget them—just be sure to label these ideas as your own, so you do not confuse them with borrowed information.
5. When you look at a source, you will need to decide whether it is useful enough to warrant taking notes. If it is, you will then need to decide what parts of the source to take notes on. You can base these decisions on your purpose and audience. For example, let's say your purpose is to demonstrate that anorexia nervosa (a psychological disorder characterized by self-imposed starvation) is caused in part by the emphasis on thinness in advertisements. In this case, you may want to take notes on a paragraph that quotes a victim who reports she first stopped eating when she noticed how thin magazine models are. However, you may pass up taking notes on a paragraph describing the typical anorexic, because this information falls outside your purpose. Similarly, your audience will influence what you take notes on. If your audience is a group of physicians, you will not need to take notes on an extended definition of anorexia nervosa. But if your audience is a magazine publisher who may not know the full scope of the illness, then you might want to take notes on this definition.

Paraphrasing

Most of the time your notes should be paraphrases, so your paper has your own distinctive style. A *paraphrase* is a restatement of the author's ideas in your own words. It is very important when you paraphrase that you *do* alter the style of the original but that you *do not* alter the meaning of the original. One good way to handle a paraphrase is to read several times the portion of original material to be paraphrased, until you are sure you understand the meaning. Then looking away from the source, write the paraphrase on your note card. Finally, check your paraphrase against the source to be sure that you *have* altered style but *have not* altered meaning.

To appreciate the difference between an acceptable and unacceptable paraphrase, study the following examples.

original source: When advertising executives are called upon to defend the advertisements they create for television, they do so by noting that such ads make consumers aware of the best products in a given field. However, this is far from the truth, for rather than informing us about the *best* products, TV ads are more likely to create in us the desire for products we don't really need.

unacceptable paraphrase: When people in advertising have to defend television ads, they do so by saying that the ads tell consumers what the best products in a particular area are. Yet, this is not the truth because these ads really make us desire products we do not really need and that is really immoral.

explanation: The above paraphrase is unacceptable for two reasons. First, the style is so close to that of the original that the author really has made no attempt to put the material in his or her own words. Second, the last sentence of the paraphrase includes an idea that does not appear in the original. Paraphrases may not alter the original author's meaning, nor may they contain ideas that did not appear in the original.

acceptable paraphrase: Television commercials have been defended on the grounds that these ads let people know which of the available products are the best ones. Actually this is not really the case. Instead, these ads cause people to want unnecessary products.

explanation: The above paraphrase has a style different from that of the original, but the meaning of the original has not been changed, nor has any meaning been added.

Quoting

Most of the material you borrow from sources should be in paraphrase form, but when you encounter material expressed in a particularly effective way, you may wish to quote it. Or sometimes material does not lend itself to paraphrase, so you may want to quote for this reason. When you are quoting, there are some guidelines for you to remember.

1. With very few exceptions (these will be noted below) you may not alter the spelling, capitalization, punctuation, or wording of anything you quote.
2. Short quotations (those fewer than five typed lines) are worked into your sentence, but long quotations (those five or more typed lines) are set off by triple-spacing before and after the quote, and by indenting the quote 10 spaces on the left. Indent 15 spaces if the quotation marks the beginning of a paragraph in the source. No quotation marks are used unless they appeared in the source, in which case double quotation marks are used. The introduction to a long quote is followed by a colon. (See p. 350 for an example of a long quotation.)
3. If you wish to leave out some portion from the middle of a quotation, use ellipses (three spaced dots) to signal that something has been omitted. Be sure when you omit words that you do not distort the original meaning.

   source material: Professional sport is in fact no more violent than it used to be.

   quotation with ellipses: ''Professional sport is . . . no more violent than it used to be.''

   Note: The word *no* cannot be omitted, for the meaning would be altered. If the omission comes at the end of a sentence, follow the ellipses with a period.

   source material: It's a poorly kept NFL secret that hooliganism increases during Monday-night games, which, when played in the east, start at the relatively late hour of 9 p.m. to accommodate west coast TV viewers.

   quotation with ellipses: ''It's a poorly kept NFL secret that hooliganism increases during Monday-night games, which, when played in the east, start at the relatively late hour of 9 p.m. . . .''

4. Sometimes it is necessary to add a word or phrase to a quotation in order to clarify something or work the quotation into your sentence. When this is the case, place the addition inside brackets.

   source material: The OTA awarded a contract to the UCLA School of Public Health for a study of adverse effects of Agent Orange on American ground troops in Vietnam.

   quotation with addition: ''The OTA [Office of Technology Assessment] awarded a contract to the UCLA School of Public Health for a study of adverse effects of Agent Orange on American ground troops in Vietnam.''

5. Sometimes part of the material you are quoting appears in italics. When this is the case, underline the part that appears in italics.

   source material: Acupuncture relieves pain *even after the needles are withdrawn.*

   quotation with underlining: ''Acupuncture relieves pain <u>even after the needles are withdrawn.</u>''

6. Sometimes all or part of what you are quoting is itself a quotation. When this

is the case, use single quotation marks wherever double quotes appear in the original. Continue to use double quotation marks to mark the place where the quoted material begins and ends.

source material: "Crowd behavior is the most sensitive issue in sports today," says a Pinkerton's, Inc. official, who coordinates security at several racetracks and arenas.

quotation with single quotation marks: "'Crowd behavior is the most sensitive issue in sports today,' says a Pinkerton's, Inc. official, who co-ordinates security at several racetracks and arenas."

7. When the quotation is preceded in your paper with an introduction that has the word *that* in it, the first word of the quotation is not capitalized and no comma is used after the introduction. However, if the introduction in your text does not have the word *that*, then a comma is used and the first word of the quotation is capitalized.

example with "that": Smith says that "few adolescents feel secure."

example without "that": Smith says, "Few adolescents feel secure."

Points to Remember about Gathering Information

1. A working bibliography (list of potentially useful sources) is compiled to identify the works you will look at.
2. To determine the titles that may be useful, look up your subject in the subject file of the card catalog, in *Essay and General Literature Index*, and in the appropriate bibliographies and indexes.
3. Every title that shows some promise should be noted on a bibliography card, which is written in the conventional form.
4. After compiling your working bibliography, look at your sources and take notes on useful material, using paraphrase and direct quotation.
   a. To paraphrase, alter the author's style but not the meaning.
   b. When you quote, spelling, capitalization, punctuation, and wording may not be altered in most cases.
   c. Quotations fewer than five typed lines are worked into the text, but ones five or more typed lines are set off.
   d. In quotations ellipses are used for omissions.
   e. In quotations brackets are used for additions.
   f. In quotations underlining is used when italics appear in the source.
   g. Single quotation marks are used for quotations within quotations.
   h. Capitalization and use of the comma are affected by whether the quotation is introduced with *that*.
5. Place one item of information on a card and indicate the source and page number(s).

6. What you take notes on will be influenced by your audience and purpose.
7. You can also take notes on ideas that strike you along the way, but label these ideas as your own.

Using Research Material Responsibly: Documentation

When writers include the words and ideas of others, they have a responsibility to do so properly and fairly. You already learned about some ways writers handle researched material responsibly when you read about how quotes and paraphrases are handled. There are also other conventions you should be aware of, and these relate to proper documentation of borrowed words and ideas.

When you *document* researched material, you are acknowledging in the conventional ways that you are using the words and ideas of others. In general, proper documentation involves introducing each borrowing, providing a parenthetical text citation for each borrowing, and citing each borrowing on the "works cited" page. Let's look at each of these documentation conventions.

Introducing Borrowings

Because your paper will include your own ideas along with those you have discovered in the library, it is necessary to distinguish what is yours from what is borrowed. This is done by introducing each of your borrowings with a phrase that indicates its source. Consider, for example, the following passage taken from a student paper. The introductions are italicized as a study aid.

> Businesses in the United States and the world over lose great sums of money because of the alcoholic employee. *Estimates of the Department of Health, Education, and Welfare and a study done by Roman and Trice show that* the number of alcoholics ranges from as high as ten out of every one hundred workers to a low of three to four out of one hundred (Williams and Moffat 7). Alcoholism, *as Joseph Follman states*, is "a problem so far reaching and so costly [it] must have an effect upon the business community of the nation." *Follman goes on to say*, "The result is impaired production, labor turnover, and increased costs of operation" (78). In terms of impaired productivity, the cost in the United States alone is said to be $12.5 billion a year, *as the National Council on Alcoholism estimates* (Follman 81–82). Obviously, someone must pay these costs, and no doubt it is the consumer who pays higher prices for goods and services. Yet reduced productivity because of alcoholic employees and the resulting higher prices could be held in check by the sound implementation of company programs to rehabilitate the alcoholic employee.

The paragraph above includes both borrowed material and the writer's own ideas. Each borrowing has an introduction to identify it clearly as someone else's words or ideas. A close look at the paragraph reveals the following points about introducing borrowed material.

1. Regardless of when the source material was written, the introduction is in the present tense. This *present-tense convention* is followed because printed words live on, even if their author died long ago.
2. Introductions often appear before the borrowing, but they can also be placed in the middle or at the end.
3. The verbs used in your introductions should be varied to avoid monotony. Instead of repeatedly writing ''Smith says,'' you can also use ''Smith explains'' (notes, estimates, reveals, demonstrates, believes, contends, feels, and so on).
4. An introduction can refer to the author of the borrowing (''Smith finds''), or to the credentials of the author (''one researcher believes'' or ''a prominent sociologist contends''), or to the title of the source (''according to *Advertising Age*'').

Writing Parenthetical Text Citations

In addition to introducing your borrowings, to document properly you must cite your source of information within parentheses immediately after the borrowing. This is true whether your borrowing is a paraphrase or a quotation. Writers who use researched material must document in this way so their readers will know exactly where the borrowings came from in case they wish to examine the sources themselves. Furthermore, it is only fair for writers to acknowledge when they use the words and ideas of others.

1. When your borrowing has been introduced with the author's name, your parenthetical note includes the page number or numbers the borrowing appeared on in the source:
   Ruth Caldersen agrees that corporal punishment is not a legitimate form of discipline in schools (104).
2. When the introduction to your borrowing does not include the author's name, your parenthetical citation should note this name along with the appropriate page number or numbers:
   One high school principal remarks, ''I've never known corporal punishment to improve the behavior of unruly students'' (Hayes 16).
3. When more than one source by the same author is cited in your paper, include the author's name in the introduction to your borrowings and use a short form of the title in the parenthetical citation:
   Rodriguez feels that a teacher who resorts to corporal punishment is acting out of frustration (Discipline, 86).
   The above title is a short form of *Discipline in the Public Schools*. It distinguishes the source from another of Rodriguez's works cited, *Education in an Enlightened Age*.
   Note: An in-text citation for a long quote that is set off appears after the period and at the right margin (see page 350 for an example).

Writing the "Works Cited" Page

In addition to introducing borrowings and providing parenthetical text citations, proper documentation requires you to furnish a "works cited" page or pages at the end of your paper. This is an alphabetical listing of all the sources from which you paraphrased and quoted in your paper—*not* all the sources you reviewed in the course of your research. For an example of a "works cited" page, see p. 351. There you will notice that entries are listed alphabetically according to the author or editor's last name. If the source has no known author or editor, then the work is alphabetized according to the first important word in the title. The form for your citations is the same that you used for your working bibliography. Thus, you can refer to the models on p. 340 when you write this last portion of your paper. If you type your paper, your citations should be double-spaced, and you should double-space between citations.

Other Methods of Documentation

The documentation procedures already described are those recommended by the Modern Language Association (MLA) for language and literature studies. There are, however, other methods of documentation used in other fields of study. In one of these systems, used in some of the sciences and social sciences, the author's last name and the source's publication date appear in the parenthetical text citation. If the author's name is used to introduce the borrowing, only the publication date appears in parentheses:

One recent study (Hacker, 1982) reveals . . .
Cornelius' view (1976) runs counter to Davis's (1974) in that . . .

The bibliography for this method of documentation is much like the one you have already studied. However, it is labeled "References" rather than "Works Cited." Also, when a single author has published more than one work in the same year, letters are used both in the bibliography and in the text to distinguish the publications from each other:

If Alderson's findings (1970 a) hold true . . .

Another form of documentation, used in some sciences, relies on numbers. Each bibliography citation is numbered. When a borrowing appears in the text, it is acknowledged with the appropriate number placed in parentheses.

Whitford's findings (4) are surprising in light of Osborne's experiments (5).

The bibliography that conforms to this method of documentation is often arranged in the order the sources are cited.

Rarely does a writer choose the method of documentation he or she uses. This is usually determined by the field of study and/or the instructor. Thus, you should always ask your instructor which method to use, and you should consult the style sheet that describes this method because what appears here by no means covers all of the conventions of the author/date or number systems.

Points to Remember about Documentation According to the MLA Style Sheet

1. Responsible documentation of borrowed material (quotations and paraphrases) involves introducing each borrowing, providing a parenthetical textual citation for each borrowing, and writing a "works cited" citation for each borrowing.
2. The present tense is used to introduce borrowings.
3. The forms for "works cited" citations are conventional and should be followed. Your "works cited" page will be an alphabetical list of the sources you quoted and paraphrased from.

Exercise: Using Research Material

1. Assume you are writing a paper on the ways magazine advertisements influence people to buy, and you are seeking explanations of specific persuasive techniques used. Your audience will be someone who succumbs easily to the influence of magazine ads. With this in mind, do the following:
   a. Check the subject file of the card catalog and write two bibliography cards for two different, promising books.
   b. Check the appropriate bibliographies and indexes and write one bibliography card for a promising journal article, one for a promising magazine article, and one (if possible) for a promising newspaper article.
   c. Check *Essay and General Literature Index*; if possible, make a bibliography card for one promising source.
2. Paraphrase the second paragraph of "The Egalitarian Error" on p. 292. Be sure to alter style but not meaning.
3. Quote directly the first sentence of paragraph 6 of "The Egalitarian Error." Introduce the quotation with the authors' names and *that*. Remember to use single quotation marks and underlining where necessary.
4. Quote directly the last two sentences of "The Egalitarian Error," omitting everything from the dash on. Remember to use ellipses. Also introduce the quotation with the authors' names but omit *that*.
5. Quote the first sentence of paragraph 3 of "The Egalitarian Error." In brackets add a

definition of "behavior of this kind." (The definition can be found in the previous paragraph.) Follow the quotation with a parenthetical text citation.

A Sample Paper Using Research

The following student essay is developed using research material to supplement the student's own ideas. As you read this piece, notice how the borrowed material is used as support and how the author follows the conventions for handling borrowed material.

How Parents Can Lessen the Effects of Television Violence

"Mommy, I'm bored."

"Don't bother me now, Junior; I have a headache. *Why don't you go watch TV?*"

Conversations like this often take place between parent and child because no parent, no matter how conscientious, can spend every minute with his or her child. And let's face it, television *is* a way to keep a bored child quiet and occupied. And yes, television *can* be a good form of entertainment and even a valuable learning tool.

Almost everyone agrees that television can have a great influence on how children view the world and how they act within it. As a result, almost everyone agrees that it is important for parents to supervise what television their children watch. Usually, this means that parents are advised to restrict the amount of violence viewed.

Anne Somers, for example, cites the National Commission on the Causes and Prevention of Violence, which published a report, *To Establish Justice, to Insure Domestic Tranquility*, in 1969. A portion of the report discloses that many of the experiments done with children show that aggressive behavior is learned by viewing violence on television. The report states that while television is a serious influence on our society's level of violence, it is not necessarily the main cause. However, it goes on to say that the influence of television on children is stronger now, when the authority of the "traditional institutions" of religion, education, and family is questionable. The concern expressed in the report is that since so much of television broadcasting expresses antisocial, aggressive behavior, and since television is such a strong influence on children, children will be learning to behave aggressively (210–11).

Certainly the literature expressing the dangers of television violence for children is abundant; one can find it published in everything from *TV Guide* to the most scholarly journals. Yet does it all mean that parents must be sure their children never view violence on the small screen? I think not, for there is evidence that not all children who view televised violence become overly

Introduction of borrowing is in the present tense.

Parenthetical text citation to document paraphrase.

aggressive. The child's interpretation of what is viewed is a crucial factor in how he or she will behave afterward. Sociology professor Hope Lunin Klapper believes:

> The child itself plays an active role in the socialization process. The consequences of television *for* a child are thus in part a consequence *of* the child. . . . It is the child's perception which defines the stimulus. . . . The consequences of television involve . . . two major steps: First, the child's perception or translation of the content, and second, his or her response or lack of response to that perception.   (427)

Quotation of more than 4 lines is set off. Ellipses signal omission.

Text citation for a long quotation is at the right margin.

Thus, whether televised violence will adversely affect a child will depend on that child. The conclusion to be drawn from Klapper is that some children will not become violent just because they have viewed violence on television. Klapper says that whether a child behaves aggressively will be, in part, a result of his or her perception of the viewed violence, and this says a lot about what the parental role should be. Parents could counteract any negative effects that television violence could have on a child's behavior by taking advantage of the opportunity presented to teach the child some of the values that they feel are important. As a child watches a violent program, the parents could explain that the behaviors displayed do not coincide with their values. In this way, a child could be taught that even though such behaviors exist, they are not desirable. After all, violence does exist in the world. If parents constantly shield their children from this fact, then the children will be unable to cope with this reality of life. On the other hand, exposure to violence, through television and parental explanation about what is viewed, can be a healthy education in the reality of violence and how to avoid it.

Professor Charles Atkin explains another reason children should not be completely restricted from viewing violence. He suggests that children will choose to watch television shows that correspond to their own tendencies toward aggression (6). Thus by observing the types of programs their children prefer, parents can gain a better understanding of their personalities. A child who continually elects to watch violence may have aggressive tendencies. Parents need to know whether their children are too aggressive so they can intervene, and one way they can discover this is to observe their children's viewing preferences. If the child is consistently choosing violent shows, the parents can, as Atkin explains, "effectively mediate their children's predispositions" (12) and make their child understand that although violence does exist in reality, there are other aspects of life as well.

Exact words appear in quotation marks, and parenthetical citation is used.

Thus, parents can help their children's personalities develop in a positive manner by observing how they respond to television violence and by influencing accordingly how they interpret what they see. Parents can use televised violence to assess their children's tendency toward violence, and they can use it to voice their disapproval to show violence is wrong. Of course, this means parents must watch violent shows *with* their children, even when they have a headache.

Works Cited

Atkin, Charles, and others. "Selective Exposure to Televised Violence." Journal of
Broadcasting 23 (Winter 1979): 5–13.

Klapper, Hope Lunin. "Childhood Socialization and Television." Public Opinion Quarterly 42 (1978): 426–30.

Somers, Anne R. "Television and Children: Issues Involved in Corrective Action."
American Journal of Orthopsychiatry 48 (1978): 205–13.

Topic Suggestions

The following suggestions are ones you can consider as you shape your essay
topic. These topics may require some narrowing to make them sufficiently
focused and to your liking. Also, be sure you select a topic you currently know
enough about, since your essay will depend only in part on research material
for its development. Most of the ideas should be yours.

1. Several topics can come from the subject area of advertising. Consider one
   impact advertising has on our lives or whether advertisers play fair or how
   advertisers persuade or to what extent advertisers shape taste and to what
   extent they influence it. To shape a narrow topic, consider selecting ads for
   a particular class of products (say, cosmetics or liquor) and a particular
   medium (such as television or magazines).
2. Several interesting topics can be shaped about the women's movement. For
   example, you might compare and/or contrast some aspect of our culture
   (family life, education, advertising, etc.) before and after the movement
   became a strong influence. You could explain why the Equal Rights Amendment failed. You could describe the effects of working mothers on the
   American family or American business. You could define the contemporary
   woman or man in light of sexual equality. You could also discuss the effect
   changing roles have had on child rearing or marriage or dating.
3. Many topics can come from the subject area, education. Should teachers be
   accountable? Should high school seniors have to pass a competency exam to
   graduate? Is a return to the basics a good idea? Should handicapped children
   be mainstreamed? Should prayer be permitted in schools? Answering these
   questions can lead to excellent topics. In addition, you could describe the
   impact of preschool education on the education system, or you could explain why there has been a decline in SAT scores, or you could define the
   ideal education. You could also compare and/or contrast the advantages of
   homogeneous and heterogeneous groupings of students.
4. The general subject of television can yield suitable topics. You might compare and/or contrast the portrayal of the role of some group (police officers,
   mothers, teachers, doctors, etc.) with the way this group functions in

reality. You might describe how television shapes our perception of something (marriage, sex roles, war, etc.). Or you could examine whether TV news provides responsible coverage of world events. Or you could argue that programs aimed at children should be free of commercials, or you could argue for or against network censorship (or argue that this censorship is or is not adequate). Answering the following questions can also lead to topics: What do you think of children's programming? Is programming too violent? Is there too much sex on TV? Should the number of hours children watch television be restricted? Does television reflect public taste or shape it?

5. It is possible to shape many topics about health and nutrition. For example, you might argue that places of business and industry should provide exercise facilities for their employees. If you are a runner or a walker, you might describe the benefits of the activity. You might explain the pros or cons of a vegetarian diet or argue for or against banning a particular food additive. You could explore whether medical schools should admit the brightest students or the most compassionate, or you could use illustrations to show whether or not the aged get adequate health care in this country. Should cigarettes be banned? Are hospices for the terminally ill and their families effective? Do school lunch programs provide balanced meals? Are birth control pills safe enough? Answering these questions can lead to interesting topics.

6. Government and politics is a general subject that many topics can come from. You could look at the advantages (or disadvantages) of the electoral college system for electing the president. You might explore whether the most able candidate is elected or the one with the largest campaign fund. You might describe how congressional lobbyists operate, or you could describe how a candidate's media image affects his or her popularity. You could compare and/or contrast the way your local schools are currently funded with an alternative method. You could describe a workable plan to halt the arms race, or you could defend or criticize the current defense budget. You could also select some current political issue on the local, state, or national level and argue for or against some aspect of it.

Writing Strategies

The suggestions below describe steps you can take as you write your paper that uses research material. In addition, Chapters 1–3 offer suggestions that may be helpful.

1. Since a good academic library has information on virtually every subject, almost anything can be narrowed to a topic to be developed using some research material. There are, however, some subjects it is best to avoid. First, if you pick a subject that is very current, you may have trouble

Topic Selection

locating information anywhere but in newspapers because not enough time has passed to allow much to be published. Second, if you pick a subject of only regional interest, you may have trouble locating information. Finally, you should avoid topics that do not really require research. A paper on how the heart pumps blood, for example, does not require much research. One good book on the subject would have all the information you need.

2. The kind of paper described in this chapter is developed mostly with your own ideas, and research material is used only to supplement your own support. Thus, be sure you select a topic you know enough about on your own.

3. If you have trouble settling on a topic, leaf through a general-knowledge encyclopedia for ideas. Another way to find a topic is to consider what you have learned in your other courses. For example, perhaps you have learned in a psychology course enough about peer pressure to write about how parents can deal with this powerful force.

Establishing Audience and Purpose

It is important to have a clear sense of audience and purpose because these will influence what you take notes on. If you do not know why you are writing and who you are writing for, you may find yourself taking notes on material you cannot really use.

Idea Generation

1. Before beginning any library work, you should discover what ideas you yourself have on your topic. To do this, use one or a combination of the idea-generation techniques you have come to favor.

2. You can also generate ideas by asking yourself these questions:
   a. What have I observed about my subject?
   b. What have I read about my subject?
   c. What have I learned in class about my subject?
   d. What have I read about my subject?
   e. What illustrations would develop my topic?
   f. What narrations would develop my topic?
   g. What descriptions would develop my topic?
   h. What definitions would develop my topic?
   i. What comparisons or contrasts would develop my topic?
   j. What persuasive points can I make to develop my topic?
   k. What cause-and-effect relationships would develop my topic?

3. After generating ideas, you may be able to identify information you would like to discover in the library. For example, say you are writing a paper arguing for stiffer penalties for drunk drivers and you have already generated quite a few ideas. A review of these ideas could lead you to decide that some statistics showing the high number of highway deaths because of drunk drivers would enhance the persuasiveness of your essay. If you can identify specific information to find in the library, make note of it for future use.

4. Do not hesitate to reshape your topic, audience, or purpose in light of problems or insights raised by your idea generation.

1. Using the ideas you have generated so far, write a scratch outline that reflects the main points you plan to cover in your essay. This outline is only tentative and can be changed later, but it can be a useful tool. You can decide whether information you encounter in the library will be useful to you on the basis of whether it treats a point in your outline.
2. If during idea generation you identified specific information you need from the library, note this on your scratch outline.

Writing a Preliminary Outline

1. To ensure efficiency when you work in the library, follow the steps described in this chapter to first compile a working bibliography and then take notes.
2. If you have identified specific information to find, compile your working bibliography and take notes with this information in mind. However, keep an eye out for other information that might also be useful.
3. If you have not yet identified specific information you are after, your research approach will be less focused; you will be looking for anything that might help your paper. Let's say, for example, you want to describe the ways teenagers use clothing and hair styles as a sign of rebellion and you already know a great deal about this subject, enough even for a well-developed essay. If this is the case, you will keep an eye out for anything that might add an interesting or useful dimension to your piece. It could be a quote from a fashion designer or a child psychologist; it could be a description of a hair fashion from the fifties; or it could be an explanation of why teens use fashion as a sign of their rebellion against adult conventions.
4. When you work in the library, remain flexible so that you can respond appropriately to the material you encounter. If, for example, you discover information you did not expect to—say, something that disproves one of your own ideas—be flexible enough to adjust your material in light of this finding.
5. What you discover in the library may lead you to step back before you go forward. Your research can cause you to reshape your topic, change your audience or purpose, add or delete ideas, and/or alter your preliminary outline.

Working in the Library

1. After you have gathered your information in the library, reread your note cards to remind yourself of what you have.
2. Because the blending and organizing of your own ideas with those of authorities is a fairly sophisticated process, you should write a detailed, formal outline. It is possible you will outline more than once before you develop an effective organization.
3. As a basis for your formal outline, add the points you discovered in the library to your preliminary outline. From this you can develop your formal outline.
4. As you outline, you may decide not to use some of the information you gathered in the library. This is not a problem, nor is it unusual. Similarly,

Organizing Your Material

you may discover you need to return to the library to find a specific piece of information to help develop a particular point.

1. Using your outline as a guide, write your first draft the best way you can without agonizing over anything. If your draft will be fairly long, you may want to write it in two or three stages.

2. When you come to the sections of your draft that include borrowed material, you can tape your note cards to the draft. If you prefer not to do this, be careful to copy the borrowing from the card accurately. Be sure to include the proper introduction and parenthetical citation.

3. When your draft is complete, write your "works cited" pages, so you are sure you have the information you need.

Writing the First Draft

1. Writers who use research material must consider many aspects of their work as they prepare it for a reader. For this reason, it is wise to revise in stages. Before beginning any revision, however, distance yourself for at least a day. It is also a good idea to distance yourself after each stage of your revision for at least an hour or two.

2. One way to break up your revising into stages is this:

   a. Stage 1—Consider the adequacy and relevance of detail and logical organization. Make whatever changes you can without too much trouble, and note the changes you will make later.

   b. Stage 2—Consider whether your borrowings are worked smoothly into your text, and consider the effectiveness of your introduction and conclusion. Make what changes you can without too much trouble, and note the rest for later consideration.

   c. Stage 3—Revise for effective expression. If any changes prove troublesome, note them for handling later. (You might want to review Chapter 4 at this point.)

   d. Stage 4—Work through the revisions you noted were necessary but have not yet handled.

3. The thought you give your draft as you revise may lead you to reconsider or change something decided earlier. It is even possible that you will decide to return to the library to find additional information.

Evaluating and Revising the Draft

1. Writers who use research material have concerns in addition to those usually a part of editing. For this reason, you should spend significantly more time editing than you usually do.

2. In addition to your usual check for mistakes in grammar and usage, you should check to be sure you have handled your borrowings properly. This means you should

   a. Be sure every quotation is accurate and that quotation marks, ellipses, brackets, and underlining are correctly handled.

   b. Be sure that long quotations are correctly handled.

   c. Be sure that your paraphrases have the meaning of the original but not the style of the original.

Editing

   d. Be sure that every borrowing is properly documented with an introduction, parenthetical in-text citation, and "works cited" citation.

   e. Be sure that your "works cited" entries are in the conventional form.

After you have typed or copied your essay into its final form, pay careful attention to your proofreading. Because of all the conventions for using borrowed material, there are additional opportunities for oversight when an essay includes research material.

Proofreading

III

A Brief Guide to Frequently Occurring Errors

14

Sentence Fragments and Run-On Sentences

Sentence fragments and run-on sentences are viewed as serious problems by knowledgeable readers. Thus if you have a tendency to make either of these errors, you should pay special attention when you edit.

Recognizing and Correcting Sentence Fragments

If you punctuate and capitalize a sentence part as if it were a sentence (that is, if you place a capital letter at the beginning and a period, question mark, or exclamation point at the end), you have written a *sentence fragment*. Take a look at the following:

> The bus driver and his wife spent over $100 on toys for their children. *Most of it on the two girls.*

In the above illustration, the italicized words form a fragment. Although the capital letter and period give the word group the appearance of a sentence, the words do not have enough completeness for sentence status. Now consider the following:

> *Since she was graceful as well as daring.* She was an excellent dancer.

Once again, the italicized words form a fragment. Despite the period and capital, the word group fails to function as a sentence because it lacks completeness.

There are two ways to correct a sentence fragment: you can connect the fragment to the appropriate sentence before or after it (the one which completes the fragment), or you can rewrite the fragment so it forms a sentence (often this means changing the verb form). These correction methods are illustrated below.

Fragment: Since she was graceful as well as daring. She was an excellent dancer.

Correction: Since she was graceful as well as daring, she was an excellent dancer. Or: She was an excellent dancer, since she was graceful as well as daring.

Method: The fragment is connected to the sentence it depends on for completion of its meaning.

Fragment: My brother believing he can learn to shoot par golf in one summer.

Correction: My brother believes (believed) he can (could) learn to shoot par golf in one summer.

Method: The verb form is altered to turn the fragment into a sentence.

If you have a tendency to write sentence fragments, the best way to proceed is to edit a separate time, looking just for fragments. Study each group of words you are calling a ''sentence.'' Read each group aloud and ask yourself if it is complete enough to be a sentence. Do not move on to the next group until you are sure the one you are leaving behind is a sentence. For this method to be effective, you must move slowly, listening to each word group independent of what comes before and after it. Otherwise you may fail to hear a fragment because you complete its meaning with a sentence coming before or after. Of course each time you find a fragment, correct it before going on.

Although there are times when sentence fragments are effective, particularly for providing emphasis, these occasions are rare. More often, fragments are a serious lapse that will undermine the effectiveness of your writing.

Exercise: Sentence Fragments

Where necessary, edit the following to eliminate the fragments. Some are correct as they are.

1. After returning from the beach. The children were exhausted.
2. The rain showed no signs of letting up, so flash flood warnings were issued.
3. After Howie had attended drama class several times and bought a subscription to *Variety*. He was sure he would become a big star.
4. Although Marie missed several training sessions. She learned to use the new computer.
5. By midnight the party was over.
6. John neglecting his assigned duties and spending time on independent research.
7. The reigning dictator, being an excellent administrator and former army officer.

8. Being the most indispensable of the Channel 27 news team. Patrick got a raise.
9. Karen dropped calculus. Which she had dropped several times before.
10. Sean went to his karate class and when he came home. He had been burglarized.
11. After awhile, the fog cleared.
12. How can you expect that of me?
13. Janine skipped breakfast. Although she needed the nourishment.
14. Working together to save our environment. We can leave the world a better place than we found it.
15. Dad cleaning the hull of the boat, helping to set the lobster traps and still finding time to teach his younger daughter how to bait her own hook.

Edit the paragraphs below to eliminate the fragments.

A. My sister, who waited two years to become a high school cheerleader. Frequently complained that the student body had no school spirit. What did she expect? Our school, Fairmont High, had the football team with the state record. For losing the most consecutive games in a row. The only people who even attended the football games being the members of the marching band and some of the players' parents. The only contest on the field was the one at halftime. When the two marching bands competed to see who was the best. Things were so bad that our team felt a sense of accomplishment when they scored 6 points. No wonder the student body was spiritless. Or was it that they just had nothing to cheer for?

B. Much literature written for adolescents is of the highest quality. For example, *IOU'S*, by Ouida Sebestyen, being a well written story of adolescent conflict that both teens and adults would enjoy. The main character is 13-year-old Stowe. A boy who lives with his divorced mother. The novel chronicles Stowe's efforts as he wrestles with an important decision, struggles with friendships, and makes peace with his family. Like most adolescents. Stowe longs for the independence of adulthood at the same time he fears it. Briskly paced, tightly narrated, and thought-provoking, *IOU'S* is a novel teens will see themselves in. And a novel that will remind adults of the struggles inherent in adolescence. It is poignant, funny, and subtle. And above all realistic.

Recognizing and Correcting Run-On Sentences

Two or more main clauses can be written as one sentence. However, to do so correctly, you must separate these main clauses with either a semicolon or a comma and a coordinate conjunction (*and, but, or, nor, for, so,* or *yet*). If you combine two or more main clauses in the same sentence and fail to separate them properly, you have written a *run-on sentence*. (For an explanation of clauses, see the discussion beginning on p. 101.) Here is an example of a run-on:

In order to become a nurse, I studied hard for my state boards passing them was not easy.

This illustration contains two main clauses: *in order to become a nurse, I studied hard for my state boards* and *passing them was not easy*. The clauses are not separated with either a semicolon or a comma used with a coordinate conjunction, so the result is a run-on. To correct the run-on, the proper separation must be included, as shown below.

separation with semicolon: In order to become a nurse, I studied hard for my state boards; passing them was not easy.

correction with comma and coordinate conjunction: In order to become a nurse, I studied hard for my state boards, but (yet) passing them was not easy.

A frequent cause of run-ons is confusing words like *however, therefore, moreover, for example,* and *consequently* (conjunctive adverbs) with coordinate conjunctions and using them with commas to separate main clauses. However, conjunctive adverbs cannot be used to join main clauses with a comma—only the coordinate conjunctions *and, but, or, nor, for, so,* or *yet* can do this.

run-on: I was certain that my interview went well and that I would get the job, therefore I was quite surprised to learn I was not even among the top three finalists.

correction: I was certain that my interview went well and that I would get the job; therefore, I was quite surprised to learn I was not even among the top three finalists.

Another frequent cause of run-on sentences is using a comma alone to separate main clauses. Again, however, the comma must appear *with* a coordinate conjunction because a comma by itself cannot separate main clauses.

run-on: The Christmas party was dull, Jan and I left at 9:30.

correction: The Christmas party was dull, so Jan and I left at 9:30.

When a semicolon or comma with coordinate conjunction is used to correct a run-on sentence, the main clauses are properly joined in the same sentence. However, it is also possible to correct a run-on by establishing each main clause as a sentence.

run-on: My car stalls when I accelerate quickly the carburetor needs to be adjusted.

correction: My car stalls when I accelerate quickly. The carburetor needs to be adjusted.

Yet another way to correct a run-on is to take one of the main clauses, recast it as a subordinate clause, and connect that subordinate clause to the remaining main clause.

run-on: Denny decided to quit smoking, it was making him dizzy and light-headed.

correction: Since smoking was making him dizzy and lightheaded, Denny decided to quit. Or: Denny decided to quit smoking since it was making him dizzy and lightheaded.

The four ways to correct a run-on sentence are reviewed for you below.

Run-on: The door slammed shut, the dog awoke with a start.

1. *correction with semicolon:* The door slammed shut; the dog awoke with a start.
2. *correction with comma and coordinate conjunction:* The door slammed shut, and the dog awoke with a start.
3. *correction with period and capital letter:* The door slammed shut. The dog awoke with a start.
4. *correction with subordinate clause:* When the door slammed shut, the dog awoke with a start.

If you have a tendency to write run-ons, edit a separate time, checking just for these errors. Study each group of words you are calling a "sentence," and ask yourself how many main clauses there are. If there is more than one, be sure the proper separation exists or supply it if necessary.

Exercise: Run-on Sentences

Correct the following run-ons using any of the methods discussed.

1. My first bike will always be special to me it was a yellow dirt bike named Thunderball.
2. Lorraine loves to gossip about others she becomes angry if she even thinks someone is gossiping about her.
3. Yesterday the fire trucks raced up our street three times it must be the summer brushfire season.
4. The large black ants marched upside down across the kitchen ceiling, I wonder where they came from.
5. The package of chicken fryer parts was obviously spoiled she returned it to the manager of the market demanding a refund.
6. My son's baseball pants are impossible to get clean, why does the league insist on purchasing white pants?
7. Randy is a terrible soccer coach, he cares more about winning than he does about the children he manages.
8. Stevie is so warm and open that it is hard to resist his charm, he seems to smile all the time.
9. Cotton material is all that they claim it is—lightweight, soft, and comfortable be careful when laundering it often shrinks.
10. My mother has often been my best friend, she is caring, supportive, and nonjudgmental.

Rewrite the paragraphs below to eliminate the run-on sentences.

A. My day off made me wish I was back at my job everything went wrong. First I overslept and neglected to get my son to day camp on time. Then there was no milk for breakfast my son ate pizza. The dog had raided the wastebasket during the night half-chewed paper and bits of garbage littered the living room carpeting. I plugged in the sweeper, one of the prongs broke off in the outlet. I drove to the local hardware store to purchase new plugs. I returned home to discover the plug was the wrong size for the sweeper cord I drove back to the store to exchange the plug for the proper size. Then I cut my finger when the screwdriver slipped while I was trying to attach the new plug. In the middle of all this chaos, the phone rang, the neighbor was calling to tell me that my German shepherd had chased the mailman away from her house. By the time I was finished listening to her, I started to itch I looked down to see the unmistakable red blotches of poison ivy rising on my arms and calves.

B. I had been on my own for 18 years by the time I was 36, but I never really thought of myself as an adult. I left for college at 18 and was earning my own living by 22. I was married by the time I was 23, I was raising a family of three by 30. But not until I was 36 did I see myself as an honest-to-goodness grownup. It was then that my parents announced they were selling the house I grew up in. Then it hit me, then I really understood. I was out on my own my old room would be inhabited by some stranger. I could not go "home" to Mother and Dad anymore my "home" would not be there. How strange it seemed that I would never again enter that familiar haven and savor the warmth of the living room or the comfort of the kitchen. I would never again return to "my" bedroom where "my" furniture remained just as I left it when I left for college. When my folks called to announce they were moving to an apartment, I realized I was indeed an adult on my own. I must confess that the awareness came as a painful jolt. I wanted to go home, however, I was already in my home.

15
Agreement Problems

Agreement means "correspondence." Grammatically, there are two kinds of correspondence that are important: agreement between subjects and verbs, and agreement between pronouns and antecedents. Most often the necessary agreement is easily achieved. However, there are some instances that do present special agreement problems, and these are discussed in this chapter.

Subject-Verb Agreement

The rule for subject-verb agreement is fairly simple and straightforward: a verb should always agree with its subject in number. That is, a singular subject requires a singular verb, and a plural subject requires a plural verb.

singular subject, singular verb: Green *ink is* often difficult to read.
plural subject, plural verb: The *desks are* highly polished.

Compound Subjects

A compound subject is formed by two or more words, phrases, or clauses joined by *and, or, nor, either . . . or,* or *neither . . . nor.*

1. If the parts of a compound subject are linked by *and*, the verb is plural.
   The *lioness and her cub share* a close bond.

365

2. If singular subjects are preceded by *each* or *every*, then a singular verb is used.
   Each lioness and *each cub faces* starvation on the drought-stricken plain.
3. Singular subjects linked by *or* or *nor* (or by *either . . . or* or *neither . . . nor*) take a singular verb.
   Drought or famine threatens all wildlife.
4. Plural subjects linked by *or* or *nor* (or *either . . . or* or *neither . . . nor*) take a plural verb.
   Neither the children nor their parents are enjoying the play.
5. When a plural subject and a singular subject are joined, the verb agrees with the nearer subject.
   Disease or predators are also a danger to newborn cubs.
   Neither the scouts nor their leader is willing to camp out on such a cold night.

Subject and Verb Separated

Words, phrases, or clauses that come between the subject and verb do not affect the subject-verb agreement rule.

> The *chipmunks*, burrowing under my flower bed, also *raid* my garden.

The subject *chipmunks* is plural, so the plural verb *raid* must be used. The phrase *burrowing under my flower bed* does not affect that.
   Here is another example:

> *One* of the demonstraters *was* fined $100.

Although the phrase between the subject and verb contains the plural *demonstraters*, the singular subject *one* still requires the singular verb *was*.

Inverted Order

1. When the verb appears before the subject in a sentence, the word order is *inverted*. When a sentence has inverted word order, be sure the verb agrees with the subject and not some other word close to the verb.
   Flowing through the steep canyons *was* the *Colorado River*.
2. Sentences which begin with *there* often have inverted order.
   There *are* many *causes* of the dreaded disease, cancer.
   There *have been* substantial *gains* in the stock market.

Indefinite Pronouns

1. Indefinite pronouns refer to some part of a group of people, things, or ideas without specifying the particular members of the group referred to. The following indefinite pronouns are singular and require singular verbs.

anyone	everybody	something
anybody	everything	none
anything	someone	no one
each	either	nobody
one	neither	nothing
everyone	somebody	

Nobody ignores an insult all the time.
Everybody retaliates once in a while.
No one likes to be the butt of a joke.

> *Note:* Although *everyone* and *everybody* clearly refer to more than one, they are still singular in a grammatical sense and take a singular verb.

Everyone is invited to the party after the show.

2. It is particularly tempting to use a plural verb with a singular indefinite pronoun when a phrase with a plural word appears after the pronoun. However, in this case too the singular verb is used in formal usage.

   Each of the boys *is* willing to help rake the leaves.
   Everyone of us *plans* to contribute a week's salary to the Christmas fund.

3. The following indefinite pronouns may be singular or plural, depending upon the meaning of the sentence.

all	some	most
any	more	

Most of the players *are* injured.
Most of the pie *is* gone already.
All of the bills *are* paid.
All of the hem *is* torn.

Collective Nouns

Collective nouns have a singular form and refer to a group of people or things. The following are examples of collective nouns.

audience	class	majority
committee	family	faculty
crew	team	jury

1. Collective nouns take a singular verb when the noun refers to the group as a single unit.
   The *number* of people attending the Who's last concert *was* staggering.
   The women's basketball *team is* still in contention for the state championship.
2. Collective nouns take a plural verb when the noun refers to the members of the group functioning individually.

A *number* of those in attendance *were* over 30 years old.

The *faculty have* agreed among themselves to promote tougher admissions standards.

Exercise: Subject-Verb Agreement

Choose the correct verb form in the following sentences.

1. Three wolves and a grizzly bear (stalk/stalks) the grazing caribou herd.
2. The hunter, not natural enemies, (is/are) responsible for the decline in the bald eagle population.
3. Only recently (has/have) we seen the possibility of the rebirth of violent protest.
4. There (is/are) few American holidays more popular than Thanksgiving.
5. None of us really (know/knows) anyone else.
6. All of us often (disguise/disguises) our real feelings.
7. Neither of the cubs born to the huge female grizzly (appear/appears) undernourished.
8. Chief among the reasons for the high unemployment rate (has/have) been the attempts to bring inflation under control.
9. Each of the campers (is/are) responsible for bringing cooking utensils.
10. A majority of people (feel/feels) insecure about something.
11. There (is/are) few presidents more admired than Lincoln.
12. Neither time nor progress (has/have) diminished the affection most Americans feel for our sixteenth president.
13. One of my favorite poems (is/are) "The Rime of the Ancient Mariner."
14. Most of the beetles (is/are) trapped.
15. Either Kool and the Gang or Billy Joel (deserve/deserves) the Grammy for record of the year.
16. Your family often (demand/demands) to know your innermost secrets.
17. Each of us (decide/decides) who we will trust.
18. Everyone (need/needs) someone to talk to.
19. Fifteen adult white-tailed deer and a single fawn (was/were) observed by the backpackers.
20. All the elements of nature (act/acts) to maintain the balance of the animal population.

Rewrite the following paragraph to eliminate problems with subject-verb agreement.

One of the islands in the Caribbean Sea is called Bonaire. A number of tourists are [*were*] attracted to Bonaire because it is a nesting sight for pink flamingoes. However, the clear waters of the sea makes [*make*] the area a perfect spot for diving. There is [*are*] numerous underwater attractions for either the experienced diver or the amateur who requires [*require*] a guide. On the coral reef is [*are*] groupies and moray eels. Also, there are small "cleaner fish," called hogfish, who eat the harmful parasites off the larger fish. The colorful reef itself is a spectacular sight where one can observe a variety of coral. Throughout the reef is [*are*] sea anemones, shrimp, and crabs for the diver to observe. Although the underwater attractions of Bonaire is not commonly known, time and word of mouth will bring more vacationers to this island off the coast of northern South America.

Pronoun-Antecedent Agreement

Pronouns must agree with the nouns they refer to (antecedents) in gender (masculine, feminine, or neuter) and number (singular or plural). Many times this agreement is easily achieved, as is the case in the following example.

Kurt lost his tennis *racket*, but *he* eventually found *it*.

The pronoun *he* is singular and masculine to agree with the number and gender of the antecedent *Kurt*, and the pronoun *it* is singular and neuter to agree with *racket*.

There are times when pronoun-antecedent agreement is not as obvious as in the above sentence, and these instances are discussed in the rest of this chapter.

Compound Subjects

A compound subject is formed by two or more words, phrases, or clauses joined by *and, or, nor, either . . . or,* or *neither . . . nor*.

1. If the parts of the antecedent are joined by *and*, a plural pronoun is used.

   His shoes and baseball cap were left in *their* usual places.
   Linda, Michelle, and Audrey finished *their* group project early.

2. If the parts of the antecedent are preceded by *each* or *every*, the pronoun is singular.

   Every citizen and group must do *its* part to elect responsible officials.
   Each school and athletic department must submit *its* budget to the superintendent.

3. Singular antecedents joined by *either . . . or* or *neither . . . nor* require singular pronouns.

   Has *either Sean or Frank* taken *his* batting practice today?
   Neither Melissa nor Jennifer has finished packing for *her* trip.

4. Plural antecedents joined by *either . . . or* or *neither . . . nor* require plural pronouns.

   Neither the teachers nor the students are eating *their* lunches.

5. If one singular and one plural antecedent are joined by *or, either . . . or,* or *neither . . . nor*, the pronoun should agree with the antecedent closer to it.

   Either Mac Davis or the Oak Ridge Boys will release *their* new album soon.

Collective Nouns

Collective nouns have a singular form and refer to a *group* of people or things. Words like the following are collective nouns:

group	committee	jury
class	society	audience
team	panel	band

1. If the collective noun is functioning as a single unit, the pronoun that refers to it is singular.

   A civilized *society* must protect *its* citizens from violence.

2. If the members of the group are functioning individually, a plural pronoun is used.

   Yesterday the *team* signed *their* contracts for next season.

Indefinite Pronouns

Indefinite pronouns refer to some part of a group of people, things, or ideas without specifying the particular members of the group referred to. Indefinite pronouns can be antecedents.

1. The following indefinite pronouns are singular, and in formal usage, the pronouns referring to them should also be singular.

each	somebody	one
everybody	someone	either
everyone	anybody	neither
nobody	anyone	none
no one		

   Anyone who has finished his or *her* essay may leave.
   Nobody on the football team should assume that *his* position is safe.
   Neither of the young mothers forgot *her* exercise class.

2. In formal usage, a pronoun referring to a singular indefinite pronoun is singular, even when a phrase with a plural word follows the indefinite pronoun.
   Each of the boys selected *his* favorite bat.

3. *Few* and *many* are plural, so pronouns referring to them must also be plural.
   Many of my friends have already bought *their* tickets.

4. The following indefinite pronouns may be singular or plural, depending upon the meaning of the sentence.

all	some	most
any	more	

   Some of the book is still attached to *its* binding.
   Some of the band forgot *their* sheet music.

Pronoun-Antecedent Agreement: Gender

When a singular noun or indefinite pronoun designates a person who can be either male or female (*lawyer, student, director, pianist, anybody,* and so on), agreement can be achieved in one of three ways.

1. The masculine pronoun can be used. This method of achieving agreement is grammatically correct, but it does not acknowledge the presence of females. For this reason, many people achieve agreement using methods 2 and 3 below.

   Each contestant must bring *his* birth certificate.

2. A masculine and feminine pronoun can be used.

   Each contestant must bring *his or her* birth certificate.

3. The sentence can be recast into the plural.

   All contestants must bring *their* birth certificates.

Exercise: Pronoun-Antecedent Agreement

Choose the correct pronoun.

1. Neither Bill nor Doug volunteered (his, their) services for the Downtown Cleanup Crusade.
2. Each teacher and principal agreed that (he or she, they) would contribute to the United Way.
3. The secretary of the scuba club urged everybody to pay (his or her, their) dues by the end of the month.
4. Anyone wanting a successful college experience must spend much of (his or her, their) time studying.
5. A dog and two cats could take care of (itself, themselves) very nicely with just our family's table scraps.
6. The hostess asked that either Cara Smith or the Dennisons move (her, their) car.
7. Both Matt and Joey lost (his, their) lunch money.
8. Few of these candlesticks are in (its, their) original boxes.
9. That tribe holds (its, their) sacred initiation rites each autumn.
10. When asked to make statements, the sheriff and his deputy insisted on (his, their) right to remain silent.
11. The company fired (its, their) inefficient workers.
12. The herd moves ever westward as (it, they) grazes.
13. The ski club held (its, their) first meeting immediately following the holiday season.
14. The squad of police antiterrorists took (its, their) positions around the abandoned warehouse.
15. The city council debated whether (it, they) should pass the new antismoking ordinance.

16. No one should force (his or her, their) vacation choice on other members of the family.
17. Questioned by the precinct worker, neither Annette nor Karen would reveal (her, their) party affiliation.
18. To prepare for hurricanes, each coastal town has (its, their) own special warning system.
19. Most of the Pep Club had (its, their) pictures taken for the yearbook.
20. Both Jeff and Greg took (his, their) lunch to camp.

Rewrite the following paragraph to eliminate problems with pronoun-antecedent agreement.

With five children to feed and get off to school, I find mornings the worst part of the day. I begin waking the kids, whose ages range from 6 to 17, at 7:00. Each child pulls the covers over their heads and refuses to get up, so I turn all their radios on full blast until every one of them is up and functioning. Then there is the complaining: Jill or Janet cannot get their hair the way they want it; Marla's favorite sweater is not washed and she *has* to wear it; Jeff refuses to change out of Peter's sweat pants. Tony cannot find his books. And of course at least one of them forgot to do their homework, so there is the last minute panic and chaos. They never agree on what they will have for breakfast, so I always prepare five different things. If they all catch his or her buses on time, it's a miracle. I almost always end up driving one of them to school. Any mother who survives mornings with five school-age kids deserves a Congressional medal.

16

Shifts in Tense and Person

Verbs should be consistent in tense, and pronouns should be consistent in person. Unnecessary shifts in verb tense (for example, from present to past) or unnecessary shifts in pronoun person (for example, from *we* to *you*) can confuse meaning.

Tense Shifts

Once you begin with a particular verb tense, maintain that tense as long as you are referring to the same period of time. The following paragraph contains unwarranted tense shifts (the verbs are underlined to help you recognize the shifts).

> When E.T. first <u>arrives</u> on earth, he <u>is met</u> by Elliot, the middle child of a suburban middle-class American family. Elliot, a sensitive and thoughtful young boy, <u>decided</u> to protect the gentle alien by keeping E.T. in his closet. Elliot <u>proceeded</u> to introduce his brother, Michael, and his younger sister, Gertie, to this strange, but wonderful creature. He then <u>convinces</u> them to help E.T. in his efforts to return "home." Committed to their task, the three <u>begin</u> a series of adventures which <u>resulted</u> in a genuine happy ending.

The verbs in this paragraph shift back and forth from present to past, interfering with an accurate representation of the action of the film. In order to prevent confusion about time sequence, pay strict attention to the time frame of the events you are relating. Once you use a verb tense, maintain that tense consistently and shift time only when the shift is justified.

A corrected version of the example paragraph reads:

> When E.T. first arrives on earth, he is met by Elliot, the middle child of a suburban middle-class American family. Elliot, a sensitive and thoughtful young boy, decides to protect the gentle alien by keeping E.T. in his closet. Elliot proceeds to introduce his brother, Michael, and his younger sister, Gertie, to this strange, but wonderful creature. He then convinces them to help E.T. in his efforts to return "home." Committed to their task, the three begin a series of adventures which result in a genuine happy ending.

Many times a shift from one tense to another is warranted because the time frame at issue has changed. When this is the case, a shift in tense is appropriate.

> When I first *began* working as a waiter, I *hated* my work. Now I *am enjoying* my job more than I *thought* possible.

In the above example, each shift (from past to present to past) is justified because each verb accurately reflects the time period referred to.

Exercise: Tense Shifts

Revise the following sentences to eliminate inappropriate tense shifts.

1. While you were turned around, a miracle happened. The line drive hits the base runner, so no runs were scored.
2. Just when Marcia thought her homework was finished, she remembers she has history questions to answer.
3. Grandma Martin seemed totally bored with the baseball game when suddenly she jumps up and screams, "Park it, Jimmy!"
4. Many educators in the United States believe in the principle of grouping students according to ability because as long as bright students were competing against other bright students, they performed better.
5. By the end of her essay exam, Jeanine had her facts all confused; she is positive, though, that she passes the multiple-choice section of the test.
6. Tracy encouraged Jeff to spend all his hard-earned money on her; leaving him after he lost his job is selfish of her.
7. Young people in the sixties demanded a religion that calls for a simple, clean, and serene life.
8. Marty asked Lynn if she wants to go out with him, but she brushed him off and left with Jerry.
9. As Dave collected his clubs and new golf balls, he thinks how difficult this tournament will be.
10. Consequently, we can see that the human race has progressed or at least seemed to have progressed.

Rewrite the following paragraph to eliminate unwarranted tense shifts.

When Ian bought his compact disc player, he shopped with caution. First, he goes to a store that had the same amplifier and speaker he owned so he could listen through brands he was accustomed to. Then he <u>listens</u> to CD music he <u>is</u> already familiar with so he could better judge the quality. He was also careful to listen to drums so he could check the quality of the bass and to brass so he could check the quality of the upper registers. While the CD player is operating, Ian <u>taps</u> on it to be sure it is not affected by slight movements such as those created when someone walks through a room. Finally, he checks to be sure the disc is easy to put in and take out. Only after such careful checking did Ian make his purchase.

Person Shifts

When you refer to yourself, you use first person pronouns. When you refer to other people directly, you use second person pronouns. When you refer to other people and things, you use third person pronouns.

First person pronouns: I, we, me, us, my, mine, our, ours
Second person pronouns: you, your, yours
Third person pronouns: he, she, it, they, his, her, hers, its, their, theirs, him,
    them

When using the above pronouns, be consistent in person because unwarranted shifts can be confusing and annoying.

Shift from third to second person: If a football player works hard, *he* has many
    chances for financial aid, and *you* might even be eligible for a full schol-
    arship.
Shift eliminated: If a football player works hard, *he* has many chances for
    financial aid, and *he* might even be eligible for a full scholarship.
Shift from second to first person: An empathetic friend is one *you* can tell your
    most private thoughts to. This kind of friend still knows when *I* want to be
    alone and respects *my* wish.
Shift eliminated: An empathetic friend is one *you* can tell your most private
    thoughts to. This kind of friend still knows when *you* want to be alone and
    respects *your* wish.

Exercise: Person Shifts

Revise the following sentences to eliminate unwarranted shifts in person.

1. In high school, I <u>liked</u> geometry because it came easily to me, and you could
   progress at your own rate.
2. I enjoy riding to the top of the city's tallest building where you can see for miles in
   all directions.

3. When we had received our boots and uniforms, you were shown how to polish and fold them according to army regulations.
4. We are all painfully aware that you can't depend on the superintendent for help.
5. While taking part in a marathon, a runner should never think about what you're doing.
6. When I ask Sybil to help with some typing, she never turns you down.
7. When a person drinks to excess, you should never attempt to drive a car.
8. In July, people welcome a cool evening, but you know that it is probably only a temporary relief from the heat.
9. By the end of a person's first term as secretary, you feel that you are finally beginning to understand the job.
10. I liked my research course better than any other this year. You were on your own searching the library for references.

The following paragraph contains unwarranted shifts in person. Locate the shifts and correct them.

As soon as we entered the room, you could sense the tension in the atmosphere. This was the day for the first in-class writing to take place. Students were quietly taking his and her places. Pencils were being sharpened; papers were being prepared. Once the class was under way, the quiet tension spread. The only sounds were of paper shuffling and pens scratching. We all hoped that your first efforts would be successful. Finally, the instructor announced, "Anybody who is finished can turn in your papers and leave." Exhausted and relieved, the tired students filed from the room leaving their papers on the teacher's desk.

17

Dangling and Misplaced Modifiers

A *modifier* is a word, phrase, or clause that describes. Writers often use modifiers to make their sentences more vivid and interesting. However, if it is not clear what word a modifier is describing, one of two problems can result: *dangling modifiers* or *misplaced modifiers*.

Dangling Modifiers

When a modifier has no stated word to modify, it is a *dangling modifier*. Dangling modifiers impair meaning and often cause silly sentences. Consider the following sentence with a dangling modifier:

While basting the turkey, the sweet potatoes burned.

While basting the turkey is a modifier, but there is no word for the modifier to refer to or describe. As a result, it seems that the sweet potatoes basted the turkey.

There are two ways to correct a dangling modifier. One way is to leave the modifier as it is and supply a word for the modifier to refer to. *This word should appear immediately after the modifier.*

dangling modifier: Listening for the telephone, the doorbell rang.

377

explanation: Because there is no word for *listening for the telephone* to refer to, the phrase is a dangling modifier. The sentence indicates that the doorbell listened for the telephone.

correction: Listening for the telephone, I heard the doorbell ring.

explanation: The word *I* is placed immediately after the modifier as a word the modifier can logically refer to.

A second way to eliminate a dangling modifier is to rewrite the modifier as a subordinate clause (see p. 101).

dangling modifier: Jogging along the side of the road, a car splashed me with mud.

explanation: Because there is no word for *jogging along the side of the road* to refer to, the phrase is a dangling modifier. The sense of the sentence is that the car did the jogging.

correction: While I was jogging along the side of the road, a car splashed me with mud.

explanation: The modifier is rewritten as a subordinate clause to eliminate the dangling modifier.

As the above examples illustrate, dangling modifiers often occur when sentences begin with an *-ing* verb form (present participle). However, a dangling modifier can also occur when a sentence begins with an *-ed, -en, -n,* or *-t* verb form (past participle) or when it begins with the present-tense verb form used with *to* (infinitive).

dangling modifier (present participle): While rocking the baby, the cat purred contentedly.

correction: While rocking the baby, I heard the cat purr contentedly.

correction: While I was rocking the baby, the cat purred contentedly.

dangling modifier (past participle): Tired from the day's work, weariness overcame me.

correction: Tired from the day's work, I was overcome with weariness.

correction: Because I was tired from the day's work, weariness overcame me.

dangling modifier (infinitive): To excel in sports, much practice is needed.

correction: To excel in sports, a person needs much practice.

correction: If a person wants to excel in sports, much practice is needed.

Exercise: Dangling Modifiers

Rewrite the following sentences to eliminate the dangling modifiers.

1. Feeling it was too late to apologize, the disagreement was never resolved.
2. While sitting at the drive-in movie, shooting stars could be seen in the clear night sky.
3. Climbing across the pasture fence, Peter's pants were torn in two places.
4. To understand the latest computer technology, these courses should be taken.
5. Faced with the possibility of suspension, studying became more attractive to me.

6. When listening to the stereo, cleaning the apartment does not seem so hard.
7. To get to class on time, my alarm is set for 6:00 a.m.
8. Struggling to earn enough money to pay next term's tuition, the job came along just in time.
9. To study in quiet surroundings, the library is the best place to go.
10. After ending the relationship with Carl, loneliness was Anita's biggest problem.

Misplaced Modifiers

A *misplaced modifier* is a modifier positioned too far away from the word it refers to. The result of such distant positioning is an unclear, silly, or illogical sentence.

misplaced modifier: The strolling musicians played while we were eating dinner *softly*.
explanation: The modifier *softly* is intended to refer to *played*. However, the modifier is too far removed from the word it is meant to describe. As a result, *softly* seems to describe *were eating*.

To correct a sentence with a misplaced modifier, move the modifier as close as possible to the word it refers to.

The strolling musicians played *softly* while we were eating dinner.

A misplaced modifier can be a word, a phrase, or a clause:

misplaced modifier (word): There must be something wrong with this cookie recipe, for it *only* requires a half-cup of sugar. (Placement of *only* indicates no other ingredients are needed.)
correction: There must be something wrong with this cookie recipe, for it requires *only* a half-cup of sugar.
misplaced modifier (phrase): Across the street, *playing far too wildly*, we saw the young children. (The phrase seems to describe *we*.)
correction: Across the street we saw the young children *playing far too wildly*.
misplaced modifier (clause): We brought the rubber tree into the house *which was at least 8 feet tall*. (The clause seems to describe house.)
correction: We brought the rubber tree, which was at least 8 feet tall, into the house.

Exercise: Misplaced Modifiers

Rewrite the following sentences to eliminate the misplaced modifiers.

1. The modern-dance class enjoyed the lecture by George Balanchine immensely.
2. Most viewers have misinterpreted the significance of the president's State of the Union address completely.
3. The Chevette's muffler fell off after we turned the corner with a loud bang.

4. Kathleen sold her bike to a neighbor with stripped gears for $25.
5. The little girl wore a flower in her hair that had pink petals.
6. We were fortunate to get a cabin by the lake with three bedrooms.
7. The child ran after the ball pulling the rusty wagon down the street.
8. I remembered that when it comes to emotional matters, arguing with Jeff logically makes him angry.
9. The missing wallet was finally found by my aunt Norma under the couch.
10. Turning to go, Lee waved to the gang in the van listening to the stereo.

18

Parallelism

Parallelism means that coordinate sentence elements (elements of equal importance) serving the same function should have the same grammatical form. The following sentence, for example, has parallel structure.

Mrs. Burton found the novel *outrageous, offbeat,* and *shocking.*

In this sentence, the italicized words all have the same function: to describe *novel.* Also, these words all have the same degree of importance in the sentence. To achieve the necessary parallelism, then, the words all take the same grammatical form—they are adjectives.

When writers fail to achieve parallelism, the result can be an awkward sentence, as in the following example.

I have always liked *hiking* and *to swim.*

Because *hiking* and *to swim* have the same function (they serve as the object of the verb *have liked*), and because they are of equal importance, they should both have the same grammatical form. Yet one is an *-ing* verb form (present participle) and one is a *to* verb form (infinitive). To be parallel, both must be present participles or both must be infinitives.

I have always liked *hiking* and *swimming.*
I have always liked *to hike* and *to swim.*

Faulty parallelism occurs most often when writers place items in a series, when they compare or contrast, and when they use correlative conjunctions. These matters are discussed below.

Items in a Series

Sentence elements forming a series serve the same function (they are part of the series), and they have equal value. Hence they should have the same grammatical form.

nonparallel: You can get to Toronto by *car, bus,* or *fly.*
parallel: You can get to Toronto by *car, bus,* or *plane.*
explanation: The nonparallel series includes two nouns and a verb. Parallelism is achieved by revising to include three nouns.
nonparallel: Before my first date Mother told me *to be in by midnight, to drive carefully,* and *she said I was to be a gentleman.*
parallel: Before my first date Mother told me *to be in by midnight, to drive carefully,* and *to be a gentleman.*
explanation: The nonparallel series includes two verb (infinitive) phrases and a clause. Parallelism is achieved by revising to include three verb (infinitive) phrases.

Comparing and Contrasting

1. When writers compare or contrast items in a sentence, these items should have the same grammatical form because they serve the same function (comparison or contrast) and because they are of equal value. Consider the following nonparallel sentence:

   I love *a day at the beach* more than *to spend a day in the country.*

   Parallelism is not achieved in this sentence because the noun phrase *a day at the beach* is contrasted with the verb phrase *to spend a day in the country.* To be parallel, the contrast should be expressed in one of the following ways:

   I love *a day at the beach* more than *a day in the country.* (two noun phrases)

   or

   I love *spending a day at the beach* more than *spending a day in the country.* (two verb phrases)

2. Sometimes parallelism problems crop up because the writer fails to mention the second item being compared or contrasted, as in the following sentence:

I like small, intimate restaurants better.

This sentence does not indicate what *small, intimate restaurants* is contrasted with. To solve the problem, a revision like the following is possible:

I like *small, intimate restaurants* better than *crowded, noisy cafeterias.* (two noun phrases)

Correlative Conjunctions

Correlative conjunctions are conjunctions used in pairs. The following are correlative conjunctions:

either . . . or	both . . . and
neither . . . nor	not only . . . but [also]

To achieve parallelism with correlative conjunctions, be sure that the same grammatical structure that follows the first conjunction also follows the second.

nonparallel construction: I want either *to spend my vacation in New York City* or *in Bermuda.*

parallel construction: I want to spend my vacation either *in New York City* or *in Bermuda.*

explanation: In the nonparallel construction, a verb (infinitive) phrase appears after *either* and a prepositional phrase appears after *or.* In the parallel construction prepositional phrases appear after *either* and *or.*

nonparallel construction: The ballet was both *well performed* and *had lavish sets.*

parallel construction: The ballet both *was well performed* and *had lavish sets.*

explanation: In the nonparallel construction, *both* is followed by a modifier and *and* is followed by a verb phrase. In the parallel construction, *both* and *and* are followed by verb phrases.

Exercise: Parallelism

Rewrite the following sentences to achieve parallel structure.

1. The boutique is known for its variety of styles, for its haughty sales clerks, and daring new designs.
2. The police car sped up the street, its lights flashing, its siren wailing, and roaring its engine.
3. I find playing tennis to be better exercise than volleyball.
4. Kim not only has bought a tape deck but also a video recorder.
5. Susan is beautiful, arrogant, and has been spoiled by her parents.

6. My neighbor wants either to resurface his driveway or be painting his house.
7. Dana plans to attend the university, study biology, and being accepted into medical school.
8. Neither is the newspaper column timely nor interesting.
9. Jerry enjoys working for a large corporation for its many chances for advancement and because of its many fringe benefits.
10. Patrick's research paper was not acceptable because it was late, it was too short, and needed typing.

19

Capitalization and Punctuation

Writers are expected to capitalize and punctuate correctly, and if they do not, their readers may lose confidence in their ability. Of course, a reader who distrusts a writer's ability will also distrust what the writer has to say.

Capitalization

Below are rules governing the most frequent uses of capital letters. In addition, if you are unsure whether to capitalize a word, you can consult a dictionary.

1. Capitalize proper nouns and adjectives derived from them.
    a. *Capitalize proper names of people and animals.*

    Harry   Rover
    Joe Popovich   Einstein

    b. *Capitalize names of nationalities, languages, and races.*

    American   Black   Chinese art
    Spanish   Italian architecture   French cooking

    c. *Capitalize names of specific countries, states, regions, places, bodies of water, and so on.*

Minnesota	Crandall Park	North Pole
Zimbabwe	Trumbull County	Fourth Avenue
Lake Huron	Europe	Brooklyn

DO NOT CAPITALIZE: the park, the beach, a large city, the town hall

d. *Capitalize proper names and titles that precede them, but not general terms.*

Judge Walters	Uncle Don
Prime Minister Gandhi	Grampa Johnson
Professor Kline	President Reagan

DO NOT CAPITALIZE: the judge, a president, the chairman

e. *Capitalize words designating family relationships only when these are not preceded by a possessive pronoun or article.*

Grampa Johnson	Mom (as in *I asked Mom to come along*)
Aunt Donna	Cousin Ralph

DO NOT CAPITALIZE: my uncle, my aunt, her mom

f. *Capitalize specific brand names but not the type of product.*

Coca-Cola	Colgate
Crisco	Nike

DO NOT CAPITALIZE: soda pop, toothpaste, oil, tennis shoes

g. *Capitalize directions when they refer to specific geographic regions.*

the Midwest	the Middle East	the South
the East Coast	the Pacific Northwest	the North

DO NOT CAPITALIZE: east on I-680, 3 miles north, the northern part of the state

h. *Capitalize names of specific courses (those with course numbers) and language courses.*

History 101	Intermediate Calculus
French	English

DO NOT CAPITALIZE: studies which do not name specific courses: math class, chemistry, drama

i. *Capitalize the names of ships, planes, and spacecraft.*

the Enterprise	the Challenger
the Queen Elizabeth	the Titanic

j. *Capitalize the names of specific buildings, institutions, and businesses.*

the Empire State Building   South Bend Water Department
Chrysler Corporation   Harvard University

k. *Capitalize names of religions, sacred books, and words that refer to God.*

the Almighty	Jewish	the Koran
Moslem	the Holy Bible	Buddha
Jesus Christ	Catholic	Jehovah
the Old Testament	the Scriptures	Mohammed
Christianity	Protestantism	the Trinity

l. *Capitalize modifiers derived from proper nouns.*

French accent   Renaissance art
Georgian hospitality   Shakespearean comedy

2. Capitalize the first and last word of a title; in between capitalize everything except articles, short prepositions, and short conjunctions.

Star Wars   *Of Mice and Men*
The Grapes of Wrath   *The Last of the Mohicans*
The Sun Also Rises   *The Sound and the Fury*

Note: For discussions of capitalization rules for direct quotation, see p. 167 and p. 342.

Exercise: Capitalization

Capitalize where necessary in the following sentences.

1. Jessica lived in the south all her life.
2. When Marie read *Gone with the wind*, she became fascinated with the old south.
3. One of our most unpopular presidents was president Nixon.
4. After my mother died, my aunt raised my sister and me.
5. When professor Blake entered the room, his sociology 505 class became quiet.
6. The Monongahela and Allegheny rivers flow into the Ohio river.
7. The Republican party's presidential nominee will be the incumbent president.
8. Most people believe that the first day of spring is march 21st.
9. Davy Crockett, a confirmed westerner, spent several years as a congressman living in washington.
10. Learning french was very difficult for harry.
11. Of all the fast-food restaurants, burger king is aunt Mandy's favorite.
12. The national center for disease control, at its Atlanta headquarters, announced its findings on Legionnaire's disease.
13. Lovers of jazz acknowledge that miles davis is the world's finest living jazz trumpeter.
14. Designed by frank lloyd wright, falling water has been acclaimed for its unique structure and its harmonious coexistence with the natural beauty that surrounds it.
15. The Golden Gate bridge is a modern architectural wonder.

Punctuation

Punctuation marks aid communication because they signal where ideas end, how ideas relate to each other, which ideas are emphasized, which ideas are downplayed, and which ideas were someone's spoken words. Most of the time, specific rules govern the placement of punctuation, but in some cases punctuation is optional, and the writer must decide which mark to use or whether to use any mark at all.

Commas

Writers who do not know the comma rules tend to place commas wherever they pause in speech. However, listening for pauses is not a reliable way to place commas, so if you have not yet learned the rules, study the next pages carefully.

Commas with Items in a Series

A series is three or more words, phrases, or clauses. Use commas to separate each item in the series.

words in a series: The gardener sprayed the *grass, trees*, and *shrubs* with pesticide.

phrases in a series: George Washington was *first in war, first in peace*, and *first in the hearts of his countrymen*.

clauses in a series: Before his first day of school, *Jane took her kindergartener on a tour of the school, she introduced him to the principal*, and *she bought him school supplies*.

If the items in the series are separated by *and* or *or*, do not use the comma.

The only vegetables Harry will eat are carrots or broccoli or corn.

Some writers omit the comma after the last item in the series, but you should get in the habit of using the comma to avoid misreading.

Exercise: Commas with Items in a Series

Place commas where they are needed in the following sentences.

1. The vacation brochure promised us fun relaxation and excitement.
2. The trouble with the mayor is that she does not delegate responsibility she does not manage city finances well and she does not work well with city council members.
3. Before you leave, clean your room and sweep the downstairs and take out the trash.
4. The instructor explained that the class could write a paper on a childhood memory on a decision recently made or on a favorite teacher.
5. When you edit, be sure to check spelling punctuation and capitalization.

Commas with Introductory Elements

1. An introductory subordinate clause is usually followed by a comma (see also p. 103).

    Although she promised to meet me for lunch, Caroline never arrived at the restaurant.

    The comma may be omitted after a relatively short introductory clause that is closely related to the main clause.

    When I left I felt sad for those I left behind.

    or

    When I left, I felt sad for those I left behind.

2. Long introductory phrases are usually followed by a comma.

    By the end of the first half of the tournament, our team had won nine games.

    The comma may be omitted after a short introductory phrase that is closely related to the rest of the sentence.

    To understand calculus a student must study hard.

    or

    To understand calculus, a student must study hard.

3. Introductory adverbs are followed by a comma when they show separation from the rest of the sentence (see also p. 124).

    Reluctantly, Mr. Simpson told his oldest employee that he was selling his business.
    Quickly yet cautiously, the store detective moved in on the suspected shop-lifter.
    Unfortunately the midterm exam grades were lower than expected.

    If you are unsure whether to use a comma after an introductory adverb, go ahead and use it; this placement of the comma is always correct.

Exercise: Commas with Introductory Elements

Insert commas in the following sentences where they are needed.

1. When Sherry arrived at the resort which her boss had recommended she was disappointed to find that there was no space available.
2. When he was 20 he believed that everything would always work out for the best.
3. Very slowly and silently the deer moved toward the water hole.
4. As a result of the devastating heat wave the death toll rose to 108.
5. Frequently we accuse others of the behavior we dislike most in ourselves.
6. After we checked to be sure all the doors were locked we left the beach house until next summer.

7. During the long, bleak evenings of winter a cozy fire in the fireplace is especially welcome.
8. At the time of the space shuttle's arrival the heavy crosswinds had finally died down.
9. Lovingly the young mother stroked her new daughter's chubby cheek.
10. Hastily the 6-year-old wiped the telltale signs of strawberry jam from the corners of his mouth.

Commas to Set Off Nouns of Direct Address

The names of those directly addressed are set off with commas.

Dorrie, you must get ready for school now.
Get away from that hamburger, *you mangy dog*.
If you ask me, *Juan*, we should turn left.

Exercise: Commas to Set Off Nouns of Direct Address

Supply commas to set off the nouns of address.

1. Ben help me carry the groceries into the house.
2. You know Son it's too cold to be outside without a jacket.
3. Friends may I have your attention please?
4. Heidi make sure you give fresh seed and water to the bird.
5. Will you be able to help me with my math tonight Brett?

Commas with Nonessential Elements

Nonessential elements are words, phrases, and clauses that do not limit or restrict the meaning of the words they refer to. In other words, nonessential elements are not necessary for clear identification of what they refer to.

nonessential element: Uncle Ralph, *who has been on the police force 20 years*, believes handgun legislation is the key to reducing violent crime.
explanation: Who has been on the police force 20 years is nonessential because the person it refers to (Uncle Ralph) is already clearly identified.
essential element: The student *who wins the state finals in speech* will get $1000.
explanation: Who wins the state finals in speech is necessary for identifying which student will win $1000; therefore, it is an essential element.

1. Use commas to set off nonessential clauses.

Sara Summers, *who is a senior*, was voted president of senior council.
My roommate collects beer cans, *which she stacks against the wall*.

but

Dr. Kingsley is a person *whose opinion I respect*. (Clause is essential.)

2. Use commas to set off nonessential phrases.

The sparrows, *hunting for food in the snow,* sensed the cat's approach and took off suddenly.

but

The child *playing in the sandbox* is my nephew. (Phrase is essential.)

3. Use commas to set off nonessential appositives. An *appositive* is a word or word group that renames the noun it follows.

nonessential appositive: My brother, an investment banker, makes $200,000 a year. (*An investment banker* renames *my brother*, so it is an appositive. However, it is not necessary for identification, so commas are used.)

essential appositive: My son the doctor is not as happy as my son the actor. (*The doctor* is an appositive renaming *my son*, and *the actor* is an appositive renaming the second *my son*. In both cases the appositives are essential for identifying which son is referred to, so no commas are used.)

Exercise: Commas with Nonessential Elements

Place commas where they are needed in the following sentences.

1. My father who worked for the Bell System for over 30 years has made many sacrifices for me.
2. A Democratic city councilman who supports his party will try to support the policies of a Democratic mayor.
3. The Luray Caverns which I visited this year are a breathtaking sight.
4. A blue wool suit sporting brass buttons and a classic, traditional cut is always in style.
5. The Empire State Building once the tallest building in the world still dominates the New York City skyline.
6. Ivan Norris a brilliant teacher will retire next month.

Commas with Interrupters

Interrupters are words and phrases that "interrupt" the flow of a sentence; they are of a parenthetical nature, functioning more as side remarks than integral parts of sentences. Sometimes transitions interrupt flow and are considered interrupters, which is why the following partial list of interrupters includes some transitions.

in a manner of speaking	after all
as a matter of fact	in fact
to tell the truth	in the first place
it seems to me	to say the least
for example	consequently
by all means	of course

Interrupters are usually set off with commas. However, commas may be omitted after short interrupters coming at the beginning of sentences.

commas used: The students' behavior at the concert, *it seems to me*, was exemplary.

comma omitted for short introductory interrupter: Of course not everyone shares my concern about this issue.

comma for short interrupter: Of course, not everyone shares my concern for this issue.

Exercise: Commas with Interrupters

Where appropriate, set off the interrupters with commas in the following sentences.

1. The children it seems will always find something to complain about.
2. As a matter of fact the lamp needs a larger-watt bulb.
3. This report I feel is inadequately prepared.
4. The customer insists for example that the ten-speed bike was never properly assembled.
5. However I am not convinced this is the right time to begin our fund-raising project.

Commas with Main Clauses

When two main clauses are connected with a coordinate conjunction (*and, but, or, nor, for, so, yet*), place a comma before the conjunction (see also p. 000).

The match was over, *but* the spectators refused to leave.
The garden was heavily fertilized, *so* the yield of vegetables was even higher than expected.

Exercise: Commas with Main Clauses

Place commas where needed in the following sentences.

1. Janice had been rejected many times yet she retained her sense of humor and her cheerful disposition.
2. The water department explained that the pipe to the house was broken and we would have to assume the cost of fixing it.
3. Marilyn wanted to fly to Montana but Betty Jo had always wanted to drive across country.
4. The students were lazy and insolent so the instructor assigned them another hundred pages to study.
5. Karen fastened red bows to the lampposts for the holiday season was fast approaching.

Commas Between Coordinate Modifiers, Commas for Clarity, and Commas to Separate Contrasting Elements

1. *Coordinate modifiers* are two or more modifiers referring equally to the same word. Commas separate such modifiers when they are not already separated by *and* or *but*. (If the order of the modifiers can be reversed or if *and* can be used to join the modifiers, they are coordinate and should be separated with a comma.)

   An *expensive, well-tailored* suit is a necessary investment for a young executive. (Order of modifiers can be reversed.)

   They ate their picnic lunch under the *blossoming apple* tree. (*And* cannot be used between the modifiers, nor can the order of the modifiers be reversed.)

   She is certainly a *happy and carefree* person. (No comma because *and* is used.)

   She is certainly a *happy, carefree* person. (*And* can be used between the modifiers.)

2. Sometimes a comma is necessary for clarity, to prevent misreading of a sentence.

   For Easter, lilies are the most popular flower. (Without the comma, a reader might read the first three words as a single phrase.)

3. Commas set off an element that contrasts sharply with what comes before it.

   Lee is only lazy, not stupid.

Exercise: Commas with Coordinate Modifiers, Commas for Clarity, and Commas with Contrasting Elements

Place commas where needed in the following sentences.

1. The muddy rough course was made even worse by the two-day downpour.
2. Ohio State's noisy enthusiastic pep club congregated in the middle section of the bleachers.
3. The twins were young not inexperienced.
4. Many new songwriters use concrete visual images to set a mood.
5. The rough manuscript is promising although rambling.
6. Of all spectator sports fans seem to enjoy football most.

When Not to Use the Comma

Below are some cautions about when *not* to use commas. Writers unfamiliar with the comma rules sometimes place commas where they are not needed.

1. Do not use a comma to separate a subject and verb.

   no: The governor-elect, promised to work to change the way public education is funded in our state.

   yes: The governor-elect promised to work to change the way public education is funded in our state.

2. Do not use a comma between a preposition and its object.

   no: The United States has a government of, the people.

   yes: The United States has a government of the people.

3. Do not use a comma between a verb and its object.

   no: Henry Aaron smacked, the ball out of the park.

   yes: Henry Aaron smacked the ball out of the park.

4. Do not use a comma between a verb and its complement.

   no: Louise will become, a concert pianist if she continues to study.

   yes: Louise will become a concert pianist if she continues to study.

5. Do not use a comma after a coordinate conjunction linking main clauses.

   no: I have tried to understand Marshall but, his behavior continues to puzzle me.

   yes: I have tried to understand Marshall, but his behavior continues to puzzle me.

6. Do not use a comma before a coordinate conjunction linking two elements that are not main clauses.

   no: Michael asked for my forgiveness, and said he would try harder.

   yes: Michael asked for my forgiveness and said he would try harder.

7. Do not use a comma before the first item or after the last item in a series.

   no: The math test covered, improper fractions, common denominators, and, mixed fractions.

   yes: The math test covered improper fractions, common denominators, and mixed fractions.

8. Do not use a comma between a modifier and the word it modifies.

   no: The faded, frayed, curtains must be replaced.

   yes: The faded, frayed curtains must be replaced.

9. Do not use a comma after *such as* or *like*.

   no: Kurt believes in some unusual ideas such as, reincarnation, transmigration, and mental telepathy.

   yes: Kurt believes in some unusual ideas, such as reincarnation, transmigration, and mental telepathy.

no: Medical technology students must take some difficult courses like,
  physiology, biochemistry, and pharmacology.
yes: Medical technology students must take some difficult courses like
  physiology, biochemistry, and pharmacology.

10. Do not use a comma between *that* and a direct quotation.

no: The school board president said that, "we are considering a ten-month
  school year."
yes: The school board president said that "we are considering a ten-month
  school year."

Exercise: Using Commas

Place commas where needed in the following sentences. You will need to draw on all the comma rules discussed in this chapter.

1. Jimmy the janitor said to pick up the paper in the halls.
2. Tommy go get the newspaper from the front porch roof.
3. I will take a small perfect carnation and a snapdragon for my mom's birthday bouquet.
4. Pam wanted to play kickball but Harry wanted to play baseball.
5. Joey and Matt by the way are excellent baseball players.
6. Although the season has just begun Matt has hit four home runs this year.
7. Joey as a matter of fact pitched his first no-hitter this season.
8. On the other hand Jeremy had made more errors than anybody in the whole league.
9. It seems to me that we worry about problems before they even occur.
10. My dad takes care of the yard, cleans the pool, coaches a pony league baseball team and still he works at a full-time job.
11. In order to stay in good condition the wide redwood deck requires a preservative stain every year.
12. The old leather chair with the matching footstool is soft and comfortable.
13. Before the heat wave we all longed for some sunshine but now we badly need rain.
14. Your novel which will be published in the fall shows promise.
15. My instructor an expert in urban affairs is an adviser to our state senator.
16. Before every race, Carla eats a light meal takes a nap and meditates.

The Semicolon

1. A semicolon is used to separate two main clauses when they are not linked by a coordinate conjunction.

The canvas raft floated smoothly near the edge of the pool; it was pushed by a gentle summer breeze.
The old uniforms were worn by the A team; the B team wore new ones.

2. Use a semicolon before a conjunctive adverb that joins two main clauses. Here is a list of conjunctive adverbs:

also	moreover	furthermore	certainly
besides	however	still	nevertheless
nonetheless	instead	indeed	similarly
likewise	therefore	thus	consequently
next	then	meanwhile	finally
subsequently			

When you join two main clauses with a semicolon and conjunctive adverb, place a comma after the conjunctive adverb.

The car I want to buy is a real bargain; furthermore, the bank is offering me an excellent financing rate.

The test grades were quite low; consequently, Dr. Barnes agreed to let us retake the exam.

3. A semicolon may be used to separate items in a list or series that already contains commas. This use of the semicolon is primarily for clarity.

The following sun-belt cities have experienced phenomenal growth in the past five years: Houston, Texas; Phoenix, Arizona; and Orlando, Florida.

Exercise: Semicolons

Place semicolons where they are appropriate in the following sentences.

1. The ideal football player is dedicated, for he must work long, hard hours intelligent, for the game is very much one of strategy and physically tough, for he must endure a great deal of punishment.
2. The hand-tied rope hammock was made to hold the weight of two people it was the hook that broke sending Christie and Jim crashing to the ground.
3. The quarterback hesitated for an instant then he passed the ball to the wide receiver, who waited in the end zone.
4. College can create anxiety because of the pressure for grades, which is unceasing the concern for future job opportunity, which is always present and the uncertainties that come from life away from home, which are most unnerving of all.
5. We tried for two hours to start the car finally we gave up and started the long trek back to town.
6. The trip was cancelled because of the snow storm however, it has been rescheduled for next weekend.

Colons

A colon signals that what follows it explains or particularizes what comes before it. A word, phrase, or clause can follow the colon; a clause usually precedes the mark.

Colon to particularize (phrase after colon): Five occupations were represented in the union membership: secretaries, data processors, maintenance workers, cafeteria workers, and bookkeepers.

Colon to explain (one word after colon): Rick writes soap opera scripts for one reason: money.

Colon to explain (clause after colon): All Terry's efforts were directed toward one goal: she wanted to learn how to skydive.

Do not use a colon between a verb and its object or complement or between a preposition and its object.

colon: The following students will compete in the debate: David Haynes, Lorenzo Ruiz, and Clara Jakes.

no colon: The students who will compete in the debate are David Haynes, Lorenzo Ruiz, and Clara Jakes.

colon: I am afraid of these: heights, small rooms, and water.

no colon: I am afraid of heights, small rooms, and water.

Exercise: Colons

Place colons where appropriate in the following sentences.

1. My courses for next semester are these political science, algebra, biology, and Advanced Composition I.
2. The basket overflowed with fresh fruit peaches, grapes, apples, and bananas.
3. Mr. Grantley seems to have one mission in life making everyone around him miserable.
4. There are complicated reasons for our company's poor safety record we do not supply incentives for employees to exercise more care on the job, our safety equipment is obsolete and ineffective, and we don't require enough proper training for new employees.
5. I knew that success in my journalism class would require curiosity, energy, and writing skill.
6. Of all the distance runners, only one seems to run effortlessly Mark.

The Dash

A dash is used to indicate a pause for emphasis or dramatic effect. It is a mark that should be used sparingly and thoughtfully, so that its emphatic or dramatic quality is not weakened by overuse. Often dashes can be used in place of commas, semicolons, colons, or parentheses; the mark used depends upon the effect the writer wishes to create.

Jake told me—I can't believe it—that he would rather stay at home than go to Las Vegas. (Parentheses may also be used.)

The cabin at the lake was spartanly furnished—two tables, eight chairs, and a single bar stool. (Colon may be used.)

I know why Tony's bike disappeared—it was stolen from the backyard. (Semi-colon or colon may also be used.)

Exercise: The Dash

Place dashes where appropriate in the following sentences.

1. The new Corvette red, shiny, and powerful was just the thing to make her friends drool.
2. Certain members of this family I won't mention any names are going to lose their allowances if they don't start doing their duties.
3. My history professor at least he calls himself a professor is the most boring teacher on campus.
4. I have only one comment to make about your room yuk!
5. There is a very obvious solution to your school problems study.

Parentheses

1. Parentheses can enclose supplemental elements the writer wants to downplay. Often parentheses signal a side comment or incidental remark.

   Louise Rodriguez (you remember her) has been elected president of the Women's Action Council.
   When I was in college (over 20 years ago), composition was taught very differently.

   Commas or dashes often set off material that could also be enclosed in parentheses. However, commas and dashes will emphasize the material, whereas parentheses will deemphasize it.

   parentheses deemphasize: This week's lottery prize (an incredible $12 million) will be split between two winners.
   dashes emphasize: This week's lottery prize—an incredible $12 million—will be split between two winners.
   commas give more emphasis than parentheses but less than dashes: This week's lottery prize, an incredible $12 million, will be split between two winners.

2. Do not place a comma before the element enclosed in parentheses.

   no: Most of the class, (easily 30 of us) felt the test was too long to complete in an hour.
   yes: Most of the class (easily 30 of us) felt the test was too long to complete in an hour.

3. A comma or end mark of punctuation that comes after an element enclosed in parentheses is placed *outside* the closing parenthesis.

The new parking deck is an imposing structure (it has 15 levels), but it has a serious drawback (people have trouble finding their cars in it).

4. Use a period and capital letter with a complete sentence enclosed in parentheses if the sentence is not interrupting another sentence.

no: After three days (Most of us wondered what took so long.) the winners were announced.

yes: After three days the winners were announced. (Most of us wondered what took so long.)

yes: After three days (most of us wondered what took so long) the winners were announced.

5. Parentheses can enclose numbers and letters in a list of items.

The Citizens' Coalition has three reservations about endorsing Smith for mayor: (1) she is inexperienced, (2) she opposes increasing city taxes, and (3) she has no clear position on minority hiring practices.

Because numbers in a list can distract a reader, writers generally try to avoid them.

The Citizens' Coalition has three reservations about endorsing Smith for mayor: she is inexperienced, she opposes increasing city taxes, and she has no clear position on minority hiring practices.

Exercise: Parentheses

Place parentheses where they are appropriate in the following sentences.

1. The police officer gave David a ticket he was traveling 50 miles per hour in a school zone.
2. Recent reports indicate that fewer white-collar workers are smoking probably because of increased awareness of the health hazards.
3. Sales of computers particularly those with word processing capabilities are at an all-time high.
4. At Debby and Don's wedding what a fiasco Don forgot the ring, Debby tripped on the hem of her dress, the best man was late, the caterer served undercooked chicken, and the band played so loudly that everyone got a headache.
5. Lee's favorite meal scrambled eggs, spaghetti, and corn disgusts most people.

The Apostrophe

The apostrophe is used most frequently to show possession. It is also used to form contractions and certain kinds of plurals.

The Apostrophe to Show Possession

The apostrophe is used with nouns and certain indefinite pronouns (see p. 366 for an explanation of indefinite pronouns) to signal possession.

Martha's hat   the teacher's lecture
children's toys   somebody's lost gloves

If you are uncertain whether a noun or pronoun is possessive, use a phrase beginning with *of* or *belonging to* as a test:

Martha's hat (the hat belonging to Martha)
children's toys (the toys belonging to children)
the teacher's lecture (the lecture of the teacher)
somebody's lost gloves (the lost gloves belonging to somebody)

but

the difficult examination (We cannot say "the examination of difficult" or "the examination belonging to difficult," so there is no possession here.)

1. To form the possessive of a word (singular or plural) that does not end in *-s*, add an apostrophe and an *s*.

   apartment   +   's
       The apartment's bedroom is much too small.
   car   +   's
       The car's fuel pump must be replaced.
   women   +   's
       The university has agreed to fund a library for women's studies.

2. To form the possessive of a word (singular or plural) that ends in *-s*, add just the apostrophe.

   Charles   +   '
       Charles' stolen car was found across town.
   boys   +   '
       The boys' football game ended in a tie.
   governors   +   '
       The governors' council on aging will examine the issue of adequate health care.

   Note: It is also permissible to add an apostrophe and *-s* to form the possessive of singular nouns ending in *s*.

       Robert brought flowers for Lois's mother.
       We will read several of Keats's poems in this class.

3. To show joint possession, use an apostrophe only with the last noun. To show individual ownership, use an apostrophe with every noun.

   Martha and Louise's committee report was thorough and clear. (one report belonging to both Martha and Louise)

Jason's and Helen's financial problems can be solved with better money management. (Jason and Helen have separate financial problems.)

4. To show possession with a hyphenated word, use the apostrophe only with the last element of the word.

The editor-in-chief's salary was cut in half after circulation decreased dramatically.
I have planned a surprise party to celebrate my mother-in-law's sixtieth birthday.

5. Do not use apostrophes with possessive pronouns (*its, whose, hers, his, ours, yours, theirs*).

incorrect: The expensive vase fell from it's shelf and shattered.
correct: The expensive vase fell from its shelf and shattered.
incorrect: The book that is missing is her's.
correct: The book that is missing is hers.

The Apostrophe to Indicate Missing Letters or Numbers

1. A *contraction* is formed when two words are joined and one or more letters are omitted. In a contraction the apostrophe stands for the missing letter or letters. Here are some common contractions. Notice that the apostrophe appears where the letter or letters are omitted.

can't (cannot)	won't (would not)
hasn't (has not)	who's (who is or who has)
they're (they are)	that's (that is)
we're (we are)	she'll (she will)
haven't (have not)	it's (it is or it has)
I'll (I will)	shouldn't (should not)

2. The apostrophe stands for missing letters in words that are not contractions.

add 'em up (add them up)
sugar 'n' spice (sugar and spice)
ma'am (madam)

Contractions are often used to stand for missing letters when dialect is written.

The drunk replied, ''Ask 'em what dey wanna do now.''

3. The apostrophe is used to stand for missing numbers.

The class of '67 will hold its annual reunion the day after Thanksgiving. (The apostrophe stands for the missing *19*.)

4. The apostrophe and an *s* form the plural of letters, numbers, and words meant to be taken as words themselves.

If I get any more D's, I will lose my scholarship.

How many t's are in *omit?*

Mark makes his 3's backwards.

Janice is too polite; I am tired of all her *yes sir's* and *no ma'am's*.

Exercise: Apostrophes

Add apostrophes where they are needed in the following sentences.

1. The panel awarding the scholarships spoke to several instructors about the three finalists grades and motivation.
2. In 85, my sister-in-laws German shepherd saved the life of a 5-year-old by dragging the sleeping child from her burning bedroom.
3. I can never read Harrys writing because his os look like as.
4. No one thought that Al and Janets business would do so well in its first 3 months of operation.
5. Todays women still dont earn equal pay for equal work, but in some ways womens lot has improved.
6. Charles older sister is encouraging him to major in computer science, but he isnt sure he wants to.
7. The hot dog vendor bellowed, "Get em while theyre hot."
8. Recent studies confirm that televisions effects on childrens attention spans should be a source of concern.
9. When I graduated in 70, students social consciousness was at an all-time high.
10. Lois new car must be a lemon, because its engine is not running well, and its been in the shop three times in a month.

Appendix I: Solving Writing Problems

One of the points made repeatedly throughout this text—and one you have no doubt confirmed on your own—is that effective writing rarely occurs quickly and easily. Writers work very hard through a series of stages to generate ideas, organize, draft, evaluate, shape, change, go back before going forward, rewrite, and so forth. And all of this takes time. Another reality is that sometimes writers get stuck. And while they may be able to identify what the problem is, they may not be able as readily to determine how to solve the problem.

Yet to be successful, writers must eventually overcome their difficulties, and they must do so in a reasonable amount of time. For this reason, some of the most frequently occurring writing problems are listed for you below, along with some strategies for solving these problems. If you get stuck and have trouble overcoming the difficulty, consult this list for a solution to your problem. However, no one can guarantee that any technique will provide results. Thus, what appears below is a selection of strategies that *may* help.

Remember one other thing when you encounter a writing problem: if you have spent a reasonable amount of time on the problem and tried several ways to overcome it but still face the problem, then cut your losses. Either alter what you are doing to eliminate the problem (perhaps by reshaping your topic) or settle for the best you can do and go on.

1. *If you have trouble coming up with ideas:*
   a. Try a prewriting technique you have never used before (see Chapter 1).
   b. Leave your writing and think about your topic while you are doing other

things. Keep a notebook with you so you can jot down ideas as they occur to you.

   c. Think about what people who disagree with your point of view might say. Use the counters to these opinions as your departure point.

   d. Have someone ask you questions about your topic (or draft, if you have one). The answers you provide can supply supporting detail.

   e. If you have a draft but need additional detail, go through the draft and check mark every generalization that is inadequately supported. Then go back and develop these generalizations with one or more examples.

2. *If you have trouble identifying an audience:*

   a. Ask yourself who would benefit the most from reading an essay on your topic.

   b. Use an enemy or someone who would disagree with you as your audience.

   c. Write to someone in authority with the power to act in accordance with the ideas in your essay.

   d. Write to the "average, general reader"—someone who knows something about your topic, but less than you do. You might consider this audience to be like the typical reader of a daily newspaper.

   e. Ask yourself who would be interested in an essay about your topic.

3. *If you have trouble establishing your purpose:*

   a. Ask yourself, "What can I accomplish with this writing?"

   b. Ask yourself, "What would I like to accomplish with this writing?"

   c. Decide whether you want to share something with your reader, inform your reader about something, or persuade your reader to act or think a certain way.

4. *If you have trouble organizing your ideas:*

   a. Try one of the outlining techniques you have not used yet (see Chapter 3).

   b. Ask yourself whether your ideas seem to follow a chronological, spatial, cause-and-effect, or progressive order.

   c. Write your draft without an outline and see what happens. When the draft is complete, check for logical ordering, and if there is a problem, number your ideas in the way you think they should appear.

   d. Check to see if instead of an organization problem, you really only lack transitional devices that signal how your ideas relate to each other and flow one to the next (see Chapter 4).

5. *If you have trouble getting your first draft down:*

   a. Skip your introduction and begin with your first body paragraph. You can always write your introduction later.

   b. Select one idea you've generated—one you know the most about or feel most comfortable with—and write up that point in its own body paragraph.

   c. Write your draft as you would speak your ideas to a close friend, or write the draft as a letter to a friend.

    d. Go back to the prewriting stage and generate more ideas; you may not have enough material yet to begin a draft.

    e. Write your draft as a form of freewriting (see p. 11), going from start to finish without stopping for anything and without evaluating your work. Feel free to ramble, write silly notions, and even write the alphabet when you are stuck—you can refine later; for now just get something down to work with.

    f. Consider reshaping your topic to yield something easier to write about.

    g. Leave your work for a while. It may be that your ideas need an incubation period before you come to your draft. However, think about your draft while you are doing other things.

6. *If you have trouble writing your introduction:*

    a. Skip it and come back to it after drafting the rest of your essay, but jot down a tentative thesis to guide and focus the remainder of your draft.

    b. Keep your introduction short and simple, perhaps writing just one or two sentences to create interest and then a thesis.

    c. Try supplying background information or making a statement about why your topic is important.

7. *If you decide you don't like your draft:*

    a. Don't make any final decisions on the worth of your draft until after you have distanced yourself to restore your objectivity.

    b. Be sure you have realistic expectations for your draft. Remember, it's supposed to be rough, so be sure you are not expecting too much. You still have to revise, after all.

    c. Do not reject your draft without trying to identify portions that can be salvaged and improved with revision.

    d. Do not reject your draft without asking a reliable reader to react to it; this reader may see merit where you do not, or the reader may be able to suggest changes that make the draft salvageable.

    e. If you decide the draft was a false start and it really is best to begin again, distance yourself first to clear your head. Take a hard look at your topic to determine if it is the source of your difficulty, and consider reshaping it. Starting over is not a tragedy; sometimes writers must discover what does not work before they discover what does work.

    f. If necessary because of time constraints, do the best you can with what you have.

8. *If you have trouble deciding what revisions to make:*

    a. Leave your work for a while to clear your head.

    b. Type your draft; weaknesses are more apparent in type than in your own handwriting.

    c. Read the draft aloud, preferably into a tape recorder, to hear problems.

    d. Ask yourself if you are trying to do too much at once by considering too many aspects of your draft at the same time. If you are doing this, consider evaluating your draft in stages.

    e. Ask a reliable reader to review your draft and make suggestions. It can be a good idea to give this reader specific content and organization questions to answer about your draft (see p. 78).

    f. Trust your instincts. If they suggest something needs to be reworked, they are probably right.

9. *If you are having trouble making your revisions:*

    a. Distance yourself to clear your head. Also, you may need an incubation period—a time to allow ideas for revising to form.

    b. Revise in stages, taking a break after each stage or two. Avoid attempting too much at one time.

    c. If you cannot solve a problem, try to get around it by expressing an idea in another way, using a different example, generating another idea to replace the one you are having trouble writing, and so forth.

    d. Work your easiest revisions first to build your momentum and confidence.

    e. Settle for less than the ideal. Once you have done your best, no more can be expected, even if your best is not as good as you want it to be this time.

10. *If you discover you have a relevance problem:*

    a. Try to reshape the detail or slant it so that it becomes relevant.

    b. Alter your thesis or topic sentence to accommodate the detail—but be careful such a change does not create a relevance problem elsewhere.

    c. Eliminate the detail—but be sure this does not create a problem with adequate detail. If it does, add what is necessary.

11. *If your detail is not adequate:*

    a. Check mark each generalization in your draft, and then look at how much support each generalization gets. For each sketchily supported or unsupported generalization, add several sentences of explanation. Make sure these sentences are specific rather than general.

    b. To show rather than just tell, try using examples to illustrate underdeveloped points.

    c. Ask a reliable reader what additional information he or she needs.

    d. Write each underdeveloped generalization on a separate sheet of paper. Below each generalization list every point that could be made about it. (To do this, you might ask yourself questions about the generalization.) Next, review your list of points and check mark the ones you will add to your essay.

    e. If you are unable to generate adequate detail, consider the possibility that your thesis is too narrow and needs to be broadened to be less restrictive.

12. *If you have trouble finding the "right" words:*

    a. Read through your draft and underline the words you want to change because they are vague or inaccurate.

    b. If after studying what you have underlined, you are unable to find the words you want, consult a dictionary or thesaurus for synonyms. Be careful, however, that you understand the meaning of words from these sources.

   c. You may not be able to take out one word and substitute another. Instead, you may have to substitute phrases and sentences for individual words to get the meaning you are after.

   d. Remember, effective word choice is specific yet simple.

   e. If you cannot express your ideas effectively one way, write a different sentence expressing your ideas in another way.

13. *If your essay does not flow well:*

   a. To help identify where the flow needs to be improved, read your draft out loud.

   b. At the points where smooth flow is lacking, look at the structure of your sentences. If too many in a row are the same length, shorten or lengthen where necessary. If too many sentences begin with the same structure, alter the beginning of some sentences (see p. 123).

   c. Use coordination and subordination to join ideas (see p. 101).

   d. Use transitions to ease flow (see p. 104).

14. *If you have trouble with your conclusion:*

   a. Try an approach other than the one in your draft (see p. 48).

   b. Try a summary of your main points if this will be helpful to the reader rather than needless repetition.

   c. Give your thesis or main points a larger application by showing their significance beyond the scope of your essay.

   d. Keep your conclusion brief—perhaps even a single sentence.

Appendix II: A Student Essay in Progress

The following pages reproduce a student essay as it progressed from idea generation to finished piece. The student's idea generation material is followed by her first draft. The second draft appears next, followed by the finished essay. Studying this work through some of its stages (the idea generation material and comments on the drafts have been simplified and the number of drafts reduced to two for ease of study) will help you appreciate how a writer works through a series of refinements to reach a satisfying finished product.

Idea Generation List

Effects of growing up in a large family

✓ food - Milk dry + canned, Beans, Soups, Oats + Mush   Audience - General
○ trips - none   Purpose - Share
✓ money - little
✓ eating out
○/ Christmas
○ Birthdays
✓ Clothing - hand me downs   Points to Bring out.
✓ Shoes 1 pr   worn a long time
✓ Haircuts
✓ teeth
✓ Nothing new

~~treats once every 2 wks payday~~
o Car – old – wouldn't go real far
Helen's Hungry Brood – Title
Commercial 50's – intro?
Mom – pregnancy – easy deliv.
Dad – ~~Bakery~~ Checker
Dad – Budgeted finances
o farthest went was to town 3 mi away
Ending
8th Grade – Father died

First Draft with Revisions

In the '50s or '60s there was a commercial on T.V. that made reference to a big family. It showed the husband and wife look-ing out their window at a car pulling up to their house with kids in it packed like sardines in a can. The wife screams, ''Here come Helen and her hungry brood, what are we gonna do for food?'' I really thought at the time that they were referring to my family. Someone in the neighborhood had to have told them about us. My mother's name was Helen. She had seven children. To get us all in the car to go anywhere was a real fiasco. The doctor told her she was built to have babies ~~kids~~. add family joke about only sleeping together on Saturday

I guess the most devastating fact about being in this large family was not enough money. My dad had a steady job at the bakery as a checker, but the pay was not very good ~~pretty crummy~~. My dad never took a vacation. We needed the money too badly. He had to do some pretty tight budgeting to pay the bills. This lack of money led to many other hardships.

Food was a problem. We never went hungry but the foods we ate were those you could make a large amount of at one time, that stretched a long way and weren't too expensive, like beans, soup, and mush. Since only nine quarts of mild were delivered to our house, we had to substitute canned milk and water or powdered milk on our cereal quite a few times. We rarely got store bought candy or sweets. We never experienced the privilege of going to a restaurant. ~~Again the culprit is lack of money.~~

We were never choosy about the clothes we wore. We couldn't afford to be choosy. Since we girls had two older brothers, we ended up wearing old faded jeans, *never dreaming that one day they would be the in thing and girls would actually want to wear them.* I can never remember getting any new clothing. It was always my brothers' or sisters' or someone elses'. The one thing I do remember getting new are shoes. We had one pair each. We wore them a long time *until* ~~till~~ they couldn't be patched and on payday we got a new pair. That was a *special* ~~great~~ feeling.

Professional haircuts were not to be had. We didn't have the money for such frivilous things. My uncle cut everyone's *tell about Uncle Charlie* hair. Regular dental work was also out of the question. We only went to the dentist when we had a toothache or when we might loose a tooth through decay.

We never owned a real nice car. My dad would keep the thing running but you couldn't depend on it to go too far. The grocery store was about the extent of our travel. *3 miles away in town, + that was*

As a member of a large family you took a few things for granted; you never took long trips, Christmas was never thought of for its material gain, and birthday parties were unheard of. ⟨These are a few of the disadvantages experienced.⟩ *?*

When I was in 8th grade, I was sitting in English class and the teacher was lecturing. Our principle appeared in the door-way and calmly said to the teacher that I was supposed to go with him. I wondered what all the mystery was about. I knew I hadn't done anything wrong. What could he want with me? When we reached the corridor I saw my older brother standing there waiting for me. I knew something was wrong. ''Dad died,'' he managed to get out. I couldn't believe it. We hugged and cried. *tell about heart attack from stress.*

Living within a large family structure had meant many hardships, but the hardship of living without a dad was one that would never be overcome. *We seven kids went without a lot, but all we really missed was Dad.*

Second Draft with Revisions

In the '50's or '60's there was a commercial on T.V. that made
reference to a big family. It showed the husband and wife look—
ing out their window at a car pulling up to their house with kids
in it packed ~~like sardines in a can~~ _as tightly as olives in a jar_. The wife screams, ''Here
comes Helen and her hungry brood, what are we gonna do for
food?'' I really thought at the time that they were referring
to my family. Someone in the neighborhood had to have told them
about us. My mother's name was Helen. She had seven children.
To get us all in the car to go anywhere was a real fiasco. The
doctor told her she was built to have babies, _and_ ~~S~~he tried to prove
him right by having two in one year. The weird thing about our
large family was that my mom and dad only slept together one
night a week. My dad was a checker in a bakery and worked all
night turn. He only had Saturday evenings off. The relatives
would always kid my parents about this. Nevertheless, seven
kids were the end result, and I don't mean lucky number seven.

I guess the most devastating fact about being in this large
family was not enough money. My dad had a steady job ~~at the
bakery as a checker~~, but the pay was not very good. ~~My dad never
took a vacation. We needed the money too badly.~~ He had to do some

pretty tight budgeting to pay the bills. This lack of money led to many ~~other~~ hardships.

Food was a problem. We never went hungry but the foods we ate were those you could make a large amount of at one time, *and that* stretched a long way and weren't too expensive, ~~like beans~~. *Soups like potato, bean and vegetable, poor man's stew, hamburgers, oatmeal, and mush were usually on the menu.* ~~soup, and mush~~. Since only 9 quarts of milk were delivered to our house, we had to substitute canned milk and water or powdered milk on our cereal quite a few times. We rarely got *We would make chocolate oatmeal fudge or ice cream from the snow in the winter.* store—bought candy or sweets. We never experienced the priv-ilege of going to a restuarant.

We were never choosy about the clothes we wore. We couldn't afford to be choosy. Since we girls had two older brothers, we ended up wearing old faded jeans, never dreaming that one day they would be the in thing and girls would want to wear them. I can never remember getting any new clothing. It was always my brothers' or sisters' or someone elses'. The one thing I do remember getting new are shoes. We had one pair each. We wore them a long time until ~~they~~ *the holes* couldn't be patched *with cardboard,* and on payday we got a new pair. That was a special feeling.

Professional haircuts were not to be had. We didn't have the money for such fri~~vi~~lous things. *sp?* My uncle cut everyone's hair. I can remember my Uncle Charlie coming over with his barber shears and electric razor. He'd start with my dad and go on down the line. ''Who's next for a trimming?'' he'd ask. Only the brave would step forward. His haircuts left something to be desired. Regular dental work was also out of the question. We only went to the dentist when we had a toothache or when we might loose a tooth through decay.

We never owned a real nice car. My dad would keep the thing running, but you couldn't depend on it to go too far. The grocery store was 3 miles away in town, and that was about the extent of our travel.

As a members of a large family we took a few things for granted; we never took long trips, Christmas was never thought of for its material gain, and birthday parties were unheard of.

When I was in 8th grade, I was sitting in English class and the teacher was lecturing. Our principle appeared in the doorway and calmly said to the teacher that I was supposed to go with him. Fill this gap I wondered what all the mystery was about. I knew I hadn't done anything wrong. What could he want with me? When we reached the corridor I saw my older brother standing there waiting for me. I knew something was wrong. ''Dad died,'' he managed to get out. I couldn't believe it. We hugged and cried.

Later I found out my dad had a heart attack. The stress of raising a large family with never enough money had taken its *final* toll.

    Living ~~within~~ *in* a large family ~~structure~~ had meant many
hardships, but the hardship of living without a dad was one
that would never be overcome. We seven kids went without ~~a lot~~ *a great deal*,
but all we really missed was our dad.

Helen's Hungry Brood

In the 1950's or 1960's there was a commercial on television
that made reference to a big family. It showed the husband and
wife looking out their window at a car pulling up to their house
with kids in it packed as tightly as olives in a jar. The wife
screams, ''Here come Helen and her hungry brood, what are we
gonna do for food?'' I really thought at the time that they were
referring to my family. Someone in the neighborhood had to have
told them about us. My mother's name was Helen. She had seven
children. To get us all in the car to go anywhere was a real
fiasco. The doctor told her she was built to have babies, and
she tried to prove him right by having two in one year. The weird
thing about our large family was that my mom and dad only slept
together one night a week. My dad was a checker in a bakery and
worked all night turn. He only had Saturday evenings off. The

relatives would always kid my parents about this. Nevertheless, seven kids were the end result, and I don't mean lucky number seven.

I guess the most devastating fact about being in this large family was not enough money. My dad had a steady job, but the pay was not very good. He had to do some pretty tight budgeting to pay the bills. This lack of money led to other hardships.

Food was a problem. We never went hungry, but the foods we ate were those that you could make a large amount of at one time, that stretched a long way, and that weren't too expensive. Soups like potato, bean, and vegetable; poor man's stew; hamburgers; oatmeal; and mush were usually on the menu. Since only 9 quarts of milk were delivered to our house, we had to substitute canned milk and water or powdered milk on our cereal quite a few times. We rarely got store-bought candy or sweets. We would make chocolate oatmeal fudge or ice cream from the snow in the winter. We never experienced the privilege of going to a restaurant.

We were never choosy about the clothes we wore. We couldn't afford to be choosy. Since we girls had two older brothers, we ended up wearing old faded jeans, never dreaming that one day they would be the in thing and girls would want to wear them. I can never remember getting any new clothing. It was always my brothers' or sisters' or someone else's. The one thing I do remember getting new are shoes. We had one pair each. We wore them until the holes couldn't be patched with cardboard, and then on payday we got a new pair. That was a special feeling.

Professional haircuts were not to be had. We didn't have the money for such frivolous things. My uncle cut everyone's hair. I can remember my Uncle Charlie coming over with his barber shears and electric razor. He'd start with my dad and go on down the line. ''Who's next for a trimming?'' he'd ask. Only the brave would step forward. His haircuts left something to be desired. Regular dental work was also out of the question. We only went to the dentist when we had a toothache or when we might lose a tooth through decay.

We never owned a real nice car. My dad would keep the thing running, but you couldn't depend on it to go too far. The grocery store was 3 miles away in town, and that was about the extent of our travel.

As members of a large family we took a few things for granted; we never took long trips, Christmas was never thought of for its material gain, and birthday parties were unheard of.

When I was in eighth grade, I was sitting in English class and the teacher was lecturing. Our principal appeared in the doorway and calmly said to the teacher that I was supposed to go with him. I rose from my seat with my books in hand and followed him into the empty hallway. ''Take your books to your locker, Emma,'' he said. I did as I was told, not saying a word. The slamming of my locker door sounded like a small bomb exploding in the quietness. ''Please come with me to the office,'' he instructed. I wondered what all the mystery was about. I knew I hadn't done anything wrong. What could he want with me? When we reached the corridor I saw my older brother standing there waiting for me. I knew something was wrong. ''Dad died,'' he managed to get out. I couldn't believe it. We hugged and cried. Later I found out my dad had a heart attack. The stress of rais-ing a large family with never enough money had taken its final toll.

Living in a large family had meant many hardships, but the hardship of living without a dad was one that would never be overcome. We seven kids went without a great deal, but all we really missed was our dad.

Acknowledgments

Russell Baker, "Bing and Elvis." Copyright © 1977 by The New York Times Company. Reprinted by permission.

Rachel Carson, "A Fable for Tomorrow," from *Silent Spring* by Rachel Carson. Copyright © 1962 by Rachel Carson. Reprinted by permission of Houghton Mifflin Company.

Jane Doe, "I Wish They'd Do It Right." Copyright © 1977 by The New York Times Company. Reprinted by permission.

Delia Ephron, "Coping with Santa," from *Funny Sauce* by Delia Ephron. Copyright © 1986 by Delia Ephron. Reprinted by permission of Viking Penguin, Inc.

Bernard Gladstone, "How to Build a Fire in a Fireplace," from *The New York Times Complete Manual of Home Repairs*. Copyright © 1966 by The New York Times Company. Reprinted by permission.

Gail Godwin, "The Watcher at the Gates." Copyright © 1977 by The New York Times Company. Reprinted by permission.

Dick Gregory, "Shame," from *Nigger: An Autobiography* by Dick Gregory with Robert Lipsyte. Copyright © 1964 by Dick Gregory Enterprises, Inc. Reprinted by permission of the publisher, E. P. Dutton, a division of NAL Penguin, Inc.

Humanities Index, Volume 9, April 1982–March 1983. Copyright © 1982, 1983 by The H. W. Wilson Company. Material reproduced by permission of the publisher.

Susan Jacoby, "When Bright Girls Decide That Math Is 'A Waste of Time.'" Copyright © 1983 by Susan Jacoby.

Robert Jastrow, "Man of Wisdom." "Man of Wisdom" is reprinted from *Until the Sun Dies* by Robert Jastrow, with the permission of W. W. Norton and Company, Inc. Copyright © 1977 by Robert Jastrow.

Index

421